MAKING SENSE OF ANARCHISM

Errico Malatesta's
Experiments with
Revolution,
1889–1900

DAVIDE TURCATO

AK PRESS
EDINBURGH · OAKLAND · BALTIMORE

T0162035

Praise for Davide Turcato and *Making Sense of Anarchism*:

"This volume is an essential read not only for anarchists eager to deepen their knowledge of one of their greatest men, but also for intellectual historians interested in nineteenth-century political thought and socialist history. Indeed, the most important lesson to be learned from Turcato's book, and one that deserves more attention, is that anarchism is, as he puts it in his concluding chapter, 'a complex, rational business' that defies easy categorizations and broad generalizations."

—Marcella Bencivenni, author of *Italian Immigrant Radical Culture: The Idealism of the Sovversivi in the United States, 1890–1940*

"Shortly before his untimely death, Nunzio Pernicone, one of the foremost historians of Italian anarchism, told me that Davide Turcato was a 'rising star' in anarchist studies. Certainly this book confirms that judgement."

—Richard Bach Jensen, in *Social History*

"Turcato's book is … something of a clarion call to historians of anarchism, providing both great insight into Malatesta's life and evolving political thought and delivering a resounding evisceration of the old stereotypes of anarchists."

—Andrew Hoyt, in *Anarchist Studies*

"Filling an undeniable historiographic gap, Davide Turcato has produced a meticulous and engrossing English-language biography of Errico Malatesta and, at the same time, a thought-provoking reassessment of the nature of classical anarchism (both as a movement and an ideology).... [T]hrough the erudite use of interpretive sociology and a determined, cogent central argument the monograph also delivers an ambitious re-examination of late nineteenth-century anarchism, with contemporary ramifications."

—Constance Bantman, author of *The French Anarchists in London, 1880–1914*

"The book skillfully interweaves Malatesta's pan-European movements with an examination of his evolving political philosophy."

—Matthew S. Adams, in *Journal for the Study of Radicalism*

"Turcato's work is a substantial contribution to our knowledge about the anarchist movement in general and, of course, about Malatesta in particular. The work's strength rests not only on the exhaustive analysis that it draws from the sources, but also on its methodological perspective."

—Lucas Poy, in *Rey Desnudo*

Errico Malatesta in his thirties.

Making Sense of Anarchism: Errico Malatesta's Experiments with Revolution, 1889–1900

@ 2015 Davide Turcato
This edition © 2015 AK Press (Oakland, Edinburgh, Baltimore).

ISBN: 978-1-84935-231-4
Library of Congress Control Number: 2015942527

AK Press	AK Press
674-A 23rd Street	PO Box 12766
Oakland, CA 94612	Edinburgh EH8 9YE
USA	Scotland
www.akpress.org	www.akuk.com
akpress@akpress.org	ak@akedin.demon.co.uk

The above addresses would be delighted to provide you with the latest AK Press distribution catalog, which features the several thousand books, pamphlets, zines, audio and video products, and stylish apparel published and/or distributed by AK Press. Alternatively, visit our websites for the complete catalog, latest news, and secure ordering.

Cover design by John Yates www.stealworks.com.

Printed in the USA on acid-free paper.

CONTENTS

ILLUSTRATIONS

Figures

Table

PREFACE

IT HAS BEEN ARGUED THAT THE HISTORIAN RESEMBLES A DETECTIVE (WINKS). The historiography of anarchism certainly lends itself to such a comparison.

In 'The Purloined Letter', one of Edgar Allan Poe's short stories featuring the Parisian detective Auguste Dupin, we make the acquaintance of Monsieur G, a type of police officer 'who had a fashion of calling every thing "odd" that was beyond his comprehension, and thus lived amid an absolute legion of "oddities" '. One day he calls on Dupin, who is sitting at home in a meditative mood, to explain to him a new case: 'The business is *very* simple indeed, and I make no doubt that we can manage it sufficiently well ourselves; but then I thought Dupin would like to hear the details of it, because it is so excessively *odd*.' 'Simple and odd', echoes Dupin doubtfully (257–8).

Such is the situation with the historiography of anarchism.

Many historians do not expect to make sense of anarchism, and therefore, like Monsieur G, they happily live amid a legion of oddities: for them, anarchists 'are moving in their sincerity, if naïve to the point of self-destruction' (Carr); 'when one argues with anarchism, one argues with an absurd point of view' (Horowitz, 589); and 'the disinterestedness and heroism of the best anarchist activists arouse our admiration, while at the same time their stupidity irritates and baffles us' (Zagorin). Naïvety, absurdity, stupidity are regarded as anarchism's obvious attributes that need not be argued. Obviously absurd, simple, and odd.

Needless to say, it was Dupin who eventually solved the case of the purloined letter, which turned out to be neither simple nor odd. His method, which is the antithesis of G's, is well illustrated by another Poe story, 'The Murders in the Rue Morgue', in which the police are at a loss with a ferocious murder committed without apparent motive by one or more individuals with puzzling physical features. Confronted with a maze of conflicting details, Dupin uses coherence as a heuristic principle and sets out to prove that 'apparent "impossibilities" are, in reality, not such'. For example, after establishing that the murderers must have escaped by the windows of a certain room, he thus reasons: 'This being so, they could not have re-fastened the sashes from the inside ... Yet the sashes *were* fastened. They *must*, then have the power of fastening themselves ... A concealed spring must, I now knew, exist...' Upon examination, Dupin finds indeed a concealed spring and eventually the solution to the mystery: the murderer was an orangutan escaped from its owner. The police, he explains, had considered the mystery insoluble

Making Sense of Anarchism

because they had fallen 'into the gross but common error of confounding the unusual with the abstruse' (148–9).

In this book I propose to take Dupin's approach to investigate whether anarchism can be made sense of and interpreted as a sensible and rational strategy of action. Anarchism is indeed unusual. Of all political movements that have ever existed, it is the only one to seek the abolishment of political power rather than its seizure. Is it abstruse, though? This may indeed be a common but gross error that stems from lack of understanding. Like Dupin in the 'Rue Morgue', I intend to embark on an exploration of anarchist ideas and action driven by coherence as a heuristic principle, in the hope of being led to an interpretation in which apparent 'oddities' and 'impossibilities' are dissolved and replaced by comprehension.

Just like detective stories do not explain their protagonist's method in the abstract, but show it at work, so I apply my approach to a historical case, that of the Italian anarchist Errico Malatesta (1853–1932).

Malatesta's figure is both prominent and underrated. He is acknowledged to be a foremost representative of international anarchism, yet his name does not always resonate, especially outside of Italy. His pamphlets—*Fra Contadini* (Between Peasants), *L'Anarchia* (Anarchy), *Al Caffè* (At the Café)—are among the greatest anarchist 'best-sellers' of all times. Yet he is regarded more as a man of action than of thought, perhaps, ironically, because his rare ability to express complex ideas in simple terms has been mistaken for lack of intellectual depth. And, of course, he has had his share of historical judgments of the simple-and-odd type. An early biographer wrote that in his old age his views remained 'simple enough and as far removed from reality as the anarchist creed of his early days. A generous creed and a humanitarian philosophy, but as effective a revolutionary weapon against the existing system as the tomahawk of an Indian brave against the tank' (Nomad, 47). The judgment has stuck. A memorial article of February 2011 in a major Italian newspaper calls Malatesta 'a champion of failures' and wonders why governments were afraid of him (Stancanelli). The emphasis of such analyses is on the abysmal gap between aims and means, ideal and reality. However, could the gap be between reality and the observer's understanding, instead?

My starting move in trying to answer this question is to grant Malatesta the benefit of common sense. This methodological presumption becomes my driving principle in attempting a complete and coherent interpretation of his intentions, beliefs, and actions.

As part of this reinterpretation process I systematically try to relate anarchists' seemingly odd beliefs to more 'reasonable' and credited ideas from political theory and social sciences. Anarchist concepts often seem to run counter to standard categorizations in those fields. This may be the fault not of anarchist inconsistency but of those categorizations. Pairs of opposite concepts, such as individualism–holism, egoism–solidarity, free initiative–planning, and capitalism–socialism, have traditionally been clustered into two mutually exclusive blocs separated by a sort of conceptual Berlin Wall. Anarchism has fallen through the cracks of such categorizations. Between the two paths of liberal democracy and state socialism, anarchism has been unanimously regarded as a dead end. One of this volume's tasks is to explain how anarchists regarded it as an open road.

The book examines 11 years in Malatesta's life, from 1889 to 1900, which he spent for the most part in exile in London, the headquarters of continental anarchism, while at the same time he made his presence strongly felt in Italy and other countries. This period is broad and central enough in Malatesta's life to allow a comprehensive view of how his ideas developed. At the same time, it is sufficiently restricted to allow a detailed empirical reconstruction of his action. This last task necessarily requires a broader study of how the anarchist movement functioned, in search of those 'concealed springs'—and anarchism had a few—which help to show that apparent 'impossibilities' are not really such.

In accounting for anarchist collective action, I identify three levels, which, for the sake of brevity, could be labeled 'anarchist network', 'anarchist party', and 'anarchist mobilization'. Roughly speaking, I use the notion of anarchist network to account for informal or underground organization, and that of anarchist party—which I take, somewhat provocatively, from Malatesta's own usage—to account for organization in formal or public form. Anarchist mobilization accounts for the anarchists' initiative within larger social movements.

The book is both a historical tracing and a systematic analysis of Malatesta's anarchism. The two tasks are orthogonal, for the former is chronological while the latter is thematic. I have striven to combine the two tasks and address them in parallel. The book's overall structure is chronological. However, in order to avoid thematic fragmentation, I discuss each theme only once and in full, in connection with the earliest suitable period. Thus, in each chapter, sections concerning Malatesta's action are interwoven with others dealing with theoretical or tactical aspects that are historically related to the chapter's main narrative. Throughout the book I constantly engage in a critical dialog with the historiography of anarchism, seeking to illustrate and contest the methodological weaknesses and historiographic pitfalls surrounding this movement.

The book has no notes. All citations are made by reference to the works cited list at the end. When a reference is not fully recoverable from the text, a parenthetical citation is added. A citation is by shortened title for Malatesta's or anonymous works. Otherwise it is by author's name.

Unless otherwise stated, all translations are mine.

ACKNOWLEDGMENTS

Portions of this book reuse materials from my earlier following publications: 'Italian Anarchism as a Transnational Movement, 1885–1915', *International Review of Social History*, 52 (3), 407–44 (2007); introduction to *Anarchism: A Documentary History of Libertarian Ideas*, ed. by Robert Graham, vol. 2 (Montréal, 2009); 'European Anarchism in the 1890s: Why Labour Matters in Categorizing Anarchism', *Working USA*, 12 (4), 451–66 (2009); 'The 1896 London Congress: Epilogue or Prologue?', in *New Perspectives on Anarchism, Labour and Syndicalism: The Individual, the National and the Transnational*, ed. D. Berry and C. Bantman (Newcastle upon Tyne, 2010); and 'Collective Action, Opacity, and the "Problem of Irrationality": Anarchism and the First of May, 1890–1892', *Journal for the Study of Radicalism*, 5 (1), 1–31 (2011). I respectively thank Cambridge University Press, Black Rose Books, John Wiley & Sons, Cambridge Scholars Publishing, and Michigan State University Press for granting permission to adapt those materials.

I would like to thank professors Mark Leier and David Laycock for their guidance in the writing of the thesis from which this book originated.

1
INTRODUCTION:
ANARCHISM, A SIMPLE AND ODD BUSINESS?

WHAT STRIKES THE ORDINARY OBSERVER OF ANARCHISM IS THE GAP BETWEEN its naïve, simple ideal and the hard, complex reality. Anarchists seem to miss some obvious point about the way people are or to make unwarranted assumptions about the way people can be. Indeed the oddity of anarchism seems to be plain to see. To increase the observer's puzzlement, the obviousness of the anarchists' cognitive shortcomings is only proportional to their obduracy in neglecting them.

This makes understanding anarchists a difficult task. It is a postulate of interpretive sociology of Weberian derivation that an action can be understood in terms of its reasons: 'observers *understand* the action of an observed subject as soon as they can conclude that in the same situation it is quite probable that they too would act in the same way' (Boudon, *Theories*, 31). In this respect, anarchism looks like a sociological puzzle. The kind of empathy required to understand it seems to be out of reach. Based on the social science common definition of rationality as coherence between desires, beliefs, and behavior (Martin and McIntyre, 283), anarchism seems to imply an element of irrationality.

HISTORIOGRAPHY AND THE IRRATIONALITY OF ANARCHISM
This common-sense perception is largely shared by the historiography of anarchism, which tends to regard this movement as inherently flawed. Consequently, much of this historiography can be synthesized in one claim: anarchists were losers and necessarily so. Anarchism is described in turn as a dead, dying, or doomed ideology, depending on one's chronological scope, and the historian's task becomes to explain why it could not be otherwise.

Marxist historiography has followed a pattern established by Marx himself, who branded anarchism a form of sectarianism typical of early stages of the proletariat's development. His judgment, issued before anarchism was even born as a movement, has become the standard pattern of marxist analyses of that movement's development during the next 70 years—a paradoxical circumstance, if one considers that an alleged cornerstone of marxism is its being based on empirical observation, not on abstract theory. In marxist theory, doom is expressed in the form of historical backwardness and obsolescence. So, within that pattern of analysis, anarchism is always found on the losing side of the march of history. Hence, the typical master narrative has been about the 'end', 'death', or 'liquidation' of anarchism.

Italy is a good example. Richard Hostetter places the 'ideological liquidation' of Italian anarchism between 1879 and 1882 (409). For Elio Conti, the markedly anarchist Italian internationalist movement died out in 1885. However, he adds, anarchism continued to endemically meander through the lowest classes (240). For Luciano Cafagna, who studies socialism in Rome from 1882 to 1891, the heyday of anarchism ended in 1891, but anarchists 'bequeathed many of their weaknesses to the Roman workers' movement for a long time'. A footnote explains that the reference is to the aftermath of World War II (770–1). Franco Della Peruta, whose topic is socialism in Rome in 1872–77, places the liquidation of anarchism at 1877, though anarchists had a revival in 1889–91 (52). For Enzo Santarelli, Italy's delayed development explains why a 'cumbersome current of utopian socialism' could survive well beyond 1914 (*Socialismo*, 7). In brief, thus goes the marxist pattern: whatever the period examined, after an ephemeral burst of activity, anarchism succumbed to the march of history right at the end of that period, lingering afterwards for an indefinite time, and often exhibiting a surprising vitality in its death struggle.

The judgment of liberal historiography is tinged with condescension. An early obituary was issued in 1911 by Ernest Vizetelly, who acknowledged that anarchism deserved sympathy, but claimed that its excesses foredoomed it to an unsuccessful ending, according to the law that 'extremist theories never secure a triumph of any permanency' (299–300). Approximately half a century later, George Woodcock set the death of anarchism to 1939 (443). The failure was irrevocable, he argued, for lost causes may be the best ones, but once lost they are never won again. Still, the anarchist idea lived on, because 'ideas do not age' (449). In a similar spirit, Irving Horowitz argued that criticizing anarchism for being politically impracticable did not do it justice. For him, 'there can be no doubt that anarchism was foredoomed to failure' (588). However, 'its very absurdities and deficiencies' proceeded not only from the anarchist position, but also from the way of life in the twentieth century (589): 'the anarchists are a romantic, absurd breed that cannot, thank goodness, come to terms with some of the oppressive excesses of civilization' (603). Finally, James Joll remarked in 1979 that the past 150 years illustrated the inconsistency of anarchism, and the impossibility of putting it into practice (*Anarchists*, 257). Yet Joll too concedes that anarchism has provided a standing threat to bourgeois complacency, concluding: 'There have been few periods in human history when we have needed this more than we do today' (*Anarchism*, 284). In sum, and in contrast with marxist historiography, which hastens to toll the bell for anarchism, liberal historiography wishes it a long life as a permanently unsuccessful movement.

Obsolescence and irrationality as the fate of anarchism are combined in the influential analysis of Eric J. Hobsbawm in *Primitive Rebels*, written in 1959. Hobsbawm interprets anarchism as a millenarian movement, characterized by a 'total rejection of the present, evil world', a standardized chiliastic 'ideology', and 'a fundamental vagueness about the actual way in which the new society will be brought about' (57–8). Abstract revolutionism and unconcern for practical politics mean, for Hobsbawm, that anarchism was not only irrational, but also unchanging. As a critic has remarked, in Hobsbawm's book anarchist 'attitudes and beliefs of 1903–05, 1918–20, 1933, and 1936 are lumped together or considered interchangeable' (Mintz, 271). In turn, immutability is Hobsbawm's ground for extending his verdict from the past to the future, concluding that anarchism, being 'a form of peasant movement almost incapable of effective adaptation to modern conditions', had a history of unrelieved failure and was bound to go down in the books with the prophets who, 'though not unarmed, did not know what to do with their arms, and were defeated for ever' (92).

In brief, the historiographical interpretation of anarchism stems essentially from the same attribution of irrationality that common sense seems to dictate.

Regarding the anarchist tradition as rational, however, is not simply a matter of replacing a dismissive analysis with a sympathetic one, or even openly advocating anarchism. In fact, after the events of 1968 and the advent of the 'new social history', renewed interest in anarchism generated numerous works that did just that, emphasizing anarchist adaptability to changing conditions, partly in reaction to millenarian interpretations á la Hobsbawm. Yet the attribution of irrationality has not disappeared, cropping up in less crude but equally serious ways. For example, Peter Marshall's encyclopedic *Demanding the Impossible* passionately argues for the relevance of anarchism, striving to rectify misconceptions, such as its association with terrorism. However, driven by such preoccupation, his discussion of anarchist violence ends up corroborating a few *pièces de résistance* of the irrationalist stereotype, as when he remarks that 'at its most violent their action has typically not gone much beyond throwing up barricades or entering a village armed with rudimentary weapons', just as the millenarian stereotype would have it (629–30).

In the spirit of social history, some authors have studied the relationship between anarchism and labor movements, focusing not on 'the trees', the anarchist leadership, but on 'the forest', the movement and its culture, which embedded the real movement's ideology. They have identified the real essence of that culture in older traditions of republicanism or 'popular' liberalism, regarding anarchism as a catalyst, a stepping stone toward the emergence of labor movements with a powerful voice in national affairs. This, they have argued, is the real, positive legacy of anarchism (Nelson; Lear).

A related stream of research has focused on the notion of anarchist counter-culture. These historians have pictured anarchism as engaged in political and cultural conflicts with their larger national societies. They have emphasized the anarchists' ability to adapt their ideas to fit the realities of their countries and to impact a wider political culture. Thus, they have argued for the realism, pragmatism, and effectiveness of anarchist action, in contrast to the idealistic, purist, and impossibilist character of their proclaimed ideology (Shaffer, *Anarchism*; M. Thomas).

The move from the institutional to the cultural terrain is even more marked in some historians of French anarchism, who have claimed that the anarchist subculture, with its diversity, was able to effectively interpret the lower-class Parisian mentality, to appeal to avant-garde artists, and to address cultural concerns central to Parisian life. However, they have argued, cultural ferment and diversity were in inverse relation to the anarchists' capacity to organize and promote their aims (Sonn; Varias).

In their diversity, all such works share a common trait: they tend to emphasize the realism of anarchism, its ability to grapple with issues in the here and now, and ultimately its effectiveness. However, effectiveness is not gauged by the anarchists' goals, but in contrast to them. For the labor movements as for the counter-cultures or subcultures under investigation, anarchist goals are ultimately regarded as a liability. As such, we are told, either they were practically, even if not nominally, disregarded by workers, or they eventually turned into a cumbersome hindrance. Realism, flexibility, expediency, and effectiveness are considered incompatible with anarchist goals, which are looked upon as synonymous with stubbornness, purism, and impossibilism. Likewise, anarchist diversity, which enabled anarchists to grapple with current issues and be in tune with the culture of their times, is also taken to be the very reason that precluded them from successfully pursuing their anarchist ends.

From the perspective of rationality, in the sense of coherence between desires, beliefs, and behavior, those who share Hobsbawm's judgment of 'monumental ineffectiveness', and those who seek to rescue anarchism from that charge are two sides of the same irrationalist coin, epitomized by the shared notion of anarchism as a necessary failure, or a permanently unsuccessful movement. The former take seriously the anarchists' stated ends and emphasize the inadequacy and futility of the means employed in their pursuit. The latter take seriously the anarchists' means, emphasizing their adaptability and effectiveness, but judge them by a different yardstick than the actors' stated goals, which tend to be regarded at best as a dead letter, or at worst as a dead weight. In either case, rational understanding of how anarchists selected their means in the light of their own ends is wanting. One way or another, the explanation process introduces an element of oddity, inconsequence, or irrationality at some point, whether in the form of impossible aims, futile means, or absurd beliefs.

From the perspective of rationality, it is irrelevant whether a movement's positive contribution is appreciated or whether—as Raymond Carr claimed about Spanish anarchism in a book review significantly titled 'All or Nothing'—a movement is regarded 'as largely a disaster, both for the workers' movement and for democracy in Spain'. The point here is not whether anarchism was a disaster, but rather that its assessment as a disaster is an evaluative statement that requires the assumption of a set of values or goals with respect to which it is established. Whose values and goals are to be chosen? Anarchism may have been a disaster for 'democracy in Spain', as Carr contends, but certainly anarchists did not intend to be beneficial to democracy, unless one intends the term broadly enough to include anarchy. And even with respect to workers, one needs to know what is good for them, in order to establish whether anarchism was a disaster, and what is good for them is not a matter that can be settled by historical analysis.

Likewise, the issue of rationality is distinct from that of effectiveness, even with respect to one's own goals. Failure to achieve one's goal does not necessarily imply irrationality. Situations may exist in which one acts rationally, but is ineffective for reasons outside of one's control. Equating rationality with effectiveness would imply that rationality is always on the side of the strongest, and ultimately of the winner. In the 1920s, Italian upholders of liberal democracy were indeed ineffective against Fascism. Nevertheless, it would be awkward to claim *ipso facto* that they were irrational. That anarchism was ineffective is a truism, given that it has not achieved its ends. However, it is one thing to attribute its ineffectiveness to exogenous factors or overpowering circumstances, and another to attribute it to endogenous factors, or inherent, inexorable flaws. As Hobsbawm's assessment illustrates, the difference is that the latter stance implies stepping out of the past into the future, which is still unwritten, and therefore is not the historian's department, notwithstanding the inveterate habit of prophesying about anarchism.

At any rate, justified or not, the attribution of irrationality has a negative impact on how historians of anarchism go about their work.

An anecdote may help illustrate this point. In a study of Italy during Fascism, the authoritative Italian historian Nicola Tranfaglia analyzes the popular support that Mussolini's colonial war in Ethiopia enjoyed in 1935. He remarks that illustrious members of Parliament, such as the philosopher Benedetto Croce, donated gold in support of the war, and even the anarchist Errico Malatesta and other former representatives of the extreme left supported the war, 'thus radically modifying their judgment on the Fascist regime'. At the crossroads between questioning or using the evidence of a chief figure of international anarchism awkwardly turned into a supporter of colonial war and Fascism, Tranfaglia briskly takes the latter path. Thus, Malatesta's new stance is exhibited as the latest instance of 'a long political-cultural tradition', spectacularly corroborating Tranfaglia's thesis: 'arousing the deepest feelings of the Italian people and identifying national honour with the redemption of its colonial inferiority was Mussolini's greatest success and the historical peak attained by his regime' (593). Unfortunately, in 1935 Errico Malatesta had been dead for three years. Mussolini's supporter was a non-anarchist namesake.

This blunder is an extreme case, but it is paradigmatic. The inclination to accept anarchist oddity as plausible and unproblematic, rather than questioning it, is common, and has vitiated the historiography of anarchism, from the ground level of factual accuracy up to historical explanation. The attribution of irrationality is a shortcut that fosters facile explanations in lieu of making sense of one's subject. Nothing is ever too odd or puzzling when irrationality is at hand as a suitable explanation. Contradictory evidence about one's behavior can always be reconciled without questioning it when irrational behavior is a matter of course.

In brief, the attribution of irrationality makes for poorer historiography.

A POLICY OF RATIONAL ACCOMMODATION

How is rationality to be assessed, though? Is its attribution a matter of choice?

In fact, the attribution of rationality to an agent is not a result of observation, but an a priori methodological assumption. This is the key tenet of a theory of interpretation that originated in the philosophy of language and extended to social sciences and philosophy. Versions of it were most notably championed by Willard V. O. Quine, Donald Davidson, Daniel Dennett, and Martin Hollis. The theory argues that a fundamental constraint for interpreting another person is to conceive of one as a rational agent. Therefore, interpretation has to proceed by necessity in a charitable manner. Rationality is not merely an empirical trait of an agent, but is constitutive for one's agency.

At the core of this theory is the methodological principle known as the 'principle of charity'. Quine resorts to it in connection with his thesis of the 'indeterminacy of translation': translation manuals can be set up in divergent ways, all compatible with the available data, yet mutually incompatible (27). What criterion should one prefer? Quine asserts the maxim that 'assertions startlingly false on the face of them are likely to turn on hidden differences of language', based on the common sense that 'one's interlocutor's silliness, beyond a certain point, is less likely than bad translation' (59). The more absurd the imputed beliefs, the more suspicious a translation is (69).

Davidson's starting point is that 'neither language nor thinking can be fully explained in terms of the other, and neither has conceptual priority' (*Inquiries*, 156). In analogy with Quine's radical translation, Davidson discusses 'radical interpretation', in which 'we must deliver simultaneously a theory of belief and a theory of meaning' (144). Attributing irrational thoughts and actions to an agent is possible, but it imposes a burden on such attributions. 'If we see a man pulling on both ends of a piece of string, we may decide he is fighting against himself, that he wants to move the string in incompatible directions. Such an explanation would require elaborate backing. No problem arises if the explanation is that he wants to break the string' (159–60).

Davidson's key to the solution for simultaneously identifying the meanings, beliefs, and evaluative attitudes, or desires, of an agent is the principle of charity, or, in Davidson's reformulation, a 'policy of rational accommodation': 'This policy calls on us to fit our own propositions...to the other person's words and attitudes in such a way as to render their speech and other behavior intelligible. This necessarily requires us to see others as much like ourselves in point of overall coherence and correctness' (*Problems*, 35). Davidson emphasizes that his policy is not one of many possible successful policies. Rather, 'it is the only policy available if we want to understand other people'. It expresses the fact that creatures with thoughts, values, and speech must be rational, are necessarily inhabitants of the same objective world as ourselves, and necessarily share their leading values with us. This is not a lucky accident, but 'something built into the concepts of belief, desire, and meaning' (36).

The principle of charity provides the criterion that will guide the present work in search of anarchism's 'good' reasons.

As Davidson explains, the process is that of constructing a viable theory of desires and beliefs from behavior open to observation, that is actions undertaken, just as a theory of meaning and belief is constructed from linguistic behavior, that is sentences held true. Davidson's key insight is that, for any constellation of beliefs and desires that rationalizes an action or sample of actions, it is always possible to find a quite different constellation that will do as well (*Inquiries*, 160). The only way for an observer to attribute desires, beliefs, and meanings to an actor, based on the latter's actions and assertions, is to assume general agreement on beliefs. The method is not designed to eliminate disagreement. Rather, its purpose is to make meaningful disagreement possible. Thus Davidson puts the matter concisely: 'all thinking creatures subscribe to my basic standards or norms of rationality.' Though this may sound authoritarian, it comes to no more than this: 'it is a condition of having thoughts, judgments and intentions that the basic standards of rationality have application' (*Problems*, 195).

Adopting the principle of charity is not a matter of benevolence or leniency toward actors. Rather, it proceeds from the acknowledgment that 'each interpretation and attribution of attitude is a move within a holistic theory, a theory necessarily governed by concern for consistency and general coherence with the truth' (*Inquiries*, 154). Accordingly, 'charity is not an option, but a condition of having a workable theory'; 'it is forced on us; whether we like it or not, if we want to understand others, we must count them right in most matters' (197).

Davidson's philosophical guiding policy, according to which we should, as far as possible, assign to a speaker's sentences 'conditions of truth that actually obtain (in our own opinion) just when the speaker holds those sentences true' (*Inquiries*, 196), goes in the same direction as the methodology that the French sociologist Raymond Boudon advocates for social sciences.

Boudon's 'cognitivist theory of action' is based on Max Weber's interpretive sociology, which assigns sociological analysis the goal of reconstructing individual behavior so as to make it meaningful and not interpret it, except in the last resort, as the effect of irrational forces ('Beyond'). For Boudon, observed behavior is often irrational only in terms of the observer's situation, whereas rationality or irrationality should be determined in relation to the actor's behavior. Thus, he rejects explanations in terms of 'alienation', 'the weight of tradition', 'resistance to change', 'false consciousness', and so on (*Theories*, 50).

Boudon's fundamental axiom is that behavior is governed by reasons. He emphasizes that social actors are socially situated: reasons may be objectively debatable, but nevertheless be perceived as good and compelling by actors (*Art*, 236). This idea shifts the focus of explaining behavior and belief from finding causes to finding reasons. Boudon's model belongs to the family of rational theories of axiological beliefs, in contrast to 'causalist' theories, according to which such beliefs would be produced in the mind of social subjects by biological, psychological, or social causes. Instead, rational theories suppose that subjects endorse such beliefs because they have strong reasons for doing so (*Origin*, 40).

In brief, both Davidson and Boudon urge us to interpret individual behavior patterns as meaningfully as possible, with irrationality as the last resort. Such notions as 'primitive' or 'pre-logical' mentality have no place in either theoretical framework. At the same time, both Boudon and Davidson emphasize the methodological, rather than ontological, character of their rationality assumption.

It is clear that much historiography of anarchism has headed in the opposite direction from a policy of rational accommodation. In contrast to Davidson's emphasis on the holistic interconnection of beliefs with desires and the world, and his methodological guideline of maximizing, or optimizing, consistency and general coherence with the truth, many of the analyses of anarchism previously illustrated utilize patterns of explanation which, at one point or another, introduce some form of detachment from empirical reality, internal inconsistency, or inconsequential beliefs. Absurdity, contradictions, inconsistencies, and practical impossibility are explicitly invoked by Horowitz (589) and Joll (*Anarchists*, 257). For Carr, anarchists approached self-destruction. The notion of a primitive mentality is central to the millenarian thesis, for which anarchists were largely unconcerned with empirical reality.

As for authors who have a positive outlook on anarchism, they often do so at the price of divorcing the anarchists' daily practice from their long-term ends, or by questioning the thoroughness of their anarchist beliefs. While charity, as Karsten Stueber remarks, is 'a principle constraining the interpretive process *globally* and *not locally*' (151), in such books rationality is found locally, not globally, in the anarchists' beliefs. Thus, we are told, Chicago anarchists are not best understood as anarchists (Nelson); Mexico City anarchists did not really aim at overthrowing capitalism (Lear); British anarchists were effective to the extent that they shed their typical anarchist impossibilism (M. Thomas); and the appeal of French anarchism stemmed from its very ineptitude (Sonn; Varias). In many cases, lame accounts from the viewpoint of rational accommodation are complemented with causalist explanations in terms of backwardness, alienation, radicalization, polarization, and so on.

Charity, in the sense of a rigorous methodological approach aimed at adequate understanding, is largely lacking in the historiography of anarchism. The more unproblematically dismissive remarks are made, such as Zagorin's one on the anarchists' stupidity, the more they speak to the 'monumental ineffectiveness' of the historiography they represent.

A charitable approach steers clear of both relativism and dogmatic egocentrism on the part of the observer. Indeed, anarchists are to be understood on their own terms. Their actions are to be related to their own desires, beliefs, and their own perception of the world. Thus, Davidson emphasizes the requirement of consistency in interpreting an actor's behavior, and Boudon emphasizes that the actor is situated. At the same time, however, interpreting an actor's behavior in his own terms can only mean accommodating as much as possible its interpretation to the observer's own standard of rationality. This is how the link between the actor's beliefs and desires and the world is retained.

Thus, making sense of anarchism in its own terms does not mean committing to a 'linguistic turn', whereby an alleged 'non-referential conception of language' is applied to one's subject, as Gareth Stedman Jones claims to have done in his study of Chartism, in order to free its politics from the 'a priori assumptions of historians about its social meaning'. For Jones, his method meant 'exploring the systematic relationship between terms and propositions within the language rather than setting particular propositions into direct relation to a putative experiential reality of which they were assumed to be the expression' (21).

Valuable and innovative as Jones's study of Chartism is, its value does not lie in the method allegedly used, which is simply untenable. Archeologists could have studied any number of inscriptions in the hieroglyphic language for any length of time in a non-referential manner, but it was only the discovery of the Rosetta Stone, a triscript in hieroglyphic, demotic, and Greek, that gave Jean-François Champollion the referential anchors enabling him to crack the code and find the key that made it possible for the texts of Ancient Egypt to be read again after 14 centuries, thus opening the door to the entire Egyptian civilization (see Solé and Valbelle).

As Martin Hollis puts it, as he describes the anthropologist's work to understand native utterances, 'to translate them into, let us say, English, he needs to relate some of them to the world, since, in relating an utterance to others he does not learn what it means, unless he already knows what the others mean. Ultimately, then, he needs a class of utterances whose situations of use he can specify', that is, a bridgehead set of utterances 'for which his specification and his informants' coincide' (214).

Understanding anarchism in its own terms means that whenever we understand it in terms that look odd or irrational, it is our understanding that must first be questioned. The appearance of oddness or irrationality is likely evidence of our using a faulty translation manual, not of anarchists being irrational. This is the essence of the principle of charity. We must indeed understand the language of anarchism, and it is indeed useful, as Jones argues, to map out 'successive languages of radicalism, liberalism, socialism, etc., both in relation to the political languages they replace and laterally in relation to rival political languages with which they are in conflict'. However, making sense of anarchism, as of any other movement, ultimately means interpreting it in terms that we understand. We need to find a translation manual. Translations must be based on the attribution of rationality, and thus they must form as coherent a whole as possible. At the same time they must make sense to us: they must be interpreted in our own terms, which are indeed referential, as they relate to our own experience of the world.

In fact, the historiography of anarchism may require an even stronger version of the principle of charity than Davidson's. His discussion concerns how beliefs and evaluative attitudes are to be related to open behavior, to which the observer has direct access. However, historians in general, dealing with the past, do not have the opportunity to directly interrogate actors. The problem is even more serious in the case of anarchism, since the anarchists' behavior was hardly open and directly accessible even to contemporary observers.

On this subject, E. P. Thompson's discussion of sources with respect to the Luddite movement is particularly relevant and enlightening. Thompson calls Luddism 'the opaque society', and remarks that any attempts to explain its actions face difficulties in the interpretation of the sources, which are unusually clouded by partisanship. First, there was the conscious partisan-ship of the authorities, which needed conspirators to justify the continuation of repressive legislation. The myth that all reformers were conspirators nec-essarily drove reformers into obscure, secretive form of activity. In order to penetrate underground activities, authorities employed spies and informers on an unprecedented scale. The more alarmist the informer's reports were, the more lucrative his trade was. This was a second form of partisanship (529). Finally, 'the third great reason why the sources are clouded is that working people *intended* them to be so' (531). For Thompson, 'if there had been an underground in these years, by its very nature it would not have left written evidence' (540).

In many respects, anarchism presents the same opacity attributed by Thompson to Luddism: scarcity or unreliability of sources and deceptiveness of evidence are not accidental, but inherent to the nature of the movement itself. This point has been often recognized by historians of anarchism, who have often circumvented rather than tackled it. For example, Sharif Gemie motivates a counter-community approach by pointing out the puzzle of an-archist organization: membership seemed to fluctuate continually, soaring in times of social struggle and dropping dramatically in times of repression, while secrecy or semi-legality of anarchist organizations prevented them from generating historical sources that would help making sense of the puz-zle ('Historians', 154). Likewise, George Esenwein justifies his study on the ideological dimension of Spanish anarchism by the availability of sources, in contrast to the lack of reliable sources concerning anarchist activism (4–5). Jerome Mintz tellingly relates how his field research on an insurrectionary episode in Spain had to confront the anarchist actors' intentional efforts to mislead observers, even decades after the fact (x–xi). Any study of anarchist action has to start by recognizing such inherent difficulties, which make the detection of continuity and sustained organization critical.

Continuity and sustained organization can also be obscured by the his-torian's scope of analysis. In their book *The Many-Headed Hydra*, Peter Line-baugh and Marcus Rediker tell the lost history of proletarian resistance to the rise of capitalism around the Atlantic, and claim that its historic invis-ibility owes not only to repression, but also 'to the violence of abstraction in the writing of history', which has been captive of the nation-state as an unquestioned framework of analysis (7). The same claim can be made about anarchism.

The history of anarchism often appears to follow a cyclical pattern of advances and retreats, with outbreaks of revolt followed by periods of qui-escence and then resurgences. For example, E. J. Hobsbawm thus summa-rizes 60 years of history of Andalusian anarchism within a paragraph: 'The movement collapsed in the later 1870s...revived again in the later 1880s, to collapse again... In 1892 there was another outburst... In the early 1900s another revival occurred... After another period of quiescence the greatest of the hitherto recorded mass movements was set off, it is said, by news of the Russian Revolution... The Republic (1931–36) saw the last of the great revivals . . . ' (78–9). Nunzio Pernicone, while rejecting Hobsbawm's millenarian thesis, similarly identifies the periods of resurgence of Italian anarchism with the years 1884–85, 1889–91, 1892–94, and 1897–98, and comments: 'As if the movement was locked in a vicious cycle of advance and retreat, every anarchist revival triggered or coincided with a new wave of government repression . . . that eradicated all that had been accomplished . . . ' (7).

Thus goes the pattern of anarchist movements that seem to disappear in the wave of arrests, exiles, shut-down of periodicals, and disbandment of groups after the onset of each struggle, only to reappear years later in a new cycle of agitations. This model fosters interpretations that identify discontinuity, spontaneism, and lack of organization as prominent features of anarchist movements, but it fails to explain what made them last. Could the seeming appearances and disappearances of anarchist movements be the fault of the historian, not of the movements? It is for charitable historians to question analyses of national scope, and investigate whether seeming entrances and exits of an anarchist movement on its country's stage may not in fact correspond to shifts of initiative between the homeland and the movement's transnational segment.

In sum, rather than just requiring that the interpretation of beliefs and evaluative attitudes be accommodated as rationally as possible to the available evidence, what may be required is to question that very evidence, when only irrationalist interpretations seem to be available. In brief, the methodological guideline that rational accommodation dictates is that whenever anarchists appear to be irrational, it is appearance that should be questioned first. In this respect, anarchist rationality, instead of being an empirical assertion to be demonstrated, becomes not only a methodological principle of interpretation, but also a heuristic principle, to be used in attempting to pierce through the deceptive appearance of anarchist action. By using the principle of charity to probe what superficially appears simple and odd, one may discover a more complex and rational underlying reality.

EPILOGUE: A CHARITABLE APPROACH TO ANARCHISM

Adopting a policy of rational accommodation, as outlined above, means shifting the uneasy burden of the attribution of irrationality: whenever the attribution occurs, the observer, not the actor, must be the first to carry that burden.

Such a shift involves questioning the arsenal of standard themes that have characterized the irrationalist historiography of anarchism: the doom of a movement that can only endlessly die and come alive again, as if by spontaneous germination; cyclicity, discontinuity, spontaneism, lack of organization, incoherence, and futile violence as the key traits of anarchism; and a 'causalist' explanation of protest as a blind reaction to economic distress by a movement to which no understandable reasons could be ascribed.

Davidson maintains that an actor's beliefs can only be made sense of in terms of an observer's own rationality. So, the task of the charitable historian becomes to investigate whether anarchism can be interpreted in terms of what we regard as rational: continuity, sustained action, evolution based on experience, planning, organization, coherence between ends and means, and sound theory. This involves questioning not only our own understanding of the anarchists' beliefs, but also the deceptive appearance of their opaque behavior.

Focusing on anarchist action in relation to the anarchists' beliefs and evaluative attitudes, and on reason-giving rather than causalist explanations, implies looking at anarchism from an internal perspective. The broader social context in which anarchist action was situated needs to be analyzed to the extent required to make sense of that action, and mainly in terms of the anarchists' own perception of that context.

An irrationalist and a rational explanation can equally fit the available evidence. However, by its very rationality, the latter is superior. An irrationalist account calls for a backing explanation of irrationality. In contrast, to paraphrase Boudon, as soon as anarchism can be explained as the outcome of rational action, the explanation invites no further question: 'rational action is its own explanation' ('Beyond', 2–3).

2
THE FIRST INTERNATIONAL:
A LASTING HERITAGE

IT IS IRONIC THAT THE BIRTH OF THE MOVEMENT THAT IS LEAST ASSOCIATED with organization and officialdom can be traced to a specific date and event—a congress, moreover. Yet anarchism as a movement unquestionably dates from the St. Imier Congress of 15–16 September 1872, where the federalist branch of the First International laid out its constitutive principles, in open contrast with those of the marxist branch.

Making sense of anarchism begins with a reflection on those origins, as this invites us to reappraise anarchism in positive terms, not just as a generic rejection of government, but as an anti-authoritarian brand of socialism. Until the split with the marxists called for distinctions, anarchists in the First International called themselves simply 'socialists'.

That first nucleus of the anarchist movement included a young student from Italy, Errico Malatesta. He would remain a protagonist of that movement for the next 60 years.

The early experience of the First International imprinted forever Malatesta's anarchism. His thought and action were constantly informed by that fundamental reliance on workers, collective action, and organization that was the common denominator of socialists of all persuasions. However, his anarchism was also characterized by another set of key themes that can equally be traced back to those years, but which specifically underpinned the anarchists' arguments in their controversies with the marxists. Those themes, which are best appreciated in contrast with their counterparts in marxist discourse, delineate the contour of Malatesta's anarchism as a distinct political philosophy. They are the proper place from which an assessment of the theoretical soundness of Malatesta's ideas ought to begin.

ERRICO MALATESTA, ONE OF THE 'BENEVENTO BAND'
When Malatesta took part in the St. Imier Congress he was 18 years old. He was born on 4 December 1853 in today's Santa Maria Capua Vetere, the small town of Southern Italy occupying the site of the Roman Capua.

At that time Southern Italy was still part of the Bourbon Kingdom of the Two Sicilies, which ended in 1860 after Garibaldi's expedition of the Thousand and the Italian unification. When Errico was ten, the Malatesta family moved to Naples. Here, at an early age, Malatesta became involved in republicanism, which had historically been the party of revolution in the Italy of *Risorgimento*. In the spring of 1871, under the influence of the Paris Commune, Malatesta turned from republicanism to socialism. At the time he was a medical student in Naples, but he soon abandoned medicine for revolution (Berti, *Errico*, 11–13). In 1872 the Italian Federation of the International was founded at the Rimini conference of 4–6 August, and a few weeks later the Federalist International, of which the Italian section became a pillar, was founded at the St. Imier Congress, where Malatesta made Bakunin's acquaintance. Malatesta soon became a leading figure of both the Italian Federation and the Federalist International.

The revolutionary character of the Italian International was apparent from the insurrectionary attempts of 1874 and 1877. In August 1874, abortive attempts to spark an armed insurrection were made, especially in Bologna and Apulia. Malatesta was arrested and jailed in the Apulian town of Trani. He remained there for several months, but at the trial he was acquitted (Luigi Fabbri, *Vida*, 87–91). In April 1877 Malatesta and Carlo Cafiero were at the head of the 'Matese band', a group of about 30 revolutionaries that penetrated the countryside around the Matese mountain range, in the Benevento province, not far from Naples, and seized a few municipalities in succession. After gathering the population in the square they publicly burned the tax registers, distributed municipal funds, and made every effort to sway the peasants to social revolution. After a few days of roaming the Matese countryside, nearly all the protagonists were arrested and jailed. However, they were acquitted at the Benevento trial of August 1878, as the charge of conspiracy was dismissed for lack of evidence (Luigi Fabbri, *Vida*, 101–5). The Benevento uprising became one of the most popular and symbolic events of the anarchist movement of those years across Europe. It represented well the anarchist focus on propaganda by the deed and on immediate insurrectionary prospects. Malatesta's characterization as 'one of the Benevento revolutionaries' lasted for many years.

The following three years, up to the International Socialist Revolutionary Congress of July 1881 in London, were years of exile and wandering across Europe and the Mediterranean Sea. In September 1878 Malatesta left Italy for Egypt, whence he was soon deported. He was embarked on a ship that took him to Beirut, Smirne, and Leghorn, finally landing him in Marseille. From France Malatesta reached Geneva, where he remained until April 1879, helping Peter Kropotkin with the editing of the first issues of *Le Révolté*. Expelled from Switzerland, Malatesta moved to Braila, in Rumania, and from there to Paris later that year. Arrested and expelled from France in November 1879, he spent the next few months moving clandestinely between

Switzerland, France, Belgium, and England. In the summer of 1880 he was arrested again in Paris, where he served time for contravening the order of expulsion. In 1881 Malatesta moved to London, where he remained until the summer 1882, when he attempted an expedition to Egypt to contribute to an uprising against the European rulers (Berti, *Errico*, 81–6, 90, 99).

By early 1883 Malatesta had finally returned to Italy, settling in Florence. However, in April 1883 the Rome Tribunal issued a warrant of arrest against him for distributing subversive handbills on the anniversary of the Paris Commune, and in May he was arrested and taken from Florence to Rome. He was released on parole in November. He returned to Florence, where he edited the anarchist periodical *La Questione Sociale* and devoted his energy to fighting the 'possibilist' turn of his former comrade Andrea Costa, who had embraced electoral tactics while maintaining his faith in revolutionary socialism. On 1 February 1884 Malatesta was convicted to a three-year detention by the Rome Tribunal for criminal association, but he appealed, thus being able to remain free. During the terrible cholera epidemic of 1884, when appeals for volunteer nurses were made in the hospitals, Malatesta and other anarchists rushed to Naples to treat the sick. Meanwhile the time was approaching for his appeal against the February sentence to be discussed. However, before that time came, Malatesta disappeared from Florence, fleeing to Argentina at the beginning of 1885. This departure marked the end of a cycle in his life (Luigi Fabbri, *Vida*, 117–21).

Two brands of socialism at cross purposes

In brief, Malatesta's activity from 1871 to 1884 was centered on the project of the International. Even after the London congress of 1881, by which time the Federalist International had practically ceased to exist, the ideal of the International remained alive in Malatesta's mind, and in 1884 he tried to revive the organization through the pamphlet *Programma e Organizzazione dell'Associazione Internazionale dei Lavoratori*, which reprinted the constitutive act of the International, followed by an extensive discussion of the International's objectives and tactics. Hence, Malatesta's formation and the political influences his anarchism underwent in the first 13 years of his militancy are best seen in the context of the ideals and debates that animated the International. Moreover, Malatesta's own analysis of the International's demise provides evidence about the lessons he learned from that long experience that spurred his later evolution.

The foundation of anarchism as a movement rather than an intellectual current is summarized by two documents: the Preamble to the Provisional Rules of the International Workingmen's Association and the third resolution of the St. Imier Congress on 'the nature of the political action of the proletariat', which respectively illustrate the anarchists' socialist belief shared within the International, and their own interpretation of it.

The Preamble's key claim was 'that the emancipation of the working class-es must be conquered by the working classes themselves; that the struggle for the emancipation of the working classes means, not a struggle for class privileges and monopolies, but for equal rights and duties, and the abolition of all class rule'. The Preamble ended by declaring that the International members acknowledged 'truth, justice, and morality, as the basis of their conduct towards each other, and towards all men, without regard to colour, creed, or nationality'; and that its founders held it 'the duty of a man to claim the rights of a man and a citizen, not only for himself but for every man who does his duty. No rights without duties, no duties without rights' (Stekloff, 446). The final version of the Preamble and Provisional Rules was the work of Marx, who nevertheless inserted two sentences about 'duty' and 'right' and about 'truth, morality, and justice' in the Preamble as a concession to the members that followed the Italian republican Giuseppe Mazzini (Hostetter, 71–2).

Ironically, of all concepts comprising the statutes of the International, the mazzinian phrases begrudgingly inserted by Marx were the ones that resonat-ed most powerfully in the Italian organs of the International. Between 1872 and 1883, 'No rights without duties, no duties without rights' was the most popular motto in that press, with 5 out of 28 periodicals inserting it in their mastheads, while two sported the phrase 'Truth, Justice, and Morality' (Bet-tini). Among these was *La Campana*, the organ of the *Federazione Operaia Napoletana*, which Malatesta helped to found. The federation's declaration of principles, signed by Malatesta as secretary, comprised seven articles, four of which were expressed in terms of rights and duties (Nettlau, *Bakunin*, 278–81).

Mazzinian republicanism is indeed a fundamental term of reference in discussing the beginning of the International in Italy: the two currents were linked by a double relationship of spiritual affinity and theoretical contrast.

In 1922, on the fiftieth anniversary of Mazzini's death, Malatesta wrote: 'at the bottom of our heart...we were Mazzinian as Mazzini was internation-alist... The animating spirit was the same: love among men, brotherhood among peoples, justice and social solidarity, spirit of self-sacrifice, sense of duty' ('Giuseppe').

At the same time, in Italy the International arose from the moral and intellectual discomfort and dissatisfaction of the idealist Italian youth to-ward mazzinian republicanism. The acknowledgment of the 'social question' was the crucial theoretical break with Italian past revolutionary traditions: 'The greatest discovery of the present century', Malatesta wrote in 1884, 'was made by the International when it proclaimed that *the economic ques-tion is fundamental* in Sociology...' ('Questione'). By focusing on the social question, the internationalists transferred the notion of freedom from a for-mal to a material ground: for them, the issue of freedom was ultimately linked to the abolition of private ownership of the means of production. This perspective was concisely emphasized by the motto that Malatesta included in 1883 in the masthead of his *La Questione Sociale*: 'Why do you speak of freedom? Whoever is poor, is a slave.' This and similar mottos eventually superseded the mazzinian ones, which disappeared altogether from the press in the following decade.

Still, republicanism is to be reckoned as a lasting cultural source of Italian anarchism. Acknowledging the elements of continuity between Italian anarchism and that older revolutionary tradition places anarchist ideas in a broader perspective and may help explaining the Italian anarchists' different attitude from the marxists' toward terms such as 'justice', 'duty', and 'morality'. Luce Fabbri, the daughter of Luigi Fabbri, who came from republicanism as Malatesta, remarks that even in her father's generation, which was next to Malatesta's, many anarchists 'brought much more of the liberal heritage of Italian *Risorgimento* than of Marx's classist one to their "subversive" work' (19).

The second seminal document that illustrates the foundation of anarchism is the third resolution of the St. Imier Congress, on 'the nature of the political action of the proletariat', which declared that 'the destruction of every kind of political power is the first task of the proletariat', that 'the organization of political power...can be nothing but deception', and that the proletarians of all lands 'must establish, independently of bourgeois politics, the solidarity of revolutionary action' (Stekloff, 259–60). These three principles were widely considered by the anarchists as the foundation of their movement. In an article published on the fiftieth anniversary of the St. Imier Congress, Malatesta quoted the third resolution and commented: 'Anarchism was born. From individual thought of a few isolated men it became the collective principle of groups distributed all over the world' ('Prima Internazionale').

The principles expressed in the third resolution of the St. Imier Congress should not be seen in contrast to the Preamble of the International, but rather as its complement. They represented the bakuninist response to Resolution IX, on the same topic of the political action of the proletariat, which the International had passed upon Marx's initiative at the London Conference of 17–23 September 1871. Marx's resolution claimed that 'the proletariat can only act as a class by organizing its forces into an independent political party', and that the conquest of political power is 'the prime duty of the proletariat' (Stekloff, 235–6). With this resolution, which gave the International a political direction clearly unacceptable to the anti-authoritarian side, the premises of the split were posed.

By comparing the two resolutions one can appreciate the depth of the contrast between marxists and anarchists: in the pursuit of the same goal, for marxists 'conquest of political power . . . becomes the prime duty of the proletariat', while for anarchists 'the destruction of every kind of political power is the first task of the proletariat'. The contrast between the two movements could not be stated more dramatically.

The fact that the two antagonistic resolutions interpreted the same principles, and aimed to fulfill the same objective, led commentators to present the split between marxists and anarchists as a controversy over tactics. The next 50 years would make it clear that the split reflected a profound theoretical divide, as marxism and anarchism branched in radically different directions from the common trunk of the workers' movement and revolutionary socialism. The respective theoretical tenets that emerged in time as most fundamental and persistent appeared to be precisely in that area of seemingly tactical initial disagreement, that of political power, while the initial common goal, revolutionary socialism, progressively turned into a special case in either branch, and sometimes into a disposable objective, as socialist reformism and anarchist individualism respectively illustrate.

The difference of outlook on political power was also at the root of the divergence between marxists and anarchists about how the International was to be organized. As Paul Thomas remarks, 'the protagonists in the Marx–Bakunin dispute were agreed basically on one thing and one thing only: that the dispute itself mattered, since its outcome would affect the direction of future society' (342). This apparent explanation leads to a more fundamental question. The International was founded as a loosely knit union of workers' associations of different countries, to give a steadier ground to the economic struggle against capitalism (Stekloff, 50). Given its initially broad-based, inclusive, and pragmatic approach, oriented to economic struggle, why did the International become the stage of an all-out theoretical antagonism between alternative conceptions of the proletarian revolution? Granted that for both opponents the outcome of their dispute would affect the direction of future society, why did that dispute take place within the International, whose initial objectives were so alien from the terms in which the dispute unfolded?

The reason may be understandable for marxists, who emphasized the link between economic and political struggles, and envisioned a disciplined and centralized organization of the working class. Marx must have deemed that the International, regardless of its initial goals, was a favorable terrain for putting his ideas in practice. Two months after the foundation of the International, he remarked to a correspondent: 'Although I have been systematically refusing to participate in any way whatsoever in all the "organizations", etc. for years now, I accepted *this time* because it concerns a matter by means of which it is possible to have a significant influence' ('To J. Weydemeyer', 44).

The answer may be less obvious for the anarchists, though. On this subject it is useful to consider the point of view of Malatesta, who was a direct witness and an actor of the events in the anarchist ranks. His analysis is all the more interesting as it offers an explanation of the International's demise that holds marxists and anarchists equally responsible.

In contrast with marxist centralism, anarchists advocated the free federation of autonomous groups, and argued that working class emancipation was to happen from the bottom up. However, Malatesta argued some 30 years later, despite the libertarian nature of their project, and without being aware, in their pragmatic attitude anarchists shared one authoritarian trait with marxists: they tended to attribute their own ideas to the mass of the associates, mistaking a more or less conscious assent for a full conversion. Therefore, one could see the International become mutualist, collectivist, communist, revolutionary, anarchist, through swift changes that were expressed in the congress resolutions and the press, but could not represent a real, simultaneous evolution of the membership. Both marxists and anarchists tried to use the International for ideological purposes. The difference was that anarchists, relying chiefly on propaganda to gain converts for their cause, favored decentralization, autonomy of groups, and both individual and collective free initiative, while the marxists, in their authoritarianism, tried to impose their ideas by way of more or less fictitious majorities, centralization, and discipline. But they each ultimately did the same: they all tried to force events rather than relying upon the force of events. As there was no distinction between organizations for economic struggle and for political and ideological struggle, the International was an all-encompassing organization that took on both functions. Consequently, Malatesta argued, the more advanced individuals were forced to either adapt to the backwardness of the mass, or keep progressing, as they actually did, with the illusion that the mass would follow and understand them. The most advanced elements investigated, discussed, uncovered the needs of the people, turned the vague ideas of the masses into concrete programs, upheld socialism, upheld anarchy, foresaw the future, and prepared for it—but in so doing they killed the association. For Malatesta what killed the International was not persecution, or personal controversies, or the way it was organized: it was that both marxists and anarchists tried to impose their program on the International, and in this struggle for hegemony they prevented the International from a slower maturation that would have more appropriately created the right conditions for change, by uplifting the minds and building up the necessary momentum ('Nuova').

DISTINCTIVE ANARCHIST THEMES

Malatesta's retrospective critique of the International, including the anarchist side, hints to the direction in which his anarchism developed in the 1890s. At the same time, the controversy in the International pointed to the fundamental differences between the two main brands of socialism. The central tenets of anarchism that the contrast with the marxists brought to the fore stayed at the core of Malatesta's anarchism throughout his life and constituted the stable foundations upon which his ideas changed and evolved, notwithstanding that such evolution partly arose from his critique of the International. Themes such as coherence between ends and means and voluntarism, which were at the root of the anarchists' controversy with the marxists, not only retained a central place in Malatesta's later elaboration, but received their fullest formulation in Malatesta's writings of years or even decades later. An outline of those formulations allows one to gauge the lasting heritage of the International in Malatesta's ideas and represents the most natural introduction to his anarchism, setting the conceptual backdrop of his later evolution.

Coherence between ends and means

One of the most contentious issues in the International and ever after was that of ends and means in collective action. A glimpse of this rift is provided by the Sonvillier circular, which the newly constituted anarchist Jura Federation sent to all federations of the International in November 1871, in reaction to the resolutions of the London Conference of September. In the circular the anarchists advocated that the organization adopted by the International be informed as much as possible by the same libertarian principles of the future society ('Circulaire'). This was in turn the application of a more general and pervasive principle advocated by the anarchists—that of coherence between ends and means, perhaps the most fundamental and universal principle of anarchist action: a non-authoritarian society could not be achieved by authoritarian means. In contrast, marxists argued that during the period of struggle to overthrow the old society the proletariat should employ means which would be discarded after liberation (Marx, 'Conspectus', 152). For marxists, by informing their action with abstract principles, anarchists gave up useful means of struggle that were available in the bourgeois society, ultimately limiting themselves, as the early Christians, 'to pray and hope instead of fighting', as Engels remarked (63–4). What was the anarchist rationale for advocating the principle of coherence between ends and means?

Malatesta provided a systematic discussion of the issue in the 1892 article 'Un peu de théorie' (A little bit of theory), reprinted shortly thereafter in Italian with the explicit title 'Fine e mezzi' (End and means). The article set off somewhat startlingly by subscribing to the popular saying that 'the end justifies the means'. Malatesta claimed that this saying—usually associated with Niccolò Machiavelli, who advocated the priority of expediency over morality in politics (48, 55)—was the universal guide to conduct. However, he immediately explained that it would be better to say that 'every end implies its means', a phrase which resembled in turn Kant's claim that 'whoever wills the end also wills (insofar as reason has decisive influence on his actions) the indispensably necessary means to it that are within his power' (70). Similarly, Malatesta maintained that 'morality is contained in the aims: the means is inevitable', further arguing that 'the big problem of life is to find the means which, in the circumstances, leads to that end most surely and economically' ('Fine e mezzi'). Each end must select its own appropriate means. In this light Machiavelli's maxim is reconciled with the Kantian rule: if one's end is to hold on to power, one has indeed to learn how not to be good, while trying to use moral means in holding on to power would be self-defeating. However, the anarchists' end was different, hence their means must also be different.

In advocating the principle of coherence between ends and means, Malatesta emphasized that the requirement that the means be not in contradiction with the end did not have an unconditional value, but was rather a matter of expediency. One had to employ self-sustainable means, given the particular circumstances in which one had to operate. This point was related explicitly to the crucial issue of violence. For Malatesta, anarchists must in no way give up violent means, as this would be self-defeating: 'we are forced to struggle in the world as we found it, on pain of remaining sterile dreamers, who leave untouched all the existing evils, and do good to no one, for fear of doing wrong to anyone.' As Marx and Engels in their criticism to the anarchists, Malatesta made a polemical reference to the Christian martyrs: 'even the purest and sweetest martyr, who let himself be dragged to the scaffold for the triumph of good, without any resistance . . . would do wrong' ('Fine e mezzi').

In the end, both Malatesta and the marxists appealed to the same principle of expediency toward the same goal of emancipating the proletariat, both polemically rejecting the adherence of Christian martyrs to an absolute ethical principle. Thus, on what ground did they respectively accept and reject the principle of coherence between ends and means? In what sense could anarchists claim that informing their collective action to the same principles of the future society was more expedient than the marxist alternative? After all, marxists had the same end, the fullest self-development, well-being, and happiness of all human beings. Why were marxist means less expedient? Malatesta claimed that 'only the widest application of the principle of solidarity can put an end to the struggle, and therefore to oppression and exploitation among men'. Marxists would definitely agree on the role of solidarity in the struggle. The whole purpose of the International was to establish solidarity among workers. However, marxists would object to the cause–effect relation implicit in the outlook on solidarity as a principle, whose spread would end oppression and exploitation. For them the terms of the relation were reversed: the abolition of oppression and exploitation would bring about a society based on solidarity. Likewise, they would likely object to the idea of solidarity as arising 'from free agreement' and 'from the spontaneous and deliberate harmonization of interests', as Malatesta put it ('Fine e mezzi'). They would rather claim that the harmonization of interests, by no means free or deliberate, arose from the spread of capitalist relations of production.

The key point was the role of knowledge.

In the *Communist Manifesto* Marx and Engels had claimed that, theoretically, the communists had 'over the great mass of the proletariat the advantage of clearly understanding the line of march, the conditions, and the ultimate general results of the proletarian movement' (256). Sixteen years later, in 1864, Marx reaffirmed the concept in his inaugural address to the First International. After claiming that the conquest of political power was the great duty of the working classes, he added: 'One element of success they possess—numbers; but numbers weigh only in the balance, if united by combination and led by knowledge' (580).

Anarchists took an opposite view. 'The aim of the Jacobins', Malatesta remarked, 'and all authoritarian parties, who believe to be in possession of absolute truth, is to impose their ideas on the ignorant masses. Therefore, even when they are sincere and no aim of personal domination is involved, they must make every effort to seize power, subject the masses, and fit humanity to the Procrustean bed of their concepts' ('Fine e mezzi'). For Malatesta, the use of authoritarian means toward emancipatory ends was based on the actors' pretensions to hold superior knowledge, as was the case for marxists, who advocated political power as a means that would eventually be discarded. For the anarchists, such presumption of knowledge was ill-founded, nor could authoritarian means be discarded. This was the essence of their claim about the self-perpetuating character of the state. Both arguments were developed at length by Bakunin in his criticism of the marxist theory of the state, and they were resumed and further articulated by Malatesta.

In *God and the State*, of 1871, Bakunin rejected as pernicious the idea of government by an intellectual elite based on scientific knowledge, even when this elite was animated by the best of intentions. Bakunin's first argument was the fallibility of science. Human science is always and necessarily imperfect. Were we to try to force the practical life of men into conformity with scientific findings, we should condemn society as well as individuals to suffer martyrdom on a 'Procrustean bed'. Second, Bakunin argued, a society which obeyed legislation emanating from an intellectual elite, not because it understood its rational character but because this legislation was imposed by the elite in the name of science, which the people venerated without comprehending it, would be a society not of men but of brutes. Third, an intellectual elite invested with absolute sovereignty, even if it were composed of the most illustrious men, would infallibly and soon end in its own moral and intellectual corruption: 'a scientific body to which has been confided the government of society would soon end by devoting itself no longer to science at all, but to quite another matter; and, as in the case of all established powers, that would be its own eternal perpetuation by rendering the society confided to its care ever more stupid and consequently more dependent upon the scientists' authority' (227–8).

Similarly, Malatesta argued in *Anarchy*, whose Italian version 'L'Anarchia' had been first serialized in 1884 for *La Questione Sociale* of Florence and finally published as a pamphlet in 1891, that even if men of infinite knowledge and goodness existed, and even supposing, against all historical evidence, that governmental power were to rest in the hands of the ablest and kindest people, government office would not add to their power to do good, but it would instead paralyze and destroy that power, by reason of the necessity men in government have of dealing with so many matters they do not understand, and above all of wasting their energy keeping themselves in power, their friends happy, holding in check the malcontents, and subduing the rebels (16). Malatesta also rejected the marxist claim that once the social conditions were changed the nature and the role of government would change, too. In a metaphorical reversal of lamarckian evolutionary law, Malatesta claimed that 'organ and function are inseparable terms. Take away from an organ its function and either the organ dies or the function is re-established. Put an army in a country in which there are neither reasons for, nor fear of, war, civil or external, and it will provoke war or, if it does not succeed in its intentions, it will collapse.' A government, that is a group of people empowered to use the collective power to oblige each individual to obey them, is already a privileged class, cut off from the people. As any constituted body would do, it will seek to extend its powers, to be beyond public control, to impose its own policies and to give priority to its special interests. In any case, even if a government wanted to, it could not please everybody, even if it did manage to please a few. It would have to defend itself against the malcontents, and would therefore need to get the support of one section of the people to do so (33–4).

In sum, anarchists rejected the idea of social engineering as a means of emancipation as ill-conceived, because it over-estimates the power of scientific knowledge and creates a privileged elite. The self-interest of this elite, the high value the elite would attribute to its own leadership for the common good, and the unforeseen side-effects of its action upon society would all contribute to lead the elite to devote an ever-increasing amount of energies to repressive functions, and to self-supporting through the creation of a privileged class around itself. The government that marxists foresaw as a means of emancipation to be discarded after the end was reached, would instead turn into a self-perpetuating and self-reinforcing end in itself.

The anarchists' arguments are closely reminiscent of the 'law of heterogony of ends', formulated in 1897 by the German psychologist Wilhelm Wundt, the founder of experimental psychology. The law states that the relation between actual effects and ideated ends 'is such that secondary effects always arise that were not thought of in the first ideas of end. These new effects enter into new series of motives and thus modify the old ends or add new ones to them' (326–7). The phenomenon described by Wundt has been widely referred to in sociology as that of 'the unanticipated consequences of purposive social action', as the American sociologist Robert K. Merton titled his 1936 seminal paper. A related aspect of the law of the heterogony of ends is the process of *displacement of goals*, whereby means tend to become ends in themselves. This aspect was emphasized by Hans Vaihinger, a philosopher often characterized as Neo-Kantian, who formulated Wundt's same idea as early as 1872, though he left it unpublished, calling it the law of the *preponderance of the means over the end* (p. xxx). The two aspects of Wundt's theory, the presence of non-purposed effects in purposive action, and the tendency of means to become end in themselves, are both present in the anarchist criticism to the foreshadowed marxist state.

In sum, far from being a mere advocacy of an abstract dogma remote from empirical conditions, the principle of coherence between ends and means was grounded on sound reasons. These received a philosophical and scientific formulation in the last quarter of the nineteenth century and gained currency in the social sciences of the twentieth, especially in connection with the critique of the totalitarian socialist states that anarchists had foreseen. The principle of coherence between ends and means notably differed from the marxist approach in three respects. First, it assigned a more modest role to anarchists than marxists attributed to themselves. As Malatesta stated, anarchists did not believe that freedom and happiness could be given to people by an individual or a party, but instead all men were themselves to discover the conditions of their freedom and happiness and conquer them. Second, it involved a more conservative and cautious outlook on science, as illustrated by the anarchists' mistrust in the idea of social engineering as undertaken by intellectual elites. Third, it exhibited greater methodological sophistication about the effects of purposive social action, in contrast to the unproblematic marxist outlook on the benign outcome of a workers' state. In brief, from the perspective of the ultimate goal of the International, the full emancipation of the proletariat, the anarchist principle of coherence between ends and means actually stemmed from a more balanced and realistic outlook on the scope and conditions of effective social action than exhibited by marxists, rather than being an expression of irrationalism and utopianism.

Voluntarism

Another trait that sharply differentiated anarchists from marxists since the First International was voluntarism. The contrast was most concisely summarized in Marx's disparaging remark about Bakunin: 'Will, not economic conditions, is the foundation of his social revolution' ('On Bakunin', 607).

How different standpoints on voluntarism translated into different tactics is illustrated by the discussion of the right of inheritance at the International's Basle Conference of September 1869. The abolition of the right of inheritance was a chief programmatic point of Bakunin's International Alliance of the Socialist Democracy, founded the previous year (Stekloff, 154–5). The committee which had been appointed to report to the Basle conference on the question had adopted Bakunin's outlook, and placed a resolution to this effect before the delegates. The General Council presented another report representing Marx's view, arguing that the right of inheritance was not the cause, but the legal outcome of the existing economic system. The disappearance of the right of inheritance would be the natural result of a social change abolishing the private ownership of the means of production, but its abolition could never be the starting point of a social transformation. Bakunin agreed that, throughout history, a legal right had always come to confirm a *fait accompli*, but he retorted that, once established, legal rights subsequently turned into causes of further effects. The chain could be broken by starting to reverse such rights (Stekloff, 142–4). In brief, the competing reports stemmed from the same contrasting views on the relation between intentional action and material conditions that separated marxists and anarchists on the issue of voluntarism.

Voluntarism was an important trait of Malatesta's ideas since the First International, but it increasingly became a distinctive feature of his anarchism over time, differentiating him not only from the marxists, but also from anarchists of other tendencies, and making him one of the most articulate and original representatives of the voluntarist strand that was always prominent in the anarchist movement. Though he probably never used this 'ism', references to *volontà* (will) were frequent in his articles. However, voluntarism became an explicit theme in his writings after the turn of the century, as he felt the urge to contrast anarchist tendencies of kropotkinian origin that he regarded as fatalist.

Though voluntarism was a central feature of Malatesta's anarchism, one finds very few discussions of voluntarism as a philosophical theory in his writings, for he refrained from philosophical debates. When he made exceptions, it was to correct pragmatic errors proceeding from philosophical beliefs. Such was the case of his contribution to the debate on determinism and free will in an article of 1913. For Malatesta, the cornerstone of determinism was the principle of causality: 'no effect without sufficient cause; no cause without its proportionate effect.' Its logical conclusion is that everything is a necessary concatenation of events, man is a conscious automaton, will is an illusion, and liberty is non-existent—a scientific conclusion that Malatesta likened to religious ones of Fate and Predestination. And it would be vain to seek to attenuate the meaning of the system and elude its consequences, trying to conciliate necessity with liberty: a 'necessity' that is not always necessary and admits exceptions can no longer be called by that name ('Liberty').

Though Malatesta did not reject determinism, he questioned its extension to human action, based on the pragmatic observation that such extension paralyzes the will and presents any effort as futile. In fact, he argued, determinists floundered about in continuous contradiction, denying responsibility while becoming indignant against the judge who punishes the irresponsible, 'as if the judge were not himself determined and therefore also irresponsible!' However, Malatesta did not try to solve the philosophical dilemma, but rather suspended his judgment. The absolute free will of the spiritualists was contradicted by facts and was repugnant to the intellect. The negation of will and liberty by the mechanists was repugnant to common feelings: 'intellect and sentiment are constituent parts of our egos and we know not how to subjugate one to the other.' However, 'we want to live a conscious and creative life, and such a life demands, in the absence of positive concepts, certain necessary presuppositions which may be unconscious but which are always, nevertheless, in the soul of everyone. The most important of these presuppositions was the efficacy of the will. All that could usefully be sought are the conditions which limit or augment the power of the will' ('Liberty').

Thus, Malatesta accepted the existence of the will as an ineliminable fact, in its pre-theoretical, common-sense evidence and immediacy. Such unresolved dualism between intellect and sentiment, which combined scientific determinism and introspective evidence without reducing one to the other, remained a constant of his thought. Some 18 years later, in a letter of 12 January 1931 to Max Nettlau, Malatesta maintained that the will must be an active force, if it is anything more than a simple illusion of consciousness: 'Does it exist, though? To claim this with certainty, one should be able to explain what it is and what all other things are, in a word one should be able to understand the Universe, which is beyond our faculties.' Malatesta reiterated that the belief in the efficacy of the will—that is, that through one's will one could effect things that would not happen otherwise—was a necessary assumption of any intelligent activity (Nettlau Papers). Then, in a follow-up letter of 21 January he concluded: 'we do not understand anything about the mysteries of the universe. Therefore we often have to act as if (*als ob*) we understood' (Nettlau Papers). The redundant insertion of the German phrase was probably a reference to Hans Vaihinger's *Die Philosophie des als ob*, where the 'law of the preponderance of the means over the end' was expounded (p. xliii).

Certainly, Malatesta acknowledged, the individual will of men was in general a very weak factor in life and history, limited as it was by the ineluctable laws of nature and by the different and sometimes contrasting wills of other men. In his letter of 12 January 1931 to Nettlau he argued that the remedies to such limitations were respectively science and association. It was the task of science to uncover the natural laws against which the will was powerless—that is, to distinguish what was necessary from what was free. And it was the task of men to try to agree among themselves for the highest good of everyone. Hence, the will, which was almost completely powerless in the isolated and ignorant man, acquired more and more force through the progress of science and association. Science seemed to limit freedom by showing what could not be done and by destroying fanciful desires and projects, but in reality it augmented people's capability and effective freedom: 'the man who ignores mechanics, physics, etc. can dream about voyages through the Milky Way, but he remains grounded to the solid surface of the earth; the engineer who has the knowledge, does not indulge in impossible dreams, but he finds the means to cross the sky by airplane or airship.' Likewise, association, even when it was free and voluntary, seemed to limit the autonomy of the individuals, but in reality it transformed a miserable savage into a man whose conditions of life improved every day through the advantages of cooperation (Nettlau Papers).

Malatesta acknowledged the primacy of material needs, expressed by the phrase 'live first, and then philosophize'. Most often those who struggled for an idea had grown up in relatively favorable conditions, accumulating a latent energy that could be released when the need came. The most active and keen members of revolutionary organizations were usually not so much motivated by their own needs as by the desire to feel ennobled by an ideal, Malatesta argued. In contrast, those in the most miserable conditions, who might seem most directly and immediately interested in social change, were often more passive or absent altogether ('Idealismo'). However, though severely constrained by material conditions, individual will was not determined by such conditions. Furthermore, to the extent that material conditions had a social rather than natural origin, they were themselves the outcome of the wills of other individuals, whose complex interplay made up social reality. This idea was at the root of both the weakness and the strength of individual will. Insofar as the interplay of wills was informed by contrast and competition, the individual was severely limited. However, insofar as competition was replaced by association, the individual will was empowered by its harmonization with the cooperating wills of other individuals. To the extent that individuals associated and established common goals, they determined the course of society. On the other hand, no social change could be expected to occur unless it was consciously willed. This was the essence of Malatesta's voluntarism and one of the most characteristic traits of his anarchism.

Anarchists and marxists agreed that purposive individual action was severely limited and unlikely to make a noticeable impact on society. However, Marx's and Malatesta's analyses diverged in describing social forces. From the acknowledgment of the isolation and powerlessness of each individual at the social level, Marx moved on to describe the relevant social forces as impersonal ones independent from any individual, and pertaining to society as a whole ('Preface', 425–6). For Malatesta, though the laws of nature were indeed ineluctable extra-human factors, social forces were constituted by the wills of other people. While no individual will could appreciably influence

the course of society, the development of society as a whole was still determined by the complex and ever-mutable interplay of the individual wills
of all members of society. For Marx, the task of the social reformer was to
understand the dynamic of society as a whole as best as possible: effectiveness
came from knowledge. In contrast, anarchist voluntarism focused on the
agency of the social actors. Rather than emphasizing how individual wills
were constrained by the development of society as a whole, the anarchist
voluntarist emphasized how society as a whole was determined by the interplay of the individual wills of social actors. Accordingly, the social reformer
aimed to aggregate as many of those wills as possible toward the same goal.
As wills were ever more united, material constraints, to the extent that they
were social, disappeared. The voluntarist's unity of goals replaced the marxist's knowledge, thus pointing again to diverging attitudes on the role of
social knowledge in collective action.

'Working Class' and 'People'

Both themes of coherence between end and means and voluntarism pointed
to contrasting views about goal-oriented action. Marxists shunned ideals and
focused on the dynamics of capitalist economy as a guide to action. For Marx
and Engels, communism was not 'a state of affairs which is to be established, an
ideal to which reality will have to adjust itself', but 'the real movement which
abolishes the present state of things' (*German*, 187). In contrast, anarchy was
indeed an ideal that informed all anarchists' action. A similar contrast of views
underpinned the respective views on class. Anarchists did share with marxists
the notions of class, proletariat, and class struggle. It was precisely the 'social
question', and not the issue of the state, that precipitated the antagonism with
mazzinians in Italy, while, conversely, the issue of the state became central in the
International, where the expropriation of capitalists was undisputed. However,
the anarchists' and marxists' respective notions of class differed significantly.

Malatesta's own view on class underwent changes since he joined the First
International as a young student. At that time Italian anarchists had an optimistic faith in the workers' revolutionary virtues that was soon disappoint-
ed. But even then their belief was not in a class consciousness of a marxist
type. Rather, as Malatesta recalled, they regarded 'the worker's condition as
morally superior to any other social position' and held 'a mystic faith in the
people's virtues, in its ability, and in its egalitarian and libertarian instincts'
(Preface, xxv, xxvii).

Malatesta's mature view on class was most clearly spelled out in 1921,
half a century after he joined the International, in the article 'Lotta di classe
o odio tra le classi? (Class struggle or class hatred?). Malatesta argued that
history had turned the proletariat into the main instrument of the next social
transformation, upon which 'those who struggle for the creation of a society
where *all* human beings are free and furnished with the means to exercise

their freedom must mainly rely'. As the present chief cause of social evils was the monopoly of natural resources and capital, it was natural that 'the chief actors of the necessary expropriation be those who, not owning anything, are most directly and obviously interested in the common ownership of the means of production'. Hence, anarchists directed their propaganda most specifically to proletarians. At the same time, and in contrast to the Italian anarchists' early belief, Malatesta argued that proletarians 'are very often prevented by the conditions in which they live from rising to the conception of a superior ideal through thought and study'.

Though Malatesta agreed with marxists about class struggle as the battleground of human emancipation, he disagreed about the link between class antagonism and class consciousness.

For marxists, the social consciousness of men was determined by their social being, which, in turn, was mainly determined by economic factors. Accordingly, the formation of the proletariat as a compact whole, conscious of its common class interests, was mainly driven by the evolution of material conditions, which produced a polarization and homogenization of classes: 'with the development of industry the proletariat not only increases in number; it becomes concentrated in greater mass, its strength grows, and it feels that strength more. The various interests and conditions of life within the ranks of the proletariat are more and more equalized, in proportion as machinery obliterates all distinctions of labour, and nearly everywhere reduces wages to the same low level...the collisions between individual workmen and individual bourgeois take more and more the character of collisions between two classes' (Marx and Engels, *Communist*, 252).

Malatesta's outlook on the relationship between material conditions and consciousness was quite different, as we can gauge from the historical narrative whereby he explains the dynamics of social antagonisms and struggles, in 'L'Anarchia', the 1884 version of *Anarchy*. For Malatesta, man's fundamental natural characteristic is the egoistic instinct of his own preservation, while the social instinct developed from the accumulated and communicated experience of generations, which 'taught man that by uniting with other men their individual safety and well-being were enhanced'. Yet man also discovered that he could achieve the advantages of cooperation by obliging the weakest to work for him and preferring domination to association: 'thus solidarity ended up in private property and government, that is in the exploitation of the labour of all by a privileged minority.' On the other hand, the oppressed did not accept their condition light-heartedly: 'and all history is the struggle between the exploited and the exploiters, and the more or less extensive forms of property and government represent nothing but the diverse outcomes of this struggle, with all its victories, its defeats, and its compromises.'

Of course, the relevance of the passage does not rest in its historical truthfulness, but rather in its illustration of the motivations and forces that

Malatesta regards as fundamental in social processes. In explaining social struggle Malatesta reaches a formula that closely resembles Marx and Engels's claim that 'the history of all hitherto existing societies is the history of class struggles'. However, a fundamental difference exists: unlike Marx and Engels, Malatesta identifies the primary factors of social processes in human dispositions, rather than in definite modes of production which impose themselves on individuals. A telling illustration of this approach is the definition of 'worker' that the Italian Federation arrived at, in an effort to determine who was entitled to join the International Workingmen's Association. As Malatesta's program of 1884 illustrates and as he recalled many years later, they concluded that 'a worker is whoever works at the overthrow of the bourgeois order' (*Programma e Organizzazione*, 59; Preface, xxvi). In this way they replaced material conditions with human dispositions in a reversal of marxist materialism.

Malatesta acknowledged that capitalist production created irreconcilably antagonistic interests. However, he rejected the idea that capitalist production also developed the conditions of its own overcoming, by creating the proletariat as a single, revolutionary subject. Instead, Malatesta tended to regard class consciousness formation not as the outcome of a material process, but rather as a consciously undertaken project. Shunning from any reliance on class polarization as determined by capitalist development, Malatesta emphasized that society could not be straightforwardly partitioned into exploited and exploiters. In the article 'Giustizia per tutti' (Justice for all) of 1897, he argued that all individuals, consciously or not, could turn at different times into oppressed or oppressors, exploited or exploiters, depending on circumstances. Hence, reducing the struggle against oppression and exploitation to the struggle of one segment of society against the other would be an oversimplification. Instead, human nature was to be respected in all individuals, by fighting them when they were oppressors and exploiters, and defending them when they were oppressed and exploited. For Malatesta, anarchist propaganda was especially addressed to workers, aiming at their organization as a class that struggled against capitalists and governments. However, it was also propaganda of solidarity addressed to everyone, with no distinction of class and social rank.

Malatesta also rejected economism, claiming instead that groups and institutions had interests that could not necessarily be reduced to those of their class, as determined by relations of production. In a letter addressed to the newspaper *Il Progresso Italo-Americano* in 1899 Malatesta denied that the bourgeoisie was a monolithic body struggling against the proletariat, and that government, army, magistrature, and churches had no other reason to exist than the defense of bourgeois interests. The bourgeoisie, he argued, was divided into fractions struggling against each other, and the various political, legal, military, and religious institutions not only defended the bourgeoisie against the proletariat, but also had their own interests, which they defended even at the cost of compromising bourgeois interests. This situation was both an advantage and a danger for workers: it split the enemy, but it might equally induce workers to forget that all bourgeois were enemies. The divisions in the bourgeoisie gave workers opportunities for alliances, provided that they avoided turning themselves into a footstool for the ambition of some fraction of the bourgeoisie. For Malatesta, the implication of social complexity was not the renunciation of class struggle, but on the contrary the effort to 'prevent workers from losing contact with the Polar star of class struggle, amidst the complex conflicts of the present hour and the near future'. Malatesta rejected the factual claim that class struggle had an exclusive influence on the multiform historical events, but concluded that the interests of the working class, which ultimately amounted to the abolition of the private ownership of the means of production, should drive the proletariat's struggle ('Signor').

In sum, given the complexity of social relationships and the absence of a clear-cut partition of society into exploiters and exploited, organization as a class becomes a guiding criterion for workers to hold on to in their struggle, in order to create that partition through conscious solidarity among workers. It is not so much daily experience that teaches workers that they have common interests. In fact the current social organization does the opposite, putting workers in competition with each other. As Malatesta argued, 'solidarity can be found in a future-oriented aspiration, in a concept of social life that negates the present society, and that does not *necessarily* arise from experience, but rather arises in some way in the minds of a minority, and must be preached and spread until it gathers sufficient support to be able to triumph' ('Dove').

In addition to 'class', the concept of 'the people' frequently appears in Malatesta's writings. What does the latter concept denote, and how does it relate to the former?

The dictionary definition of 'the people', in the sense relevant here, is 'the mass of people in a country etc., not having special rank or position' (*Concise*). In the same spirit, Margaret Canovan noted in her book *Populism* that the notion of 'the people' is one of those collective ideas that make sense only through an implied contrast with something else (59). The generic and negative character of the definition probably captures what is essential here about this concept. 'People' has a broader connotation than 'proletariat': the latter implies a reference to the capitalist society, while the former covers every society in which governmental oppression exists. The appeal to the people expresses a universal egalitarian stance that encompasses all forms of oppression, of which capitalism represents a specific instance. In this respect, the appeal to the people implicitly claims the relevance of anarchism for all societies where some form of oppression exists, not just for those where workers' exploitation is the main form of oppression.

On the other hand, a definition of the people in a negative form also covers a connotation of people as an unconscious, passive mass that has not arisen from its condition of subjection. In fact, consciousness seems to be the main characteristic that discriminates between 'the people' and 'class' in Malatesta's writings. When Malatesta refers to the passive and submissive character of the masses, he tends to refer to them as 'the people'. For example, in an article of 1902 where he discusses the delusory character of arbitration in labor disputes, he remarks that 'the people is unfortunately the most credulous bird that one could imagine; it rushes most eagerly to any bait set by any fowler' ('Arbitrato'). Conversely, references to the consciousness of the masses are usually made in terms of 'class consciousness', as in the following example: 'It is our task, the task of socialists in general, to cultivate in the proletariat the consciousness of class antagonism, of the necessity of collective struggle ...' ('Anarchismo nel movimento'). Thus, Malatesta's linguistic usage is another indication of his outlook on class as a project substantiated by human dispositions, rather than a fact determined by material conditions.

Notwithstanding their different connotations, in the context of bourgeois society the concepts of 'proletariat' and 'the people' arguably have the same denotation. If the bourgeois state is the defender of capitalist interests, the masses politically oppressed by the bourgeois state and those economically exploited by capitalism are by and large the same, thus making 'proletariat' and 'the people' coterminous. A test bed of this hypothesis is represented by those manifestos directly addressing the masses, which Malatesta signed or was involved with. Such documents show that the terms 'people' and 'workers' were freely, though not randomly, intermixed. For example an abstentionist manifesto of November 1890 was titled *I socialisti-anarchici al Popolo Italiano: Non votate!* (The anarchist-socialists to the Italian People: Don't Vote!) and addressed 'workers and peasants'; a manifesto *Al popolo d'Italia* (To the people of Italy) of March 1894 contained four sections in the form of invocations, the first of which called upon the Italian workers, while the others called upon the people; and another abstentionist manifesto of November 1897, *I socialisti anarchici ai lavoratori italiani in occasione delle elezioni* (The anarchist-socialists to the Italian workers on the elections), repeatedly addressed workers, but ended with the following appeal: 'No socialists in Parliament. Whoever wants to struggle for the people must remain among the people.'

However, 'proletariat' and 'the people' are not coterminous in every society. Their different senses may yield different denotations in different contexts. A case in point is the dictatorship of the proletariat. If 'proletariat' is contrasted to 'bourgeoisie', while 'the people' is contrasted to 'government', or more generally to those 'having special rank or position', then the 'proletarian' character of a party dictatorship can be argued for more easily than its 'popular' character. While the class character of party dictatorship is a debatable issue, its coercive character makes it almost tautologically belong to the latter side of the people–government dichotomy. Hence, the concept of 'the people', always current in the anarchist language, made itself readily available to the anarchist criticism of Bolshevik dictatorship. Indeed, references to the masses in Malatesta's articles of the 1920s about Bolshevik rule in Russia were most often made in terms of 'the people'. Malatesta himself emphasized and justified his usage of the term in a controversy of 1921 with an Italian communist periodical: 'the day the communists attempted to impose their tyranny upon the people, they would meet the opposition of all anarchists . . . And I say *people* and not proletariat, because in my opinion the first act of a revolution must be the direct expropriation of the exploiting class by the proletarians and therefore the merge of all social classes, linked together by the common necessity of work' ('Nemico'). In the last sentence one can still discern an echo of Bakunin's 'equalization of classes', a most controversial concept in his arguments with Marx, for whom it was a voluntaristic oxymoron that failed to recognize that the abolition of classes would be a process, not a resolution ('To P. Lafargue', 46).

In sum, Malatesta's notion of class was subsumed by a broader humanism. Most importantly, his emphasis on class consciousness as arising from a future-oriented aspiration and not necessarily from experience alone pointed again to his construing collective action as guided by values. This was also the essential trait of coherence between ends and means and voluntarism, in contrast to the marxist emphasis on knowledge. Such prominence of values was signaled since the rise of the International by the Italian anarchists' predilection for moral language, as witnessed by the popularity of the mazzinian phrases reluctantly inserted by Marx in the statutes of the International.

The different roles respectively attributed by marxists and anarchists to knowledge and values points to a deep theoretical divergence between the two camps, which contrasts with the view that the controversy was mainly tactical or even proceeded from a clash of personalities between Marx and Bakunin. A charitable interpretation of a rift that divided marxists from anarchists for decades calls for more thorough explanations than ones based on contingent or temperamental factors.

In fact, both marxists and anarchists knew better than uncharitable interpretations imply. The standard charges of utopianism, individualism, and voluntarism that marxists leveled against anarchists captured fundamental traits of anarchist theory: anarchist action was driven by ideals and values that were ultimately individual in nature and were intentionally chosen and pursued. Notwithstanding the misleading interpretations that marxists gave to those ideas and the slanderous form that their attacks took, their disparaging attributions were perceptive and based on a substantially correct appraisal of anarchist theory.

EPILOGUE: THE ANARCHIST PROJECT

Just as the controversies between anarchists and marxists can be made sense of without recurring to irrationalist explanations, so can anarchism at large.

Anarchism was neither the extreme expression of a perennial human aspiration to freedom, nor a recurrent blind reaction of alienated crowds to displacement and economic distress. What started with the First International was a collective, conscious revolutionary project. It had cultural roots in an earlier revolutionary tradition in Italy, and it was part of that broader worldwide movement that began to address the 'social question' in the second half of the nineteenth century. The anarchist project's aim was a brand of socialism antithetical to the centralist type with which the term has come to be identified in time, and whose implications anarchists were fully aware of. And its means were underpinned by a theoretically sound and sophisticated core set of beliefs, which, often unacknowledged, were consistent with or akin to 'sensible' theories widely accepted in the social sciences.

Those beliefs circumscribed the space within which anarchist action ranged. Malatesta's following six decades were a constant exploration of that space.

The heritage of the First International for Malatesta's anarchism was marked by both continuity and change. The fundamental traits of anarchism that emerged from the contrast with the marxists were made explicit and fully developed in Malatesta's theory and tactics from 1889 on. At the same time, such developments were based on Malatesta's critique of the International. In retrospect, Malatesta argued that the contrast between marxists and anarchists broke out because of differences and similarities alike, for the anarchists' engagement in a struggle for hegemony stemmed from residual authoritarianism. He often claimed that anarchists 'were still too marxist' at that time (Preface, xxvi). In outlining the errors that wrecked the International, Malatesta also hinted to the direction that his anarchism would take in the new cycle of struggles that began in 1889, when he returned from Argentina to Europe, and lasted a decade.

How that cycle of struggles and the new direction of Malatesta's anarchism shaped each other is the subject of the rest of this work.

3

An 'Anarchist Rarity' Reappears, 1889

In Malatesta's return to Europe in 1889 one can see paradigmatically reflected several issues that have generally troubled the historiography of anarchism as a movement. When Max Nettlau met Malatesta for the first time that year, he thus described the encounter: 'Right there, then, I finally had in front of my eyes, in the flesh, one of the most notable anarchist rarities, the disappeared Malatesta' (*Errico*, 146–7). The perception of Malatesta's stay in South America as a 'disappearance' and his return to Europe as a 'reappearance' is common in standard accounts, reflecting a more general tendency to describe the history of Italian anarchism as following a cyclical pattern of appearances and disappearances. Moreover, Malatesta's decisions and movements, such as changes of residence, often seem to have a chance character in his biographies, conveying an image of anarchism as being at the mercy of events.

At the same time, a more thorough account reveals circumstances that illustrate how the Italian anarchist movement functioned, thus dispelling stereotyped images. Malatesta's return to Europe, the establishment of *L'Associazione* in Nice, and its subsequent move to London illustrate a recurrent pattern of transnational organization, which involved five countries in the space of a year: Argentina, Spain, France, Italy, and England. A reconstruction of Malatesta's life during that brief time span provides an introduction to key themes of the present work, illustrating by example the typical mode of operation of Italian anarchism during the next decade.

Opaque planning across borders

Malatesta had fled to Argentina in early 1885 to escape conviction in Italy. His stay in South America was initially planned to be short, as Malatesta himself recounted to Max Nettlau in a letter of 12 January 1931, but things turned out otherwise (Nettlau Papers). The historian's knowledge of Malatesta's South American years is indeed spotty, but the available evidence is more than sufficient to show that he was by no means inactive. In 1885 he edited a new run of *La Questione Sociale* in Buenos Aires. In 1886 Malatesta and a few comrades made an unsuccessful attempt to prospect gold in Patagonia—the episode for which his stay in South America is best known in romanticized accounts. In the following two years Malatesta made a powerful contribution to the foundation of the Argentinean labor movement, cooperating with Spanish anarchist immigrants in labor agitations (Zaragoza, 98–105). Through their meetings, regularly reported by such Spanish anarchist periodicals as *El Productor* of Barcelona, *La Bandera Roja* of Madrid, and *La Solidaridad* of Seville, he kept in touch with the Spanish movement ('Universales'; G. A.; S. N. T.; 'Noticias'). As for his ongoing contacts with the Italian movement, evidence about them comes precisely from events linked to his return to Europe.

Describing Malatesta's return to Europe in 1889 his biographer and friend Luigi Fabbri dryly relates that 'in October 1889 Malatesta was already in Nice, where he started the publication of *L'Associazione*'. However, Fabbri continues, 'he could not remain in Nice for long, due to the fact that he had been expelled from France ten years before. The police looked for him after he exposed in *L'Associazione* the old spy Terzaghi... However, Malatesta could easily take refuge in London before being caught', continuing there the publication of the periodical (*Vida*, 126–7). Nothing is said about Malatesta's reasons for choosing Nice, his contacts, and his plans. Likewise, the move to London looks like a hasty remedy to a situation suddenly gone awry. However, such appearance of casualness was often the effect of the opacity of anarchist action. The scarcity of sources is not accidental, but inherent to the nature of a movement that in most cases could not operate in broad daylight. Moreover, militant biographers such as Fabbri shared such preoccupations and filtered their writing through a cautious reserve.

This is a case in which an empirical investigation driven by the heuristic principle of rationality may lead the historian emulous of Auguste Dupin to make discoveries with broad interpretive implications. In fact, by probing the appearance of fortuitousness of contemporary accounts, a different reality looms up, made of planning and organization sustained by a dense and steady web of militant contacts cast across the Atlantic Ocean.

According to Italian police records, Malatesta disappeared from Buenos Aires on 22 June 1889 (*Processo*, 64).

In contrast to the standard account that Malatesta settled right away in Nice, his first stop was Barcelona. *El Productor* of 19 July reported two recent meetings with Malatesta, in which 'the most momentous subjects of militant socialism were discussed, especially those related to the communist and collectivist schools' ('Miscelánea'). Thus, it was a brief but significant stop. *El Productor* was a key organizational center for Spanish anarchism, and Malatesta's stop in Barcelona was part of his web of contacts with the Spaniards. This is a first instance of a recurring theme: the crossnational mutual involvement in each other's movements by anarchists of different nationalities, which was one of the characteristic aspects of anarchist trans-nationalism. Malatesta's involvement with Spanish anarchism was deep. As will be seen, his preoccupation with the Spanish anarchist controversy between collectivists and communists would be a key motive of his theoretical turn of 1889.

On the occasion, Malatesta was probably instrumental in bringing about the International Anarchist Meeting that took place in Paris on 1 and 8 September of that year. The meeting brought together notable figures of Italian, Spanish, and French anarchism, as well as German and British representatives ('Résumé'). Malatesta attended it (Sernicoli, 9 September 1889). The idea of the congress had been launched by Italian anarchists in Paris the year before (Excerpt), and had been hesitantly entertained by various European groups. Eventually, *La Révolte* published a letter of 19 July 1889 from Barcelona, expressing the Spanish anarchists' intention to carry out the initiative: 'We got news from certain groups from abroad that have our same desire and same regret that the date has not been set yet' ('Réunion'). The date of the letter and the reference to groups from abroad suggests that the initiative was discussed during Malatesta's visit. It was indeed this letter that set in motion the arrangement of the conference. Malatesta had already a grip on the events of European anarchism before his return was even known.

What was Malatesta's final destination upon his return to Europe? The question is important in order to assess the chance or planned character of his moves.

All evidence indicates that London, not Nice, was Malatesta's destination. As early as April 22, the ministry of foreign affairs had informed the London embassy that Malatesta and Francesco Pezzi had left America for London (Puccioni). The information was incorrect, but it points to Malatesta's early plans involving London. Then, a telegram of August 9 from the Italian foreign under-secretary, Damiani, to the London embassy reported that Malatesta was in Paris, possibly heading for London. Damiani's further note of August 15 reported that Malatesta had indeed arrived there.

Further evidence of a protracted stay in London in August 1889 is revealed by the story of a passport. This was found on Malatesta upon his arrest in Switzerland two years later. It bore the name of Felice Vigliano (Commissariato di Lugano, 12 June 1891). Along with the passport, a reader's ticket of the British Museum issued on 27 August 1889, also in Vigliano's name, was found on Malatesta (Commissariato di Lugano, 15 June 1891). The Italian police did considerable research on the passport. However, it is the reader's ticket that is revealing. Vigliano was an Italian anarchist emigrated to South America. It turns out that, at the time the reader's ticket was issued, he was editing the periodical *Il Socialista* in Montevideo (Bettini, 2: 269). Thus, someone else obtained that ticket at the British Museum on 27 August 1889, and that was Malatesta. A comparison between the signature on the British Museum's register for temporary admission (Register) and samples of Malatesta's handwriting leaves little doubt even to an untrained eye. The most obvious explanation is that Vigliano never left South America, and Malatesta came in possession of his passport before leaving that continent, holding on to it until his arrest of 1891.

In brief, Malatesta's return was carefully planned and arranged well ahead of time. Most importantly, far from being a makeshift solution to an emergency situation, London, the great capital of revolutionary exile, where Malatesta had already resided in 1881–82, was his destination of choice from the beginning. By establishing this point a different image, made of effective planning and organization, begins to replace the standard one made of spontaneity, lack of organization, and powerlessness in the face of events.

Upon his arrival in London, Malatesta was not alone and isolated, but could count on a network of militants. In addition to acquaintances from his previous stay, by the time Malatesta returned to Europe, Francesco Saverio Merlino, one of his co-defendants in the Rome trial of 1884, was also in London. He had fled there after conviction, approximately at the same time that Malatesta escaped to Argentina. Merlino would be a chief contributor of L'Associazione, as well as Malatesta's closest partner in all undertakings of the next years, until his arrest in Naples in January 1894.

Nice came into the picture only the next month. In September 1889 Malatesta, Merlino, and Pezzi reached the French city to arrange the publication of L'Associazione, only a month before the first issue appeared. A telegram of September 11 from the Italian vice-consul in Nice, Beauregard, informed the foreign ministry of their imminent arrival. How was the project of the periodical brought about, and why was Nice its place of publication? Addressing such questions helps dispel the impression of fortuitousness and isolation that surrounds Malatesta's undertaking.

Arrangements for a periodical had started in Nice well before Malatesta's arrival, although it is not known whether he had a part in them. What is known, and quite significant, is that most people involved in the project came from an 'old guard' of Internationalists who were active around 1876–84 in Florence—as Pezzi and his wife Luisa Minguzzi also were. Florence was also Malatesta's center of operations in 1883–84. Among those militants were Giovanni Talchi, who had fled Florence for Nice years before (Di Lembo, 'Talchi'); Giuseppe Cioci, a former editor of Malatesta's La Questione Sociale in 1884, who arrived in Nice around May 1889 (Di Lembo, 'Cioci'); and the typesetter and printer Giuseppe Consorti, who arrived the next month, as the Italian consul in Nice, Centurione, duly reported to the Italian foreign minister on 15 June. In an earlier memo of 20 May the same consul had informed the minister of Talchi's projected publication of a socialist periodical by the familiar title La Questione Sociale, to be printed clandestinely and smuggled into Italy. This was all well before even Malatesta's return to Europe.

On 10 September the Italian Consulate in Nice reported the imminent publication of Talchi's projected periodical, with the participation of Cioci and other Nice anarchists. The same report added that 'the dangerous Malatesta, Merlino, and Pezzi, who landed in Marseille on their way from America, would appear to have come to this city for purposes of anarchist propaganda, joining the editor group of said periodical' (Beauregard, 18 October 1889). Indeed, ten days later announcements started to appear in the anarchist press that *L'Associazione* would appear in Nice by October ('Nelle', 21 September 1889). The first issue did appear on 6 October, with the erroneous date 6 September. Most likely this was a trick to divert police attention, by concealing that the publication was fresh off the press. Both Cioci and Consorti were in the editing group. Another element of continuity was the periodical's manager, Giacomo Faraut, who in 1887 had managed *Lo Schiavo* (Bettini, 2: 93), an anarchist periodical edited in Nice by Malatesta's friend Nicolò Converti, now emigrated to Tunis.

In sum, there is a clear continuity between Talchi's and Malatesta's projects, though it is not clear at which point the latter's involvement began. At any rate, it is evident that upon returning from South America Malatesta resumed his web of militant contacts from where he had left them before his departure—assuming he had interrupted them—and that such links were instrumental in bringing about his editorial project. The 'disappeared' Malatesta 'reappeared' with a new project, in which the key comrades were the same of the early 1880s, who had never left Europe.

The Nice location must also have been attractive to Malatesta for the purpose of smuggling the periodical in Italy, given its proximity to the Italian border. The key role of this city as a conveniently located hub of Italian transnational anarchism is described by an alarmed article appeared in an Italian newspaper five years later. The article remarks that Nice does not have a proper anarchist *club* as London, nor does any anarchist leader reside there. However, 'it cannot be denied that anarchy has a considerable number of representatives . . . in transit, as it were'. In fact, the article continues, 'to and from the nearby border certain wicked fellows come and go, smuggle anarchist press, easily dispatch their correspondence from here, and confer here with their bosses, who, coming from Paris or London, sometimes choose the *cosmopolitan* Nice area for their shady gangs'. Among such 'bosses', Malatesta and Merlino are explicitly mentioned ('Covo'). In a few lines, the article vividly captures the transnational and mobile character of Italian anarchism.

Thus, the project of *L'Associazione* had been conceived and carried out across several foreign countries on both sides of the Atlantic Ocean, but its focus remained the struggle in the homeland. As will be seen, this was one of the most fundamental traits of Italian transnational anarchism.

LONDON: DIRECT ACTION ON A MASS SCALE

That Malatesta lived in London, and not in Nice, from early August to early September, has the important implication that he directly witnessed an extraordinary event that had a profound influence on his outlook on strikes as revolutionary weapons: the Great Dock Strike, which took place in London from 14 August to 16 September 1889. This is generally acknowledged as the start of British 'new unionism', which differed from the older craft unionism for its effort to achieve a broad base of unskilled and semi-skilled workers and its focus on industrial action.

This episode illustrates another fundamental aspect of anarchist transnationalism, that is, the acquisition of a broad, first-hand experience of advanced capitalism and working-class struggles worldwide, in contrast to stereotypes of anarchist backwardness and detachment from empirical reality. The relevance of the Great Dock Strike for Malatesta was witnessed by the first issue of *L'Associazione*, which featured an article on the strike that provides Malatesta's perception of the events ('A proposito di uno sciopero').

As a result of a short but active propaganda, Malatesta relates, the casual workers of the London docks, approximately numbering 50,000, organized into a union and went on strike, in contrast to the traditional belief that the uncertainty and competition inherent to their employment made them unsuitable for organization. The strikers' main demands were an hourly pay of sixpence instead of fivepence a day, and the abolition of the subcontracting system. As soon as the casuals' strike was called, all other trades connected to the loading and unloading of cargos stopped work, some of them purely in sympathy. At the same time other trades outside the docks advanced grievances and struck, with the total number of strikers peaking at 180,000. The Gas workers offered to come out on strike, with the prospect, as *L'Associazione* put it, that London be 'plunged into darkness at night' and the homes of the bourgeois be 'exposed to great danger'. Analogous offers of support came from other workers. In brief, 'an outburst of enthusiasm, an impulse of solidarity, and a reawakening of dignity were about to bring forth a general strike: the stoppage of production, transit, and public services in a city of five million people!'

Malatesta was impressed by the collective might and maturity displayed by the British workers. In the space of a few weeks, and against anyone's expectation, the great mass of London and British laborers were putting their strength into the field, lining up in formidable, organized, and largely spontaneous ranks in unprecedented ways. The strikers' self-discipline and ability to get organized were also remarkable. Feeding a population of over half a million, managing donations and collections, keeping up correspondence, organizing meetings and demonstrations, and keeping watch against the bosses' attempts to employ scabs: 'all this was done marvelously and spontaneously, by the work of volunteers.' Above all, the strike illustrated the indeterminacy and open-endedness of collective action, presenting fertile ground for the revolutionary option: 'those workers were not lacking a broad and often instinctive notion of their rights and social usefulness; nor did they lack the combativeness required to make a revolution; a vague desire of more radical measures arose in them...' The situation was tense and open to different outcomes: 'the city was in a state of alarm; most of the food provision was at a standstill; a large number of factories were closed for lack of coal or raw materials; and irritation grew with discomfort.' In sum, 'a breath of social revolution blew through the streets of the great city' ('A proposito di uno sciopero').

The idea of a general strike got as far as a 'No-Work' manifesto issued by the strike committee after two weeks of the strike, as workers faced a serious shortage of strike funds and with no settlement in sight. The manifesto called upon all London workers to come out on strike on 2 September. However, the call was withdrawn before the general strike could begin. Meanwhile, other developments brought the strike toward its conclusion. The influential Cardinal Manning, who had family connections with dock companies, undertook the role of mediator. Another portentous event was the unexpected arrival of unprecedented financial support for the strikers from Australian unions. With the further intervention of the London mayor, negotiations began. The workers' demands were substantially accepted on 14 September, to be implemented as of November. The Port of London was reopened on 16 September (Tsuzuki, 61–6).

For Malatesta, in an open-ended situation such as the climax of the strike, the role of conscious minorities was crucial in tipping the scales in one or the other direction. Thus, he contrasted the actual behavior of the strike leaders with a conjectural insurrectional scenario. The strike leaders were indeed praiseworthy for their role in preparing the strike, but also inadequate to the position in which the circumstances had placed them. 'In the face of a situation that went beyond their aspirations and their boldness, they lacked the courage to take on their incumbent responsibilities and push things forward,' he wrote. 'Nor did they have enough abnegation and intelligence to draw aside and let the masses take the initiative.'

In contrast, if the general strike in London had been encouraged and not prevented, the situation would have become critical for the bourgeoisie, and revolution would have presented itself as a solution: 'shut-down of factories, stoppage of railways, trains, streetcars, cabs, and carriages, interruption of public services, suspension of the provision system, nights without gas, hundreds of thousands of workers in the streets: what a situation for a group of people with ideas and a little courage!' Malatesta thus depicted how collective action might have taken an insurrectional path:

If clear and plain propaganda for violent expropriation had been done earlier; if groups of daring people had started to take and distribute foodstuff, clothes, and all commodities that fill the stores but run short for proletarians; if other groups or isolated individuals had forcibly or cunningly penetrated banks and government offices to set them on fire, while others had entered the houses of well-off people and used them for lodging women and children from the populace; if others had given the most greedy bourgeois what they deserve, and others had made power-less and inoffensive the government chiefs and those who could replace them in times of crisis, the police officers, the generals and high-ranking army officers, taking them by surprise in their sleep or when they left their homes—in brief, if few thousands of resolute revolutionaries had existed in London, which is so large, today this immense metropolis and the whole of England, Scotland and Ireland would be in a revolution.

Though such things, Malatesta concluded, were nearly impossible to bring about if they had to be planned and preordained by a central commit-tee, yet they became easy 'if revolutionaries—in agreement about end and means—take action by their own initiative in the direction that they see fit, as soon as there is an opportunity, together with those comrades that they need for accomplishing their task, and without awaiting anyone's opinion or order'. Such a scenario clearly illustrates the dynamic interplay envisaged by Malatesta between the spontaneous action of the people and the initiative of conscious minorities, both of which were necessary, but neither of which was sufficient for a revolution to be accomplished.

The positive implications of the Great Dock Strike and the tactics of new unionism for Malatesta can hardly be over-estimated. He came to regard strikes as the most promising path to revolution, in contrast to any other means that anarchists had practiced or entertained until then.

Plots and conspiracies, he argued, were unable to determine popular ag-itations sufficiently broad to stand a chance of victory. Conversely, purely spontaneous movements were seldom allowed by the authorities to last long enough to develop into general insurrections. Caught in this conundrum, anarchists tended to reach the conclusion that political movements initiated by the bourgeoisie and wars provided the best opportunities to attempt a social revolution. However, in addition to many other shortcomings, both wars and political movements had the drawback that their outbreak did not depend on the initiative of revolutionaries, and therefore reliance on them as revolutionary sparks eventually engendered inertia and fatalism. 'Fortu-nately', Malatesta concluded, 'there are other ways by which a revolution can come, and it seems to us that the most important among these are workers' agitations that manifest themselves in the form of strikes... The most fruitful lesson of all was the huge dock labourers' strike, which recently occurred in London' ('A proposito di uno sciopero').

The effect of the Great Dock Strike on Malatesta was strengthened by the internationalization of the dockers' struggle in the next months. Not only did the London dockers' strike enjoy international support, but dock workers in other countries followed in their footsteps. The most notable example was the strike of the Rotterdam dockers, which on 27 September 1889 was met by harsh police repression, after it had extended to about 5,000 workers. The strike lasted until 10 October, when the workers' request of a salary increase was accepted. Malatesta commented upon the Rotterdam strike in the second issue of *L'Associazione*, reporting that during the strike Dutch socialist leaders, who had rushed to Rotterdam to defuse the tension and to offer their leadership to the workers, were met with hostility and rejected. The Rotterdam dockers, eager to banish any suspicion of socialism, got to the point of throwing out of a meeting a worker who had spoken in socialist terms, and of cheering the Orange reigning house. For Malatesta the strike was another lesson, which questioned the attitudes of conscious minorities to patronize the masses or, at the opposite extreme, to hold inflated expectations about the latter's revolutionary instincts ('Altro').

The dockers' struggles of those months furnished ample evidence that, between those dogmatic excesses, workers' movements offered a wide field for anarchist action that was both pragmatic and revolutionary. Malatesta's next decade was devoted to experimenting on that field, which the Great Dock Strike had shown to be so promising. During that decade, London was the place where he lived for the most part and returned to from revolutionary engagement in Italy and elsewhere.

An official 'reappearance'

It is not clear where Malatesta resided right after the periodical's launch of early October in Nice, but it seems that he returned to London soon. On 21 October 1889 the Italian foreign ministry informed the London embassy that a letter had been mailed by Pezzi on 8 October from Harrow, a London suburb (Ministero degli Affari Esteri); a further note of 24 October added that 'the known Malatesta and Pezzi receive from Nice, under another name, many general delivery letters at Harrow'; again on 26 October the ministry confirmed to its London embassy that 'from further intelligence it would appear that Malatesta remains in hiding in London'; and on the same day the consulate in Nice was informed by the same ministry that 'Malatesta and Pezzi appear to be in London, where they keep in regular contact with Cioci in Nice'. According to the same note, *L'Associazione* was smuggled into Italy by Cioci's partner, Leonilda Giacchetti.

Finally, on an October Monday Malatesta made what Max Nettlau—who made his acquaintance on that occasion—recorded as his entrance on the London revolutionary scene:

I saw [Malatesta] for the first time on a Monday, after a session of the *Socialist League Council* in the League's headquarters, in Great Queen

Street, W.C. These sessions were attended by members, and visitors and delegations were also admitted. He and another Italian came in, and silently sat down in the back. I was sitting next to Victor Dave, who, I believe, had already seen him in the morning in the League's office. He told me that that was Malatesta. I was deeply amazed. Through the old periodicals from 1872 to 1884 I kept memory of him as one of the few who had remained faithful to the movement through all those years, until he later disappeared, or rather, as I came to know, emigrated to South America. Some English comrades recalled him from the 1881 congress. However, to all the others, except for Dave, whose recollection spanned across the whole International, he was unknown, including William Morris, who cared little or nothing of the continental movements. Morris then made Malatesta's acquaintance, although the scope of his action and his sphere of interests remained distant. That night I was introduced to Malatesta by Dave, as someone who had an antiquarian interest in anarchism. The situation was quite extraordinary. In everyone else's eyes, including probably his own, Malatesta was then a young man of 35 years of age. Instead, for me he was one of the greatest antiques of the international anarchist movement that I could have met.... Right there, then, I finally had in front of my eyes, in the flesh, one of the most notable anarchist rarities, the disappeared Malatesta.

(*Errico*, 146–7)

Nettlau was then a young member of the Socialist League, still far from becoming the foremost historian of anarchism. His perception of Malatesta was probably common in socialist circles acquainted only indirectly with the latter's activity. That perception is significant for its characterization of the Italian anarchist as a 'disappeared anarchist rarity', which conjures up an image of Malatesta as a historical figure, associated with the experience of the extinct International, rather than an active militant.

That perception was not unjustified, for Malatesta had been engaged in the struggle for 18 years, a lifetime for many revolutionaries. Only by looking at Malatesta's 60-year militancy in hindsight can that period be regarded as a prologue. Given the perception expressed by Nettlau, its complement could only be surprise at the viability of Malatesta's anarchist project in the years to come, the same surprise that historians exhibit at the 'reappearances' of anarchism. Yet the very perception of Malatesta as a 'disappeared anarchist rarity', with its implicit emphasis on the gap between an irretrievable past and the present, eloquently speaks to the sustainability and adaptability to changing conditions of his anarchist project. It is for the historian to replace surprise with an understanding of the intellectual and material resources that made that project viable.

The last issue of *L'Associazione* to come out of Nice was that of 27 October 1889. The next one was published out of London on 30 November. In the meantime Malatesta moved his London residence from Harrow to Fulham, into the same premises where *L'Associazione* set office. On 7 November Malatesta wrote to Gustave Brocher, who also lived in London: 'I no longer live in Harrow; I'll give you my new address. I would be grateful if you could write me of any legal formalities that need to be fulfilled in order to set up a printing house and publish a periodical' (*Epistolario*, 57). The message confirms that Malatesta had lived in London well before his 'official' appearance of October 1889. Accordingly, the transfer of *L'Associazione* should perhaps be seen not as a simultaneous change of residence and office, but rather as the reunion of the periodical's office with Malatesta's residence. The motives of the transfer of office may look different in this light. Usually they are identified with Malatesta's personal safety after his denunciation of the spy Terzaghi. However, Malatesta was probably already back in London by the time the Terzaghi case was brought up. The real motives may have had more to do with the management of *L'Associazione*. Nice was attractive for the purpose of smuggling the paper into Italy. However, the plan encountered difficulties from the outset, as the first issue was seized at the border crossing ('Nelle', 12 October 1889). Apparently, even the printing process was harassed by the French police, with the result that the second issue had to be printed by hand ('Mouvement', 26 October 1899). Therefore, the strongest reasons for printing in Nice may have failed soon, making the trouble of remote editing useless. An explanation of this sort was given by *El Productor*: 'The comrades who edit and manage our dear colleague *L'Associazione* were forced to establish their place of publication in London, in order to better guarantee the distribution of the issue' ('Miscelánea', 15 November 1889).

With the transfer of the periodical's office, Malatesta's settling in London was complete.

A TRANSNATIONAL NETWORK

The story of *L'Associazione* nicely illustrates the anarchist movement's transnational mode of operation.

Anarchist militants were mobile. They often had only a loose link to the place where they physically resided, while keeping strong ties to comrades in other countries. Such mobility was partly due to persecution. Anarchists were often persecuted as such, as best exemplified by the 'criminal association' charges in Italy, and exile was often their ordinary status. Another relevant factor was emigration, a lot that befell anarchists as workers, and that they shared with Italian workers in general. Accordingly, transnational ties were denser along ethnic and linguistic lines, but they were by no means limited to those. Anarchists were also internationalist. The international anarchist network could be likened to the 'many-headed hydra' described by Linebaugh and Rediker. By that term they refer to the mobile, transatlantic, motley proletariat that resisted expansionist capitalism between the seventeenth and the early nineteenth century. The anarchist hydra, which Italians and their ethnic network were part of, had its origins in Italy, Spain, and France, and spread around the Atlantic Ocean, from continental Europe and Britain to South and North America, and throughout the Mediterranean Sea, especially in Egypt and Tunisia.

In standard accounts, a wandering Malatesta crosses the Atlantic Ocean, lands in Nice, founds an Italian periodical there, then packs up again and goes to London. However, none of these places was terra incognita. In a transnational perspective, Argentina, France, England, and Italy were part of the same, large, anarchist map. By the time Malatesta and his companions—Francesco and Luisa Pezzi and Galileo Palla—left Buenos Aires, Talchi was already in Nice, Merlino was already in London, and Cioci and Consorti were still in Italy. Each of them played a role in Malatesta's editorial project.

In the same way that a transnational perspective reveals the geographical continuity of the anarchist movement, appraising that movement as a network of militants makes it possible to detect its chronological continuity.

Borrowing from graph theory, a social network is represented in terms of points, or nodes, representing actors, and lines, or edges, representing ties or relations. In the anarchist network the nodes were individuals and small groups, and the ties consisted of exchanges of information, including practical agreements for action. By allowing the coordination of activity, the anarchist network was thus a form of organization, though an informal one.

A transnational network is an elusive object of study. The traditional institutional approach to history focuses on formal organizations, usually of national scope. A transnational network is the antithesis of that: it is informal, and it crosses national borders.

A formal organization has a structure with fixed roles. Different individuals occupy different roles at different times, but the structure remains the same. Incidentally, it should be noted that formal organizations, too, fit the definition of social network. However, when I use the term 'network' without further qualifications, the reference is to informal ones.

In contrast to formal organizations, nodes had no fixed configuration in the anarchist network. There was no articulation of center versus periphery, or top versus bottom. Information had no fixed direction. Certainly, distinctions can be made within the anarchist network, too. Social network analysis defines various notions of 'centrality' in a network: 'degree centrality' is based on an actor's number of direct ties; 'closeness centrality' on an actor's distance from all others; and 'betweenness centrality' on the number of indirect ties in which an actor's intervenes as intermediary (Hanneman and Riddle, ch. 10). Such concepts certainly apply to the anarchist network, where some individuals enjoyed greater prominence, prestige, or influence. These can be characterized as the movement's leaders, though it should be added that other militants, whose relevance can probably be measured in terms of 'betweenness', could typically fulfill an effective liaison role by keeping a relatively low profile in the movement. Still, no institutional roles existed.

The temporal continuity of a formal organization is most naturally followed through its structure, which persists across the changes of individuals occupying its positions. Conversely, in a network the individuals may remain the same, while the configuration may keep changing. Therefore, while the search for organization in a formal sense is elusive, continuity of action is best studied by following actors and their connections in the long term. This may bring up a strong level of sustained integration that could not easily be detected otherwise.

I do not attempt a systematic study of the anarchist network. However, to the extent that I investigate it, my approach resembles 'ego-centric' methods. Rather than tracking down a full network, I select a 'focal ego', that is Malatesta, and identify the nodes to which it is connected. A further step would be to check 'alter connections', that is, to determine which of the nodes identified in the first stage are connected to one another (Hanneman and Riddle, ch. 1). I undertake this latter step only occasionally. My focus is mainly on tracking the persistence of ties, in order to detect temporal continuity.

For example, tracing Malatesta's local network over time reveals continuity of action between his first *Questione Sociale* and *L'Associazione*, between his work in Florence and in Nice and London five years later. It is illuminating to compare the tiny size and tightness of this local network with its geographical spread. It may not surprise that eight actors—Malatesta, the Pezzis, Palla, Merlino, Talchi, Cioci, and Consorti—shuttled between four locations. What is more surprising is that the four locations—Florence, Buenos Aires, London, and Nice—spanned as many countries in two continents.

The importance of transnational networks to understand how Italian anarchism functioned in the motherland has been pointed out by the British historian Carl Levy, who remarks that exile 'created hidden organizational and financial mobilization networks, which explains to a great extent why the movement could suddenly snap back to life in Italy after years of torpidity' ('Italian', 44). The concept of network has been used only occasionally by historians of anarchism, but the situation is changing (see, e.g., Bouhey; Bantman; and Shaffer, 'Havana'). Networks as anarchist means of organization have generally received increasing attention, especially with the spread of the Internet. Thus, a report of the Canadian Security Intelligence Service about the anti-globalization movement remarks that 'the Internet has breathed new life into the anarchist philosophy, permitting communication and coordination without the need for a central source of command, and facilitating coordinated actions with minimal resources and bureaucracy'. Perhaps it would be more correct to say that the anarchist philosophy has breathed new life into the Internet, for decentralized communication and coordination have characterized anarchism for much longer than the Internet.

The carriers of information were mobile militants and migrant workers instead of fiber-optic cables.

Network organization has even come to be seen as a defining trait of anarchism. For George Woodcock, 'it seems evident that logically pure anarchism goes against its own nature when it attempts to create elaborate international or even national organizations' (256). Perhaps Malatesta lacked in logic or purity, by Woodcock's standards, but it should be stressed that he was a strong advocate of organization, even in the form of a party. Organization was a prominent theme in *L'Associazione*, as it would be in Malatesta's all subsequent periodicals. So, notwithstanding the central place of network organization in the anarchist movement, Malatesta's reliance on the anarchist network rather than on formal structures made a virtue of necessity. This certainly owed to the constraints arising from persecution and exile, but it was also a result of internal opposition to his effort to build permanent organizational structures.

It is necessary for the historian to study informal organization to understand how anarchist movements functioned. Whether informal organization is necessary for anarchist movements to function is a different question, though, which the historian need not address.

Epilogue: three paradigmatic months

Along with the relevance of the anarchist network, a number of other important themes were foreshadowed by the three months separating Malatesta's return to Europe from his definitive settlement in London: his relationship with the Spaniards; the founding of a periodical, a key tool of both propaganda and organization; Malatesta's focus on Italy, which influenced his choice of Nice; and London as his stable place of residence. Each theme remained prominent in the following quarter of a century.

That brief span was a period of intense evolution in Malatesta's theory and tactics, at a time when his public persona was still associated with the history of the International. The influence of the Great Dock Strike on that evolution shows that Malatesta's anarchism was not a fixed and unchangeable doctrine, but evolved under the lesson of experience. The impact of that struggle on Malatesta also illustrates how transnationalism brought Italian anarchists in contact with diverse aspects of capitalist development, broadening their perspective and making them aware of the need for tactical flexibility.

By the time the 'anarchist rarity' Malatesta made his official reappearance in London, his anarchism had already undergone profound changes under the influence of events he had directly witnessed in that very city. Such is the nature of anarchist opacity.

Over the next three equally fruitful months, those changes were spelled out in the brief but intense run of Malatesta's periodical *L'Associazione*.

4

A SHORT-LIVED, MOMENTOUS PERIODICAL, 1889–90

IF THE CONTROVERSIES IN THE FIRST INTERNATIONAL ARE THE BEST BACK-ground to an outline of the themes that Malatesta shared with most anarchists, the periodical *L'Associazione* gives the opportunity to illustrate Malatesta's own distinctive themes, which often depart significantly from the anarchist cliché. As Luigi Fabbri remarks, it was from 1889 that 'Malatesta's thought took on those ever clearer and more coherent character and directions that constitute a very different way of presenting and interpreting anarchism from those commonly accepted in the anarchist camp, especially outside of Italy, and mainly inspired by Bakunin's and Kropotkin's theories' (*Malatesta*, 8).

L'Associazione was a short-lived periodical. After the first three issues published in Nice, only four more appeared in London. In January 1890 the publication was suspended due to financial difficulties, after one of the editors, Giuseppe Cioci, fled to the continent with the periodical's funds (Luigi Fabbri, *Vida*, 127).

Despite its short life-span, *L'Associazione* was a turning point. Malatesta had been away from Europe for almost five years and had published almost nothing for four. With the International now long gone, Malatesta's new periodical was an opportunity to articulate his changed outlook on the road to revolution. *L'Associazione* was only a beginning. Through the 1890s Malatesta's tactics kept evolving, often with dramatic turns. Still, *L'Associazione* was the juncture at which Malatesta introduced, sometimes inconspicuously, the theoretical cornerstones of his entire subsequent evolution.

Malatesta's novel views concerned the pluralism of models for the anarchist society, anarchism as a method rather than as the pursuit of a specific blueprint, the role of solidarity as an anarchist disposition, and the relation between conscious minorities and masses. One can fully assess the import and fertility of such ideas in hindsight, in the light of Malatesta's ideas of over 30 years later. They are best discussed here, though, for tracing their source in *L'Associazione* lays the ground for understanding Malatesta's later evolution.

A similar argument holds for Malatesta's tactics. The flexibility and pragmatism that characterized them can be best appreciated by looking at their evolution over time. Yet they were based on a set of coherent principles. Since these principles proceeded from Malatesta's outlook on conscious minorities and masses they are best introduced in connection with that theme. The concrete form those principles took will then be illustrated throughout the next chapters.

Finally, at the core of Malatesta's reformulation of anarchism was a methodological shift about the relation between individuals and social wholes. This had pervasive and long-term implications on his appraisal of collective action. Bringing forth the common methodological foundation of Malatesta's novel ideas reveals their unity and conceptual interdependence.

ANARCHIST PLURALISM

Malatesta's reflections on anarchist pluralism originated from a controversy among anarchists that had its roots in the First International. How should an anarchist society be organized? Should it be communist or collectivist? Which model best realizes anarchist principles? The two competing theories agreed on the common ownership of the means of production but differed about distribution, which for collectivism was to be done according to work performed, while for communism was to be done according to needs, thus amounting to free consumption.

The debate arose early in the anarchist movement and Malatesta was among those responsible for it. Anarchism was born collectivist in the Federalist International, under Bakunin's influence. However, in 1876 the Italian Federation decided to give up collectivism for communism (Nettlau, *Short*, 138–9). The debate thus initiated occupied the anarchist movement for years, especially in Spain. The onset of the controversy occurred during Malatesta's stay in South America. Malatesta's new determination to overcome the controversy was already evident at that time, when he stated that his communism was exactly the same as the collectivism of the Spanish anarchists, the differences being more formal than substantial (S. N. T.). Such claims attest that Malatesta's ideas of 1889 had roots in a long reflection. When he returned to Europe, his views on the subject took not only a pluralist turn, but also a central role in his political program.

Such views were outlined in *Appello*, a declaration of principles printed out of Nice in September 1889, before *L'Associazione* began publication, and promptly translated in Spain by both the communist *La Revolución Social* and the collectivist *El Productor*. After discussing the pitfalls of both collectivism and communism, Malatesta argued that a new moral consciousness would develop in the future society, such that men would find wage labor repugnant, just as they presently found slavery repugnant. Therefore,

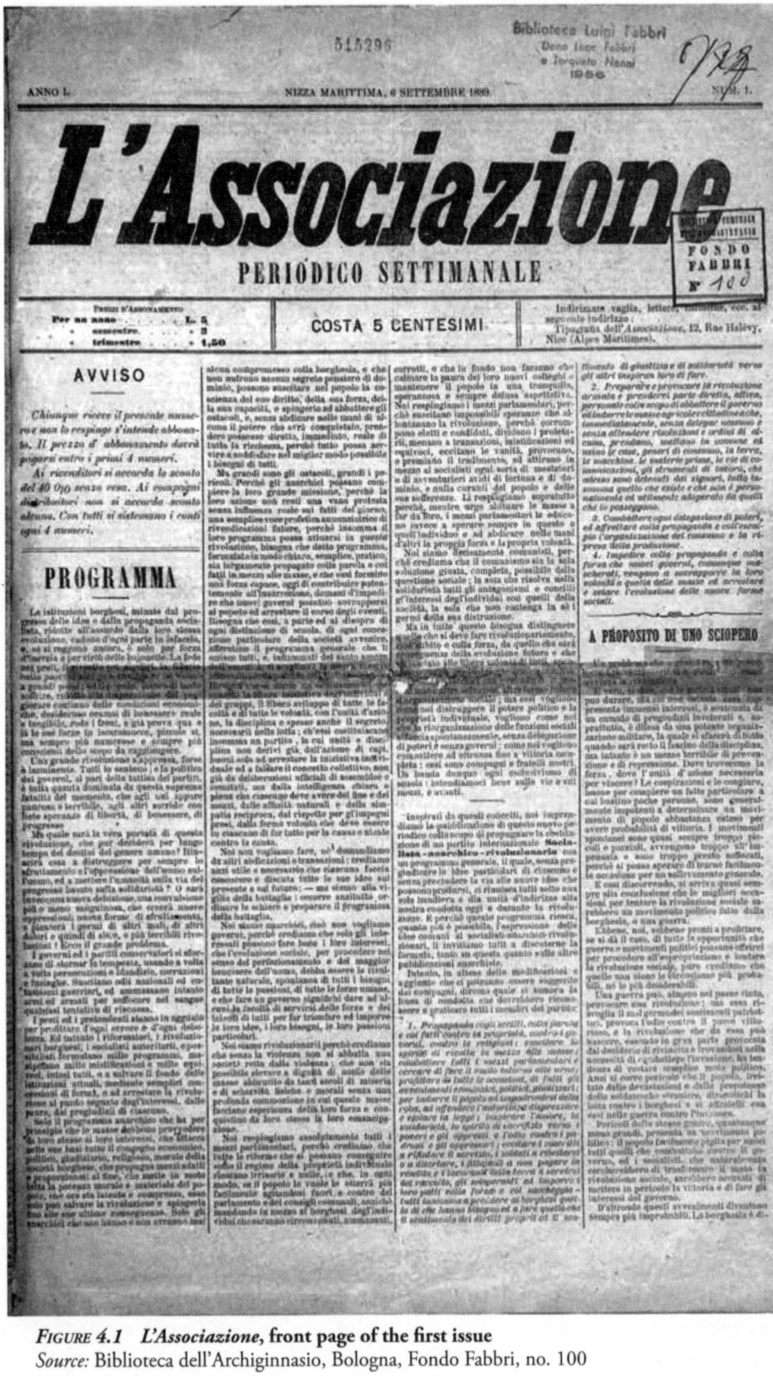

ANNO I. NIZZA MARITTIMA, 6 SETTEMBRE 1889 NUM. 1.

L'Associazione

PERIODICO SETTIMANALE

PREZZI D'ABBONAMENTO
Per un anno . . . L. 5
" semestre . . . " 3
" trimestre . . . " 1,50

COSTA 5 CENTESIMI

Indirizzare vaglia, lettere, manoscritti, ecc. al seguente indirizzo:
Tipografia dell'*Associazione*, 12, Rue Halévy, Nice (Alpes Maritimes).

AVVISO

Chiunque riceve il presente numero e non lo respinge s'intende abbonato. Il prezzo d' abbonamento dovrà pagarsi entro i primi 4 numeri.

Ai rivenditori si accorda lo sconto del 40 0/0 senza resa. Ai compagni distributori non si accorda sconto alcuno. Con tutti si sistemano i conti ogni 4 numeri.

PROGRAMMA

A PROPOSITO DI UNO SCIOPERO

FIGURE 4.1 ***L'Associazione*, front page of the first issue**
Source: Biblioteca dell'Archiginnasio, Bologna, Fondo Fabbri, no. 100

whatever its details, the organization of the future society would be animated at bottom by a communist spirit: 'Let's be content', Malatesta concluded, 'with this moral and fundamental communism, which, all things considered, is more valuable than the material and formal one.' The import of this apparently facile way out will be discussed shortly.

Malatesta returned to the subject in the article 'Programma', published in the first issue of *L'Associazione*. After confirming his personal belief in communism as the only full solution to the social question, he added that it was nevertheless necessary to make a distinction between what needed to be done by way of revolution, that is immediately and forcibly, and what would be the result of the future evolution of the new society. The latter was to be left to the free wishes of everyone, which would spontaneously and gradually harmonize.

The argument was further developed in the article 'I nostri propositi: I. L'Unione tra comunisti e collettivisti', specifically devoted to the proposed union between communists and collectivists. A novel emphasis on 'the anarchist method' was introduced. Malatesta expressed the key concept that the coexistence of collectivists and communists in the same party is a logical, necessary consequence of the anarchist idea and method: 'If anarchy means spontaneous evolution; if being anarchist means believing that nobody is infallible and that only through freedom can humanity find the solution to its problems and reach harmony and general well-being, then by what right, by what logic could one elevate to the rank of dogma and impose the solutions that one prefers and advocates? And by what means, then?' If anarchists were an authoritarian party, that would be conceivable. Being an anarchist party, the only means to get one's solutions to triumph were propaganda and example. Anarchists could hold the most diverse ideals about the reconstruction of society. However, what determined the attained end would always be the method, since one did not get where one wished, but rather where the taken path led. 'To create a party it is necessary and sufficient to have the same method. And the method, that is the practical line of conduct that the revolutionary anarchist socialists intend to follow, is common to all, be they communist or collectivist.'

In contrast to stereotypes of anarchism as a static and unchanging doctrine, the debate provides an example of ideas in evolution, from the novel advocacy of communism by the Italian anarchists in 1876, through the debate in Spain, to Malatesta's pluralist solution. Most importantly, at the same time that there was a substantial continuity in Malatesta's outlook on collectivism and communism, with his preference remaining for communism, a significant change of perspective occurred. This may best be detected by comparing Malatesta's arguments of 1889 with those made on the same subject in his 1884 pamphlet *Programma e Organizzazione dei L'Associazione Internazionale dei Lavoratori*, the last writing of his Internationalist period.

In that program Malatesta foresaw that after the revolution collectivism would be experimented with in some places and communism in others; and that errors, and possibly acts of abuse and injustice, would be committed. However, so long as no power was established to thwart the process of social experimentation, the method of trial and error would eventually yield the best solution, that is communism. Malatesta acknowledged that communism needed a high degree of moral development in people, which the revolutionary impetus might be insufficient to generate at once. Therefore, collectivism would be accepted somewhere as a transitory solution. However, collectivism carried with it the bourgeois spirit intrinsic to the principle of competition. It was 'powerless in bringing about that revolution, that profound moral transformation of men, whereby nobody will do and wish anything that could damage others'. Hence, in order to prevent collectivism from generating a bourgeois spirit, it would be necessary for it to rapidly evolve toward communism in those places where it was transitorily accepted. In sum, though the program already contained elements of pluralism and experimentalism, collectivism was ultimately rejected as 'incompatible with anarchy', and it was recommended that the International 'advocate communism everywhere' (32–3, 57). That rejection was based on the negative moral effects of collectivism. Ultimately, in 1884 Malatesta's focus was primarily on the configuration of society as a whole and on its effects on the moral dispositions of individuals.

With respect to that assessment, a key change occurred in 1889 with the argument of 'moral communism'. With this phrase, Malatesta meant the spirit of solidarity, that is the moral attitude that eventually would lead to communism. In other words, regardless of the contingent social arrangement in which that spirit manifested, its presence already provided a sufficient moral foundation for communism, even before communism was realized. In Malatesta's argument of 1889, the presence of that spirit, or 'moral communism', was all that really mattered for the establishment of an anarchist society. In its presence, the controversy between collectivism and communism became secondary and derivative. Malatesta kept advocating communism and judging collectivism incompatible with anarchy. Yet the terms of the relation were now reversed. He no longer argued that there could not be anarchy where there was collectivism, but rather that there could not be collectivism where there was anarchy, that is, a society driven by solidarity. He no longer claimed that collectivism would be powerless to bring about a moral transformation, but rather that a moral transformation would prevent collectivism from bringing back privilege and wage labor.

In brief, a methodological shift in Malatesta's appraisal of social transformation had occurred. His focus was no longer on social configurations as causes and individual dispositions as effects; rather, individual dispositions, such as 'moral communism', were now the causes and social configurations the effects.

Anarchism as a method

Malatesta's pluralist way out of the debate on collectivism and communism brought considerations of method to the foreground of anarchist theory. Method had been central to anarchism since its inception. After all, the split in the First International was over the method to achieve emancipation, or between the anarchist method of freedom and the marxist political method. In the 1884 version of 'L'Anarchia', Malatesta pointed out that the aim of a society based on solidarity was not sufficient to determine the program of a party. Ideals may be abstract and distant enough for everyone to agree on them: 'to be able to act, to be able to contribute to the realization of one's cherished ideas, one has to choose one's own path. In parties, as more generally in life, the questions of method are predominant. If the idea is the beacon, the method is the helm.' Thus, Malatesta continued, 'we are anarchist in our goal . . . but we are anarchist in our method too'. After returning to Europe, Malatesta placed even greater emphasis on method. In 1884 he claimed that a specification of method was necessary to determine a party program. In 1889 he claimed that it was sufficient ('I nostri propositi: I').

This evolution is illuminated by a comparison between the original 1884 version of 'L'Anarchia' with the final one of 1891. The changes that Malatesta made to the text reveal changes in his views.

In the final edition Malatesta provided a very general definition of anarchy, free of references to specific solutions to social problems, stressing instead that solutions cannot be provided in advance. At the outset, as in the previous version, anarchy was defined according to etymology, as 'the condition of a people who live without a constituted authority, without government' (*Anarchy*, 11). Pages later, Malatesta described it as a 'society of friends', in which the spontaneous grouping according to requirements and sympathies, bottom-up and from simple to complex, would give rise to a social organization aimed at the greatest welfare and freedom of everyone, and would be modified according to circumstances and experience (31).

Significantly, in the 1891 edition, unlike the previous one, communism was never mentioned. Instead, to a hypothetical reader who asked how the anarchist society would be organized, Malatesta responded that those who expected detailed answers in advance, beyond what could be only personal opinions, lacked a real understanding of what anarchy was: 'We are no more prophets than anyone else; and if we claimed to be able to give an official solution to all the problems that will arise in the course of the daily life of a future society, then what we meant by the abolition of government would be curious to say the least . . . It is just as well that not having the stake or prisons with which to impose our bible, mankind would be free to laugh at us and at our pretensions with impunity!' Anarchists were indeed concerned with the problems of social life, for which they had solutions. However, these were no longer definitive plans to be inscribed in the party program, but individual and possibly transitory opinions, whose implementation depended on what experience and discussion would dictate (44–5).

Accordingly, a program concerned with the very foundations of society 'cannot do other than suggest a method'. For Malatesta, it was method that differentiated parties and determined their historical importance, not their abstract claims about pursuing the welfare of humanity. Therefore, 'one must consider anarchy above all as a method'. The methods of non-anarchist parties could be reduced to two, 'the authoritarian and the so-called liberal'. The former entrusted to a few the management of social life and led to the exploitation and oppression of the masses by the few. The latter relied on free individual enterprise and proclaimed the reduction of governmental functions to an absolute minimum. Anarchists offered a new method: 'free initiative of all and free compact when, private property having been abolished by revolutionary action, everybody has been put in a situation of equality to dispose of social wealth. This method, by not allowing access to the reconstitution of private property, must lead, via free association, to the complete victory of the principle of solidarity' (45–6).

The more problems were put forward in order to counter anarchist ideas, Malatesta added, the more they turned into arguments in favor of those ideas, because the core of anarchism was precisely a superior method to solve social problems. This was the method of trial and error, by which the solutions could be found that best satisfied the dictates of science as well as everybody's needs and wishes. In brief, anarchy was the only form of society which left open the way to achieving the greatest good for humanity, since it alone destroyed every class bent on keeping the masses oppressed and in poverty (46–7).

Malatesta concluded his discussion of the anarchist method with a third and last definition of anarchy, the most complete. The definition admirably summarizes in a paragraph a whole view of anarchism: 'Anarchy, in common with socialism, has as its basis, its point of departure, its essential environment, *equality of conditions*; its beacon is *solidarity* and *freedom* is its method. It is not perfection, it is not the absolute ideal which like the horizon recedes as fast as we approach it; but it is the way open to all progress and all improvements for the benefit of everybody' (47).

SOLIDARITY AS A VALUE

Malatesta's apparently obvious and uncontroversial reference to solidarity as the 'beacon of anarchy' was instead of crucial importance. It drew a line not only between anarchism and marxism, which despised abstract ideals and values, but also between different brands of anarchism.

This is illustrated by an article devoted to the subject in *L'Associazione* of January 1890, under the title 'La lotta per la vita: Egoismo e Solidarietà' (The struggle for life: Egoism and solidarity). The article resumed an argument that Malatesta had already broached in the 1884 first draft of *Anarchy*, where he had outlined history as a struggle between two fundamental human dispositions, egoism and solidarity, and the corresponding principles of competition and cooperation. In the article of 1890 that narrative was reiterated, and the concepts of egoism and solidarity were further discussed, in polemic with anarchists imbued with a positivistic spirit and influenced by Darwinian evolutionism, who attempted to construe anarchism on the basis of egoistic tendencies.

Malatesta claimed that the ongoing controversy about egoism and solidarity was largely a question of words. To the extent that the feeling of sympathy toward others was an individual moral need, its satisfaction could be regarded as a form of egoism. However, it was a very different and superior form of egoism from the mere instinct of self-preservation and disregard of others which usually went by the same name. Therefore, it was convenient to have different names for them, 'altruism' being the readily available name for the superior form of egoism.

Even assuming self-interest as people's sole motivation, Malatesta argued, the rise and development of solidarity could still be explained in a utilitarian fashion, along the lines already drawn in *Anarchy*. By associating among themselves, individuals and groups animated by altruism get the upper hand in the struggle for life, all the rest being equal. In sum, self-interest and moral sentiment head in the same direction: 'If socialism and revolution have their material *raison d'être* in the proletarian's impossibility of individually reaching his own emancipation, they also have their moral force and attraction in the *will* of socialists and revolutionaries to only seek their individual emancipation in the collective emancipation' ('Lotta per la vita').

Malatesta's reference to 'the will' points to the relevant implications of his emphasis on solidarity, which dovetailed with his voluntarism. Both became qualifying traits of Malatesta's anarchism, in contrast to determinist tendencies that grew popular among anarchists, especially under the influence of Kropotkin. For the latter, anarchism was 'a world-concept based upon a mechanical explanation of all phenomena', both natural and social ('Modern', 150); and the anarchist conception was 'not a Utopia, constructed on the *a priori* method, after a few desiderata have been taken as postulates', but was derived 'from an *analysis of tendencies* that are at work already' ('Anarchism', 285). Unlike the anarchists challenged in Malatesta's article, Kropotkin emphasized mutual aid as an evolutionary factor. However, Malatesta's target was not any specific evolutionary theory, but the scientistic tendency as such. Though Malatesta always refrained from directly attacking Kropotkin, he explained the depth of their divergence and the negative influence he attributed to Kropotkin's theories in an article published toward the end of his life, years after Kropotkin's death.

For Malatesta, Kropotkin's mechanical conception of the universe was more paralyzing than the marxist fatalism Kropotkin criticized. Since all that happens has to happen, communist anarchism had necessarily to triumph. In Malatesta's opinion, this took all incertitude away from Kropotkin and hid every difficulty. Undoubtedly Kropotkin's influence as a propagandist was due considerably to how he showed the evolution to anarchism to be so simple, easy, and inevitable that his audience was seized by enthusiasm. However, his optimistic fatalism was, according to Malatesta, a form of wishful thinking. Kropotkin conceived nature as a kind of Providence thanks to which harmony must reign in everything, human societies included. This led many anarchists to repeat the phrase of kropotkinian flavor: 'Anarchy is natural order.' However, Malatesta countered, 'one might ask how is it that if Nature's law is really harmony, Nature has waited for Anarchists to come into existence, and still waits until they are victorious, before destroying the terrible and murderous disharmonies which at all times men have suffered'. Then he concluded: 'would it not be nearer to truth to say that Anarchy is the struggle within human societies against the disharmonies of Nature?' ('Peter').

The contrast with Kropotkin's theories throws into relief the originality of Malatesta's voluntarist appeal to solidarity, which also flies in the face of the claim, made current by postmodernist scholars of anarchism, that 'classical anarchism' posited a universal benign human nature. Precisely because Malatesta did not posit any natural tendency toward anarchy he committed anarchism to a conscious choice between egoism and solidarity that confronted every individual. Natural harmony, the natural marriage of the good of each with that of all, was the invention of human laziness, which rather than struggling for an objective assumed its spontaneous fulfillment by natural law. How such ideas, clearly stated as early as 1890, were still at the core of Malatesta's thought three decades later is illustrated by the article 'La base morale dell'anarchismo' of 1922. Malatesta dropped therein any historical or sociological explanation as to how egoism and solidarity arose in society, but he confirmed his outlook on society as the outcome of the interplay between those two fundamental dispositions: 'How the feeling arose which is expressed by the so-called moral precepts and which, as it develops, denies the existing morality and substitutes a higher morality, is a subject for research which may interest philosophers and sociologists, but it does not detract from the fact that it exists, independently of the explanations which may be advanced.' Whatever one's explanation, the problem remained intact: 'one must choose between love and hate, between brotherly co-operation and fratricidal struggle, between "altruism" and "egoism."'

Malatesta's voluntarism and outlook on solidarity as a conscious choice did not mean that he regarded such choice as free from external constraints. On the contrary, he believed it was a choice that could only be made in favorable conditions. Though the advocacy and practice of solidarity and association were ultimately in the best interest of the oppressed and exploited classes, still the spirit of solidarity characteristic of socialism was a moral force that could not be equated with the mere defense of material interests. Throughout his life, Malatesta frequently emphasized the discrepancy between the day-to-day defense of immediate material interests and a broader spirit of solidarity among workers. In August 1893, for example, a tragic episode occurred at Aigues-Mortes, in Provence, where 30 Italian workers were killed by French workers enraged by the competition that foreign labor was bringing in the local salt industry (Masini, *Storia . . . nell'epoca*, 15). A French anarchist periodical approved as natural the aggression against the 'polenta-eaters', guilty of lowering wage rates. In contrast, Malatesta and Merlino called the aggression a crime. While the periodical conceded that 'it would have been "more expedient" for the workers of the two nationalities to ally against the bosses', Malatesta and Merlino retorted that, on the contrary, 'it is perhaps "more expedient" to take it out on poor foreign workers than to revolt against the bosses'. However, this was also more reactionary and more detrimental to the workers' cause ('A propos').

The contrast between class solidarity and immediate interests in relation to foreign workers was addressed again ten years later with reference to Great Britain, where unemployment and poverty were rampant. Part of the mainstream press launched a campaign against 'the foreign invasion', and a similar sentiment spread among workers, who called for 'good laws' against immigration. Malatesta regarded this viewpoint as mistaken; still he understood it, remarking that 'the damages that each individual suffers or could suffer from immigrant competition, in terms of lack of work or lower salaries, are immediate, direct, and readily palpable damages, while the general damages coming from disregarding solidarity among workers of all places of origin, and possibly from the artificial arrest of immigration flows, are a complex phenomenon, which cannot be easily understood without intellectual effort'. For Malatesta, all the workers of the world had the same interests in the class struggle. However, he understood that such arguments could not easily find a way in the minds of hungry people. In times of crisis, when the alternative to even the most exploitative job may be starvation, 'the economic science loses its rights, and it is no wonder—nor the object of blame—that those who are, or fear to become, unemployed overlook what might happen tomorrow, and look upon any new competitor with dislike, or even with hate'. Equally understandable was the fact that the capitalists encouraged the fratricidal war. What was inexcusable, though, was for socialist leaders to encourage such popular prejudices ('Guerra').

In sum, Malatesta held realistic views on class consciousness formation, which he did not expect to arise necessarily from material interests. In spite of the standard dichotomy between 'idealism' and 'realism', Malatesta's 'idealistic' advocacy of solidarity was precisely dictated by realism. He did not believe that anarchy was the natural order or that capitalism would dig its own grave. Anarchist and marxist theories that posited progressive historical tendencies were equally rejected as pernicious forms of wishful thinking. Nor did Malatesta believe that the defense of interests would automatically generate revolutionary consciousness. The beacon of solidarity was his substitute for either unjustified optimism or resignation.

At the same time, he realistically acknowledged that the practice of solidarity, though ultimately justifiable even from a utilitarian point of view, could require sacrifices in the immediate and might not be within the reach of those who struggled for survival.

Malatesta's realism and idealism were the two faces of the same coin.

CONSCIOUS MINORITIES AND MASSES

Realism was also at the core of Malatesta's outlook on the relationship between conscious minorities and masses. This theme, brought into sharp relief by the dockers' strike, was at the center of Malatesta's critique of the International and remained central thereafter. The knot of the matter was that conscious minorities could not substitute for the masses if a revolution was to be truly emancipatory, and at the same time the action of the masses could not be forthcoming at the will of the conscious minorities.

The increasing recognition of the gap between conscious minorities and masses spurred much of Malatesta's theoretical and tactical thinking. The International had been an association of both workers and revolutionaries in which, Malatesta argued, the conscious minorities were either forced to adapt to the backwardness of the mass, or fell under the illusion that the mass followed and understood them. In contrast, the first issue of *L'Associazione* featured the program of a prospective anarchist party, the organization of a specific conscious minority, which staked no claim to representing all workers.

In turn, the acknowledgment of anarchism as a party presented the question of how to act among workers in a new perspective. Malatesta's discussion of the question was occasioned by the strike of the Rotterdam dockers, in which frictions between conscious minorities and masses had dramatically emerged ('Altro').

In his commentary to the strike Malatesta elaborated the theme of 'going to the people', claiming that in order to exert influence among the masses one had to live among them, not offering leadership, but preaching by example. Rather than caring about theoretical, abstract claims, 'one must take the viewpoint of the mass, reach down to its starting point, and thence push it forward'. Malatesta's polemical targets were the Dutch socialists who had rushed to the Rotterdam docks as outsiders to offer their leadership and preach moderation. In later years he would raise the same issue even more frequently against those anarchists who isolated themselves from the masses.

How then should propaganda and agitation be done among the masses?

Malatesta's response was informed by a realistic awareness of the limited degree of consciousness of the masses and an emphasis on the open-endedness and indeterminacy of collective action. For Malatesta, history showed that revolutions almost invariably start with moderate demands, more in the form of protests against abuses than of revolts against the essence of institutions, and often with displays of respect and devotion to the authorities. However, it is in action itself that revolts can radicalize: 'a strike, if it can last and spread, can end up undermining the legitimacy itself of bosses; likewise, any attack on a town hall or a police station, can end up in open insurrection against the monarchy, even if it is made amidst shouts of "Long live the king! Long live the queen!" '

Propaganda and agitation should take into account such characteristics of collective action, he argued. In the anarchist press and any vehicle of propaganda that addressed the public in general, anarchists were to spell out their ideas and always state their whole program loud and clear, without any concern about tailoring their message to specific people and circumstances. However, in the one-to-one propaganda and amid popular unrest, in order to do useful work, the anarchist must adjust to the intelligence, conditions, habits, and prejudices of the individuals and masses, to draw them as directly as possible to the socialist belief and action:

> If one is afraid of naming things, let's not mention names, when this is useful to do the things.
>
> Who cares if the people shout 'Long live the king!' if they are revolting against the king's forces?
>
> Who cares if they do not want to hear any talk of socialism, if they are attacking the bosses and taking back stuff from them?
>
> The people of Paris, unaware of the irony, welcomed with cheers to the king every victory against the monarchy. Did this prevent Louis Capet from being beheaded?
>
> Let's take the people as they are, and let's move forward with them: abandoning them just because they do not understand our formulas and our arguments in the abstract would be foolishness and betrayal at the same time.

This, however, should not turn into a pretext for abandoning the anarchist program and both names and things. In certain circumstances, one could avoid mentioning socialism and anarchy, but only insofar as one was putting socialism and anarchy in practice ('Altro').

Thus, Malatesta set a double task for anarchists: as an autonomous conscious minority, they should fully advocate their ideas; as a segment of the masses they should aim to be as flexible as possible in order to steer collective action in an emancipatory direction. How crucial this differentiation was is witnessed by the fact that Malatesta repeatedly resumed the theme in the next years, further sharpening the distinction between organization as anarchists and agitation among the masses.

In the article 'Questions de Tactique', of October 1892, Malatesta reiterated the theme of 'going to the people', and elaborated on the twofold organizational task for anarchists. He quoted approvingly the apparently paradoxical opinion expressed by a comrade, who argued that anarchists must enter workers' associations, or, where these do not exist, create them first and only afterwards spread anarchism in them. In their own groups, Malatesta argued, it made sense for anarchists to get together only with likeminded anarchists, and to remain together only as long as agreement lasted. On the other hand, outside of the anarchist groups, when it came to making propaganda and taking advantage of any popular movement, anarchists were to endeavor to make their presence felt wherever they could, and use any possible means to draw the masses together, to educate them to revolt, and to get an opportunity to preach socialism and anarchy, as long as such means did not contradict anarchist ends.

Two years later, in the article 'Andiamo fra il popolo' (Let's go to the people), Malatesta maintained that anarchists could not and did not want to wait for the masses to become fully anarchist before making a revolution. As long as the present economical and political social order existed, the vast majority of the population was condemned to ignorance and brutishness, and it was only capable of more or less blind rebellions. First the present order had to be overthrown, by making a revolution in whatever way one could, with the available forces. The anarchist could not expect to organize workers only after these had become anarchists. How could they become anarchists, if they were left alone with the sense of impotence that came from their isolation? Anarchists were to organize among themselves, among people with firm beliefs and in full agreement; but around their groups they had to organize as many workers as possible in broad and open associations, accepting those workers for what they were, and getting them to progress as much as possible.

The theoretical distinction between workers' associations for economic struggle and political organizations, already clear in the above articles, became increasingly sharp in Malatesta's writings, thus illustrating the fertility of his early distinctions of 1889. For him, that distinction was not only to be accepted as unavoidable, when a gap between conscious minorities and masses existed; it was also to be promoted as desirable, even in the favorable situations in which that gap was less perceptible.

Thus, in the 1897 article 'L'anarchismo nel movimento operajo' (Anarchism in the labor movement) Malatesta commented on the French union congress held in September 1897 in Toulouse, in which the French workers had expressed their leanings toward the positions of the anarchists. While rejoicing in the circumstance, Malatesta remarked: 'Certainly the Toulouse congress was not an anarchist congress—and it is good that it was not.

Anarchist congresses must be held by the anarchists, not by workers in general . . . except when the latter have already become anarchist, in which case anarchy would have triumphed.' Then, in clear contrast to the authoritarian spirit that he ascribed to both the marxist and anarchist sides in the old International, he added: 'We do not intend to impose our program to the still unconvinced masses; even less we want to look strong by making workers vote declarations of principles that they do not fully accept, through sleights of hand and more or less clever maneuvers. We do not want our party to replace popular life; but we strive for that life to be broader, more conscious, and livelier, and for our party to exercise on it as much influence as comes naturally from the activity and intelligence that the party is able to put in its propaganda and action' ('Anarchismo nel movimento').

In Malatesta's reconsideration of the whole question of conscious minorities and masses, based on his criticism of the past experience of the International, we see again realism and pragmatism at work, in contrast to the cliché of anarchism as impossibilist and unconcerned with empirical reality. The most prominent aspect is a disenchanted outlook on the people and a rejection of inflated expectations about the people's revolutionary instincts. The masses, however, were one side of the equation, conscious minorities being the other. The interplay that Malatesta posited between masses and conscious minorities was an instance of a more general dynamic relationship between the possible and the desirable, neither of which could be derived from the other.

As Malatesta most concisely put it, 'one must aim at what one wants, doing what one can' ('Ideale').

TACTICAL PRINCIPLES

The same mutual dependence between the desirable and the possible was present in Malatesta's tactical principles, which are summed up by five concepts: insurrectionism, coherence with ends, inclusiveness, 'going to the people', and anarchist autonomy. Such concepts, which were already clearly outlined in Malatesta's discussion of conscious minorities and masses in *L'Associazione*, would remain the foundation of his tactics ever after.

Insurrection, or the violent overthrow of government, was the central concept in Malatesta's tactics. For him insurrection was an inevitable step in a struggle for the expropriation of the means of production, which inevitably had to confront the force of government, the 'gendarme' of privilege. Insurrection was the watershed of revolutionary tactics, the event that separated 'before' from 'after'. By removing the obstacle of governmental armed forces and by enabling workers to take possession of the means of production, the insurrection opened up a whole new social scenario. As with most of his ideas, Malatesta's outlook on the role of insurrection in the revolutionary process changed over time, on the ground of past experience and in response to changing conditions. In his early view, insurrection was largely identified with revolution. In time, he reached a more cautious outlook, according to which the insurrection required patient preparation, and it was to be regarded as a mere start, not as the full accomplishment of the revolutionary process. However, this more realistic outlook on insurrection and revolution, rather than weakening Malatesta's focus on insurrection, provided further motivation for advocating that a successful insurrection should happen as soon as possible. In brief, Malatesta was adamant in regarding insurrection as a key tactical objective. This aspect of his thought remained unchanged throughout his life, though his outlook on the overall revolutionary process did change.

While insurrection was the main objective, coherence between means and ends was the key principle that informed anarchist tactics. As discussed earlier, this principle is not to be intended as a form of ethical purism, but rather as a methodological principle that ensures the adequacy of the means to the intended end. In discussing pluralism we started to see how considerations of method acquired prominence in Malatesta's views on the anarchist party. In the article 'Questions révolutionnaires', which appeared in *La Révolte* of Paris few months after the demise of *L'Associazione*, Malatesta remarked again that 'in social struggles, as well as in scientific research, it is method that counts most and determines the results; parties are constituted on the basis of what they want to do, not on the basis of what they desire or foresee'. The principle of coherence between means and ends and the focus on method posited a direct link between current tactics and the outlook on future society, not in terms of a blueprint of society, but in terms of the method of collective action that characterized it. While revolution constituted a dramatic break in social life, there was no break or discontinuity in the anarchist method of collective action.

The complement to the principle of coherence between ends and means is what we might call the principle of inclusiveness. If, on the one hand, any struggle relevant to anarchists must be coherent with their ends, any struggle coherent with their ends is relevant to anarchists, no matter how limited or partial it is. The combination of these two principles, coherence and inclusiveness, was a mainstay of Malatesta's tactics, and was clearly expressed as early as his 1884 program, where he wrote: 'the International, whose immediate goal is the simultaneous insurrection against political power, for its abolition, and against owners, for the common ownership of wealth, must choose those means that are instrumental to prepare the insurrection and to ensure its anti-authoritarian and anti-property character.' Then he condensed the tactics of the International in the following principle: 'Everything that draws the socialist insurrection closer and makes it easier is good; everything that pushes it farther, or makes it more difficult, or alters its anarchist-socialist character is bad: this is the criterion that guides the International in its conduct' (*Programma e Organizzazione*, 50). The same concept was frequently repeated in later writings. For example, Malatesta wrote in *L'Associazione*: 'Deeds perhaps insignificant in themselves but repeated frequently and widely are more useful than momentous ones undertaken once every so many years' ('Propaganda').

Unlike coherence between ends and means, the advocacy of inclusiveness in anarchist struggles was more characteristic of Malatesta than of anarchism in general, and subjected him to polemics and misunderstandings by anarchists of different tendencies. The same can be said for another of Malatesta's basic tactical tenets, the urge of 'going to the people'. In 'Questions révolutionnaires' Malatesta thus expressed his point in a short paragraph that well summarizes the tactical principles illustrated so far:

> We must mingle as much as possible with the popular life; we must encourage and push every movement that contains a seed of material or moral revolt and gets the people used to managing themselves their own matters and relying only on their own force. However, we must do this without ever losing sight of the following facts: that the revolution for the purposes of expropriating and collectively owning property and the demolition of power are the only salvation of the proletariat and of Humanity; and therefore anything is good or bad depending on whether it draws that revolution closer or farther, whether it makes it easier or more difficult.

Malatesta advocated anarchist autonomy as a way out of the apparent conflict or contradiction between anarchist coherence and participation in every struggle. Anarchists should organize among themselves, he maintained, and claim their ideas and programs in their entirety. At the same time, they should join or promote any struggle that did not clash with their principles and objectives, even when the struggle was not explicitly anarchist. This did not exclude that, whenever they had sufficient strength, suitable opportunities, and chances of success, they should also undertake initiatives on their own behalf. These could also be the deeds of small groups and individuals, when they had a good chance to be useful and effective. Explicitly anarchist and collective action was the ideal case. However, in the same way that Malatesta was inclusive with respect to collective initiatives that were not explicitly anarchist, he was also inclusive with respect to explicitly anarchist initiatives that were not collective. In contrast to the exclusiveness of other anarchists, who conceived collective action as a sum of individual actions of a purely anarchist type, and tended to despise mass movements, Malatesta's advocacy of participation in mass movements, especially in the labor movement, did not imply ruling out individual or affinity group action.

These five tactical principles—insurrectionism, coherence with ends, inclusiveness, 'going to the people', and anarchist autonomy—account for much of the tactics that Malatesta advocated over time. They do not define a single tactic, but rather stake out the ground of anarchist action. Within their boundaries different tactics could be devised, depending on the specific context. Such principles are general enough as to make many tactics available within them, but also restrictive enough to rule out all those deviations from anarchism that Malatesta criticized. The principles of insurrectionism and anarchist autonomy on the one hand, and inclusiveness and 'going to the people' on the other hand, placed different demands on the anarchist militants. While each of those principles was individually shared by other anarchists, their coexistence gave Malatesta's tactics their distinctive character of flexibility and pragmatism.

At the same time, Malatesta was aware of the exaggerations that a rigid interpretation of one or the other principle could engender. Thus, in 'Questions révolutionnaires' he also remarked: 'We must avoid two pitfalls: on the one hand, the indifference to everyday life and struggles, which brings us farther from the people and makes us stranger and incomprehensible to them; and on the other hand, letting ourselves be absorbed by such struggles, giving them a greater importance than they have, and ending up forgetting about the revolution.' The importance attributed to partial struggles, which in other socialist and anarchist militants was accompanied with the tendency to defer the revolution to a time when conditions would be ripe, was counterbalanced in Malatesta by his voluntarism, which regarded revolution as an occurrence that had to be not only awaited, but also prepared and consciously aimed for.

METHODOLOGICAL INDIVIDUALISM

With the exception of insurrectionism, Malatesta's tactical tenets did not advocate specific tactics, but provided guidelines for choosing tactics. In their methodological nature, those principles were consistent with Malatesta's redefinition of anarchism as method, whose importance for anarchist thought can hardly be over-emphasized.

In the transition from the 1884 version of 'L'Anarchia' to that of 1891 one can discern at the same time the continuity of themes and the novelty of the conclusions Malatesta eventually reached. Anarchy was no longer defined, more or less statically, as a blueprint, an ideal description of how a perfect society would be organized as a whole. Instead, it was dynamically described as a method defining an open-ended process, which guaranteed that the best possible society be reached, without describing what its specific traits would be. Such a method was the method of freedom; its pre-requisite was that private ownership of the means of production and government be abolished; and the driving force of social evolution was solidarity. The relationship between the solidarity of individuals and the organization of society as a whole had been inverted: it was no longer the case that the best organization of society ensured the solidarity of individuals, but rather the latter engendered, through free initiative, the best possible social organization. Ideas about specific solutions to social problems were still relevant, but they pertained to individuals, and as such they contributed to shape the new society, as long as they were inspired by the beacon of solidarity. In sum, the anarchist method became not only the essence of the anarchist party in the present, but also of the anarchist society in the future.

At the core of Malatesta's transition from defining anarchism in terms of blueprints of society to defining it in terms of method was an even more fundamental turn in his thought, which provides unity to the themes discussed so far. Concepts such as collectivism and communism were inherently collective, while method was individually applicable. Correspondingly, the turn in question was a methodological shift from a holistic to an individualistic outlook on society. The terms 'methodological holism' and 'methodological individualism' belong to the philosophy of social science of the twentieth century. In a nutshell, the former explains the behavior of individuals in terms of the influence and constraints that social wholes place on each of them; the latter explains social wholes as the end result of the complex interactions among actors (Watkins, 729). Though Malatesta never used such terms and cannot be claimed to be a forerunner of ideas advanced decades later, a methodological-individualistic outlook is evident in his writings after 1889. For example, in the final version of *Anarchy* he wrote:

> The real being is man, the individual. Society or the collectivity—and the *State* or government which claims to represent it—if it is not a hollow abstraction must be made up of individuals. And it is in the organism of every individual that all thoughts and human actions inevitably have their origin, and from being individual they become collective thoughts and acts when they are or become accepted by many individuals. Social action, therefore, is neither the negation nor the complement of individual initiative, but is the resultant of initiatives, thoughts, and actions of all individuals who make up society; a resultant which, all other things being equal, is greater or smaller depending on whether individual forces are directed to a common objective or are divided or antagonistic. And if instead, as do the authoritarians, one means government action when one talks of social action, then this is still the resultant of individual forces, but only of those individuals who form the government or who by reason of their position can influence the policy of the government. (36)

Unlike methodological individualism of the twentieth century, which is explanatory and descriptive, Malatesta's methodological individualism also bore a prescriptive character, becoming the basis of his model of purposive social action. However, appraising society is equally required in the descriptive and prescriptive domains, therefore the extension of methodological concepts from one domain to the other is justified. The distinction between methodological and ethical individualism should also be emphasized, for Malatesta was not an individualist in the latter sense, as his advocacy of solidarity as the basis of socialism clearly shows.

Elements of methodological individualism already existed in the tradition of political thought that influenced Malatesta, thus suggesting that such a stance was not a mere, contingent addition to Malatesta's ideas, but rather it was logically connected to them. For example, Carlo Pisacane, a federalist socialist who had a strong influence on Italian Internationalists, wrote in 1857 that there was no denying that the revolution had to be made by 'the country'. However, he added, 'the country is made up of individuals . . . If everybody were to say: the revolution must be made by the country and I, being an infinitesimal part of the country, have my infinitesimal portion of duty to do and will do it, the revolution would be immediately huge' (qtd in 'Pisacane').

Furthermore, opposite methodological attitudes were already implicit in the respective outlooks on human will held by marxists and anarchists since the First International. Marxists focused on understanding the developmental laws of autonomous social processes. Instead, the voluntarist anarchists focused on the individual agencies of social actors and their interplay. Such a contrast, which readily lends itself to be described methodologically in terms of holism versus individualism, underlay the different ways in which collective goals were set. For the holists the object of the purposive action of proletarians was the 'historical mission' assigned to them by the laws of social development. In contrast, the individualists emphasized that the goals of purposive action were chosen.

After 1889 Malatesta's methodological individualist stance became explicit and pervaded every theme he dealt with in *L'Associazione*.

For example, though he had always drawn a distinction between conscious minorities and masses, the new emphasis placed on the consciousness gap between minorities and masses signaled a reorientation of his perspective on their mutual relationship. In the International the proletariat was held to be the revolutionary subject, and the International was meant to be the proletariat's organization. A holistic assumption underlay such perspective, from which, as Malatesta later acknowledged, the tendency proceeded to overlook the gap between the proletarian masses and the conscious minority that actually formed the International. Malatesta's novel acknowledgment of that gap went hand in hand with his rejection of any holistic assumption. The organization he advocated in 1889 was no longer the organization of the entire proletariat, but an anarchist party. The latter was made up of workers, but only claimed to represent itself, not the proletariat as a whole. It claimed autonomy at the same time that it reasserted its aim to work among the masses and to 'go to the people'. The distinction between anarchist and workers' organizations was not an adjustment to a contingent consciousness gap between minorities and masses. Rather, it took on a prescriptive character, as Malatesta made clear in 1897, remarking that 'anarchist congresses must be held by the anarchists, not by workers in general' ('Anarchismo nel movimento').

Malatesta's methodological reorientation was also evident in his new outlook on collectivism and communism. In 1884 he had maintained that collectivism was powerless to bring about people's moral transformation. In contrast, in 1889 he maintained that people's moral transformation would prevent collectivism from bringing back privilege and wage labor.

On the subject of pluralism, too, Malatesta did not just take an instrumental stance for the sake of unity, but gave pluralism a prescriptive character. Dropping the collectivist–communist controversy was not just a tactical possibility, but also a necessity dictated by the anarchist method.

Finally, by moving from a concept of anarchy as description of the optimal social organization, to that of anarchy as method, Malatesta fully resolved the concept of the anarchist society into individual dispositions and actions. The end result of the interaction among actors was left unspecified; but to the extent that the interaction was informed by anarchist dispositions, and therefore conducted by anarchist method, the result could only be an anarchist society.

Epilogue: pragmatism and coherence

Malatesta's novel views expressed in *L'Associazione* both represented a methodological shift and provided fertile ground for the continuing development of his ideas. They began to weaken a black-and-white outlook on society, according to which either a society was anarchist or it was not, either government and private property existed or they did not. The future society was no longer regarded as statically perfect, as 'the absolute ideal which like the horizon recedes as fast as we approach it'; instead, it came to be regarded as a process, as 'the way open to all progress and all improvements for the benefit of everybody' (*Anarchy*, 46–7). As for the present society, methodological individualism opened the door to a more graded view of society. Government and private property might have a greater or lesser strength, depending on the strength and intransigence of the opposition they encountered. Malatesta foreshadowed such a view in the final paragraphs of the 1891 version of *Anarchy*, where he argued for the value of anarchism in bringing about social progress, regardless of whether or not anarchy and socialism would triumph in the next revolution:

> In any case we will have on events the kind of influence which will reflect our numerical strength, our energy, our intelligence and our intransigence. Even if we are defeated, our work will not have been useless, for the greater our resolve to achieve the implementation of our programme

in full, the less property, and less government will there be in the new society. And we will have performed a worthy task for, after all, human progress is measured by the extent government power and private property are reduced. (53–4)

In Malatesta's new appraisal of anarchism were the seeds of ideas that he would fully formulate in the 1920s. Those formulations were the result of decades of revolutionary experiences, struggles, and defeats, thus contrasting with the irrationalist stereotype of anarchism as unchanging and detached from reality. The dynamic interplay between ideal and reality and between conscious minorities and masses that Malatesta posited in 1889 called for pragmatism in adapting one's tactics to contingent situations. Those later formulations would be the outcome of three decades of revolutionary experiments. At the same time, that Malatesta's ideas of the 1920s were rooted in his theoretical turn of 1889 speaks to the coherence of his anarchism, thus defying another side of the irrationalist cliché, that of anarchism as contradictory and inconsequent.

Both the tactical flexibility and the theoretical unity of Malatesta's anarchism were well illustrated by his trajectory during the 1890s, beginning with the insurrectionary activities of 1890–92. This is where our investigation of Malatesta's action begins.

5
OPAQUE INSURRECTIONARY TRIALS, 1890–92

For Malatesta, the early 1890s, following the end of *L'Associazione* in January 1890, were years of intense agitations with insurrectionary objectives. The cycle of struggles of 1890–94, covered by the present and the next chapter, illustrates both the continuity and diversity of Malatesta's anarchism.

Continuity is relevant in three respects. First is the continuity of Malatesta's action over time, in contrast with the historiographical pattern of cyclical appearances and disappearances of anarchism. The historiographical problem is particularly acute for this cycle of struggles, which were largely forced underground by their insurrectionary objectives. Second is continuity in space, or the interconnection of anarchist struggles across national borders. Malatesta's activity over five years involved as many countries: England, France, Italy, Spain, and Belgium. The neglect of the transnational and cross-national dimensions of anarchism is another historiographical shortcoming that has fostered interpretations in terms of appearances and disappearances. Third is the continuity of Malatesta's thought, in terms of both interdependence between theory and tactics and solidity of theoretical foundations over time.

At the same time, the struggles of 1890–94 illustrate the diversity of Malatesta's tactics, which both adjusted to different circumstances and changed in time, based on the lesson of experience. Among agitations with insurrectionary objectives, a first differentiation, reflected in Malatesta's tactics, can be made between anarchist autonomous initiatives and participation in ongoing agitations that did not have explicit anarchist content. The agitations of 1890–92, centered on the First of May and its competing interpretations by socialists and anarchists, were examples of the former type.

THE INDETERMINACY OF SOCIAL ACTION

The theoretical foundations of the insurrectionary tactics that underpinned Malatesta's action of the early 1890s were illustrated in a series of articles that

appeared in *L'Associazione*. In these articles Malatesta explained his positive
outlook on uprisings. His outlook was based on theoretical notions, such
as the indeterminacy of collective action and the precedence of deeds over
ideas, that were already implicit in the tactics of propaganda by the deed
that Italian anarchists began advocating in the mid-1870s. In *L'Associazione*
Malatesta reiterated his belief in propaganda by the deed, at the same time
that he thoroughly reviewed this concept, in the light of past experiences and
changed conditions.

Malatesta articulated his appreciation of uprisings as steps on the path
of revolution in the article 'La sommossa non é rivoluzione' (An uprising
is not a revolution) of October 1889. This was Malatesta's response to an
article by the same title published in the Italian socialist revolutionary periodical *La Rivendicazione*, in which N. Sandri claimed that 'every partial
uprising is an aborted revolution'. Malatesta retorted that uprisings played
an immense role in provoking and preparing revolutions. For Malatesta, 'it
is always deeds that provoke ideas, which in turn act upon deeds, and so
on'. He pointed to the history of past revolutions, which were all preceded,
provoked, and determined by numerous uprisings that prepared people's
minds to the struggle: 'The great French revolution would not have occurred if the countryside—worked up by a thorough propaganda—had
not started to burn castles and hang masters, and if the people of Paris in
tumult had not committed the sublime folly of attacking the Bastille with
pikes.' The history of socialism itself provided further evidence with the
Paris Commune, which arose from an uprising in Montmartre, and which
in turn originated a splendid movement of ideas, and a whole period of
feverish socialist activism. Revolutions had nowhere to start from than uprisings: 'Certainly, while all uprisings make propaganda, only few have the
good fortune to arrive at the right time to determine a revolution. Yet who
can say what is the right time?'

The key concept outlined here by Malatesta is the indeterminacy of collective action. No one can fully foresee the outcome of one's intentional social action, nor is the outcome of collective action necessarily what its participants had initially envisioned.

Similar ideas dotted Malatesta's writings from 1889 on. Commenting
upon the Rotterdam strike of September 1889 Malatesta had remarked that
'history shows that revolutions start almost invariably with moderate demands, more in the form of protests against abuses than of revolts against
the essence of institutions, and often with displays of respect and devotion to
the authorities' ('Altro').

In 1894 he expressed the same concept, with reference to the French
Revolution and to the recent movement of the Sicilian Fasci: 'Let us remember that the people of Paris started off by demanding bread to the king
amidst applauses and tears of affection, yet—having received bullets instead
of bread, as it was natural—after two years they beheaded him. And it was

only yesterday that the Sicilian people were on the verge of making a revolution while cheering to the king and his whole family' ('Andiamo').

Malatesta still reiterated the idea in writings of two decades later. In 1914 a strike of the railway workers in Italy was creating serious difficulties to the government. In the article 'É possibile la rivoluzione' Malatesta started by claiming, 'Naturally we do not know what could happen in the near future.' He then emphasized how a minor issue over salaries had escalated into a serious crisis, and pictured a hypothetical scenario, which really looks like a disguised call for action: 'If really—people wonder—the railway workers refused to work; if ill-intentioned people made even a limited service impossible, sabotaging the rolling stock and the railway tracks; if the most conscious part of the proletariat supported the movement with general strikes: what would the government do with its soldiers, even supposing that the latter failed to remember that they are forcefully enlisted proletarians, and that their fathers, brothers, and friends are among the strikers? How could the current order continue?' Malatesta argued that revolution would impose itself as a necessity, for it alone could ensure the continuation of social life. 'Perhaps this will not happen today. Still, why could not it happen tomorrow?' After maintaining that nobody knows in advance when the times are really ripe and that the fateful hour could strike at any moment, Malatesta concluded: 'Everybody keep ready for tomorrow . . . or for today.' Only a few weeks later the insurrectional movement of the Red Week broke out, in which Malatesta had a leading role. It would be problematic to retrospectively determine whether Malatesta's prediction should be read descriptively as that of a perceptive sociologist or prescriptively as that of an effective agitator.

PROPAGANDA BY THE DEED REDEFINED

Another key point raised by Malatesta's argument about uprisings was the precedence of deeds over ideas. This concept had already been put forward by Carlo Pisacane in his 1857 'Political Testament':

> The propaganda of the idea is a chimera; the education of the people is nonsense. Ideas result from deeds, and not the latter from the former; it is not the case that the people will be free once it is educated, but rather it will be educated once it is free. The only work a citizen can undertake to benefit his country is to contribute to the material revolution: conspiracies, plots, insurrectional attempts, etc. constitute the trend of events through which Italy progresses towards its goal. The flash of Milano's bayonet was a more effective propaganda than a thousand volumes written by those doctrinaires who are a real plague to ours as to any other country.
>
> (qtd in 'Pisacane')

'Milano's bayonet' is a reference to Agesilao Milano, a Calabrian soldier who made an attempt on the king of the Two Sicilies' life in 1856.

The precedence of deeds over ideas meant that deeds themselves had a propaganda value, regardless of their victorious outcome, as the Paris Commune demonstrated. Therefore deeds were consciously undertaken by anarchists not only for their immediate effects, but also as a form of propaganda, in order to build a revolutionary consciousness in the people. This was the idea of propaganda by the deed, which anarchists inherited directly from Pisacane and turned into a cornerstone of their tactics. The Benevento uprising of April 1877 was itself an instance of propaganda by the deed.

Indeterminacy of collective action and precedence of deeds over ideas jointly provided the ground for Malatesta's dynamic outlook on insurrection in two respects: the relationship between anarchist and popular collective action and the relationship between partial struggles and insurrection.

In the first respect, one could not determine a priori how a successful insurrection would come about. Anarchist and popular collective action neither preceded nor necessarily followed each other. On the one hand, anarchists had the task of creating the opportunities for insurrectionary collective action. The First of May movement was a case in point. On the other hand, they were to seize any insurrectionary opportunity offered by popular movements, without shunning them when these did not have explicit anarchist content.

As for the relationship between partial struggles and insurrection, Malatesta blurred the distinction between them. On the one hand, he refused to regard a failed uprising as simply an aborted revolution, since even a failed uprising might have propaganda value. On the other hand, he believed that insurrections could arise from open-ended initiatives that were not originally meant as insurrections. From these beliefs taken together, a continuum resulted that ranged from local revolts and attacks on property to fully fledged insurrections.

Malatesta redefined propaganda by the deed in the two articles 'A proposito di uno sciopero' and 'La propaganda a fatti', which appeared consecutively in the first two issues of *L'Associazione*, in October 1889. Malatesta's increasing emphasis on 'going to the people' led him to a retrospective criticism of earlier tactics of the Italian Internationalists. The two articles were complementary.

The first article, prompted by the London dockers' strike, focused on the workplace and criticized the attitude of Internationalists toward strikes, which overlooked the strike as economic weapon, and neglected to attribute its due importance as a factor of moral revolt. In contrast, Malatesta emphasized that 'the masses get to advance broad demands by way of small complaints and small revolts'. The anarchists' task was to join them and push them forward, to provoke and organize as many strikes as possible, striving to make them contagious. However, each strike should have its revolutionary mark; in each of them there should be people resolute enough 'to castigate the bosses, and above all to attack property and show to the strikers how much easier it is to take than to demand'. These tactics would put anarchists in direct and continuous contact with the masses, provide opportunities to spread anarchist ideas, and to practice that propaganda by the deed that, Malatesta lamented, anarchists often preached but seldom practiced. In addition, a revolution arising from a wave of strikes would have the advantage of directly placing the question of human emancipation on its proper ground, the economic one.

The second article focused on propaganda by the deed outside of the workplace, while retaining a strong anti-capitalist character. Malatesta argued that classical armed band warfare, as attempted in the Benevento uprising of 1877, was no longer suitable to the present conditions and aspirations of the anarchist party. The armed band, with its marked military character, was in conflict with the idea of a popular revolution, which required means at everyone's reach. Malatesta proposed to replace armed bands with temporary flying squads, which would focus on direct attacks on private property, such as appropriating an employer's cash funds or a farmer's crop and distributing them to the workers, attacking landlords and tax collectors, and so on. Such tactics would not only be more sustainable, but also accessible to everyone, and flexible enough to be applicable in nearly every circumstance.

In both cases the redefinition of propaganda by the deed pointed in the same twofold direction. First, it drew propaganda by the deed closer to the immediate interests and antagonistic feelings of the popular masses, by shifting focus from lofty ideals to everyday complaints, and from military action to the attack on private property. Second, it emphasized the inclusive character that Malatesta believed anarchist action should bear, by shifting focus from single sensational events to small-scale, diffuse actions within everyone's reach.

While insurrectionary goals should not prevent anarchists from joining or promoting all forms of small-scale struggle at any level, neither should the latter lead anarchists to lose sight of their ultimate goal. Malatesta did not expect that a successful insurrection would arise from a sheer multiplication of local acts of attack on property. Though he believed that mass insurrection would 'come as a consequence of an incessant propaganda and of a huge number of individual and collective revolts', he also claimed that such acts were to be carried out 'waiting for the day in which we will be able to get to the streets with the popular masses to deal the final blow' ('Propaganda'). Coordination and preparation on a different scale were definitely required for an insurrection to be successful. This, in turn, did not mean that a popular insurrection could be planned as if anarchists could expect to turn the popular masses into a disciplined army at their disposal, waiting for the sign of revolt from their leaders. This is another aspect of Malatesta's dynamic outlook on the relationship between anarchist and popular, or organized and spontaneous collective action. A successful insurrection could be neither fully planned nor fully spontaneous. Instead, it could only arise from a combination of anarchist planning and popular spontaneity.

Malatesta's outlook on propaganda by the deed sheds light on the cyclic pattern of anarchist struggles, which historians of anarchism have often described in terms of repetition without progress or evolution. By refusing to simply look upon partial uprisings as aborted revolutions, Malatesta tended to attribute to them a progressive role in preparing a revolution and bringing it nearer, though no one could foretell if and when a revolution was about to come. Uprisings had value regardless of whether they were successful, or even when a lasting success was simply out of the question from a merely tactical perspective. For Malatesta, partial uprisings, local revolts, and acts of propaganda by the deed were valuable in instilling a struggling habit and forming a revolutionary consciousness in workers. His appraisal of direct action was not based on anarchist dogmas, but on reasons drawn from the logic of collective action, such as the precedence of deeds over ideas and social indeterminacy, the latter of which has become a current theme in today's sociological literature (see, e.g., Hardin, *Indeterminacy*). By emphasizing the open-endedness of partial struggles and the progressive value of unsuccessful revolts, Malatesta inclusively looked upon the whole gamut of direct action as a continuum. Local revolts and failed uprisings were useful in their own right as acts of propaganda by the deed and steps toward the final insurrection.

For Malatesta, each revolt made sense in view of the ultimate insurrectionary goal, while no revolt needed to explicitly aim for that goal to make sense. Such continuity has been obliterated in stereotypical representations of anarchism. On the one hand, propaganda by the deed has been trivialized through identification with individual deeds, and preferentially the most senseless ones, such as bombings that most anarchists themselves disavowed. On the other hand, anarchist uprisings have been trivialized into an equally senseless all-or-nothing pursuit of a heaven-on-earth to be immediately realized. While Malatesta's notion of propaganda by the deed bridged the gap between here-and-now direct action means and ultimate insurrectionary ends, stereotyped trivializations of anarchism have precisely severed that link, representing anarchist action as either aimless or aiming for the impossible. Unsurprisingly, the only explanations left open have been in terms of chiliastic mentality, purism, or stupidity.

FRANCE: THE FIRST OF MAY

Malatesta's ideas about the indeterminacy of social action, the precedence of deeds over ideas, and the propaganda value of direct action are practically illustrated by his attitude toward the First of May movement, and by his action in the first three years of this annual event.

The origin of the First of May was bound up with the eight-hour movement that started in America, escalating to the Haymarket affair of 1886 in Chicago. During a workers' demonstration three days after a 1 May strike for the eight-hour day, a bomb thrown from the crowd killed a policemen, leading to the hanging of four anarchist labor leaders held responsible for the bomb. In December 1888, a year after the execution, the American Federation of Labor decided to resume mass demonstrations for the eight-hour day on 1 May 1890. The following year, one of two competing international socialist congresses held simultaneously in Paris, from which the Second International was to arise, followed suit, deciding that mass demonstrations be organized in all countries for the same day. The First of May's character of annual demonstration was eventually established by the Brussels international socialist congress of August 1891 (Trachtenberg, 11–14).

In an essay on the First of May, which she interprets as a working-class ritual, or 'the High Mass of the working class', Michelle Perrot remarks: '*Doing the same thing at the same time*: this great principle of religious practice was now, by a stroke of genius, transferred to the labor movement, a new Moses leading the way to a new Promised Land' (149). However, the idea of 'doing the same thing at the same time' was also, for Malatesta, the principle of effective revolutionary practice and collective action in general, the general strike being an example. The very characters that Perrot regards as ritual, especially the contrast between the paucity of instructions and the grandiose vision, constituted for Malatesta a promising basis for collective action, by making the demonstration amenable to different outcomes. Large masses of workers gathered together under an anti-capitalist banner in an ideologically highly charged context; at the same time, no immediate practical objectives were provided to the demonstrators. A great energy was being accumulated that could be released in different directions.

During the first years of the First of May, when the event had not crystallized into a ritualized tradition, Malatesta placed hope and invested great energy in the movement. In contrast to socialist parties, which aimed to channel the movement into institutional forms in support of legal demands, from the outset Malatesta interpreted the First of May as an opportunity for a less predictable and controllable escalation of class struggle through direct action. Thus, at the end of April 1890 he traveled from London for Paris with the hope of taking part in a combative mass demonstration with momentous consequences. However, Malatesta's hope did not materialize, and days later he returned to London (Luigi Fabbri, *Vida*, 127–8).

Malatesta's attitude and expectations in Paris clearly emerge from his article 'Les Leçons du 1er Mai', written for *La Révolte* in the wake of the demonstration, which he regarded as a missed opportunity. On the occasion, some anarchists had made an effort to demonstrate the uselessness of an eight-hour law, others had undertaken isolated pillaging actions. Malatesta's criticism focused on the anarchists' lack of organization and their wrong attitude toward the masses. If anarchists felt that the demonstration would not or should not be peaceful, they should have got ready to set the masses in revolt, foreseen means of attack and defense, made plans, and distributed tasks. As for their attitude toward the masses, Malatesta argued that the uselessness of an eight-hour law could well be true in general, since the workers' conquests were secured by resistance rather than laws, but emphasizing it as useless on the eve of the demonstration was a bad idea, as this boiled down to inviting workers not to demonstrate. In brief, Malatesta appreciated the eight-hour struggle, but advocated its move from the legislative terrain to collective direct action, where it was open to various outcomes, depending on workers' participation and determination.

The article also hinted at what Malatesta thought anarchists could have done: attract part of the demonstrators to some unguarded uptown district of Paris, entrench themselves, erect barricades, and defend themselves. They might have remained in control for only few days, or even hours, but meanwhile expropriation might have started, showing to the masses what the triumphant revolution would bring them. Malatesta's scenario is a clear example of his concept of propaganda by the deed: 'Can you imagine', he wrote, 'what the effect would have been, in France and abroad, of the news that Paris had risen up, and that the anarchists had been in control of Montmartre or Belleville? ('Leçons').

More generally, Malatesta's analysis of the Paris demonstration is an example of what he regarded as an effective relationship between conscious minorities and masses. The former were to organize among themselves and take a leading role, but they could do so only by 'going to the people': mingling with popular life, preaching by example, 'taking the people as they were, and moving forward with them' ('Altro').

The relation between conscious minorities and masses was made not only of demonstrative actions, but also of day-to-day organization work, as illustrated by another initiative addressed to French workers that Malatesta promoted in September 1890. After the strikes in the ports of London and Rotterdam the year before, considerations about the relevance of dock workers' struggles across Europe induced Malatesta to regard French dock workers as a privileged target of his agitation efforts.

In a letter of 24 September, he asked Gustave Brocher, a French longtime fellow exile in London, to revise the draft of an enclosed appeal in French addressed to dock workers (Brocher Papers). Malatesta's hand-written draft, bearing the title 'Aux ouvriérs du Port de...' and generically signed 'Un groupe de travailleurs', urged dock workers to organize on the workplace, reminding them in plain language that the cause of their exploitation was that 'instead of loving each other like brothers, instead of uniting and agreeing on what should be done, as the workers of other countries have done, among which our fellow workers of Le Havre, we are jealous and hate each other like enemies. By remaining divided we will never have the force to remedy the ills that afflict us'. Then the flyer announced that a group of workers of the port had created an association to defend the workers' interests and urged dockers to join it, issuing the battle-cry of the International: 'The workers' emancipation must be undertaken by the workers themselves.' Workers were then invited to an upcoming meeting.

The draft was meant for simultaneous distribution in different ports. The cover letter to Brocher contained a significant recommendation: 'Feel free to change it as you like, but please note: no socialism, revolution, anarchy, etc., since that, it seems, would frighten and turn away the workers to which it is addressed.' The recommendation was clearly prompted by the events of London and Rotterdam, where the strikers had rejected red flags and socialist language.

The episode speaks to Malatesta's pragmatism and to the mutual influence between his tactical evolution and practical experience. It also provides a concrete example of how he intended propaganda among workers, which was altogether different from the proselytizing effort aimed at making anarchists.

AN ANARCHIST PARTY

Meanwhile Malatesta's main focus was shifting to Italy, in a series of events that culminated with the First of May 1891.

The start of this mobilization effort was a manifesto of November 1890, calling for workers to abstain from voting in the general elections in Italy. As Luigi Galleani recalled years later, the decision to issue the manifesto was taken 'together with Errico Malatesta, Saverio Merlino, Paolo Schicchi, Augusto Norsa, Peppino Consorti, Galileo Palla and a number of other comrades exiled in France, Switzerland, and England' ('É morto'). The initiative must have originated in the very days around the First of May 1890, during Malatesta's stay in Paris, where all the militants mentioned by Galleani had converged, scattering shortly thereafter in different directions: Merlino, convicted in connection with the First of May, left France in July, as Schicchi also did (Musarra, 'Schicchi'); Norsa was expelled during the very month of May (Antonioli, 'Norsa'); the same lot fell on Galleani after a four-month imprisonment, followed by another arrest in Switzerland in October (Scavino).

The manifesto, titled *I socialisti-anarchici al Popolo Italiano: Non votate!*, was signed by 75 militants 'on behalf of Anarchist Groups and Federations'. As Luigi Fabbri points out, these were militants living abroad, among whom the manifesto had been circulated between May and November (*Vida*, 128). Thus the manifesto documents the role of transnational Italian anarchism for propaganda and mobilization in the motherland. Although no location was associated with the signatories, available biographical information for 25 of them—in addition to those already mentioned—illustrates their geographical spread: between 1890 and 1900 seven are found in London; four each in France, Switzerland, Tunisia, and Egypt; and two in the United States. In addition to 'the best-known comrades of the time', as Fabbri remarked, the majority were obscure figures. Yet in many instances their militancy had a sustained character. It was precisely their ability to remain inconspicuous that enabled them to effectively protract their militancy for a considerable stretch of time. To a significant degree, this kind of militancy provided the backbone of the transnational anarchist network, providing logistic support to propaganda and organization, and contributing to the continuity of the anarchist network over the next decade and beyond.

The key event of the organization effort that occupied Italian anarchism from mid-1890 on was a congress aimed at establishing a country-wide federation. Anarchists could neither afford to hold their congress on Italian soil nor let the government know about its time and place. Thus it was decided that the congress would take place in Tessin, a Swiss canton bordering with Italy. A public call was made for 11 January 1891 in Lugano, and socialists of all tendencies were invited. However, the date and place were only meant to deceive the authorities. On 7 January the news came instead that the congress had already taken place in the small town of Capolago. It lasted from 4 to 6 January 1891, with the participation of numerous delegates, including Malatesta, Merlino, Pezzi, Pietro Gori, and Ettore Molinari. After the congress Malatesta returned unscathed to London (Luigi Fabbri, *Vida*, 129–30).

The congress was the founding act of the *Partito Socialista-anarchico-rivoluzionario*. The relevance of the event has been emphasized by participants and historians alike. For the first time since the 1876 congress of the Italian Federation of the International in Florence, Italian anarchists gathered together again on a national basis to establish a common program and a common organization. For Merlino, the resolution marked a new phase of the anarchist movement in Italy: 'anarchy, which certain opponents consider synonymous with chaos and disorganization, proves to be the organization that makes the greatest use of human resources while respecting individual freedom' (qtd in Santarelli, *Socialismo*, 202). For the historian Nunzio Pernicone, 'Capolago represented the highest point the movement had reached since the heyday of the International' (257). For the marxist Enzo Santarelli the Capolago congress 'certainly represents one of the most original and interesting initiatives of the anarchist socialists around the end of the century'. Santarelli's comment implies a further element of novelty in the very fact that anarchists organized as a party, though such novelty is based on the false but often alleged contrast between anarchism and organization. Significantly, Santarelli adds that the party founded at Capolago seemed to foreshadow the socialist party that would be founded in Genoa the following year: 'an evident sign' he concluded, 'that the force of attraction and expansion of the class-based socialist movement is very strong in this period' (*Socialismo*, 74–5).

Instead, in the minds of the Capolago participants the program of the new party recalled in broad outline the old program of the anarchist International approved at St. Imier in 1872, as explicitly stated in the Capolago congress proceedings ('Congresso Socialista').

ITALY: 'AN UNKNOWN YOUNG MAN . . . '

The congress placed great emphasis on the upcoming 1 May agitations, approving a resolution to join in the celebration, call workers to launch a general strike on 1 May, and call anarchists to carry out suitable propaganda ('Risoluzioni', 192).

When 1 May arrived, the most notable incidents occurred in Rome, at the meeting in the Piazza Santa Croce in Gerusalemme. The London *Times* of the next day thus described the events in a report on 'The Labour Question':

> A meeting of workmen was held to-day in the Piazza Santa Croce. The proceedings passed off quietly, and the speeches delivered by the several leaders had been peaceful, when a workman named Vincenzo Landi mounted the platform, and, after proclaiming himself an Anarchist, called upon the assembly to attack the troops drawn up near the meeting. Then ensued a scene of terrible confusion, the mob pelting the soldiery with stones, and, the cavalry charging the mob, several shots were fired at the troops and many soldiers wounded. Several of the mob were also killed and wounded.

The report represents a widespread perception of the events, as featuring an inflammable crowd ignited by the sudden appearance of an unknown individual coming out of the blue, who thus came to bear much of the responsibility for the events. Such accounts engender an obvious and odd contrast between the two highlights of Italian anarchism in 1891: on the one hand, the high-sounding formal propositions of the Capolago congress, seemingly a prelude to a country-wide, articulate mobilization effort aimed at 1 May; on the other hand, the unplanned, impromptu character born by the most notable 1 May occurrence. What is the historian to make of such a contrast?

It soon emerged that things were not exactly as they seemed. Venerio Landi—not Vincenzo, as the *Times* reported—was actually Galileo Palla, a prominent Italian anarchist and friend of Malatesta. Though the discovery dispelled the suspicion of Palla being an *agent provocateur*, the perception of the disturbances remained that of a spontaneous riot sparked off by his impromptu intervention. Anarchist sources tended to support this version, probably in an effort to avert legal charges and to emphasize the unadulterated popular spontaneous character of the events. In an article published 45 years later, a direct witness to the events, Aristide Ceccarelli, a young republican in 1891, still recalled Palla as 'a tall and strong young man unknown to anyone'.

Most notably, many historians, especially marxists, have characterized the Rome events as unplanned, backing the appearances described by the *Times* with underlying historical analyses, and variously attempting to link the Rome events to the Capolago resolutions. For example, Luciano Cafagna argues that those resolutions revealed insurrectionary intentions for the First of May, but that the increasing isolation of the Roman anarchists persuaded them that insurrection plans were nonsensical (729–71). Enzo Santarelli argues that congress leaders such as Cipriani and Malatesta rejected the insurrectionary idea, but were not able to control the *barricadero* tendencies within the movement (*Socialismo*, 77–84). The contrast between 'responsible leadership' and 'anarchism' is also argued for by Renzo Del Carria, for whom anarchist leaders did not want to unleash the revolution 'at a fixed date', but were thwarted in their efforts by the anarchists' inability to lead the Rome workers in revolt (1: 171).

All such interpretations reconcile the Capolago resolutions and the Rome events by attributing incoherence and inconsistency to an anarchist movement overwhelmed by events: the indecisiveness and change of mind of the Roman anarchists, the impossibility for 'thinking anarchists' to tame blind individualism, or the powerlessness of 'responsible leaders' before the chronic anarchist incapability to lead workers.

In contrast to the attribution of irrationality, a charitable historian is to question superficial evidence so as to dissolve oddity, rather than integrating it in one's explanations. We start from the end, by questioning the odd circumstance of a prominent figure such as Palla, who apparently took the gravest initiative in total isolation, unbeknownst to his comrades. Following Palla's movements will reveal a web of connections and underground activity, involving Malatesta himself, which will shed a very different light on the Rome events.

Indeed, Palla did not come out of nowhere. He left Paris for Italy nearly a month before the Rome demonstration (Negri). What was he up to during that period? On 12 April he attended the Milan international congress 'for labour rights' (Sernicoli, 13 May 1891). This was a large convention held at the Canobbiana theater, in which trade union, democratic, and socialist organizations were represented, along with delegations from France, Germany, and Spain. Pietro Gori and Luigi Galleani spoke for the Italian anarchists. An energetic revolutionary speech was delivered by the Spanish anarchist representative, Fernandez (Fedeli, *Luigi*, 16, 23–4). Another Capolago anarchist, Giovanni Bergamasco from Naples, was also in attendance (Aragno). Clearly, such events were opportunities for militants to meet inconspicuously and lay out plans, as they had done in Paris a year before. Even in Rome Palla was no stranger. He was there days before 1 May, meeting the socialist Cesare Ciurri, the anarchist Pietro Calcagno, and Cipriani himself (Felzani, 14 May 1891).

In brief, the version of Palla as 'a tall and strong young man unknown to anyone' does not hold water. Some historians, such as Giampietro Berti, have indeed rejected Palla's sole responsibility, drawing instead a straight line connecting Capolago to the Rome events, regarded as 'a nearly predictable outcome' of a considerable organizational effort (*Francesco*, 153). However, this interpretation raises its own questions.

One question concerns the propaganda activities emanating from Capolago. According to Galleani, the congress decided that Cipriani and he would undertake extensive propaganda tours from Piedmont to Sicily ('É morto'). Though little is known about Galleani's tour in Northern Italy, information is available, especially from police sources, about Cipriani's tour, which had a more official character. The tour started in March and lasted approximately six weeks, spent half in Sicily, and half between Naples and Rome, ending on 1 May with the Piazza Santa Croce meeting (Felzani, 21 May 1891). During the tour, Cipriani's preoccupation was not the promotion of insurrectionary movements, but their prevention (Romano, *Storia*, 385). A confirmation of Cipriani's misgivings about insurrectionary prospects comes from Malatesta's letter to Merlino dated 29 [*sic*] February 1891 (*Epistolario*, 60). Upon arrival in Rome, Cipriani spoke in the same terms to the local anarchists, some of which insisted instead on direct action (Cafagna, 768). Finally, 1 May arrived, and again Cipriani recommended caution to the crowd in the square: 'I say to you painfully: today we are not ready to fight, for if you dare to move you will be massacred . . . ' The questor of Rome regarded Cipriani's speech as 'very violent' and 'inciting to revolt', and his recommendations as 'a subterfuge to avoid a greater criminal liability' (Felzani, 14 May 1891). However, unless one accepts this Machiavellian theory, the conjecture that his tour was part of insurrectionary plans was consistently contradicted by his attitude and actions.

Another question concerns Malatesta's role. Unlike Palla, Malatesta is conspicuous for his absence in the events' accounts. Yet if Palla had shared plans with anyone at all, it would have been his long-standing comrade Malatesta. Considering Malatesta's militant outlook on the First of May, lack of contact between the two would be odd. Aside from Palla, Malatesta's activity around 1 May looks incongruous. According to the Italian authorities, he left London in mid-April and spent time in France, to reach Italy only on 4 May. Such an account has been unproblematically taken at face value by most historians (Gestri, 311; Pernicone, 264; Berti, *Errico*, 175).

Yet Malatesta had spelled out his intentions in his 29 February letter to Merlino: 'if one wants to undertake serious organization and get anything accomplished, one must go to Italy; now, I intend to go myself as soon as I free myself from the jobs I have in hand, that is around the beginning of April...' (*Epistolario*, 60). In the light of this, it would be odd if Malatesta had left London only to keep away from Italy until after 1 May. According to the London Metropolitan Police, Malatesta stuck to his plans instead, as he was reported to have left in mid-April 'en route for Italy, and supposedly for

Rome, for the purpose of fomenting disturbances on the 1st of May' (Little-child). This is confirmed by Malatesta's biographers. Fabbri plainly states that 'Malatesta had clandestinely arrived in Italy in April, and remained there for some time after the events' (*Vida*, 130). Likewise, Nettlau writes: 'Malatesta went on a clandestine trip to Italy, before and after that First of May 1891—between April and the beginning of June' ('Prólogo', 22).

Another clue as to Malatesta's whereabouts in those days comes unexpect-edly from an interview with a Spanish anarchist immigrant in the United States, taken 80 years later by the historian Paul Avrich and published in his *Anarchist Voices*. Speaking about his old friend Pedro Esteve, Marcelino García noted incidentally: 'In 1891 he met Errico Malatesta at a convention in Milan...' (391). Given the timeline of Malatesta's movements that year, the only possible convention in Milan where they could have met was the meet-ing for labor rights of 12 April 1891. Of course, such indirect testimony after such a long time demands caution. Yet an 1891 report by the Italian consul in Barcelona, Stella, reveals that Fernandez, the fiery Spaniard who spoke at that convention, was no one else than Pedro Esteve.

Figure 5.1 **Malatesta in his thirties, during a sojourn in Italy.**
Source: Schweizerisches Bundesarchiv, Berne, E21, 1000/131, no. 9157

Malatesta's presence in Milan as early as 12 April 1891 would leave a three-week period completely unaccounted for, during which he could have carried out activity in Italy—a circumstance of great consequence in reconstructing the events leading to 1 May. What is more, Luigi Fabbri claims that on 1 May Malatesta was either in Rome or in Florence, the two cities where the most serious incidents occurred. Either way, Malatesta would have been at the heart of the agitations. A more coherent picture of consequent planning and opaque organization based on the anarchist network rather than on the official party structures begins to emerge.

Thus it is plausible that Malatesta had a role in Palla's preparations. Further investigation on Malatesta and Merlino's activity corroborates the hypothesis. The two had started insurrectionary preparations well before Capolago. Since August 1890 Merlino had been in Malta, from where he landed in Sicily to undertake an extensive and successful tour, aiming to organize and prepare groups for a possible armed insurrection. The questor of Rome reported on insurrectionary plans involving the Roman anarchists, including Malatesta's help in London with a shipment of Sicily-bound weapons to Malta. From Sicily, Merlino eventually returned to the continent, with Capolago as final destination (Berti, *Francesco*, 126–9).

Insurrectionary preparation did not stop there. Besides Galleani's and Cipriani's tours, a third tour was planned at the time of the Capolago congress, to be undertaken in Calabria by the Roman delegate Ettore Gnocchetti, so as to extend the work initiated in Sicily by Merlino. Though eventually the tour aborted, it provides evidence about plans and connections (Gestri, 309–10). The letters of credentials, prepared by Merlino for Gnocchetti and addressed to Calabrian militants, were all dated 6 January 1891, thus they were indeed written at the time of the congress (Gestri, 315–16). Actually, they must have been written from Capolago, and the decision to undertake the tour was likely taken there, too.

We seem to have come up against an apparent 'impossibility': the Capolago congress spokesman, Cipriani, consistently discouraged insurrectionary propositions; yet insurrectionary plans seem to have emanated from Capolago. Here is where it becomes important not to confound the 'unusual' with the 'abstruse'.

The question of what was actually decided at the Capolago congress becomes crucial, if one is to establish a link between those decisions and the events of 1 May. While Berti claims that the congress resolution 'confirmed the intention to give an insurrectionary character' to the demonstrations, one cannot find explicit signs of that in the resolution's wording, which called only for a general strike and propaganda activity. Of course, one cannot expect an explicit call for insurrection in official party resolutions; and the resolution had no doubt a revolutionary tone. Still, one should distinguish generic revolutionary appeals from specific insurrectionary calls, on pain of reading a call for insurrection in every public statement issued by a revolutionary party—as the Italian authorities did in interpreting Cipriani's speeches.

So far, there is no evidence that the decision to undertake the tour emanated from the congress. Even Merlino's letters of credentials for Gnocchetti made no mention of any mandate from the Capolago congress. Again, this suggests that insurrectionary organization and planning proceeded on a separate track from official party initiatives. The issue of public versus secret resolutions is crucial in discussing a movement's opacity, and one needs to look beyond the congress public documents for evidence of planned undertakings. In fact, a report from Capolago signed 'A Comrade who was present' and published in *Freedom* tellingly revealed that, in addition to the congress resolutions, 'agreements of a practical nature were ratified that are not meant for publication'. Fabbri explicitly states that 'secret agreements were made' to the effect of giving an insurrectionary character to the 1 May demonstrations (*Vida*, 130). Was Gnocchetti's tour part of such secret agreements? This is consistent with his mandate not being issued by the congress. In turn, the continuity of his tour with Merlino's, and the project's extraneousness to the congress, points to a different causal chain for the 1 May events, proceeding from circles around Malatesta and Merlino, and pre-dating the Capolago congress, in contrast to accounts that take that congress as their starting point.

That the Calabrian tour was entrusted to the Roman congress delegate leads us to the role played by the Roman anarchists. They had been in contact with Merlino and Malatesta since at least August 1890. After Capolago they immediately started building the new party's local organizations. In addition, they were being entrusted by the congress with the publication of the prospective party organ, *La Questione Sociale* (Cafagna, 763–4). Their central national role is corroborated by a list of correspondents of the Roman Anarchist-Socialist Federation seized by the police, which covered the entire national territory (Gestri, 310). Contacts with Malatesta are attested by his correspondence throughout the months after Capolago, for example by Malatesta's letters of 21 February 1891 to Gnocchetti and of 29 February to Merlino (Gestri, 321–3). Finally, a Roman anarchist, Cesare Bedogni, was also present at the Canobbiana theater meeting of 12 April (Felzani, 14 May 1891). In brief, unity of intents, cooperation, and a dense web of contacts existed between Malatesta, Merlino, and the Roman anarchists.

In the quest for insurrectionary plans through the smoke screen of anarchist opacity the focus has moved from Palla to Malatesta and Merlino, and from them to the Roman anarchists. It is time to come back to Rome and analyze the role of the Roman anarchists in the riots. In contrast to Cafagna's thesis that they had given up insurrectionary plans by the time 1 May arrived, evidence from his own article speaks to a different frame of mind: for example, they called on workers to register at anarchist headquarters for the purpose of organizing all forces for 1 May. Here, enrolling people were asked whether they had served in the army, and in what corps. In their conversations with Cipriani in Rome, Calcagno and other Roman anarchists still insisted on the call for insurrectionary action (765–9).

According to a detailed memo of 6 May 1891 from the questor of Rome, Felzani, to the minister of interior, the police officer-in-chief reported that the anarchists 'were greeted with prolonged applause, after they almost militarily wedged themselves into the thick crowd of the other associations to take possession of the area next to the speakers' platform, in order to be ready for any immediate maneuver'. When Palla–Venerio Landi appeared on the platform, he addressed the crowd: 'It is useless to keep wasting time with chatter. Revolutions were always made without discussions and meetings. Deeds are what it takes. It all comes to seizing the moment, and this can be tomorrow, today, or when you like.' Then, 'at once hurling himself from the platform amidst the by-standers, he gave the signal of revolt by example'. It was utter confusion. 'The officer-in-chief, realizing that the anarchists had surrounded the officers that stood closest to the platform to begin the fight, and thus persuaded that any delay could be fatal, gave order for the bugle blasts . . . ' This was the signal of the police attack.

The meeting was over and the fight started, lasting for several hours, and including attempts to erect barricades, an assault on a prison during which a demonstrator was killed, and several attempts by groups of demonstrators to penetrate the city center. As a result, Cipriani and numerous other anarchists were arrested (Felzani, 14 May 1891). Police reports outline the tactical side of the anarchist presence in the square, as the audience that Palla addressed most immediately and that started the fight was not an angry mob, but rather a disciplined contingent of anarchist militants, who had intentionally taken the position they occupied.

To fully close the circle, the behavior of the 'mob' needs to be finally reconsidered. The *Times*'s account conforms to a pattern of explanation of the 'crowd psychology' type, with leaders exercising a 'hypnotic' influence that spreads by 'mental contagion' over a non-rational crowd dominated by instinctive emotions (Nye, 12). However, models of collective behavior that assume rational actors with complete information can alternatively be applied. In particular, Mark Granovetter proposes a 'threshold model' in which each actor has a lower or higher disposition to riot, defined by a threshold: 'a person's threshold for joining a riot is defined here as the proportion of the group he would have to see join before he would do so' (1422). In Piazza Santa Croce everyone could see what everyone else was doing: a textbook situation. Assuming that nobody had a zero percent threshold, nobody would have spontaneously made the first move. Yet the prolonged applause to the anarchists' entrance in the square speaks to people's dispositions. Palla's speech was the signal for his comrades; in turn, their starting the riot led individuals with low thresholds to join in; and then, as more people went joining the riot, more and more thresholds were reached and more and more people joined in, in a sort of domino effect. In brief, according to this model, everybody may have been rational, with Palla still being decisive: another example of dynamic relationship between conscious minorities and masses.

Finally, various tactical aspects of ensuing actions, however unsuccessful, were reminiscent of what Malatesta had earlier advocated for the 1890 Paris demonstration, thus suggesting that organization went beyond the lighting of the initial spark.

In sum, a very different reality from the spontaneous riot reported by the *Times* emerges here, based on planning and organization by the Roman anarchists, who enjoyed the support of the workers in attendance. Their action was part of a wider insurrectionary project involving a significant part of the Italian anarchist movement, especially its transnational segment, with relevant figures such as Malatesta and Palla supporting that action, attending the demonstration, or being instrumental in carrying out the plan.

That the insurrectionary plan involved key participants in the Capolago congress, while proceeding on a separate and underground track, makes plausible an explanation that no previous account has even taken into consideration: that the riots were planned, but the plans were not made by the Capolago congress. This explanation resolves the apparent 'impossibilities' in the empirical evidence: if we admit that plans may have been made at Capolago, but not by the congress, then Fabbri's claim about secret plans can be reconciled with Cipriani's lack of support for any such plans. The key to resolving contradictions in the patent evidence lies in exploring the opaque circumstances, and in that way we are led to better historical explanations.

In fact, it would have been odd if the congress had acted otherwise. A significant congress component was represented by the Romagna socialist associations led by Germanico Piselli, the editor of the Forlí periodical *La Rivendicazione*. Their slogan was 'neither unreasonably intransigent, nor absolutely legalitarian', and they set themselves the task of bridging the gap between anarchists and revolutionary socialists who participated in elections. Considering their self-attributed role, they would not have subscribed to any insurrectionary plans. Their position had already been announced in *La Rivendicazione* on the eve of the congress, by claiming that 'the congress can only provide directions for the moment of the action, and unify its impulse and forces, but it cannot set the date and time for rising up by improvident and rash arrangements' (Sandri, 'Congresso'). Weeks ahead of the First of May, they eloquently called for demonstrations 'disregarding stupid provocations that over-zealous or ignorant government agents may try to throw amidst peaceful demonstrations' (Sandri, 'Festa').

The debate on the First of May in the revolutionary press was asymmetrical. While the advocates of peaceful demonstrations could openly express their viewpoint, the supporters of insurrectionary initiatives could not. Hence, there are no open responses to articles such as the one above that counseled caution. Still, the next issue of *La Rivendicazione* contained a short article by Merlino celebrating the Paris Commune and obliquely but unmistakably outlining the case for more militant action: 'neither the people nor the Bourgeoisie, *at that time*, were aware of the importance of the struggle. It was only afterwards... that it was really felt that *something exceptionally important had happened in the world...*' Merlino went on listing the reasons why the Paris Commune did not succeed. Significantly, the final item in the list was that 'it did not succeed because 1871 is not 1891' ('Marzo'). The message was clear: one did not know for sure when the times were ripe for a revolution; at the same time, 1891 offered more favorable conditions than 1871. Taken together, the two arguments denied that 1891 was unripe for a successful insurrectional movement: instead, a new Commune might indeed be successful.

Thus, the Capolago anarchists' apparent contradictions between words and deeds should be appraised as disagreements asymmetrically expressed, through overt propaganda on one side, and covert activism on the other. Support for this interpretation comes from Max Nettlau, who emphasized that lack of support for Malatesta's insurrectionary project was a relevant factor in 1891, though few historians seem to have heeded his remarks. Nettlau identifies a generational gap at the root of the contrast between Malatesta's optimism about the possibility of overthrowing the state and the pessimism of younger generations. In a self-fulfilling process, the latter's criticism of insurrectionary projects engendered failures, used in turn as argument against Malatesta's alleged chimeras of revolutionary possibilities. For Nettlau, 'this was the deep tragedy of his efforts', demonstrated both in the Capolago congress and in the preparations and plans for the First of May 1891, and possibly determined, in Nettlau's opinion, by both the degeneration of revolutionary socialists and the anarchist lack of confidence in collective action and organization ('Prólogo', 21–2).

This contrast is further illustrated by the debate in the revolutionary press after the Rome events. Now that everything was over, both sides could more openly express the respective viewpoints. *La Rivendicazione* contrasted the nearly unanimous agreement on a peaceful demonstration with Palla's act, likened to that of a cowardly *deus ex machina* (Sandri, 'Fatti'). Malatesta responded by defending Palla's integrity. His deed may have been untimely, Malatesta conceded, but the greatest criticism should be for his detractors, who 'talk incessantly of revolution', but 'take little or no action'. He reaffirmed that no one could determine the right time for an insurrection, and wished that 'the events of Rome and Florence be a lesson'. 'The time is right for us', he concluded: 'if we are not able to act and win, it is our fault' ('Galileo').

SPAIN: A SPEAKING TOUR?

After the events of 1 May 1891 Malatesta remained in Italy for some time, visiting northern Italy and part of the central regions, including the Tuscan city of Carrara, an anarchist stronghold for long thereafter. After leaving Italy, on his way through Switzerland, he made a stop in Lugano to meet the Italian anarchist Isaia Pacini. There the Swiss police, tipped off by an Italian spy, arrested him on 22 July 1891. Prosecuted for violation of an earlier expulsion, Malatesta was convicted and sentenced to 45 days of detention, after which he was kept in jail, because the Italian government had requested his extradition in the meantime. The motivation was that the riots of 1 May, which the Italian authorities regarded as common crimes, allegedly originated from the Capolago congress, in which Malatesta had participated. However, the Swiss federal court refused the extradition. In mid-September, after serving his time, Malatesta returned to London (Luigi Fabbri, *Vida*, 130–1).

Revolutionary agitation knew no interruption. As soon as the series of events connected to the First of May 1891 came to a conclusion, Malatesta directed his planning and organizing to the First of May of the next year, turning his attention to Spain. If the Italian movement was Malatesta's

FIGURE 5.2 **Malatesta during his 1891 detention in Switzerland**
Source: Schweizerisches Bundesarchiv, Berne, E21, 1000/131, no. 9157

primary concern, Spanish anarchism was the one with which he had the greatest affinity. Malatesta's relationship with the Spaniards dated back to 1872, at the time of the First International. The key concepts of the International—collective action, organization, and reliance on the workers' movement—remained the essence of that affinity. In October 1891 Malatesta expressed his optimism and hopes about Spain at a London anarchist conference, holding up Spain as an example of effective anarchist agitation among workers ('Anarchists'), and claiming 'that anarchists were the life and soul of the labour movement in Spain' (W. B. P.). On 8 November Malatesta was in Barcelona, to embark with Pedro Esteve on an extensive propaganda tour, promoted by the anarchist newspaper *El Productor*.

The tour was the first of two trains of events that unfolded in Spain between November 1891 and January 1892. The second was the uprising that occurred in the Andalusian town of Jerez on 8 January 1892. As in the case of the Capolago congress and the Rome riots in Italy, historians have wondered about the respective internal connections in the two trains of events and about Malatesta's role in each insurrectionary episode. While Malatesta was a protagonist of both the Capolago congress and the propaganda tour in Spain, I will argue that he stood in opposite relationships to the two subsequent episodes, being involved in the Rome riots, but extraneous to the Jerez uprising. However, beyond this asymmetry, there is a deeper similarity between the events of Italy and Spain. Through different circumstances in different countries, the two cases illustrate the same contrast between the appearance of anarchism, made of sensational but ephemeral outbursts of spontaneous revolt, and its reality, made of opaque but sustained and coherent organization and planning.

In order to probe the appearances, it is first necessary to investigate the goal of Esteve and Malatesta's itinerant project.

After a month spent touring in Catalonia, the 'propaganda committee' comprising the two anarchists set out on a countrywide tour scheduled to touch Saragossa, Bilbao, Valladolid, Madrid, Córdoba, Granada, Málaga, Cadiz, Cartagena, Alicante, Alcoy, Valencia, and possibly Corunna. For Max Nettlau, 'that propaganda tour was undoubtedly motivated by the objective of uniting anarchists toward some activity of a general character starting from 1 May 1892' ('Prólogo', 24). Nettlau's claim is confirmed by Malatesta himself: recalling the events of Spain in a letter to Nettlau of 12 January 1929, he mentioned 'the plans we had for 1 May 1893 [*sic*]' (Nettlau Papers). The year mismatch is simply Malatesta's typo. We get a sense of the project's far-reaching scope by considering its itinerary. The portion of the tour that actually took place covered in approximately a month only the first four of the planned main centers: Saragossa, Bilbao, Valladolid, and Madrid. If one considers that eight more main centers were scheduled, one can appreciate the proportions of the propaganda drive being undertaken.

What could have been the 'activity of a general character' Nettlau refers to? A letter that, according to the Italian ambassador in Madrid, Maffei, Malatesta sent to comrades in Italy before leaving Spain, made explicit reference to insurrectionary activity, stating 'that the uprising of the Jerez anarchists was too hasty and therefore it could not achieve the results expected by the party; that the agitation should have taken place later, in six Spanish provinces simultaneously; that, however, the revolution is simply postponed. . . . '

Insurrectionary objectives were not a necessary corollary of anarchist tactics. A look at the tactics adopted by the Spanish anarchists for May Day of the two previous years shows that their ultimate revolutionary goal neither implied a commitment to violence nor a disregard for the palliative improvement of working conditions. Rather, they were committed to direct action means, within which there was room for different tactics. Looking at May Day 1892 in this context points to discontinuities as well as continuities with earlier tactics. Insurrectionary objectives were not simply associated with every First of May, but were the result of tactical considerations based on an assessment of changing conditions. Had Spanish anarchists specifically made insurrectionary plans for the First of May 1892, Malatesta's trip at that juncture would acquire a sharper contour in their light.

In the month before 1 May 1890 *El Productor* enthusiastically focused its propaganda on the eight-hour issue. Indeed, this was 'an episode of the war, but not the object of the war' ('Víspera'). However, the achievement of the final objective was presently out of the question. No mention of insurrectionary activity was made, while great emphasis was placed on direct action, in the form of a general strike. The workers were to address not the state, but the bourgeoisie directly, and 'demand the eight-hour day, and if this is refused to us, we refuse in turn to work' ('Huelga'). Workers' mobilization on May Day was extensive, with major general strikes in Catalonia and elsewhere. On 4 July, a 12-page issue of *El Productor* was entirely devoted to May Day reports. In Spain, as elsewhere in Europe, the degree of participation and combativeness displayed by the workers immediately made May Day a crucial date of anti-capitalist struggle.

The following year was spent organizing and preparing the general strike for May Day 1891. Numerous meetings were held, workers' societies were organized, and new federations among workers' societies were established. A country-wide trade union congress held in Madrid in March 1891 unanimously confirmed its commitment to the eight-hour struggle for the next May Day ('Congreso'). On 1 May important strikes occurred in many cities. However, in the aftermath *El Productor* tended to stress that 'events cannot occur twice in exactly the same way' ('Movimiento obrero de Mayo'), that there had been 'neither victors nor vanquished' ('Ni vencedores'), and bitterly remarked that 'legality is a farce', when it comes to the workers' rights of association, assembly, and speech ('Legalidad'). The following months provided the opportunity to reassess the entire issue of May Day. In the article 'El movimiento de Mayo' *El Productor* asked a crucial question: 'What shall we do the next May Day?' A dilemma was posed: 'two paths are presently available...one is to persevere in the pursuit of the eight hour; the other, recently emerged with great seriousness, is the threat of going bankrupt that hangs over several European States.' The forthcoming events would show which path to follow. In the former case, the general strike would be the only available means. In the latter case, 'it will come to attempting plainly and simply the dissolution of the States, the expropriation of the bourgeoisie, and the return of the universal wealth to the proletariat'.

Evidence that the eventual answer was in the insurrectionary direction comes from an analysis of the speeches held during the propaganda tour, as regularly reported by *El Productor* between 19 November 1891 and 14 January 1892 in its columns 'El 11 de Noviembre' and 'Movimiento Obrero'. Reports from Logroño, Zaragoza, and Santander also appeared in *La Anarquía* of Madrid, on 18 and 24 December 1891 and 8 January 1892, respectively. These reports represent an insightful source, because between the lines they provide a glimpse on themes that could hardly be openly discussed in the press. The eight-hour workday was mentioned only occasionally and marginally. Likewise, only a couple of references to May Day can be found. The theme that recurred most frequently in Pedro Esteve's speeches was the need for organization. As for Malatesta, the most outstanding theme was insurrection. At a Barcelona meeting of 11 November he claimed that 'when the bourgeoisie have bayonets, rifles, and many other powerful means to gun us down, it cannot be denied that the same means of defence cannot be disregarded by revolutionaries. The struggle of ideas is sufficient when we are not physically attacked, but when we are knocked down, it is only natural to defend ourselves'. Equally explicit references were made in other meetings, such as those in Manresa, Sabadell, Sallent, Palafrugell, and Madrid. Such references were not generic elements of the standard anarchist repertoire, nor were they dropped casually. In contrast to other standard themes, such as anti-republicanism, anti-parliamentarianism, the futility of reforms, and social revolution, that were used by all speakers, insurrection and expropriation were almost exclusively addressed by Malatesta, who tended to concentrate those themes in specific areas, especially Catalonia. In brief, references to insurrection were governed by careful planning.

For the charitable historian, it is reasonable to assume that Malatesta's speech planning was driven by a purpose; that such purpose was shared by the Spanish anarchists that entrusted him with the responsibility of a propaganda tour on their behalf; and that the initiative was part of broader plans laid out in the previous months.

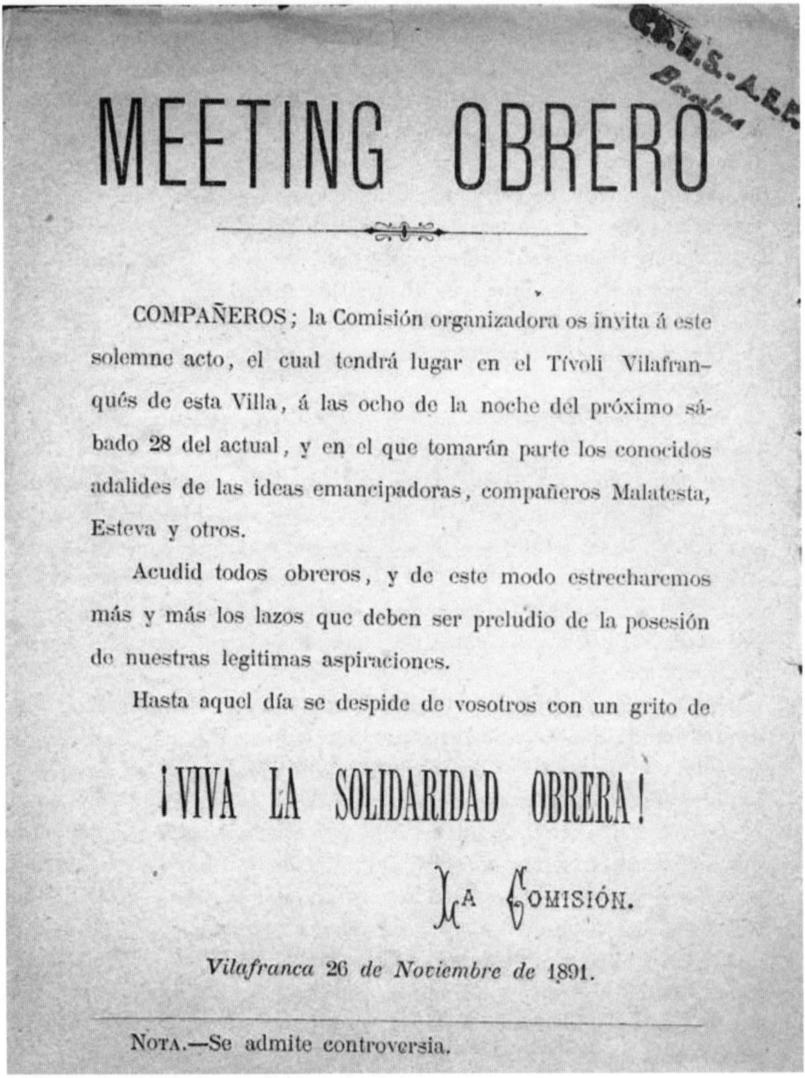

MEETING OBRERO

COMPAÑEROS; la Comisión organizadora os invita á este solemne acto, el cual tendrá lugar en el Tívoli Vilafranqués de esta Villa, á las ocho de la noche del próximo sábado 28 del actual, y en el que tomarán parte los conocidos adalides de las ideas emancipadoras, compañeros Malatesta, Esteva y otros.

Acudid todos obreros, y de este modo estrecharemos más y más los lazos que deben ser preludio de la posesión de nuestras legítimas aspiraciones.

Hasta aquel día se despide de vosotros con un grito de

¡VIVA LA SOLIDARIDAD OBRERA!

La Comisión.

Vilafranca 26 de Noviembre de 1891.

Nota.—Se admite controversia.

Figure 5.3 **A handbill announcing a meeting with Malatesta and Esteve**
Source: Ateneu Enciclopèdic Popular, Barcelona

In sum, the changed attitude of Spanish anarchists toward the objective of the eight-hour day, the references to an insurrectionary solution in their press, and the undertaking of a far-reaching propaganda tour in which the insurrectionary theme was prominent, all indicate that an insurrectionary project was in the wings.

The question about the relationship between the tour and its objectives can also be reversed: How was a speaking tour instrumental to the objective of an understanding for insurrectionary activity?

Despite their inconspicuous characterization as 'propaganda' tours, such tours often had organizational objectives. As Luigi Galleani recalled about the speaking tours entrusted to him and Cipriani at Capolago, their task was 'to put out feelers, to test who the best comrades were as to seriousness and activism, to join them in a strong chain, providing that this web be put to good use at the first opportunity' ('É morto'). A decentralized network model of organization was at work. It was less conspicuous than centralized ones, when it came to coordination for insurrectionary objectives. For the same reasons, it was also historiographically more opaque. A striking contrast existed between the scale and ambitions of the Esteve–Malatesta tour, and its lack of prominence in the anarchist press, confined as it was to the small print of short reports in internal pages. Moreover, such reports were obviously limited to the public part of the tour. However, similarly to the Capolago congress, private understandings were possibly even more important than public statements, especially when insurrectionary projects were at stake.

In this respect, the Esteve–Malatesta tour really provided the opportunity to cast a country-wide organizational web. During the tour, whose plan covered the entire Spanish territory, Malatesta had contacts with chief representatives of Spanish anarchism, such as José Llunas, Teresa Claramunt, José López Montenegro, Fernando Tárrida del Mármol, Adrián del Valle in Barcelona, and Vicente García in Bilbao. Besides establishing or strengthening contacts with existing groups and individuals, new nodes in the network were created. Reports mention the formation of various new anarchist groups or workers' associations after the passage of Esteve and Malatesta.

Unsurprisingly, the tour worried the Spanish government. A significant episode occurred in Valladolid on 26 December. Esteve and Malatesta were received in the premises of the local anarchist federation and given accommodation in its caretaker's apartment. Soon thereafter the police surrounded the premises, barring access to anyone until the following day. The two guests were taken to the civil governor, but were soon released ('Misceláneas'). However, the caretaker was charged for hosting a meeting aimed at conspiring against the government, though he was eventually acquitted ('Movimiento Obrero. Interior'). The episode points to an underground sphere of activity that occurred in parallel with public meetings. Most importantly, it provides evidence of police preoccupations with the tour activities. In fact, the tour was interrupted shortly thereafter, in the wake of the Jerez uprising of 8 January 1892, to which we now turn to analyze its characteristics, Malatesta's alleged role in it, and its impact on the propaganda tour.

The overall scenario can be summarized as follows. Between November 1891 and January 1892 two trains of events occurred in Spanish anarchism: on the one hand, a superficially quiet, but articulated and far-reaching organizational drive; on the other hand, a clamorous, but isolated and shortsighted uprising. There is evidence that the authorities let the latter initiative happen, and then blew the event out of all proportion, attributing to it the widest possible implications. One of the consequences was that the former initiative was suppressed as quietly as it was unfolding. The Jerez uprising went down in history as the anarchist highlight of this period, while the propaganda tour was relegated to a minor episode of biographical interest.

The significance of the story is that the historiographical agenda of anarchism may end up being dictated not so much by the anarchists, as by their enemies. Conversely, what is relevant to the history of anarchism may not necessarily be under the light of the street lamp, but lie instead somewhere in the surrounding darkness, as the historiographical debate about the rationality of the Jerez anarchists well illustrates.

George Woodcock characterizes the Jerez uprising as a paradigmatic example of anarchist oddity. He describes it as part of 'a sudden upsurge of insurrection, bomb throwings, and assassinations' that characterized Spain as well as France. On this occasion, the country districts 'sprang to life again' in one of those 'periodical surges of enthusiasm' that were 'characteristic of Andalusian anarchism': 'four thousand peasants, armed with scythes and shouting "Long Live Anarchy!" marched into Jerez and killed a few unpopular shopkeepers. After a night of sporadic fighting between the insurgents and the Civil Guard, a force of cavalry arrived and the rebellion was quickly crushed.' The result was that 'four of the peasant leaders were executed and many others were sentenced to long terms of imprisonment'. Woodcock packs in a few lines the whole repertoire of anarchist irrationalism: spontaneity, cyclicity, chaos, futility of means, senseless violence, lack of plans or goals, and lack of impact, all of these together constituting the regional 'character' of Andalusian anarchism (346).

E. J. Hobsbawm's millenarian interpretation, as Woodcock's account, emphasizes the spontaneity and ultimately the irrationality of the Jerez anarchists, characterized by an abysmal inadequacy of means to ends. Their revolutionary belief did not turn into an effort to understand conditions, to organize workers, and to plan agitations, but rather into a simple, spontaneous urge to rebel, with no knowledge of how the great change would come about. Hobsbawm's analysis of the Jerez uprising extends to the history of Andalusian anarchism, Spanish anarchism, and ultimately, anarchism in general (74–92).

In contrast, Temma Kaplan emphasizes the rationality of the Andalusian anarchists, their high level of organization, tactical sophistication, and effectiveness (172, 204). Kaplan's account has been criticized in turn by Antonio López Estudillo, for whom 'the questionable and excessively imaginative work of Temma Kaplan cannot be used as a reference, as it is riddled with epic assertions devoid of any foundation'. For López Estudillo the uprising arose in the context of contrasts between two currents of Spanish anarchism, one engaged in unionism, and the other comprising affinity groups advocating the urgency of revolutionary action (692–5).

Fresh insight into the uprising can be gained by analyzing it in the broader context of Spanish anarchism, as López Estudillo does, especially by contrasting it with the ongoing organizational drive represented by the propaganda tour. In this context, the most prominent characteristic of the Jerez uprising was its isolation. The accounts of anarchist commentators, such as Ricardo Mella (184), Fortunato Serantoni, and Pedro Vallina (35), almost unanimously emphasize its narrowness. The immediate reaction of anarchist newspapers such as *El Productor* ('Lo de Jerez') and *La Anarquía* of Madrid ('Que ha sido') reveals a complete lack of any information, which points to the insurgents' isolation. *El Corsario* of Corunna even cast doubts on the conduct of the authorities, not in terms of their repressiveness, but of their permissiveness, given that the authorities had preventively made 60 arrests and knew about the insurrectionary preparations, but did nothing to prevent the uprising ('Lo de Jerez'). Pedro Vallina turned such doubts into explicit accusations, identifying Félix Grávalo Bonilla, an agitator who appeared in Jerez few months before the uprising, as an *agent provocateur* (37).

There is a narrowness to the historians' debate about the millenarianism of the Jerez insurgents, which comes from neglecting a larger context.

Hobsbawm takes the uprising for what it appeared to be, a spontaneous, isolated rebellion, but he arbitrarily attributes such characters to anarchism in general. His generalization is unwarranted, especially considering that the Jerez uprising occurred at the same time as a wider initiative that conflicted with the former precisely on those issues of spontaneism and lack of organization that Hobsbawm considers anarchism's universal features.

Kaplan's emphasis on rationality, organization, and planning is equally problematic and incongruous in the light of the Jerez insurgents' isolation and lack of cooperation, if not open conflict, with a broader organizational effort simultaneously occurring across Spain. In her effort to refute Hobsbawm and to show the existence of a wide organizational network, Kaplan turns to an inflated account, just as the authorities of the time had done.

Both Hobsbawm and Kaplan unquestioningly take the Jerez uprising to exhaustively represent what anarchists were up to in that area at that time, and then proceed to assessing the adequacy of anarchism to the given circumstances, with opposite conclusions. Ultimately, despite their diametrical divergence, the respective shortcomings have a common source, which is precisely their focus on Jerez. Neither scholar takes into account that there were alternative views and different options available within anarchism.

The same narrowness affects the debate about whether Malatesta was involved in the Jerez uprising. Simply because Malatesta was in Spain at that time, the question of his role in the uprising has naturally tended to turn up. Such discussions usually neglect to consider Malatesta's own plans and those of the editors of *El Productor* who brought him to Spain. Malatesta's link with the Jerez uprising is simply hypothesized on the ground of his presence in the country.

However, recollections published by Pedro Esteve many years later vouch that no such involvement existed. The night of the uprising Malatesta was in Madrid, taking part in a public meeting with Esteve and others. Also, news from Jerez came absolutely out of the blue ('Constatazione'). Moreover, Malatesta deemed the uprising untimely. As a matter of fact, not only was the uprising itself unsuccessful, but it also spoiled Esteve and Malatesta's plans. If Malatesta had had contacts with the insurgents, most likely he would have advised them to change their course of action. Conversely, if the uprising had had insurrectionary objectives, coordination with Esteve and Malatesta would have been the most obvious course of action, given the commonality of objectives. In fact, Fermín Salvochea advised a group of Jerez anarchists to wait for Malatesta's imminent arrival in Andalusia, in view of concerted action (Vallina, 34).

Thus, in all likelihood Malatesta had no acquaintance of the uprising being hatched in Jerez, while the insurgents were acquainted with Esteve and Malatesta's project. If any relation can be posited at all, it would seem to be one of conflict, rather than coordination. Accordingly, a possible interpretation would be along the lines suggested by López Estudillo, in terms of a tactical conflict between affinity groups and *societarismo*, or unionism (692–5). Furthermore, *agents provocateurs* may have had a role. If police manipulation occurred, one could reasonably conjecture that undermining the tour's organizational drive may have been an objective.

In sum, standard accounts of the events in Spain involving Malatesta have been fraught with the historian's mental laziness. The superficial and sensational appearance of Spanish anarchism has been unquestioningly put in the foreground, while the handy view of anarchism as an undivided whole has left no room for distinctions and multiple narratives. As a result, what has remained in the background, such as Malatesta's presence, has received consideration only to the extent that it fitted into that simplified picture, rather than on its own terms.

A more complex picture is also more rational. It presents anarchist insurrectionism not as an aimless and spontaneous outburst of rebellion, but as a conscious project based on the assessment of previous First of May experiences, on a change of tactical direction, and on plans carried out through sustained activity. Divisions, lack of coordination, and possibly police provocation undermined the project. Nevertheless, lack of effectiveness does not diminish the project's rationality. Its opacity, which was the rational pre-requisite of its success, determined its erasure from the history of Spanish anarchism, the center-stage being taken by a local and isolated revolt, usually interpreted in the most irrationalist terms.

EPILOGUE: THE CONTINUITY OF ANARCHISM

The events that unfolded in Italy and Spain within the space of a year concurrently demonstrate that the continuity of anarchism is an elusive bird when opacity is not adequately taken into account: historians look for it in the wrong places. Focusing on the movement's highlights and conveniently regarding anarchism as an ideological monolith have led historians to posit continuity where continuity does not exist, as the parallel attempts to link the Capolago congress with the Rome riots and the Malatesta–Esteve tour with the Jerez uprising illustrate. Relatedly, Malatesta's 'absence' from Italy and presence in Spain have misled historians in opposite directions.

Focusing on the movement's highlights is prone to missing the real action, and considering anarchism an ideological monolith generates irrationalist interpretations, by attributing incoherence in the presence of seemingly inconsistent behaviors.

In contrast, assuming anarchism to be capable of intellectual sophistication and fine-grained distinctions leads the historian to actively seek and become aware of theoretical and tactical differences, as existed both at the Capolago congress and among Spanish anarchists, thus making the anarchists' alleged ideological uniformity and irrationality vanish together. Undoubtedly the disagreements among both Italian and Spanish anarchists weakened their effectiveness. However, they made neither side irrational, thus confirming that effectiveness and rationality are distinct questions.

The continuity of anarchism is illustrated instead by the cycle of struggles connected with the First of May. Preparations were carried out from one First of May to the next without interruption. Initiatives aiming at the First of May 1891 in Italy started at the very same time of the 1890 demonstration in Paris, and arrangements aimed at the First of May 1892 in Spain followed Malatesta's release from prison that ensued from his presence in Italy in 1891. Continuity also had a spatial dimension, not only in terms of the transnationalism of Italian anarchism, but also of the links and cooperation between the anarchist movements of different countries. Malatesta focused on three different countries in three years.

The anarchists' focus on direct action did not mean that they were generically inclined to staging violent demonstrations in a repetitive and unchanging manner, whatever the circumstances. Direct action was undertaken where and when conditions were deemed favorable. This was the case of Italy in 1891. Thus, as Maurice Dommanget relates, 'outside of France, it is mainly in Italy that the First of May 1891 was characterized by violence' (162). The next year, after the insurrectionary project in Spain was foiled, Malatesta quietly spent the First of May speaking from an anarchist platform in Hyde Park ('Movimiento Obrero. Exterior'). Organization was a pre-condition of insurrectionary projects. The opening act of the agitations in Italy in 1891 was the foundation of an anarchist party, and Spain was the country where anarchists had the most prominent role in the organized labor movement.

Most importantly, the cycle of struggles of 1890–92 points to Malatesta's continuity of thought, for those struggles illustrate the tactical principles he put forward in *L'Associazione*. For Malatesta, the First of May movement provided a good opportunity to set in motion a revolutionary process by escalating class struggle. It was for anarchists to initiate such a process through autonomous initiatives, such as Malatesta advocated in Paris in 1890, promoted in Rome in 1891, and planned in Spain in 1892. The theme of anarchist autonomy was clearly reflected in those tactics. At the same time that anarchists were to act autonomously, their initiatives could not be self-sufficient and isolated. They were to 'go to the people' and act among workers. The First of May agitations gave anarchists an excellent chance to do so, especially because they bore an anti-capitalist character from the outset. This is what made the eight-hour movement so promising for Malatesta.

However, in 1892 his insurrectionary expectations about the First of May began waning, though he continued to warmly support anarchist participation in the movement. Thus, in an article for the *Commonweal* of 1 May 1893 he argued that the First of May movement was 'the more significant as being the direct work of the masses' and that it was 'for revolutionists to save this movement . . . which it would be folly to give up'. However, he concluded the article by making clear that the First of May was not 'the revolution day', though it remained 'a good opportunity for the propagation of our ideas, and for turning men's minds towards the social revolution' ('First of May'). Malatesta's language was still revolutionary, but not insurrectionary.

As the First of May became more and more an 'invented tradition', Malatesta's revolutionary hopes turned elsewhere. The two years following his return from Spain were still a period of intense insurrectionary agitation, but rather than focusing on anarchist autonomous initiatives, Malatesta directed his efforts to another side of his tactics and another way of 'going to the people', the anarchists' participation in ongoing agitations that did not have explicit anarchist content.

6
OPEN-ENDED POPULAR MOVEMENTS, 1892–94

AS THE INSTITUTIONALIZATION OF THE FIRST OF MAY MOVEMENT BEGAN STI-fling anarchist hopes, the insurrectionary opportunities to which Malatesta mainly turned his attention were popular movements that had not been initiated by anarchists, but that nevertheless he urged anarchists to join. Malatesta's attitude to such movements throws into relief another aspect of his tactics, the flexibility and open-minded inclination to take advantage of any opportunity. Inclusiveness rather than anarchist autonomy came to the forefront of his tactics in these years. Even when popular struggles had no anarchist goals, Malatesta believed they could be potentially revolutionary, as a result not of the stated aims of the participants, but of the radicalizing logic of collective action.

Malatesta's tactics and attitude toward collective movements in the years 1892–94 are best understood in their contrast with those of anarchist currents that criticized his ideas and gained momentum in those years. The comparison allows one to appreciate the specific characters of Malatesta's anarchism; it shows that disagreements about participation in collective movements were connected to diverging views on a broader range of issues, thus illustrating the internal theoretical links both in Malatesta's and in alternative versions of anarchism; and it partly explains the limited success of Malatesta's initiatives in those years.

THE ANARCHIST TACTICAL CHASM
As Luigi Fabbri recalls, the early 1890s 'marked the beginning of a period of long, ardent, and sometimes harsh polemics between Malatesta and the anarchists who dissented from him on a number of diverse issues: organization, syndicates, morals, individual deeds . . . ' (*Vida*, 132).

In Italy the controversy took the form of a contrast between organizationists and anti-organizationists. Aversion to and mistrust for organization by many anarchists dated back to the immediate aftermath of the First International and was clearly manifested at the London International Congress of 1881. However, Fabbri remarks, while dislike for organization became a widespread tendency outside of Italy, it was especially among anarchists of Italian language that anti-organizationism developed into a theoretical and practical current (*Malatesta*, 197–9). Many historians, such as Pier Carlo Masini, describe anti-organizationism as a form of individualism (*Storia... Da Bakunin*, 226). Certainly, all anarchist individualists, in whatever sense of this very vague term, were opposed to organization, but the reverse did not hold. No doubt, anti-organizationists emphasized individual autonomy. In fact, the 1880s' early opponents of organization used to call themselves 'autonomists'. Moreover, a focus on individual autonomy was a trait that anti-organizationists shared with Malatesta's opponents in the various controversies mentioned by Fabbri, which otherwise were waged from a diverse range of viewpoints. However, Italian anti-organizationists were alien from individualism in their working-class orientation and advocacy of anarchist communism.

The main issue at stake was whether anarchists should organize in any permanent, structured form. Anti-organizationists opposed the idea, and rejected organization in institutional forms such as parties, programs, and congresses. As *L'Ordine* maintained in an 1893 article significantly addressed to 'pseudo-anarchists', for anti-organizationists organization was illogical, because 'anarchy aims for the absolute autonomy of the individual, and organization constitutes the negation of it'; organization was useless, because 'it adds nothing to the sum of individual activities and it almost always subtracts considerably from that sum'; and it was harmful, because 'every organization presupposes one or more organizers and these fatally assert themselves as an authority, stifling individual initiative' ('Franca'). In a protracted controversy with Malatesta in the columns of *La Révolte* between August and September 1892, the anti-organizationist Amilcare Pomati argued that the role of anarchism was to be 'that force, that moral power, that current of ideas that, outside every system, outside every rule or convention, is exerted and acts among the masses, with the variety and energy that the individuals who embody that force can give it . . . In the presence of a popular event or commotion, anarchists will always agree on the course of action to be taken, without any need for previous agreements' ('Communications', 10 September 1892).

The contrast had far-reaching ramifications which involved such issues as participation in labor organizations. The anti-organizationists' preoccupation was that anarchists would compromise and ultimately lose their anarchist identity in trade unions, becoming progressively involved in questions of palliative improvements that diverted them from their real focus, the pursuit of the anarchist ideal (Colombo, 24). In general, anti-organizationists were critical not only of attempts at anarchist organizations, but also of tactical alliances with non-anarchist parties and of anarchist efforts to take a leading role in organized collective movements. Their arguments often pointed to the theme of the displacement of goals, and the tone of their polemics toward organizationists was akin to the tone that anarchists at large used toward the socialist advocates of parliamentarian tactics. Such controversies agitated Italian anarchism throughout the 1890s and beyond.

Anti-organizationist tendencies soon manifested themselves as attacks on Malatesta's revolutionary project begun with the Capolago congress. For Malatesta's biographer Armando Borghi, Capolago was 'not so much a congress of theoretical debates, as an attempt to reach practical agreement for immediate action' (81). If the tendency to stretch the concept of anarchism so as to include simple anti-parliamentarians such as Cipriani was a weakness of the party, another weakness was that the same concept was already too broad to be a solid basis for practical agreements. Malatesta aimed at combining insurrection and organization in the party's tactics. The former element found obstacles in anti-parliamentarian socialists, but the latter element found obstacles in anti-organizationist anarchism. The focus on the First of May movement equally came under attack. Anarchists as Malatesta came to be disparagingly called 'primomaggisti' (MayDayers) that allegedly advocated 'revolution at a fixed date'. Such criticisms implicitly emphasize the inherent link between Malatesta's insurrectionism and organization, in contrast to the cliché of anarchist insurrectionism as spontaneistic. Similar contrasts, of which the Jerez uprising was probably evidence, also undermined the insurrectionary project in Spain.

A measure of the anti-organizationist opposition to the Capolago tactics is given by Pomati's controversy with Malatesta. For him, Merlino and Malatesta's 'evolution towards the legalitarian parties [was] becoming every day more pronounced' ('Mouvement', 13 August 1892). The term 'legalitarian' referred to parties that focused on parliamentarian tactics, regarding mass mobilization mainly as a support to electoral and legal struggles. In the ensuing debate, Malatesta acknowledged the existence of great differences among anarchists about tactics and perhaps even about the way of conceiving anarchy, and remarked: 'I even believe that the error that we committed at Capolago consisted in failing to be fully aware of such differences, and in believing it possible to march all together, just because there was agreement on the general formulas.' For Malatesta, the main differences concerned the attitude toward the labor movement and the relative importance attributed to individual deeds versus collective movements ('Communications', 3 September 1892).

Nowhere was such contrast sharper than in the respective attitudes to movements that did not have an explicit anarchist content. Unlike anti-organizationists, Malatesta attributed great value to such movements. He reiterated his viewpoint in his article of 1 May 1893 in *Commonweal*, arguing that 'popular movements begin how they *can*; nearly always they spring from some idea already transcended by contemporary thought . . . If we wait to plunge into the fray until the people mount the Anarchist Communist colours...we shall see the tide of history flow at our feet while scarcely contributing anything toward determining its course . . . ' ('First of May').

By the end of the 1892–94 cycle of struggles the contrast between Malatesta's inclusiveness and anti-organizationist tendencies would only be sharper and the pitfalls warned against by the *Commonweal* article more acute, leading Malatesta to a thorough rethinking of the direction in which anarchism was to be taken.

BELGIUM: WORKERS ON STRIKE FOR UNIVERSAL SUFFRAGE

The clearest example of Malatesta's tactical attitude was an expedition he had just returned from when the *Commonweal* article was published. Though he was banned from Belgium by an order of expulsion of 1880, in mid-April 1893 Malatesta went to that country with Charles Malato, on the occasion of the political general strike for universal suffrage led by the *Parti Ouvrier Belge*, or POB. The expedition is relevant not for its practical outcome, which was non-existent, but because it helps shed light on the link between theory and practice in Malatesta's tactics. The strike is an extreme example, as at first sight anarchist participation to a struggle for universal suffrage might look paradoxical. Yet by showing that Malatesta's participation was grounded on theoretical principles, it helps dispel stereotypes of random, impromptu participation to any riot, or, conversely, charges of anarchist exclusivism.

The agitation for universal suffrage in Belgium had a long history. Though the lower classes had a significant role in the Belgian revolution of 1830 that brought independence to the country, the new electoral law gave them little representation (Pierson, 19–21, 57). The Liberal Party's electoral defeat of 1863 gave the signal for electoral reform agitation. Universal suffrage rapidly became the objective of the agitation. From this moment until the war of 1914, this demand would dominate Belgian political life, soon finding the working class rallying behind its banner (69). A turning point in working-class politics was the formation of the POB in April 1885. Universal suffrage soon became the party's main focus. At the same time, advocacy of the general strike as a form of struggle became predominant. As Madeleine Rebérioux remarks, the POB worried about the anarchist tones of the Walloon movement, but the party's links with the base and with the struggling unions prevented the POB from disavowing the call for a general strike (323–4).

These dynamics between a cautious leadership and a militant base marked much of the struggle for universal suffrage leading to the events of April 1893. For example, in 1886 a strike started in the industrial area of Liége rapidly spread to other regions, turning into a spontaneous *jacquerie*. The military and judiciary repression was brutal, but the events drew public attention to the 'social question'. For the first time the Throne speech announced a program of reforms, but the clerical government put in practice only a small number of them (Pierson, 88–90). From 1890 the agitation for universal suffrage intensified and extended. In April of that year 80,000 demonstrators marched in Brussels, ending the demonstration with a collective solemn oath to be irreducible in their struggle for universal suffrage. In May 1892, three weeks into a general strike called by the POB that turned into an impressive display of strength and discipline, the Parliament decided that the revision of the electoral law would take place. However, no agreement could be reached in the Chamber. The situation was at a standstill. To get out of the deadlock, on 12 April 1893 the POB declared the immediate general strike (104–7).

In a long article published in April 1897, Malatesta provided a retrospective outlook on the entire Belgian struggle for universal suffrage, which he personally witnessed in the days of April 1893. In the article, eloquently titled 'Come si conquista quel . . . che si vuole' (How one obtains what . . . one wants), Malatesta remarked that it was through insurrection that Belgium obtained independence and the constitution in 1830. Likewise, the violent strikes of 1886 were 'marked by the formation of armed bands, destruction of machinery, pillaging of workshops, and castles on fire'. The 'order' was restored, repression was terrible, but the first 'social laws', Malatesta noted, dated from that year. In brief, the article emphasized the reforming power of direct action, in contrast to the ineffectiveness of legal struggles, as well as its revolutionary value in getting workers accustomed to obtain what they wanted by direct action, regardless of whether they were led by a parliamentarian party and were struggling for reformist aims.

In the days following the strike declaration the tension between workers and authorities rapidly escalated, with the strike extending from the capital to the provinces and with clashes between police and demonstrators, including armed confrontations and an attack on the burgomaster of Brussels, while at the same time the POB leaders exhibited a sense of responsibility by condemning their followers' excesses. A leading article on the Belgian crisis in the London *Times* of 18 April 1893 thus opened: 'Since the Commune of Paris was crushed by the Government of M. Thiers, so grave a crisis as that which now threatens Belgium has not arisen in Western Europe.' However, the article ended on a hopeful monarchist note, remarking 'that, in the midst of these fierce strifes, the personal popularity of the King is unshaken'.

Such was the situation at the time of Malatesta's trip to Belgium. The *Times*'s apprehension was the counterpoint to Malatesta's expectations. The gravity of the situation and the sense of its open-endedness to dramatically different outcomes are palpable from the *Times*'s reports. In particular, there was a sense of a potentially revolutionary outcome, though no revolutionary goal had been formulated by the strikers. In this situation one sees a concrete instance of Malatesta's oft-repeated concept that revolutions in history started almost invariably with moderate demands, more in the form of protests against abuses than of revolts against the essence of institutions. Even the reassuring remark of the *Times*'s columnist about the king's popularity found a sinister match in Malatesta's frequent references to the fate of Louis XVI in the French Revolution, despite the cheers to the king from the Parisian revolutionary crowds ('Altro'). Historians may explain why the events had to unfold the way they did, but no such awareness was available to the actors.

Malatesta and Malato's trip was recounted by the latter in his recollections *Les Joyeusetés de l'Exil*, though his account, reflecting the general style of the book, tends to dwell more on humorous digressions than on historical details. The whole expedition unfolded within the space of a week, approximately coinciding with the week of 12–18 April, during which the general strike itself unfolded. Together with Malatesta and Malato was another anarchist living in London, Louis Delorme. They joined a group of local anarchists, but the available human and material resources were inadequate for any initiative (Malato, *Joyeusetés*, 62–75). Meanwhile, the agitations were timely and rapidly defused by the April 18 news that the Chamber adopted a scheme of manhood suffrage and the POB leaders accepted the decision ('Belgian'). As a French spy by the code name of 'Z N° 6' promptly reported, on that day Malatesta, Malato, and Delorme were already back in London.

From Malatesta's anarchist point of view, the characteristics of struggles like the Belgian strike were inverse and complementary to the First of May ones. The First of May demonstrations were explicitly anti-capitalist, but they were undetermined as to their means, ranging from festive demonstrations to general strikes. Conversely, the Belgian agitation used the right means, as it resorted to direct action and open revolt, but its declared goals were not shared by anarchists. In this respect, it could be likened more to the London Dock Strike than to the First of May. Like the Great Dock Strike, the Belgian agitation for universal suffrage coupled an impressive display of collective might by a determined and united working class with a great deal of restraint, encouraged by the leaders in view of non-revolutionary goals of limited scope. In such situations, characterized by the indeterminacy and open-endedness of collective action, the role of minorities in steering the agitations in one or another direction could be crucial.

Despite the non-insurrectional outcome of the Belgian agitation, its success was a glaring confirmation of Malatesta's appraisal of the reforming power of direct action and even violence. This aspect was not lost on the bourgeois press either. For example, the Parisian *Temps* regretted that the extended franchise had been adopted 'under mob pressure, for concessions that are extorted lose much of their grace, and the precedent may leave dangerous traces in a nation hitherto honourably distinguished by respect for law and order' (qtd in 'Situation').

At the same time, from an anarchist perspective, the agitation was a lost opportunity. According to the historian of Belgian anarchism Jan Moulaert, data on anarchist participation in the struggle are scarce, 'but it is certain that one can hardly expect an orchestrated action that would depart from the anarchist tradition' (135). Anarchist participation may have been scarce, but whether or not an orchestrated action was to be expected is a different issue. In Moulaert's expectation one can discern the bias of anarchism as necessarily doomed, while his reference to a single 'anarchist tradition' is unwarranted. In contrast, Malato reports Malatesta to have regretfully commented during their fruitless attempt: 'If instead of living aloof from the working masses, our friends had made an effort to penetrate them, talking with them in ordinary language of everyday interests and not of metaphysics, it would be us steering this movement today!' (*Joyeusetés*, 72). This comment provides the context to Malatesta's remark of a few days later to the effect that anarchists would 'see the tide of history flow at [their] feet' if they deferred acting until 'the people mount the Anarchist Communist colours'.

In a similar vein, the outcome of the general strike was commented on in an anonymous article appeared in *La Révolte* of 3–10 May, eloquently titled 'Sommes-nous a la hauteur des événéments?' (Are we equal to the events?), which analyzed the anarchists' inadequacy in steering the events in a different direction. Max Nettlau attributes the article to Kropotkin, but adds that Malatesta's impressions of the Belgian events, as he reported directly to Kropotkin, probably formed the article (*Erste*, 173–4).

According to the author, the Belgian movement had all the characteristics that a revolutionary movement could possibly have in its initial phase. It was a popular movement. Hundreds of thousands of people took part in it and took to the street. There was enthusiasm, especially at the beginning, and the mass of workers kept their promise: they had promised a general strike, and they nearly accomplished that, paying for their decision in hardships and blood. However, did the socialists, and especially the anarchists, keep their own promise? Did they throw themselves into the movement, resolve to instill broader ideas in it, and give it a more revolutionary character? In such a circumstance, even recriminations against the social democrats were futile. If the social democrats had lulled the masses to sleep, the anarchists had not done enough to wake them up, penetrating among them and mobilizing them toward wider goals than universal suffrage: 'We have had our period of isolation, which was necessary for the elaboration of ideas. However, it is high time to return among the masses.' Anarchists had had their own martyrs, but they had not had popular agitators, who, 'identifying themselves with the workers' popular movements, would cross every town and every village of the whole country and would get to be recognized everywhere as brothers—as John Burns, unfortunately a social democrat, had done in England—living the same life and harboring the same hatred, but also carrying a broader revolutionary conception; ready to pay a personal price for their participation in the smallest strike or workers' riot, no matter how negligible their results, so long as they are relevant for their participants; and thus loved and kept in high regard like better informed brothers'.

Malatesta's theme of 'going to the people' clearly resonates in these words.

SICILY: PEASANTS IN REVOLT AGAINST TAXES

Similar hopes, disappointments, and criticisms to those Malatesta manifested about the general strike in Belgium also characterized his involvement with the agitations that occurred in Italy in 1893–94, in connection with the Fasci movement in Sicily. If Malatesta's involvement in the Belgian strike was episodic and his contribution null, he had a greater and more sustained role in Sicily. Moreover, it was not an individual role, but part of the collective involvement of the Italian anarchist movement. Hence, while the Fasci movement shared with the Belgian strike the lack of a specific anarchist character, it provides the opportunity to assess not only the tactics that Malatesta advocated, but also those put in practice by the Italian anarchists. Moreover, coming two years after the Italian agitations of 1891, it provides the opportunity to test the historiographical assumption of Italian anarchism as cyclically disappearing and reappearing. Finally, assessing the outcome of anarchist participation in those agitations is crucial for understanding further developments in Malatesta's tactics, for the events had a profound impact on him.

Malatesta's direct involvement in Italian events had stopped at the Rome riots of 1 May 1891. On that same day, a federation of trade unions called *Fascio dei lavoratori* (Workers' Fasces) was founded in the Sicilian city of Catania by Giuseppe De Felice Giuffrida. By the end of 1893 the Fasci movement—'fasci' being the plural for 'fascio' (bundle), a term that symbolized the strength of union and bore no relation but etymological with the later Fascist movement—had developed into a mass movement, with 181 associations throughout the seven Sicilian districts—Palermo, Trapani, Messina, Catania, Syracuse, Caltanissetta, and Girgenti (Musarra, 'Dati', 77)—with a membership that government sources estimated at approximately 300,000 (Romano, *Storia*, 226), and with De Felice, now a member of Parliament, as chief leader. Thus, the very same day that seemed to put an end to Malatesta and Merlino's year-long organizational and insurrectionary effort, during which they devoted much attention to Sicily, also marked the beginning of a spectacular organizational growth on that island, which led to the dramatic events of 1893–94.

A hard-and-fast ideological map of the Fasci cannot be drawn. Ideological boundaries were blurred among the leaders themselves. Suffice to mention the unorthodox socialist De Felice, who stood by the inclusive principle of gathering all workers with no specific party characterization in contrast to the idea of creating a marxist-type party in Sicily (Romano, *Storia*, 29), and the anarchists Petrina and Noè, elected as Fasci representatives in the town

ERRICO MALATESTA.

FIGURE 6.1   **Malatesta's photograph, presumably from the mid-1890s**
Source: International Institute of Social History, Amsterdam, BG A8/783

council of Messina (Cerrito, 85). The political allegiance of the base was also far from definite. An 1893 breakdown of the Fasci by the socialist newspaper *La Giustizia Sociale* shows that only a minority of them joined the socialist party (qtd in Musarra, 'Dati', 70). Moreover, Salvatore Romano laments that the task of creating disciplined socialist Fasci, as pursued by the orthodox Palermo leader Rosario Garibaldi Bosco, proved difficult, as many Fasci carried out activities of local scope, keeping only loose ties with the central committee, and neglecting to obey rules and instructions (Romano, *Storia*, 188). While the Fasci were a growing working-class movement, they had no definite party affiliation, nor were their political leanings sharply defined.

The Fasci's struggle started on the ground of economic demands, with the greatest unity of action in the 1893 peasant strikes (Romano, *Storia*, 289). Another crucial aspect of the agitations concerned the reduction or abolition of taxes, a demand traditionally associated with riotous forms of struggle in Sicily (313). The agitations of 1893–94 were no exception. They started by the summer 1893 and peaked between October and December (330–1). Despite the methods employed, the Fasci historian Salvatore Romano argues that 'the demonstration that took place at the cries of "Long live the King!" and "Down with taxes!" ending up in the destruction of custom-houses, clearly reveal that the intentions of the masses in agitation were non-revolutionary, aiming instead at the satisfaction of demands' (*Storia*,

463). Nevertheless, their characteristics turned them into a riskier struggle for the Fasci leadership than the peasant strikes, which were kept within legal boundaries (314).

Thus, the Fasci's evolution spoke to Malatesta's claim that 'popular movements begin how they can' and nearly always 'spring from some idea already transcended by contemporary thought' ('First of May'). Such movements could be potentially revolutionary, Malatesta believed, for revolt had its own logic that transcended the initial aims of the actors, as the escalation of the struggle in Sicily and the socialist leadership's difficulty to control it showed.

In London, Malatesta, Merlino, and Cipriani started making preparations for agitations in Sicily in early 1893, well before the Fasci movement reached its onset, as their French associate Charles Malato recalled years later: 'Since the first half of the year, Malatesta, Merlino, and I knew that a revolutionary situation would present itself in Sicily around August or September. Malatesta felt that certain field equipment (including firearms) would not be useless, and wished to purchase some Maxim machine-guns, to be sent to Italy disassembled and mixed with farming tools. Cipriani took several trips from Paris to London to confer with us' (qtd in Borghi, 99).

However, much of their activity in 1893–94 focused not so much on Sicily itself, as on the rest of Italy. Now that the fire was catching on in the island, their preoccupation was to spread the agitations to the rest of the country as a necessary condition for a successful insurrection. Thus, in February 1893 the Italian anarchist socialists in London printed the placard *Agli Operai Italiani* (To the Italian workers), to be sent to Italy (Herschel de Minerbi). The manifesto addressed workers, but it touched upon themes such as hunger, the cost of foodstuff, and heavy duties, that struck traditionally sensitive popular chords. It also made a reference to the government's plunders and massacres since the unification of Italy, thus striking the chord of the betrayed ideals of *Risorgimento*, still alive in many minds (*Agli Operai*). Nonanarchist motives were not only pragmatically accepted, but also actively appealed to.

The Italian anarchists in London also sought to mobilize the transnational section of Italian anarchism. Around April 1893 the anarchist-socialist group *La Solidarietà* was formed in London, with the threefold goal of 'propagating the anarchist-socialist principles among the Italian workers in London; getting in contact with the groups and comrades of both England and other countries to the end of constituting a federation of Italian anarchists residing abroad; and helping by all possible means and constantly the revolutionary propaganda in Italy and everywhere the activity of the group can be effectively carried out' ('Communications', 8 April 1893). One of the first initiatives of the group was to issue a circular 'To the Italian Workers Abroad', in which they reiterated the necessity of 'uniting, forming anarchist groups everywhere, actively corresponding between group and group and with the comrades of Italy' ('Á los anarquistas').

A testimony of the anarchist activism linked to the Sicilian agitations comes from Antonio Labriola, 'the most robust mind of the Italian social-ist movement of that period', according to Romano (*Storia*, 6). In July 1893 Labriola wrote to Engels: 'Here, in Italy, the so-called anarchists are beginning to take action once again. What they are, you already know. They are a mixture of all revolutionary passions. A secret circular from Malatesta urges them to remake the *Federations*, which were ruined by the famous trials of 1 May 1891.' Labriola dismissed 'the illusion of a coming revolt in Sicily' and 'the alleged Sicilian agitation', calling the Fasci 'labors of fantasy' (488). However, within a few months his assessment had dra-matically changed. In another letter to Engels of November he declared: 'These Fasci are the second great mass movement after that of Rome in 1889–91, and the former is certainly rooted in more permanent causes' (qtd in Cortesi, 1094–5). By December his reports to Engels had become enthusiastic: 'How *perceptive* and swift these Sicilians are! Every authority is questioned, and the monarchy has no more strength. The proletariat is coming to the forestage' (1097). Labriola omitted to retrospectively credit Italian anarchists, too, with perceptiveness in their early appreciation of the Fasci movement's revolutionary potential.

The anarchists' agitation on the continent was encouraged by a general atmosphere of revolt, which found an outlet in widespread popular agita-tions after the Italian workers' massacre of 17 August 1893 at Aigues-Mortes. Numerous anti-French and nationalist popular demonstrations took place, promoted by patriotic and student associations. As the demonstrations grew in number each day, they also changed in character, turning into clashes with the police and mass riots. The most serious incidents occurred in Naples, where street clashes raged across the city for three days, ending only with the intervention of troops and 2,000 arrests (Masini, *Storia . . . nell'epoca*, 16–17). Besides giving a measure of the popular discontent, such episodes of 'spontaneous anarchy', as Labriola called them, speak again to the social indeterminacy of collective action emphasized by Malatesta, corroborating his claim that 'revolt has its own logic', independent from self-proclaimed motivations, and despite initial 'displays of respect and devotion to the au-thorities' ('Altro').

Malatesta's focus on the continent materialized in the manifesto *Agli An-archici d'Italia* (To the anarchists of Italy), issued from London in November 1893 by the *Gruppo La Solidarietà*. The manifesto called upon 'the audacious' to give the signal of revolt, 'whatever choice the other parties may make'. The link between Sicily and the rest of Italy was emphasized: 'once Sicily is de-feated, it will be the turn of the continent.' On the other hand, the manifesto claimed, 'if we want, we can win. Victory never looked as likely as now. It is up to us to make it certain.' The manifesto urged anarchists to organize rev-olutionary Fasci everywhere and 'arouse such an agitation as to prevent the Government from sending whole regiments of soldiers to Sicily'. Anarchists were urged to struggle beneath their own banner, without compromise, but also without intolerance, 'which is always harmful, but outright disastrous at this moment'. In brief, the manifesto outlined the anarchist insurrectionary strategy of wearing down the army's military power by extending the struggle to the whole country.

The manifesto met with mixed reactions in Italy. In some places Malatesta's call for tactical coalition was heeded, though his mistrust in other parties proved justified. Agreements with socialists and republicans took place, but they generally broke down at the moment of taking up arms. On the other hand, the manifesto's urge to organize Fasci was not uncontroversially accepted. Anti-organizationist periodicals, such as *Sempre Avanti* of Leghorn and *L'Ordine* of Turin, had a different view and harshly criticized the 'fascist regimentation' and 'Sicilian Fasciocracy', while supporting grassroots agitations (Pernicone, 284; 'Franca'; 'Comunicati'; 'Fasti'; 'Bava').

While Malatesta's tactics were opposed by part of the anarchist movement, they were in agreement with the revolutionary tactics of De Felice, who also believed that an insurrection on the island could not be successful unless a similar revolt broke out on the continent at the same time. Thus, a meeting of 7 November 1893 at the Fascio of Catania resolved to send a propaganda committee to the continent (Romano, *Storia*, 398). By then, a number of Fasci already existed on the continent in Apulia and Calabria, and more were formed between November and December in Naples, Rome, and all over the peninsula (399). As Romano sums up, 'De Felice, with the direct support of the anarchists, cast a network of new Fasci in the peninsula, ready to back the Sicilian movement and come from the peninsula to the aid of the Fasci insurrection on the island' (*Storia*, 401–2).

In turn, the insurrectionary network being built in the homeland was firmly connected with anarchists abroad. After his release of early 1893 from the imprisonment for the 1891 riots, Cipriani had returned to Paris, from where he was in contact not only with the London anarchists but also with De Felice, Noè, Petrina, and others in Sicily (Nicotri, 138–9). In November 1893 a French informer by the code name of A40 reported: 'Malatesta has written to several comrades in Italy, especially in Sicily, for the organization of armed bands. The anarchists of Northern Piedmont have responded to him very favourably.' On 16 December Cipriani met De Felice in Marseille (Ressman). In contrast to millenarian stereotypes, revolution was not simply preached or expected to happen spontaneously. It was actively planned and prepared through tactical alliances across ideological lines. The weapon to overcome the enemy forces was the extension of the struggle to the whole country.

By the time De Felice met Cipriani, repression had dramatically escalated in Sicily, after the resignation of prime minister Giovanni Giolitti and his replacement by Francesco Crispi. Throughout December 1893 the armed forces opened fire on demonstrators in various towns and villages of the island, killing and wounding tens of workers. In the first three days of January 1894 massacres of workers occurred on a daily basis (Romano, *Storia*, 427–8).

In contrast to Malatesta's and De Felice's wholehearted support, the prevailing tendency of socialist newspapers at this juncture was to disavow the 'socialist' character of the Fasci movement, notwithstanding that more than half of the over 100,000 members of the socialist party were in Sicily. This attitude was evident in a chilling advance eulogy appeared in *Lotta di Classe* on 31 December 1893, at the climax of the Sicilian struggle:

> By this time the chronicle of the events loses almost any relevance for Sicily. It is a revolution, the most spontaneous, natural, legitimate revolution: the revolution of a people that prefers to die by lead than by starvation. What makes it most solemnly tragic is the certainty of its destiny: it will be bloodily repressed by the armed force at the service of the bourgeoisie. The fraternal sympathy that we express to the rebels is, alas! but an advance eulogy of the victims. Although the socialist party has the right to be sensitive to the cry of pain of a whole proletariat, it realizes that its action will be null, or nearly so, in the face of a movement that does not proceed from a determined thought, and is not the expression of a clear and precise consciousness of its goal. The revolt of hunger is not the revolt of a party.
>
> (qtd in Romano, *Storia*, 407–8)

The distance between the perspective of the socialist leadership and Malatesta's could not be greater. For the latter, as he had written five years earlier, 'any strike, if it can last and spread, can end up undermining the legitimacy itself of bosses; likewise, any attack on a town hall or a police station, can end up in open insurrection against the monarchy, even if it is made amidst shouts of "Long live the king! Long live the queen!" ' His closing argument was: 'Let's take the people as they are, and let's move forward with them: abandoning them just because they do not understand our formulas and our arguments in the abstract would be foolishness and betrayal at the same time' ('Altro').

For *Lotta di Classe* the Fasci movement was doomed, and hence it was to be left to its fate. For Malatesta its victory or defeat depended on whether the revolutionary forces, including socialists, would leave it to its fate or side with it.

On 2 January 1894 Crispi was empowered to invest General Morra di Lavriano with full power to re-establish order. The following day a dramatic meeting of the Fasci central committee took place in Palermo, where De Felice made an impassioned appeal to take up arms. The insurrectional option was rejected by the central committee. Instead, a manifesto was issued, containing demands to the government and a call for workers to regain their calm (Romano, *Storia*, 406–15). On 4 January a state of siege was proclaimed in Sicily. The same day De Felice was arrested in Palermo ('Disturbances in Sicily'). In the next fortnight other Fasci leaders were arrested, the Palermo Fascio was dissolved ('More'), mass arrests ensued, and approximately a thousand people were sent to *domicilio coatto* (internment) without trial (Romano, *Storia*, 471).

Lotta di Classe's prediction had finally come true.

In the following days, while socialists staged peaceful protest demonstrations, the initiative on the continent passed to the hands of the anarchists, though their action was sporadic. Demonstrations akin to those of Sicily for the abolition of octroi duties caused arrests in the Cosenza district, where Fasci had formed weeks before (Romano, *Storia*, 400). In Milan and Rome clashes with the police occurred. Riots took place in the Apulian towns of Ruvo and Corato, where the anarchist Sergio De Cosmo operated: octroi guards were attacked, fire was set to a town-hall, tax collection offices, and public registers, railway lines were torn up, telegraph wires cut, and gendarmerie barracks assailed (Vatteroni, 40–1; 'Italy').

The most serious uprising by far was the one that occurred on 13–16 January 1894 in the area around Carrara, a city in Lunigiana, the northernmost tip of Tuscany. Because of the city's strong anarchist presence, centered on the marble industry of the Apuan mountains, the uprising provides the opportunity to analyze the anarchists' mode of operation in the context of the ongoing agitations. Was the Carrara uprising an isolated initiative, as the Jerez uprising of two years before? Was it an impromptu reaction to the news from Sicily or was it planned? What was its goal?

The most recurrent interpretation, sometimes from a sympathetic standpoint, has been that the insurrectionary outcome exceeded the leaders' intentions, who only meant to stage a protest demonstration (Masini, *Storia . . . nell'epoca*, 27–8; Bertolucci, 62). This interpretation exonerates anarchist leaders from responsibilities but also, often unwittingly, reinforces stereotypes of anarchist collective action as spontaneistic and reactive. A local historian, Gino Vatteroni, has challenged the mainstream interpretation, arguing instead that the demonstration had insurrectionary goals (25–6).

Vatteroni's detailed reconstruction starts from the months preceding the uprising, which recorded an increased organization effort in the Carrara area, practical agreements with the collectivist republicans, a series of meetings held by the visiting anarchist Luigi Molinari at the end of December 1893, and the appearance of numerous placards of insurrectionary tone on the walls of Carrara on 7 January 1894 (41–8).

On the night of 13 January insurgents assembled in six meeting points around Carrara, with the plan to gather further participants and enter the city simultaneously. Telegraph wires were cut, custom-houses attacked and set on fire, weapons seized, barricades erected on strategic roads, and work stoppages imposed by armed groups in various sawmills. However, unexpected early clashes with the police induced the insurgents to change their plans. The insurgents dispersed in the mountains, falling back on defensive tactics of guerrilla warfare for the next two days. On Monday 15 January, many workers abstained from work, while Carrara was occupied by over 3,000 soldiers. On that day the struggle intensified, recording demonstrations and episodes of insurgency. On the morning of 16 January a general strike was proclaimed, and work at the quarries came to a standstill. The troops opened fire on a crowd that was marching in the direction of Carrara, killing 8 people and wounding 13. Widespread repression ensued, with house searches and arrests (Vatteroni, 11–36). On 17 January all the quarrymen remained on strike, but the uprising was virtually over. On the same day the state of siege in the district of Massa–Carrara was proclaimed, and General Heusch was invested with full powers to re-establish order ('Disturbances in Italy').

The Carrara anarchists, Vatteroni argues, intended to arouse an insurrectionary movement that would lead by example and spark revolts in the rest of Italy. However, in contrast to Crispi's conspiracy theory, which sought to explain the uprising by 'a broader subversive plan that linked the Apuan insurgents to those of Sicily, to the libertarian centres in Italy and abroad, and through the latter to the dark maneuvers of foreign powers' (qtd in Vatteroni, 59), Vatteroni argues that the uprising was undertaken 'in a completely autonomous and independent manner, outside of any kind of influence from or agreement with other "revolutionary centres" in Italy or abroad'. For him, even Molinari knew nothing about what was being hatched in Carrara. However, Vatteroni acknowledges that the initiatives of the Carrara anarchists followed a line of conduct similar to that of a large section of the Italian anarchist movement. 'In practice', Vatteroni concludes, 'Carrara followed more or less consciously this political tendency', which sought 'a united front for a general insurrection' starting from Sicily and spreading to the whole country (61–2).

Analyses of this kind stop halfway on the path of charity. Interpreting the uprising as both autonomous and in step with a broader project is like wanting to have one's cake and eat it. Vatteroni's explicit contrasting his own interpretation with Crispi's conspiracy theory exhibits a preoccupation, typical of much militant historiography, to play down the anarchists' legal responsibilities and argue for their victimization, but at the price of playing down their rationality, too. However, legal and historical evidence lie on different planes. Certainly Crispi had little ground for legal charges, and his references to foreign powers were a figment of the imagination. Still, his hypothesis was historiographically more charitable than Vatteroni's. Of course, one need not posit a centralized direction. Malatesta himself had claimed in *L'Associazione* that the most effective insurrections were those in which everyone knew what to do and acted autonomously. However, a common line of conduct could not arise by chance, but only through prior communication ('A proposito di uno sciopero').

The manifestos sent from London, such as *Agli Anarchici d'Italia* of November 1893, which was an explicit, public call for the very sort of insurrectionary tactics that the Carrara anarchists undertook, were themselves a clear message. Moreover, prominent actors in the uprising, such as Ezio Puntoni, Garibaldi Rossi, Primo Ghio, and Raffaele De Santi, had steady contacts with Malatesta and other anarchists: in 1891 Puntoni and Rossi received Malatesta during his clandestine stay in Italy, while De Santi was the Roman anarchists' contact in Carrara (Gestri, 310–3); a country-wide list of contacts sent in 1892 from Milan to the Palermo anarchists included Rossi's name (Romano, 'Alcuni documenti', 191–2); in April 1893 a placard 'coming from abroad' was posted in Carrara, whose description matches *Agli Operai Italiani*, sent from London a few weeks earlier (Vatteroni, 38); and less than two months after the Carrara uprising Primo Ghio received a bundle of placards from Malatesta's group in London ('Elenco'). Ghio and Puntoni's names were still in Malatesta's address book at the turn of the century (Pages), when the two lived in the United States, after escaping the repressive backlash of 1894. Most importantly, Berti provides evidence that Luigi Molinari knew about the plans being made in London (*Francesco*, 223). That no communication on the subject occurred during his stay in Carrara would be odd, unless one subscribes to the interpretation of the uprising as wholly spontaneous, which at this point seems highly implausible.

Not only were the tactics of the Carrara anarchists in tune with a broader tendency, but they make sense only if interpreted in a national context. A tenable objective could hardly be attributed to such initiatives on a local level. In contrast, the uprising's tactics become transparent in the light of a country-wide strategy aimed at overcoming the government's repressive power by wearing it thin through the sheer extension of the insurrectionary agitations. In this light, the uprising itself, not its local result, would really matter: engaging as many troops as long as possible and hampering their communication would be the objective, provided that the same is also done elsewhere. A common pattern can be discerned in the anarchists' attempts in Apulia, Lunigiana, and later Piedmont: the interruption of means of communications; more or less symbolic attacks on government targets; and retreat to defensive position or transfer to other towns. What seems spontaneistic and aimless at a local level, acquires sense in a broader context.

The plan to arouse country-wide insurrectionary agitations was also reflected by the movements of Malato, Malatesta, and Merlino, who all left London in January 1894 for different parts of Italy. The first to leave was Malato, on 12 January. He was to operate in the northern regions of Piedmont and Lombardy; his departure predated the beginning of the Lunigiana uprising by one day. Malatesta and Merlino left in its aftermath (Tornielli). Meanwhile, a handbill titled *Solidarietà con la Sicilia* was printed by the

London anarchist-socialists for distribution in Italy. The manifesto addressed again the workers of Italy, but it avoided any reference to anarchism, in an effort to appeal to as many workers as possible, especially socialists and republicans: 'If we cannot do better, *let us stop working*.... Let us go on a *general strike*. Let no one go to work! Let no one pay taxes anymore!' And whereas the manifesto of February 1893 ended with the words 'Long live anarchist socialism! Long live the workers' revolution!' this one ended with 'Long live the workers' solidarity!'.

Charles Malato's movements in Italy are known with reasonable accuracy, mainly through his autobiography *Les Joyeusetés de l'Exil*. Malato visited Turin, Biella, and Milan. After a few more days spent between the Biellese and the Montferrat areas in mostly fruitless talks and meetings, Malato's presence was requested in Turin, where the local anarchists believed that opportunities for action did exist in the Biellese. The plan, in Malato's words, was to 'take to the countryside, blow up bridges, cut telegraph wires, blockade roads, attack isolated police stations, endeavour to hold out in the mountains for a month, long enough to allow the winter agitations of the unemployed to spread out to the industrious cities of Northern Italy' (121). A band was formed, which reached Biella on 7 February, its leading spirit being Romualdo Pappini, whom Malato describes as 'leaning towards Stirner's individualism' (qtd in Borghi, 100). The band held out in the Biellese mountains for several days, but did not succeed in arousing the population. Eventually, after destroying numerous telegraph lines, they returned to Turin, where they were reached by the news of Émile Henry's bombing of Café Terminus in Paris on 12 February. A month after his departure, Malato made his way back to London (Malato, *Joyeusetés*, 123–5).

Merlino's mission was short-lived. On 30 January, a few days after his arrival in Italy, he was arrested in Naples, betrayed by the spy Giovanni Domanico. Merlino's arrest and conviction practically ended his collaboration with Malatesta, for after release he began distancing himself from anarchism.

Malatesta's movements in Italy are hard to reconstruct, as much information comes from police sources, which partly relied on Domanico. Luigi Fabbri states that he met Turati in Milan (*Vida*, 133), and Pietro Gori confirms that he was there in late January (qtd in Marucco, n. 11). Domanico states that Malatesta made a stop in Bologna, then in Romagna and later in Ancona (38). Though no notable agitations occurred in Romagna, Malatesta's presence determined Crispi's apprehension, which may explain his sending two army corps in that region, 'where the situation might become grave', as he still maintained in late March ('European'). According to other sources, Malatesta was also in Tuscany (Berti, *Errico*, 216). In Ancona he contributed to the local anarchist press. The article 'Andiamo fra il popolo', of 4 February, drew a balance sheet of the anarchist contributions to the agitations, showing that by then Malatesta had abandoned hopes to revive the movement. By 20

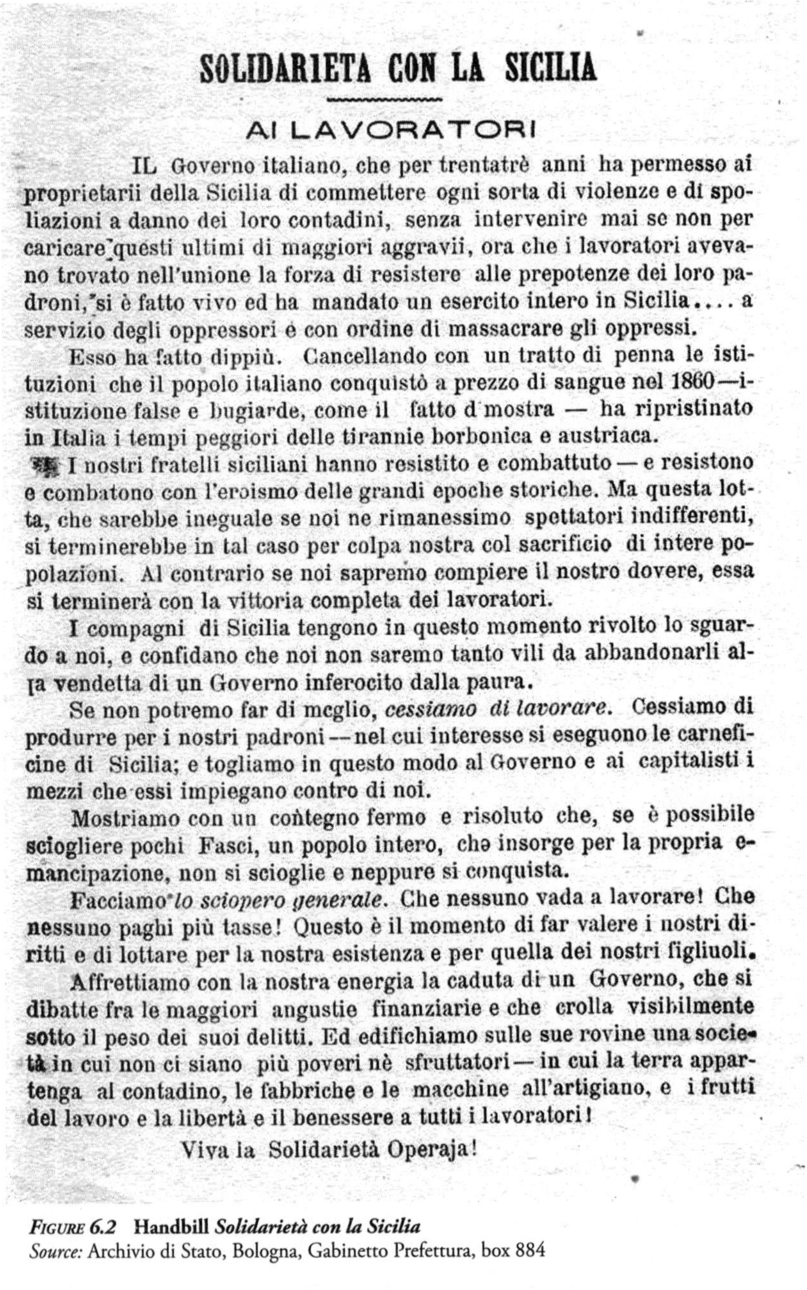

SOLIDARIETA CON LA SICILIA

AI LAVORATORI

IL Governo italiano, che per trentatrè anni ha permesso ai proprietarii della Sicilia di commettere ogni sorta di violenze e di spoliazioni a danno dei loro contadini, senza intervenire mai se non per caricare questi ultimi di maggiori aggravii, ora che i lavoratori avevano trovato nell'unione la forza di resistere alle prepotenze dei loro padroni, si è fatto vivo ed ha mandato un esercito intero in Sicilia.... a servizio degli oppressori e con ordine di massacrare gli oppressi.

Esso ha fatto dippiù. Cancellando con un tratto di penna le istituzioni che il popolo italiano conquistò a prezzo di sangue nel 1860 — istituzione false e bugiarde, come il fatto d'mostra — ha ripristinato in Italia i tempi peggiori delle tirannie borbonica e austriaca.

I nostri fratelli siciliani hanno resistito e combattuto — e resistono e combatono con l'eroismo delle grandi epoche storiche. Ma questa lotta, che sarebbe ineguale se noi ne rimanessimo spettatori indifferenti, si terminerebbe in tal caso per colpa nostra col sacrificio di intere popolazioni. Al contrario se noi sapremo compiere il nostro dovere, essa si terminerà con la vittoria completa dei lavoratori.

I compagni di Sicilia tengono in questo momento rivolto lo sguardo a noi, e confidano che noi non saremo tanto vili da abbandonarli alla vendetta di un Governo inferocito dalla paura.

Se non potremo far di meglio, *cessiamo di lavorare*. Cessiamo di produrre per i nostri padroni — nel cui interesse si eseguono le carneficine di Sicilia; e togliamo in questo modo al Governo e ai capitalisti i mezzi che essi impiegano contro di noi.

Mostriamo con un contegno fermo e risoluto che, se è possibile sciogliere pochi Fasci, un popolo intero, che insorge per la propria emancipazione, non si scioglie e neppure si conquista.

Facciamo *lo sciopero generale*. Che nessuno vada a lavorare! Che nessuno paghi più tasse! Questo è il momento di far valere i nostri diritti e di lottare per la nostra esistenza e per quella dei nostri figliuoli.

Affrettiamo con la nostra energia la caduta di un Governo, che si dibatte fra le maggiori angustie finanziarie e che crolla visibilmente sotto il peso dei suoi delitti. Ed edifichiamo sulle sue rovine una società in cui non ci siano più poveri nè sfruttatori — in cui la terra appartenga al contadino, le fabbriche e le macchine all'artigiano, e i frutti del lavoro e la libertà e il benessere a tutti i lavoratori!

Viva la Solidarietà Operaja!

FIGURE 6.2 Handbill *Solidarietà con la Sicilia*
Source: Archivio di Stato, Bologna, Gabinetto Prefettura, box 884

February he was back in London, as can be gathered from his correspondence (Postcard).

Let us review the evidence collected so far.

Anarchism, in its stereotyped image of spontaneous and aimless rebellion, allegedly disappeared after the events of 1 May 1891 in Piazza Santa Croce in Gerusalemme and reappeared on the Apuan mountains in January 1894. In fact, throughout that period there was a stream of continuous activism, planned and proactive rather than impromptu and reactive. Since 1890 anarchists such as Malatesta and Merlino focused on Sicily as a fertile ground for the revolutionary struggle. In the next three years Sicilian anarchists gave a significant and steady contribution to the formidable working-class movement that developed on the island, of which they had been among the early founders. There was continuity between the anarchist groups active in Sicily around 1893 and those that endorsed the Capolago congress of 1891, which in turn had roots that went as far back as the First International. Well before the Sicilian Fasci had developed into a full-blown mass movement, anarchists on the continent and abroad had started focusing on the extension of the struggle to the whole country. Contemporary observers such as Antonio Labriola and historians such as Salvatore Romano have recorded early anarchist activism throughout 1893 in connection with the Sicilian movement. Though anti-organizationists supported the popular agitations but harshly criticized the Fasci form of organization, organizationists such as Malatesta favored the extension of the Fasci to the continent and established alliances with Fasci leaders such as De Felice.

The extension of the Sicilian struggle to the continent and the alliance with De Felice were part of an overall anarchist insurrectionary strategy consistently pursued throughout 1893. Though insurrectionary agitations in early 1894 were sporadic and inadequate, being limited to Apulia, Lunigiana, and Piedmont, they shared a pattern of action that fits an overall strategy outlined by both Malatesta and De Felice. In particular, the most notable of such agitations, the Carrara uprising, often depicted as a protest demonstration that got out of hand, fits that common pattern in its mode of operation and makes sense only if its objectives are interpreted on a national scale. In Carrara, too, there was considerable continuity between the key figures that were in contact with Malatesta and the Roman anarchists in 1891 and the main actors of the 1894 uprising. As in the rest of the country, revolutionary propaganda in Carrara increased throughout 1893 and insurrectionary plans were laid out well before the uprising occurred. In sum, between 1891 and 1894 anarchists never disappeared or stopped agitating. Instead, a dense web of links can be identified between the events of those two years, in terms of both people and activity. Moreover, conscious planning, not spontaneous reaction, was the key factor in the 1894 events.

The tactics pursued by Malatesta exhibited both coherence and flexibility, as the four manifestos issued by the London anarchists in 1893–94 illustrate.

The first two, *Agli Operai Italiani* and *Agli Anarchici d'Italia*, openly advocated insurrection. However, they differed in content, as they respectively addressed workers and anarchists: the first manifesto surveyed the social ills that afflicted Italy and recalled the unfulfilled revolutionary ideals of *Risorgimento*; the second manifesto outlined the tactics that anarchists were to follow. The third manifesto, *Solidarietà con la Sicilia*, issued in early 1894, when insurrectionary prospects were becoming less bright, no longer called workers to insurrection, but to the general strike. Shortly after Malatesta's return to London, hundreds of copies of a fourth manifesto, *Al Popolo d'Italia* (To the people of Italy), dated London, 1 March 1894, and signed by the group *La Solidarietà*, reached Italy. The manifesto conceded defeat and blamed the lack of support to the areas in revolt from the rest of Italy. Then, it addressed the Italian people in strikingly explicit terms: 'Attack and disarm all police stations, set fire to courtrooms, archives, city halls, town halls, and prefect offices, burning all documents kept therein concerning ownership claims, sentences, and convictions. Take possession of everything...' The manifesto ended with the phrase 'Long live anarchist communism!'

Each manifesto illustrates a different aspect of Malatesta's tactics. By addressing workers and anarchists differently, the manifestos reflected Malatesta's distinction between masses and conscious minorities. The manifestos to workers contained little or no reference to anarchism and socialism. In the first of them the only such reference was in the signature phrase 'Long live anarchist socialism!' In the third one, even that reference disappeared. In the coherent pursuit of the same insurrectionary project, the manifestos exhibited tactical flexibility, changing focus from open insurrection to the general strike. The focus changed again with the fourth manifesto, which illustrates another aspect of Malatesta's tactics, the difference between propaganda for immediate action and the propaganda of ideas. The former was to pragmatically adjust to specific contexts, omitting references to anarchism when these could be counterproductive. The latter was to fully convey the anarchist message. Thus, at the same time that the fourth manifesto conceded defeat, it was also the one that most explicitly spelled out insurrectionary tactics and made reference again to the ideal of anarchy. In issuing that manifesto, the London anarchists had already turned to the preparation of the next insurrection.

The contrast between the tactics of the socialist party and Malatesta best illustrates the latter's originality and the tight connection between anarchist theory and practice.

The socialists invested greater effort and gained more prominence than the anarchists in organizing the Fasci. Yet, despite their greater involvement, they abandoned the movement to its fate when class struggle escalated to open conflict with the authorities. The two apparently contradictory attitudes were complementary, both proceeding from the socialists' preoccupation with hegemony. Socialists made every effort to control the movement, but disavowed it when it got out of control. They identified themselves with the cause of the proletariat, but in turn they identified the latter with the cause of their party—an example of heterogony of ends.

Instead, for anarchists such as Malatesta the Sicilian agitations might have been only 'the revolt of hunger' and not of a party, but that might have been just as well. The movement might not have 'proceeded from a determined thought', but people were to be taken as they were. Despite the anarchists' lesser involvement in the organization of the Fasci, the movement was to be fully supported, and its action extended by autonomous action on the continent. Participation in popular movements was not conditional upon anarchist hegemony, so long as the movements were not in contrast with anarchist goals. Malatesta found good reasons for joining movements that did not have an anarchist character in the logic of revolt, which had its own dynamics that transcended the explicit aims of actors. The events of 1893–94, in which social conflict escalated from non-revolutionary demands and traditional forms of struggle as in Sicily, or even from patriotic demonstrations as in Naples, showed that Malatesta's reasons were not based on wishful thinking, but were grounded on empirical reality.

The socialist party's doctrinarism was acknowledged in an article that appeared in Filippo Turati's *Critica Sociale* of 16 January 1894. The article recalled that the Sicilian movement raised disbelief among socialists, who argued that 'it was not conscious, that it was not a socialist movement'. It looked strange to them 'that the people could rise up without Marx's name on their lips, and instead they carried around the portraits of the king and queen and the icon of Our Lady'. However, the author acknowledged, 'it was a proletarian movement', though 'it was not as we would have wanted it, as it should have been according to the pure doctrine'. In sum, the author concluded, 'our historical prejudice blinded us to true history' (qtd in Romano, *Storia*, 529–30).

In the anarchist camp, the task of self-criticism was undertaken by Malatesta himself, who characteristically addressed the anarchists' inadequacies in his article 'Andiamo fra il popolo': 'Let us confess it at the outset: the anarchists have not been up to the situation.' With the exception of Carrara, which gave evidence of courage and devotion, but also of inadequate organization, anarchists had had a minor role amid such a popular upheaval. Malatesta targeted the rising anti-organizationist tendency, and the isolation that proceeded from it. He drew a comparison between the Fasci and the French Revolution:

> Let us remember that the people of Paris started off by demanding bread to the king amidst applauses and tears of affection, yet—having received bullets instead of bread, as it was natural—after two years they had already beheaded him. And it was only yesterday that the people of Sicily have been on the verge of making a revolution, while still cheering to the king and all his family.

For him, ridiculing the Fasci because they were not organized as anarchists wished, 'or because they were often named after Mary Immaculate, or because they kept in their rooms the bust of Karl Marx rather than that of Bakunin' revealed a lack of understanding and revolutionary spirit.

Thus, in the end, the charge of doctrinarism fell upon socialists and anarchists alike, and both had some responsibility in the defeat of the Fasci movement.

AN UNEVENTFUL YEAR OF DEEP CHANGE

For the historian Giampietro Berti, 'the general failure of the 1894 revolts marks an important turning point in Malatesta' thought and action...Popular spontaneism could not get anywhere by itself. It was necessary to change tune, laying down the foundations of a methodical work of propaganda... it was necessary to "go to the people"' (*Errico*, 218). Indeed, the defeat of the Fasci and the related anarchists' inadequacies led Malatesta to a thorough reassessment of anarchist tactics. However, Berti's remark conflates two separate themes, 'going to the people' and the theme of a methodical work of propaganda. 'Going to the people' was not a new theme; Malatesta had voiced it at least since 1889. At this time, 'going to the people' was felt increasingly urgent in the face of anti-organizationism. A similar criticism had already been expressed in January by *L'Art. 248*—the same periodical in which Malatesta's article appeared—still amid the agitations: 'what are we doing? Nothing at all. We have a revolution in the living-room, and we keep splitting hairs about free initiative and organization' ('Sicilia'). However, Malatesta's references to a long and patient work—as spelled out in 1897–98 in *L'Agitazione*—would only begin months later.

Malatesta's intense reworking of his tactics is revealed by two documents that he published in the year following his return from Italy. These have remained unheeded by commentators.

The first is the article 'The Duties of the Present Hour', which appeared in August 1894 in the London anarchist periodical *Liberty*. The article has never been translated into Italian or any other language, though in the late 1920s Malatesta himself included it in a list of his own works to which he attributed special importance (Luigi Fabbri, 'Per una raccolta'). What were anarchists to do, Malatesta asked, in the face of the reaction let loose upon them from all sides? 'Before all', he responded, 'we must as much as possible resist the laws; I might almost say we must ignore them.' The degree of freedom under which people lived, he argued, depended less on the letter of the law than on resistance and customs. If anarchists offered energetic resistance to anti-anarchist laws, these laws would at once appear to public opinion as a shameless violation of all human rights and would be doomed to extinction or to remaining a dead letter. Conversely, those laws would gain the status of political customs if anarchists put up with them. The disastrous result would be that the struggle for political liberties would gain priority over the social question. 'We are to be prevented from expressing our ideas: let us do so none the less and that more than ever. They want to proscribe the very name of Anarchist: let us shout aloud that we are Anarchists. The right of association is to be denied us: let us associate as we can, and proclaim that we are associated, and mean to be.' Before anything else anarchists were to go among the people. While their ideas obliged them to put all hopes in the masses, they had neglected all manifestations of popular life, thus becoming isolated: 'hence the want of success of what I will call, the first period of the Anarchist movement.' The anarchists' ordinary means of propaganda, such as the press, meetings, and groups, would become increasingly difficult to use. The alternative was the involvement in the labor movement:

> It is only in working-men's associations, strikes, collective revolts where we can find a waste [*sic*] field for exercising our influence and propagating our ideas. But if we want to succeed, let us remember that people do not become Anarchists in a single day, by hearing some violent speeches, and let us above all avoid falling into the error common to many comrades, who refuse to associate with working men who are not already perfect Anarchists, whilst it is absolutely necessary to associate with them in order to make them become Anarchists.

The comparison between 'Andiamo tra il popolo' and 'The Duties of the Present Hour' is especially instructive. There was continuity in the advocacy of 'going to the people', but at the same time different arguments were made. The two articles were written only six months apart, yet their arguments, language, and imagery were respectively reminiscent of two periodicals edited by Malatesta, *L'Associazione* and *L'Agitazione*, that were nearly a decade apart. The February article had the same emphasis of *L'Associazione* on the social indeterminacy of collective action, expressed through the same references to the French Revolution. The August article, the first after Malatesta's return from Italy and months of silence, made novel references to economic and legal resistance and to the idea of laws as resulting from the balance of antagonistic forces, foreshadowing concepts that he fully developed in 1897–98 in *L'Agitazione*. Clearly, that six-month interlude was a period of transition and elaboration. Malatesta showed full awareness that the 'present hour' was a momentous watershed between two phases, as his reference to 'the first period of the Anarchist movement' made clear.

The second relevant event in the 12 months after Malatesta's return to London was his attempt to create the International Federation of Revolutionary Anarchist Socialists. In February 1895 the London anarchist periodicals *Liberty* and *The Torch* published a manifesto titled after the recently formed federation, which had started in Italy. The manifesto contained the federation's program. *Liberty* stated that the federation was now seeking to extend itself, while *The Torch* claimed that it had been 'largely adhered to in Spain, Portugal, Southern France, and South America'. As frequently happened with Malatesta's initiatives, the manifesto was best received by the Spanish-language anarchist press. It was promptly translated, under the same title 'Federación Internacional Socialista Anárquica Revolucionaria', by *El Despertar* of New York and *El Corsario* of Corunna, which explicitly attributed it to Malatesta. There is no evidence of a French edition. However, the French syndicalist Fernand Pelloutier took notice of the document—quoting it from *Solidarity* of New York—in an overview of the current situation of socialism for *Les Temps Nouveaux* ('Situation'). The project was short-lived, thus pointing to the difficulties that Malatesta's organizationist ideas encountered. However, it is valuable as a way to assess the evolution of his ideas on anarchist organization.

The manifesto comprised three main sections: preamble, aims, and rules. The aims of the Federation were: (i) to propagate anarchist-socialism and the necessity for violent revolution; (ii) to inspire the people with a consciousness of their rights and sentiments of love and solidarity; (iii) to encourage the working-class movement and stimulate workers to organize with the threefold purpose of resisting employers and authorities for immediate gains, taking part in a general strike or insurrection to overthrow the present institutions, and taking over production and distribution on the day of the revolution; (iv) to encourage and profit by all movements of emancipation to the advantage of anarchist-socialist propaganda, and by all progress in ideas and facts which may be realized by the action of other individuals or parties; and (v) to coordinate the revolutionary efforts to attain a general insurrection. The section ended with a statement on violence: 'The Federation declares that its work is one of love. It rejects every action inspired by the spirit of hatred and vengeance, and admits violence only as a hard necessity imposed on it by present conditions and limited by the same necessity.'

The manifesto's significance in Malatesta's evolution is best grasped by comparing it with the Capolago program of four years earlier. The means advocated by the latter were expressed by generic phrases such as 'propaganda in all forms', 'participation in all agitations and all workers' movements', and 'revolutionary initiative'. In the Federation's manifesto ends and means were more sharply defined. Participation in the labor movement was spelled out in terms of both struggles for partial gains and insurrectionary general strikes. Participation in collective movements was qualified by an inclusive reference to the usefulness of 'all progress in ideas and facts' coming from 'other individuals or parties'. Finally, a line was drawn between different kinds of violence. The sharpening of the Federation's program concerned exactly those issues that divided anarchists but had been left hidden in the Capolago program: participation in the labor movement, the relative importance of collective versus individual action, and the revolutionary value of violent deeds. In brief, the Federation manifesto was the outcome of Malatesta's acknowledgment of the errors made at Capolago.

The manifesto's 'Rules' showed great similarity with those of Capolago, but here, too, the few differences were significant. In general, there was stronger emphasis on party discipline and a positive definition of duties. In his program of 1889, Malatesta had maintained that an anarchist party should reconcile free initiative with unity of action and discipline ('Programma', *Associazione*). Both elements were present in both the Capolago and the International Federation's rules. However, the Capolago organization scheme placed greater emphasis on free initiative: no terms evoking duty were used; unity of action was generically expressed by the intention 'to cooperate to the accomplishment of the stated principles by the stated means'. At the same time, there was a preoccupation to protect the free initiative of groups: groups were 'autonomous' and district Committees did not 'interfere in the internal matters of the groups'. In contrast, the language of unity and discipline was more prominent in the Federation manifesto: members 'must accept' the Federation's aims, remaining free to leave when such commitment lacked; they engaged in the labor movement, 'save in impossible circumstances'; and new members were subject to approval. The Federation had a more centralized structure. National federations were foreseen, and since federations were expected to nominate 'correspondents', it seems that national correspondence committees were also foreseen. Greater detail was also provided about the decision-making process: most notably, 'a common line of action' was decided not only by correspondence, but also 'by congress or by special delegates', that is by processes shunned by anti-organizationists. Finally, there was stronger emphasis on secrecy, in the face of circumstances that threatened the Federation's survival.

The Federation's organizational guidelines resulted not only from Malatesta's evolution and experiences after Capolago, but they also confirmed ideas that he had consistently held since earlier times. Some ideas that differentiated the Federation's from the Capolago organization scheme could already be found in the *Programma e Organizzazione dei L'Associazione Internazionale dei Lavoratori* of 1884: for example, federal committees and congresses were foreseen at both national and international levels; new members needed to be approved; and strict adherence to the program was explicitly required (59–64). What was new in 1895 with respect to 1884 was a keener awareness of the disruptive effects of government repression, and accordingly a greater preoccupation with continuity of action, as Malatesta's concern for secrecy shows. A cross-comparison of organizational schemes suggests that the weak formulation of the Capolago program was a concession to anti-organizationist currents, for the sake of building a broad-based anarchist party. In contrast, the manifesto of 1895 focused no longer on uniting all anarchists, but on acknowledging irreconcilable differences. Malatesta was explicitly and intentionally drawing the line that divided him and Merlino from anti-organizationist opponents such as Pomati. A 'Declaration' at the end of the manifesto made that clear:

> The members of this Federation know well that many Anarchists, or men calling themselves so, will fight their program and their organization. They do not complain. What they want is to unite for a common purpose with those who agree with them, and will be content if their initiative will contribute to destroy prevailing equivocations and will show the difference between principles, tendencies, and aims, often essentially opposed to one another and that go by the general name of Anarchy.

Perhaps because of its lack of success, Malatesta's project has been discussed by historians in hasty and dismissive terms. Pier Carlo Masini calls it 'an attempt to revive the old International' (*Storia . . . nell'epoca*, 75), while Giampietro Berti describes its manifesto as 'a sort of reissue—very cut-down and simplified—of the Capolago programme' (*Errico*, 233).

Actually, it was neither. With respect to the International, Malatesta longed for the revolutionary thrust that the International had been able to express, but he had systematically criticized its program and organization since at least 1889. The main difference, already visible in the Capolago program, was a different outlook on the relationship with the labor movement. The anarchist party no longer aimed at hegemonizing the labor movement, but rather at being part of it, as an influential but autonomous component. As the respective names made clear, the International gathered workers, the Federation anarchists. As for the Capolago program, the 1895 program was significantly different, and by all evidence such differences were exactly the result of Malatesta's learning the lesson of Capolago.

In contrast to revivalistic interpretations, Malatesta's project was part of a new phase in his anarchism.

Epilogue: the tide of history

Malatesta's new phase came in the wake of a biennium during which he had invested energies in popular movements that had no explicit anarchist goals. His positive outlook on those movements was coupled with a realistic view of both the movements themselves and the anarchists' tasks in them.

'It is absurd', he argued, 'to hope that in the present condition of the proletariat the great mass are capable before they stir of conceiving and accepting a programme formulated by a small number to whom circumstances have given exceptional means of development.' Yet anarchists were to plunge into the fray of those movements, or they would see the tide of history flow at their feet. There would be no pure anarchist movements to await, for an advanced program 'can only come to be consciously accepted by the great number through the action of moral and material conditions which the movement itself must supply' ('First of May').

History had no inexorable line of march. The future was indeterminate, and social action was open-ended. Popular movements began how they could, and nearly always sprang from obsolete ideas. But equally revolt had its own logic that transcended the actors' self-proclaimed motivations. When those movements engaged on the terrain of direct action, the employed means were of greater consequence than the stated aims. The anarchists' task was to struggle along with the masses, 'pushing them forward by reasoning and example' ('First of May').

Workers who suffered but understood little or nothing of theories had no time to wait, and were naturally disposed to prefer any immediate amelioration than wait for a radical transformation of society. It was for anarchists to persuade those workers that, if small concessions were obtained instead of great ones, it was not because they were easier to get, but because the people contented themselves with them ('First of May').

This was Malatesta's theoretical ground for crediting the popular movements of 1893–94 in Belgium and Italy with great potential for anarchist action. This is also why, in retrospect, he regarded them as lost opportunities and began a thorough reworking of anarchist tactics.

The metaphor of tides is also appropriate for a final remark about the history of anarchism. Analyses that tend to focus on high-tide moments, especially sensational ones such as the Jerez and Carrara uprisings, gloss over Malatesta's year after his return from Italy as uneventful. Yet it was a crucial year for understanding his evolution. In the day-to-day inconspicuous elaboration of ideas, in obscure projects and false starts, historians can trace the continuity that enables them to bridge the gap between highlights, avoiding the pitfall of thinking that these were as many rebirths and deaths of anarchism.

The new phase of Malatesta's anarchism, whose highlight was the project of *L'Agitazione*, did not start in 1897, when Malatesta returned to Italy three years after the Fasci's defeat. It started in 1894, right after that defeat, and it started abroad, while Crispi's reaction was raging over Italy.

7

PATIENT WORK IN THE LIGHT OF DAY, 1894–98

CHANGE IS A PROBLEMATIC CONCEPT FOR THE HISTORIOGRAPHY OF ANARchism.

Uncharitable historians maintain that change was a problem for anarchism itself. The reality is that understanding anarchist change is a problem for uncharitable historians. The various ways in which they misunderstand correspond to as many interpretations of anarchism as necessarily doomed.

Some, as E. J. Hobsbawm, simply deny change in anarchist theory and practice and claim that anarchism was irredeemably incapable of adaptation. Others acknowledge change, but interpret it as deflection from an abstract notion of 'anarchism' of their own making, narrowly and arbitrarily characterized as 'impossibilist' or 'purist'. In other words, when it comes to anarchism, change and continuity are regarded as mutually exclusive, for continuity is identified with immutability and change with a breakaway from 'anarchism'.

Conversely, other historians search for continuity in the wrong places, because they are traditionally attached to the national level of analysis and study a country's anarchist movement as an undifferentiated and insulated whole. We have already seen examples concerning Italy and Spain in 1891–92. Another case in point is the transition from illegalism to syndicalism in France in the years covered in this chapter. As F. F. Ridley notes, it has been often suggested that 'syndicalism was something especially French, born of, or reflecting, the peculiar character of the French people' (11). Partly subscribing to this view, Ridley sketches a simplistic picture: 'The anarchists found themselves isolated and helpless: they had come to a blank wall where no further progress seemed possible. Their leaders recognized the futility of individual action and of the bomb as a revolutionary weapon' (43). Richard Sonn makes the equally implausible argument that the transition was not precipitated by the anarchists themselves, but rather by government repression (19), and that French anarchists 'shifted from a predominantly cultural to an economic orientation' as they realized 'the need to bridge the gap between libertarian ideals and organizational necessity' (26). So long as a movement is regarded as a monolith that evolved en bloc solely under the pressure of domestic factors, unlikely explanations are bound to crop up.

In contrast, change, continuity, cross-fertilization, and controversy are the key themes of Malatesta's evolution in 1894–98. In this period Malatesta undertook a change in tactics that stemmed from two sources: the disappointing outcome of the agitations of 1893–94 and the acknowledgment of differences among anarchists, divided by a rift on questions of organization and participation in the labor movement.

The highlight of that half-decade was the biennium 1897–98, when Malatesta returned to Italy to edit *L'Agitazione* in Ancona. This periodical is widely regarded as a high point in Malatesta's anarchism. Luigi Fabbri considered it Malatesta's most important periodical, both historically and theoretically (*Vida*, 138). For the marxist Enzo Santarelli, *L'Agitazione* expressed 'open, and, to some extent, unitary and advanced positions', in contrast to a later alleged anti-socialist involution (*Socialismo*, 48). As Giampietro Berti explains, 'the insurrectionary objective is now subordinated to the indispensable pre-condition of a patient propaganda work among the working classes' (*Errico*, 240). From the columns of *L'Agitazione* Malatesta preached novel tactics for Italy, advocating the intervention of anarchist-socialists in labor struggles for immediate economic gains.

The biennium 1897–98 is often simplistically viewed as another dramatic rebirth of Italian anarchism spurred by the 'reappearance' of Malatesta with new tactics in mind. However, what tends to be regarded as a relatively sudden and circumscribed event was actually part of a more complex process, which can be fully understood by extending the scope of analysis, chronologically, from 1897 back to 1894 and, geographically, from Italy to Europe.

As we have seen, Malatesta's rethinking of anarchist tactics began in London, right after the defeat of the Sicilian Fasci. Moreover, Malatesta's trajectory was not isolated and individual, nor were his new tactics a solitary invention. His initiative in the mid-1890s to assert his new tactical orientation involved wider circles of Italian anarchists abroad. In order to grasp the continuity between the defeats of 1894 and the new phase of 1897–98 one has to look at the transnational dimension of Italian anarchism.

Most importantly, the new tactics advocated by Malatesta were part of a wider current of change including French anarchism, where syndicalism became prominent in those years.

The parallel evolutions of the Italian and French anarchist movements were interrelated and partly came to maturity in the London international milieu of anarchist exiles. The analysis of the characteristics and functioning mode of that milieu reveals the importance of another form of continuity, the collaboration and mutual influence between different anarchist movements outside of their respective countries. The new labor-oriented tactics progressed in parallel in the two movements. An important venue where Italian and French anarchists made a common front to publicly assert their new tactics was the International London Congress of 1896, in which Malatesta had a prominent role.

By showing that labor-oriented tactics in Italy and France had common origins in the years of illegalism, both arose in contrast to alternative conceptions of anarchism, and progressed in step, the new phase of Italian anarchism and the rise of French syndicalism can be placed in a broader context, which prevents misinterpretations of new anarchist tendencies as sudden rebirths or unlikely shifts of supposedly monolithic movements. Change and continuity can be reconciled, if they are seen in the context of dynamic relations between alternative anarchist currents.

Besides chronological continuity and cross-national affinities, theoretical continuity is another key issue. Malatesta's turn was not a deflection from his former anarchism, nor a move toward other currents of socialism previously alien to him—notwithstanding biased comments from anti-organizationist anarchists and parliamentarian socialists alike, as well as interpretations by historians assuming that anarchism is inherently impossibilist.

Malatesta's theoretical continuity can be gauged from his theoretical controversies of those years. While the anarchists' struggle at the London congress was waged from a new standpoint rather than simply re-enacting the First International's old contrasts, it was also a restatement of the fundamental tenets that separated anarchism from marxism. And at the same time that Malatesta expounded his new tactics in *L'Agitazione*, he engaged in a protracted debate with his friend and former comrade Saverio Merlino in which he clarified the theoretical foundations of anarchism and the reasons why anarchists rejected parliamentarianism as firmly as ever.

In contrast to interpretations based on a narrow idea of anarchism, Malatesta's evolution was a trajectory within anarchism, fully coherent with his theoretical principles and tactical basic tenets, yet heading in a novel direction.

THE CROSSROADS OF COSMOPOLITAN ANARCHISM

A good starting point for reconstructing the parallel rise of labor-oriented anarchist currents in Italy and France in the mid-1890s is a description of the international community of anarchist exiles in London, of which Malatesta had been a notable member for half a decade.

That community swelled after repression against anarchism swept across Europe in connection with anarchist uprisings and *attentats* that occurred from 1892 on, the latter being often undertaken as responses to previous acts of repression: in Spain the Jerez uprising of 1892 and the bombings by Paulino Pallás and Santiago Salvador the next year; in Italy the Sicily and Lunigiana uprisings of 1893–94 and Paolo Lega's attempt on Crispi's life in June 1894; and in France, the bombings of Ravachol, Vaillant, and Émile Henry between March 1892 and February 1894, and Sante Caserio's assassination of president Sadi Carnot in June of the same year. Repression tended to strike the anarchist movement and its press indiscriminately. In Spain an anti-anarchist police force was created, militants were rounded up, and innocents executed. After the bombing of the Corpus Christi procession in Barcelona in June 1896, such a massive campaign of arrests, tortures, and deaths in the Montjuich prison ensued as to raise international protests (Woodcock, 346–8). In Italy, exceptional laws were passed in July 1894. By the end of the year thousands of anarchists and socialists were in jail or *domicilio coatto* (Pernicone, 287–9). In France, the *lois scélérates* were passed after Vaillant's attempt. Anarchist leaders and intellectuals, such as Jean Grave, Sébastien Faure, Paul Reclus, and Émile Pouget, were brought before the courts along with a gang of illegalist anarchists in the so-called Trial of the Thirty of August 1894 (Woodcock, 288–95).

In the face of such repression, exile was one of the anarchists' options. While Spaniards tended initially to emigrate to the Americas, London was a destination of anarchists from France and Italy, who joined the exiles of earlier times. The London international milieu of anarchist exiles provides the opportunity to study not only the transnationalism of the anarchist networks of individual countries, but also what might be termed their crossnational dimension, that is the cooperation, involvement in the affairs of each other's country, and cross-fertilization among anarchists of different countries. In that way the historian is in a better position to account for the rise of new currents in specific countries, which cannot be fully explained by analyses of national scope. Three circumstances favored the coalescing of refugees into a political milieu of effective activism: rootedness in colonies of immigrants; transnational ties with respective homeland movements; and cosmopolitan cooperation across national and linguistic lines. Late Victorian London provided opportunity for each of these, and so its international anarchist community became the headquarters of continental anarchism (see Oliver).

In the second half of the nineteenth century, Europeans dominated foreign immigration to Britain. However, their numbers remained small. Lack of assimilation and separateness from the native population meant that relatively few pockets of foreigners coexisted with a vast majority of native British or Irish origin (Holmes, 84). Rudolf Rocker, the German anarchist who became prominent in the Jewish labor movement in London, recalled that in the 1890s a small area in the City of Westminster, approximately corresponding to the area known as Fitzrovia in the twentieth century, was almost exclusively inhabited by Germans, French, Austrians, and Swiss, so that the language spoken there was more often German or French than English (*London*, 69).

The concentration of foreign anarchists was even more pronounced than that of their ethnic communities. An 1896 report to the police prefecture of Paris lists 227 anarchists of various nationalities resident in London

('Anarchistes'). Of the 193 militants whose addresses can be identified, more than half resided in a West London rectangle covering less than half a square mile, comprising Fitzrovia and Soho. A slightly wider area around this West London core accounts for nearly 80 percent of the total. For anarchist exiles, lack of assimilation and separateness were not disadvantages. At the same time that they could rely on immigrant colonies to draw support and resources, the colonies' insularity made them impenetrable to direct police surveillance, which had to resort mainly to spies and informers from those immigrant communities. The drawback for the anarchists was that the concentration of militants in restricted areas made the work of spies and police easier.

Not only did anarchists in London have roots in local colonies; they also kept ties with the homeland and with anarchist colonies around the Mediterranean and the Atlantic Ocean. The Fabian Edward Pease describes anarchist communism in London in the 1880s as an influential doctrine, remarking that its rank and file, mostly continental refugees, 'had direct relations with similar parties abroad, the exact extent and significance of which we could not calculate' (66). According to a French police report of December 1893, more than one-fourth of those who corresponded with Paris anarchists were from foreign countries in Europe, North Africa, and the Americas. In turn, over one-third of the abroad correspondents were from London, which ranked first in absolute numbers, preceding the top-ranking French cities (Unsigned). This was months before the Trial of the Thirty. After the Trial, London gained further prominence as a center of French anarchism.

The flux of French militants, as the Italians', was bidirectional, depending on the homeland situation. For example, in 1894 Pouget resumed the publication of *Le Père Peinard* in London, to be smuggled back to France. However, the next year intervening political changes led him and other French anarchists to return to France, where Pouget became a key figure of revolutionary syndicalism (Rocker, *En la Borrasca*, 23–4). The incessant interest of the French police, through a network of spies in London, points to the influence that anarchists could exert from there. In 1895 there were no less than three agents in London, as many as in Paris, all six sometimes responding simultaneously to the same requests from the Paris prefecture (Jackson; Lapeyre; Eureka; Bornibus; Caraman; Guillaume; André). In other words, the two cities received equal consideration from the French police, and this indicates the importance of London as an anarchist center.

Part of the reason why London became the headquarters of continental anarchism is that it was at the crossroads of transatlantic routes. Anarchists en route between Europe and the Americas would spend time in London and meet local exiles, providing a link between anarchists across the Atlantic. In turn, the residents' rootedness in colonies was a logistic asset in receiving and providing assistance to transient comrades and newcomers. Luigi Fabbri remarks that the house and shop of the Defendis, where Malatesta lived, were a meeting point for all the new arrivals in London. In addition, the shop offered a discreet venue for sheltered meetings. 'How many stormy and fraternal discussions', Fabbri recalls, 'in that makeshift athenaeum that was the small kitchen in the back of Defendi's delicatessen shop!' Fabbri states that Defendi even raised the attention of the French police, which placed his address under mail surveillance (*Vida*, 134). Similar shops fulfilled the same function for French exiles, such as Victor Richard's grocery in Charlotte Street, where Charles Malato recalls that all refugees turned (*De la commune*, 276), and Armand Lapie's bookstore, also in the French district. The latter's key role is revealed by an 1894 list of 34 anarchists resident in London compiled by the French police, which included cross-links to each individual's associates ('Anarchistes'). In the miniature social network thus described, Lapie was the most densely connected individual, far outnumbering the likes of Pouget, Malatesta, and Malato, thus illustrating the inconspicuous but fundamental liaising role that less prominent figures played in the anarchist movement.

Anarchist cosmopolitanism in London found expression in the movement's public life, including mass demonstrations, where speakers customarily included representatives of exile groups who spoke in their native languages, and club life, which was markedly international in such clubs as Rose Street, Berner Street, and Autonomie. Aside from the East End clubs of Jewish workers, almost all such clubs were in that half square mile area where foreign population was most dense and where the club life of foreign exiles intersected with a long-standing local tradition (Shipley, 2; 'Club Life'). In addition, places as the shops and dwellings of Defendi, Richard, and Lapie complemented club life in accounting for the activism of London exiles. Club life was more conspicuous. Its public character made it appear more defiant and threatening, but also made it more easily targeted by the police (Dipaola, 'Italian', 214). The back-rooms of shops were more inconspicuous venues of political activism, but by the same token they may have been more effective.

In sum, the study of exile anarchists in London provides insight into the relevance of transnationalism for the working of anarchist networks. Mundane and unconventional venues as shop back-rooms epitomize even more clearly than clubs the correlation between political exile, rootedness in colonies, and transnational links with the homeland. They also epitomize the opacity of anarchism, for which kitchens and back-rooms became more dependable 'institutions' than convention halls. In all these respects, London exhibited a pattern that was probably common to other cities around the world. Such militants as the dairyman Constant Martin in Paris (Moreau) and the hatter Cesare Agostinelli in Ancona (Giulianelli) fulfilled a fundamental function in anarchist networks both abroad and at home, made possible by their pattern of militancy in which low profile and lasting residency were coupled with sustained commitment.

Not only was London an example of a city where transnational anarchism thrived, but it also fulfilled a unique role as a cross-national hub of cooperation and exchange among continental anarchists, which proceeded from its being a junction in the anarchist networks of different countries. The transnationalism of each country's movement, along with international exchange and integration among anarchist exiles in London, determined a pattern of cross-national involvement in each other's movement. Bantman has illustrated the cooperation between French and British anarchists across the Channel. Even more characteristic was the mutual involvement between French and Italian anarchist exiles in London. The frequent cooperation between Malatesta and Malato is an example. Because of the entwinement of French and Italian anarchists, the French police monitored the two groups with equal zeal and reports often dealt indistinctly with both. For example, the abovementioned 1894 list of 34 London anarchists lumped 8 Italians with the remaining French ('Anarchistes'). Similarly, more than half of the larger 1896 list, which was multinational but certainly biased toward those of greatest concern to the French authorities, comprised French- and Italian-sounding names, with Italians being nearly 40 percent of that subgroup ('Anarchistes'). Finally, an 1897 report by the title 'Anarchism in France', included biographies of Malatesta and Merlino among the 'Profiles of some leaders of the anarchist party' (Moreau).

The exchange and cooperation between Italian and French anarchists in London was instrumental in setting in motion a process by which the currents of anarchism that believed in organization, collective struggle, and participation in the labor movement increasingly regained initiative in the respective countries, after the setbacks of 1894. In France, 1894 was a turning point between a three-year period predominated by individual deeds, ending with the Trial of the Thirty, and an era in which anarchists acted as conscious minorities amid the masses. Thus for Jean Maitron, syndicalism 'was precisely a reaction against that infantile disorder of anarchism that was terrorism' (259), in contrast to the continuity posited by Sonn. In Italy anarchism was at low ebb in 1894, after Crispi's repression had disbanded its ranks. That year, after his return to London, Malatesta began subjecting anarchist tactics to a thorough reconsideration, lamenting the failure caused by the progressive detachment of the anarchist movement from popular life, and the resulting neglect of sustained agitation among the masses ('Duties').

The mutual influence between Malatesta and two key figures of syndicalism, Émile Pouget and Fernand Pelloutier, in a crucial phase of their intellectual evolution illustrates the cross-fertilization of ideas among anarchist exiles in London and the part that such cross-fertilization played in setting in motion a new tactical orientation in the anarchist movements of the respective countries. In mid-1893 Pouget traveled from Paris to London to confer with Malato and Marius Sicard, according to a spy, about giving a revolutionary direction to the *Bourses du Travail*. On the occasion he also visited Malatesta and others (Z N° 6, 3 July 1893). Pouget's links with the Italians in London were indeed close, for the next year, upon moving to that city, he lived at Defendi's, where Malatesta also lived (Z N° 6, 5 and 21 February 1894). Both Pouget and Malatesta contributed to *The Torch*, an anarchist periodical edited in London. Significantly, the issue of August 1894 contained articles from both, but it was Malatesta's article that advocated the general strike as a revolutionary weapon ('General'). The next month, the new syndicalist orientation was signaled in France by a split that occurred at the Nantes union congress between the marxists and a syndicalist majority that voted for general strike tactics (Maitron, 290–1). In 1895 Pouget returned to France. For Jean Maitron, one reason why Pouget's stay in London was a turning point in his syndicalist trajectory was the influence of trade unions, as witnessed by the London run of Pouget's periodical, *Le Père Peinard* (273). According to Pierre Monatte, Pouget established strong relationships with British trade unionists that he kept up after his return to France (qtd in Maitron, 273). In 1895 Pouget and Pelloutier undertook an intense propaganda of the new syndicalist tactics among French anarchists. That year Pelloutier published a series of articles in *Les Temps Nouveaux* advocating anarchist engagement in syndicates (Julliard, 131). In the first article, 'La situation actuelle du socialisme', he backed up his appeal for new tactics with a reference to Merlino's ideas and to their implementation in Malatesta's International Federation of Revolutionary Anarchist Socialists (346–7). Pelloutier would restate his affinity with Malatesta four years later in a 'Lettre aux anarchistes', which he opened by claiming that his ideas found a perfect illustration in Malatesta, who could 'combine so well an indomitable revolutionary passion with the methodical organization of the proletariat' (415).

At the time of Pouget's return to France Malatesta remained in London. His own return to his country would only take place two years later. However, there is evidence that in early 1896, a year after Pouget's homecoming, Malatesta's plans to return to Italy were already taking shape, too. In a letter from London of 10 March 1896 to Nicolò Converti, Malatesta mentioned a recent aborted plan to leave for Italy. In the letter he clearly outlined his motivation for a tactical turn, summarizing the disappointing situation of the movement in Italy and lamenting the Italian anarchists' inability to take initiative and their division and lack of preparation even when external circumstances created opportunities for action. Such a state of internal strife and paralysis, he argued, could only be overcome by splitting and regrouping according to tactical affinity (*Epistolario*, 74). Then, in a letter of 21 May 1896 to Victorine Rouchy-Brocher, Malatesta stated that he would probably return to Italy at the beginning of the next year, as he actually did (Brocher Papers).

Malatesta's tactical elaboration and early plans of this period, in parallel with the elaboration and plans of the French anarchists, help bridge the gap between his return from Italy in 1894 and his departure for Italy in 1897.

A straight, uninterrupted line connected the experiences of 1894 to the new tactics of 1897. Malatesta's own evolution and the new phase of Italian anarchism were part of a broader trend based on organization and participation in labor struggles, which was also gaining momentum in France through syndicalism. Any account of the national anarchist movements in Italy and France in the second half of the 1890s would be incomplete without including developments that not only occurred outside the countries' borders, but also involved cooperation and cross-pollination of ideas among anarchists of different nationalities in London. Only by taking heed of such elements do processes that appear separate and unrelated from a national perspective reveal their interconnection and parallel progression.

A PLURALIST VIEW ON THE LABOR MOVEMENT

The labor-oriented currents of Italian and French anarchism not only arose in parallel, but also publicly and jointly asserted their new ideas when they made a common front at the International Socialist Workers and Trade Union Congress that took place in London from 26 July to 2 August 1896, where they waged a battle on the anarchists' right to participate.

The congress was a milestone in the process of reorienting anarchist tactics that Malatesta and his comrades promoted. The anarchists' participation well signified the change, continuity, and distinction that marked that process. Their ground for participation in a congress of the Second International had changed from the old struggle in the First International. At the same time, there was continuity between the two controversies, owing to the deep theoretical rift between marxists and anarchists. Finally, by choosing a socialist and workers' congress as a venue to assert their new tactics, labor-oriented anarchists stated their distinction from currents of anarchism that traditionally shunned such gatherings.

The congress was dominated by the issue of the anarchists' exclusion from participation. Though controversies over this question had occurred in all previous congresses of the Second International since 1889, anarchist opposition was episodic until their exclusion was formalized at Zurich in 1893 (Joll, *Second*, 45, 68, 71). Only with the London congress did a coordinated opposition to the anarchists' exclusion take place. The initiative partly owed to anarchists now facing a formal exclusion. Another factor was the choice of London as the host city, because of the presence not only of a strong international contingent of anarchist exiles, but also of a socialist and labor movement of non-marxist tradition (Masini, *Storia . . . nell'epoca*, 78–9). Finally, the anarchists' organized participation and combativeness in that congress were made possible by the ascendancy that currents advocating organization and labor involvement were gaining among them.

The controversy over the anarchists' admission to the Second International's congresses is usually depicted as a revival of Bakunin's struggle with

Marx, with anarchists fighting once more the old battle and losing it once and for all. For example, James Joll writes that 'as soon as the survivors of the old International began to take practical steps [to create another international organization] ... they at once came up against two difficulties: the increased hostility of governments ... and the fundamental division between marxists and Anarchists that had wrecked the First International' and 'was to dominate the early years of the Second International as it had the end of the First'. For Joll, the ultimate root of that division was 'a profound psychological difference, a contrast of types of political temperament' (*Second*, 23–4). The cliché underlying Joll's analysis is that anarchists were backward-looking, unchanging, disruptive, and doomed. In contrast to such analyses, placing the anarchist opposition in the context of the new trends that were arising in the anarchist movement in that period shows that their battle in London was forward-looking, novel, and constructive.

The very denomination 'International Socialist Workers and Trade Union Congress' epitomized the new orientation that Malatesta wanted to give to the anarchist movement. This was summarized by the label 'anarchist socialism', which came to characterize his brand of anarchism. Malatesta proclaimed the socialist character of anarchism and urged anarchists to regain contact with the working masses, especially through involvement in the labor movement. Even the circumstance that the arena of the struggle was a congress reflected Malatesta's belief in organization. Demanding the anarchists' admission to the congress meant reasserting socialism and labor movement as central to anarchism; conversely, the marxists' effort to exclude anarchists aimed at denying that they had a place among socialists and workers. In brief, Malatesta's struggle for admission to the congress was a statement of his new tactics.

Moreover, the terms of the question had changed since the First International. A fortnight before the congress, Malatesta recalled in the *Labour Leader* that in the old International both marxists and bakuninists wished to make their program triumph. In the struggle between centralism and federalism, class struggle and economic solidarity got neglected, and the International perished in the process. In contrast, anarchists were not presently demanding anyone to renounce their program. They only asked for divisions to be left out of the economic struggle, where they had no reason to exist ('Should'). Thus, the issue was no longer hegemony, but the contrast between an exclusive view of socialism, for which one political idea was to be hegemonic, and an inclusive one, for which multiple political views were to coexist, united in the economic struggle. Kropotkin well summarized the anarchist argument: 'Had the Congress been announced as a Social Democratic Congress, Anarchists would evidently not have gone... But the Congress is announced as a *Universal Workers' Congress*, and therefore—either trade unions only are admitted, or all Socialist and Revolutionary groups that care to come must be admitted' ('Workers'). The matter of the question had changed: the controversy was no longer with the anarchists, but about the anarchists.

Accordingly, the struggle was presently between two larger fronts, or at least between a compact one, led by the *Sozialdemokratische Partei Deutschlands*, or SPD, for which parliamentarianism was a *sine qua non* of socialism, and a diverse one including not only the anarchists, but also the majority of the British Independent Labour Party, the Allemanist fraction of French socialism, the 'young' German socialists expelled from the SPD Erfurt congress of 1891, and the Dutch, anti-parliamentarian *Socialistenbond* of Ferdinand Domela Nieuwenhuis and Christian Cornelissen (Rocker, *En la Borrasca*, 37–9). Hence, if continuity existed with the First International, it was on the marxist side, as Engels's comment on the 1891 Brussels congress confirms: 'Voting the exclusion of the anarchists was the right thing to do: thus had ended the old International, and it is thus that the new one is being launched. It confirms, purely and simply, the resolution taken at The Hague nineteen years ago' (qtd in *Congrès International Ouvrier*, 14).

The London congress was a step in a new direction for French anarchists, too. Their continuity was not with the First International but with the Nantes congress of two years before. As Jean Maitron remarks, the London congress, where the majority of the French delegation voted against the anarchists' exclusion, was the 'continuation and completion' of the split occurred at Nantes between marxists and syndicalists (Maitron, 291). Carl Levy rightly emphasizes the forward-bound character of the antiparliamentary congressional opposition in London, arguing that it was 'a transitional link between an older bakuninism, and other varieties of populist socialism, and conscious syndicalism' ('Malatesta in London', 34). However, even Levy's remark does not fully do justice to that opposition. The transition pattern was not so much a linear evolution of anarchism as a whole, as the result of the interplay between coexisting currents. The rise of syndicalism is best contrasted not to a distant bakuninist past, but to the spread of anti-organizationist tendencies. Moreover, the process did not simply consist of the rise of syndicalism, but more generally of the resurgence of organizationist tendencies, including those in Italy, committed to collective action in the labor movement. Seen in this light, the process represented more a resumption than a rejection of the bakuninist tradition.

By demanding admission to the London congress, Malatesta and his comrades faced not only the opposition of marxists, but also set themselves apart from anarchist currents opposed to organization and involvement in the labor movement. That anarchist forces coalesced around a congress was itself a declaration of intent about their tactical orientation. Though the struggle with marxists was a clash of ideas, it took the form of an extenuating battle over mandates, letterhead, stamps, voting systems, that is the very machinery that many anarchists dreaded as outward symbols of the authoritarianism inherent in organization. For example, in 1893 *La Révolte* had sarcastically remarked that the Zurich expulsion served anarchists right ('Mouvement Social. Suisse'). Kropotkin's absence from the 1896 congress was also telling. Malatesta's letters to Hamon of 3 and 8 July 1896 reveal repeated but vain efforts to secure his participation (Hamon Papers, file 109). In a further letter of 11 July, Malatesta conjectured that Kropotkin's reluctance proceeded from a deep-seated aversion to voting, coupled with the anticipation that not voting at the congress would be perceived as playing in the opponents' hands (Hamon Papers, file 109). Thus, the anarchists' congressional initiative was engaged on a double front, aiming to assert the anarchists' place among socialists and workers and to propagate an organization and labor-oriented attitude in the anarchist ranks.

Meetings in London to organize the anarchist presence at the congress started a year earlier. In July 1895 the Freedom Group expressed the unanimous opinion to attend *en masse* (Kropotkin, 'Congrès'). In the following months, the initiative was taken by the English anarchists, though it was fraught with dissension and ineffectiveness (Quail, 202–4). In August–September 1895 the *Torch* group issued an appeal and a manifesto for free admission to the congress ('England'), which received a wide echo in the anarchist press. The comments by the Italian Antonio Agresti and Pietro Gori in *La Questione Sociale* of Paterson, New Jersey, expressed the novel context of the foreseen opposition in London ('Congresso Operaio'). Both regarded participation as part of new tactics focused on propaganda among workers. In contrast to past methods, they argued, anarchists were to seek an understanding on broad demands with anti-parliamentarian socialists and British trade unions, and spread among workers not only anarchist communism, but also the idea of the general strike, as a step toward insurrection. Both Agresti and Gori had recently come to the United States from London, where such ideas must have been debated. Thus, for organizationist anarchists, the demand to join the congress was not just a disruptive maneuver to contrast marxist hegemony, but was part of broader, inclusive tactics based on participation in the labor movement. The initiative of the *Torch* was a false start, for internal dissension among British anarchists deprived it of support ('Between'). A new committee was appointed, but its progress remained slow ('International Workers', February 1896). At any rate, between February and April 1896 initiatives were taken in London, as the anarchist periodicals *Freedom* and *Liberty* reported in their February and March issues. They ended with a West End meeting at the end of April, with which the committee wound up its activities ('International Workers', May 1896).

However, other anarchists in London believed that much remained to be done. By late June a new 'Anarchist and Anti-Parliamentary Committee' was formed, with Malatesta as the most active member. While the previous committee had focused on domestic propaganda, Malatesta liaised with anarchists abroad, especially in France. Throughout July 1896 a nearly daily correspondence went on with Augustin Hamon, through which Malatesta was also in contact with Pelloutier. According to Hamon, these three militants were the main organizers of the anarchist opposition (qtd in Maitron, 293). Malatesta's correspondence with Hamon provides valuable insights on his activities, expectations, and congressional tactics.

A key task was to ensure mandates for anarchists in London. Malatesta discussed the matter at length with Hamon in his letters of 30 June, 9, 17, and 20 July 1896 (Hamon Papers, file 109). As a result, the list of French delegates contained the names of several British anarchists (*International Socialist*, 249–51). The distribution of mandates at the congress is a telling indicator both of the role of international anarchist exiles in London and of the affinity and cooperation between Italian and French anarchists. Malatesta himself, who held mandates from workers' organizations in both France and Spain, was eventually admitted in virtue of a mandate from the Amiens metal workers; Pelloutier represented the Italian Federation of Labor Chambers (Hamon, 78); Louise Michel carried a mandate from an anarchist-communist association in Northern Italy (Gori, 'Congresso', 207); Agresti represented a workers' association of Morez, in France; and Isaia Pacini, another Italian exile in London, also represented a French group (*International Socialist*, 249–51). Considering that the French delegation voted against the exclusion of anarchists by a narrow margin, such mandates proved crucial.

Malatesta's commitment to the struggle for admission at the London congress well illustrates the breadth and adaptability of his tactics. The advocate of insurrectionary tactics was equally at ease with congress politics, fully appreciating its procedural nuances. Anarchist principles are often regarded, by supporters and opponents alike, as a Procrustean bed that severely limits anarchists' options. Malatesta's inclusiveness shows that the principle of coherence between ends and means did not prevent any effective action and that within its scope a broad range of tactics were available. Malatesta was aware that procedure would be the congress battleground and he was ready to enter it without reservations. Thus, in a letter of 8 July 1896 he remarked to Hamon that formal requirements were to be taken seriously, for only those with unexceptionable mandates would be initially admitted. For him, anarchists were to carry mandates from both unions, so as to gain admission, and anarchist groups, so as to be able to put the Zurich resolution on the agenda (Hamon Papers, file 109).

Malatesta's congressional tactics displayed a remarkable pragmatism and political moderation. He regarded unity of action as paramount, stating in a letter of July 11 that he would even prefer that 'a stupid course of action be taken', rather than each acting in a different way. The importance of unity and the role of the British delegation counseled restraint to him. Thus, he expressed doubts about the Allemanists' idea of resisting by force. 'I believe', he countered, 'that we will have the majority of the English on our side if we do not commit intemperances' (Hamon Papers, file 109). A final decision on a common line of conduct was expected to be taken at a private meeting of delegates on the eve of the congress. English trade unionists, representatives of the French syndicates and labor chambers, Dutch delegates, and members of Italian groups and labor organizations attended the meeting. However, Hamon stated, 'the discussion was quite vague, though it all took place peacefully. No resolution was taken and nothing came out of the meeting' (Hamon, 83, 95).

The meeting's indecisiveness illustrates the divisions and biases that hindered the effectiveness of anarchist opposition. In his letter of 11 July to Hamon, Malatesta reported a telling debate with Kropotkin, Nettlau, and others, about voting systems to be proposed at the congress. No agreement was reached, leaving the question unsolved. Malatesta commented that for many anarchists, possibly the majority, 'the mere word "voting," no matter how and why, has the same effect that the devil would have on a bigot'. He argued that 'they would prefer to leave even the most important and necessary thing undone, rather than going through a vote.' Thus, he concluded 'at the congress as anywhere else, they would like not to vote and not to join any discussion about the question of voting' (Hamon Papers, file 109). In a letter of 17 July—wrongly dated 1895—ten days before the congress, Malatesta already expressed to Hamon his disappointment about the gap between what anarchists could have done and what they actually did: 'Certainly, if we win or just come out well, we will owe it to the French labor organizations and the Allemanists. You know that the anarchists in a strict sense have been very divided throughout on the question of the congress, and because of this they have done almost nothing' (Hamon Papers, file 109).

The anarchists did not win, but they did come out well. Various British newspapers, including the mass circulation radical liberal *Star* and the literary weekly *The New Age*, sympathetically reported the libertarians' battles (Levy, 'Malatesta in London', 34). Most notably, the anarchists won the sympathy of the *Clarion*, the main newspaper of British socialism, with a circulation of 60,000 ('Blatchford'). Its editor Robert Blatchford sternly remarked that the congress proceedings were conducted with 'intolerance and contempt' and presented socialism as 'a cast-iron creed administered by a dictatorship or priesthood of superior persons of the conference platform type'. Moreover, the vote of the French delegation was an important event that foreshadowed the predominant role that anarchists would have in the labor movement in the following years. For the French anarchists as for Malatesta and the Italians, the congress was a step in the constructive path toward asserting anarchism as a significant force in workers' collective struggles.

Two methodological approaches at cross purposes

Malatesta was guided along the labor-oriented path by his view of the re-lationship between conscious minorities and masses, which he had evolved from his criticism of the First International and which his article for the *Labour Leader* hinted to. This view sharply contrasted with the marxists'. The struggle at the London congress stemmed from radically different outlooks on the relationship between conscious minorities and masses, which in turn proceeded from opposite perspectives on the relation between theory and practice, or knowledge and action. In order to make sense of the struggle between marxists and anarchists those theoretical foundations need to be explained, so as to understand how the respective stances were both inter-nally coherent and mutually exclusive. This way one can avoid causalistic explanations in terms of irrational motives, such as the psychological and temperamental differences purported by Joll, or in terms of contingent or opportunistic reasons. In turn, illustrating how Malatesta's theoretical foun-dations differed from those of marxism makes it clear how his novel tactical orientation represented both change and continuity in its departure from the anarchist stances of the First International and its reassertion of anarchist principles in contrast with marxism.

Explanations of the London congress controversy in terms of contin-gent reasons tend to present the contrast asymmetrically, the stronger side having the stronger reasons. The anarchists' expulsion would result from the marxists' desire to get on with their own business, in the face of the anarchists' aimless disruptiveness. However, the marxists' exclusionary at-titude was not accessory, but essential to their theory. An apparently mar-ginal example helps set the terms of the question. In January 1896, as congress preparations were in full swing, the London Jewish anarchist L. Baron asked the secretary of the congress committee Will Thorne whether a trade union not believing in parliamentary action was entitled to send a delegate to the congress. Thorne responded: 'all Trade Unions recognize the necessity of political action: that being so, the Zurich resolution covers them' (Baron). This might seem a throw-away response dictated by contin-gent reasons. Yet a straight line connects that response to the theoretical tenets of marxism.

The marxist relation between theory and practice rested on a conflation between the positive and normative spheres. Any contrast between 'is' and 'ought' was rejected. As early as 1843 Marx urged: 'it is out of the world's own principles that we develop for it new principles' ('Correspondence', 44–5). In *The German Ideology* he and Engels argued that communism was not 'a state of affairs which is to be established, an ideal to which reality will have to adjust itself', but 'the real movement which abolishes the present state of things', whose conditions resulted 'from the premises now in existence' (187). And in the *Communist Manifesto* they explained that 'the theoretical conclusions of the Communists are in no way based on ideas or principles that have been invented, or discovered, by this or that would-be universal reformer'; rather, 'they merely express, in general terms, actual relations springing from an existing class struggle, from a historical movement going on under our very eyes' (256). As Steven Lukes notes, marxism rejected all moral vocabulary (3), regarding moral thinking as stemming from cognitive inadequacy (6). In rejecting abstract ideals, marxism placed great emphasis on knowledge as a guide of action.

The marxist conflation of positive and normative was characteristically expressed by the notion of 'historical mission', a normative concept arising from objective, historical circumstances. The proletariat was not to set itself abstract goals, but to become aware of and embrace the aim that the development of productive forces had set for it. The same conflation of positive and normative was present in Marx and Engels's discussion of workers organizing as a political party. It was a marxist axiom that every class struggle was a political struggle. This meant that the workers' interests became class interests only when the economic struggle became political. The notion of the proletariat 'constituting itself as a class' or 'organizing itself into a class' essentially amounted to the constitution of a political party. The process was characterized as necessary, where 'necessity' was interpreted both descriptively and prescriptively. For example, in *The Poverty of Philosophy* Marx aimed to provide a study of 'strikes, combinations and other forms in which the proletarians carry out before our eyes their organization as a class', remarking that combination had 'not yet ceased for an instant to go forward and grow with the development and growth of modern industry' (232). Marx dealt with workers' purposive action, but described the process as historically necessary. Yet at the 1866 Geneva congress of the International, he penned a resolution on trade unions, in which he lamented that these concentrated too exclusively on immediate struggles, and urged them to undertake just what, in *The Poverty of Philosophy*, he had claimed that proletarians were carrying out before everyone's eyes: the promotion of the political organization of the working class (Lozovsky, 17–18).

The marxist equation between class struggle and political struggle, as implied by the Zurich resolution (*International Socialist*, 194), informed the whole London congress. The equation was most clearly represented by the demand that Jean Jaurés and other French socialists put forward to be admitted without credentials, on the sole ground of being socialist members of Parliament. The assumption underlying such obliteration of any distinction between political and labor representation was that political representation was the strongest form of workers' mandate. Shortly before his own case was discussed, Jaurés had supported the Zurich resolution arguing that 'trade unionism of itself and by itself is powerless... Trade unionism must be a political movement; it must capture political power...' (*International Socialist*, 202). Thus, when marxists argued that social-democrats and anarchists were distinct parties, and the former had every right to separately convene, they ignored the real objection ('Congress'; Pearson). As Kropotkin stated, anarchists would have not objected to an explicitly social democratic congress ('Workers'). The point was that the congress was meant to involve the whole working class, with trade unions and social democrats respectively representing the class 'in itself' and 'for itself'. Anarchism was thus denied a place in the working class, as per the claim that 'every class struggle is a political struggle'. The claim was both descriptive and prescriptive: a historical process was both acknowledged and enforced. Thus, when Will Thorne stated: 'all Trade Unions recognize the necessity of political action: that being so, the Zurich resolution covers them', he was conflating an allegedly descriptive statement about trade unions with its normative counterpart represented by the Zurich resolution, thus providing an example of the marxist unity of theory and practice.

Malatesta shared with marxists the advocacy of the socialists' involvement in the labor movement, but he differed from them on all key points concerning the role of a political organization, and its relation with other parties, unions, and workers. In turn, tactical differences proceeded from opposite theoretical and methodological approaches. While marxist theory was based on the conflation of the positive and normative spheres, Malatesta's theory was based on a sharp distinction between them. Such distinction was closely linked to his voluntarism and had important ramifications on his view on class. The contrast between marxists and anarchists on such themes had already arisen at the time of the First International, but the theoretical roots of such contrast became increasingly explicit in Malatesta's later elaboration. Similarly to his voluntarism, the distinction between the descriptive and prescriptive domains was already fully at work in Malatesta's ideas of the 1890s, but he expounded it in detail only much later. The most comprehensive exposition can be found in the same series of articles, which appeared in *Volontà* in 1913–14, in which he dealt with voluntarism, in reaction to the positivistic scientism made popular among anarchists by Kropotkin.

The premise of Malatesta's distinction between positive and normative was the mutual exclusion between determinism and voluntarism. Determinism, he argued, was a sure guide in the study of the physico-chemical world, but its consequential application in the social sphere undermined the very possibility of conceiving purposive action, in contrast to the plain fact that any individual undertook purposive action. Malatesta neither denied the logical cogency of determinism, nor the pragmatic cogency of the will's efficacy, even if they contradicted each other. He acknowledged the dualism, but made no attempt to resolve it. Accordingly, Malatesta looked upon attempts to infer practical aims from empirical observation as instrumental. Arguments about 'revolution not being made by the caprice of man' and 'coming only when the time is ripe for it', he argued, were just expedients to steer efforts in one or the other direction ('Liberty').

Even the positivistic pretense of giving anarchism solid scientific foundations, despite its best intentions, made such foundations shakier, based as they were on mutable hypotheses. If an anarchist was really such because of scientific convictions, he would have to 'continually consult the latest bulletins of the Academy of Science in order to determine whether he can continue to be an anarchist'. For Malatesta, science 'does not tell man what to desire, whether he should love or hate, be good or bad, just or unjust. Goodness, justice, and right are concepts which science ignores completely' ('Science').

Though science could not provide normative statements, purposeful action did not escape scientific analysis. Malatesta drew a distinction between natural sciences, which dealt with the physical world, and social sciences, whose task was 'to uncover, to determine what are the necessary facts, the fatal laws resulting from people living together in the diverse circumstances in which they can find themselves, thus preventing vain efforts and enabling the wills of all men to concur to a common aim, beneficial to everyone, instead of paralyzing each other'. Yet anarchy could not be demonstrated, for it was based upon sentiments such as respect of the human person and love. Unlike an argument, which was logically cogent, a sentiment could only be communicated by awakening a similar sentiment in one's mind. Science could not create sentiments, and human redemption could only be the work of 'the will of those who wish such redemption' ('Volontà').

Malatesta's anarchism and marxism looked at the relation between positive and normative from opposite perspectives, which were rooted in opposite methodological stances. The marxist method of looking at social reality as a concrete totality aimed precisely at overcoming the dichotomies between subject and object, normative and positive, voluntarism and determinism. Conversely, such dichotomies were ineliminable for Malatesta, who founded upon them his approach to social action. In contrast to marxist holism, Malatesta's point of departure was methodologically individualist. For him, individual aims and intentional action were the elements of social reality, which was the resultant of the interaction of individual forces acting in different directions, sometimes concurring to a common aim and sometimes paralyzing each other.

In contrast to the idea that history had a knowable line of march, with change spurred by endogenous 'contradictions', Malatesta emphasized indeterminacy and unforeseeable exogenous factors. At an anti-parliamentarian debate on 'agricultural propaganda' in margin to the London congress, Malatesta and Pouget joined forces against the opinion that the rural population was worth the anarchists' attention only insofar as it was proletarianized, thus being turned into a revolutionary force. For Pouget, such beliefs revealed that 'fallacious marxist ideas' were still lingering among anarchists; instead, these 'must not wait for an impossible development sketched out by

Marx; but take matters as they really are'. Malatesta added that the marxists' rule of conduct toward rural populations was 'to contrive to bring them on a level with the English labourers', for which Marx had 'laid down the further course of development'. Were socialists to 'wait for a hundred years', he asked, 'until the alleged concentration eliminates the last peasant?' Not even this was certain, 'for anything, such as the invention of a new electric motor decentralizing machine power might turn the whole course of events another way' ('Report').

The pragmatic implications of the methodological and theoretical divide described thus far were manifold. From the marxist holistic perspective, there was one line of march of history, hence there was one effective course of action, the one fulfilling the 'historical mission' of the proletariat. For Malatesta, there were as many courses of action as aims collectively pursued by social actors. Not each one was viable, though. Given one's aim, its achievement depended on the non-arbitrary selection of the appropriate means. Finding such means was an empirical problem, to be solved experimentally. Social sciences helped precisely to determine the possible forms of social life.

Another difference concerned revolutionary minorities. Marx and Engels claimed in the *Communist Manifesto* that communists 'do not form a separate party opposed to other working-class parties' and 'have no interests separate and apart from those of the proletariat as a whole' (255–6). For Marx, every class struggle was political, and it was only on the political terrain that workers acted as a class. Thus, marxists posited continuity between trade unions and 'the working class organized as a party'. As the working class was one, there could only be one such party, representing the interests of the whole class.

Malatesta's views were diametrically opposed. For him, only in the economic terrain could workers act as a class, because only there did they share the common interest of resisting capitalists, while there were as many political aims as working-class parties. Accordingly, Malatesta kept apart workers' organizations for economic resistance and revolutionary parties aiming at the overthrow of capitalism. Unions were to be independent from revolutionary ideals, or else there would be as many of them as political ideals, with an unnecessary fragmentation even in the economic struggle. Anarchists were to 'go to the people', but unions were not and could not be anarchist. Conversely, anarchists were to organize autonomously, without dampening ideals for the sake of class unity thrust upon them on the terrain of revolutionary aims.

In sum, Malatesta's urge that anarchists get involved in the labor movement and in economic struggles and his consequent battle for their admission to the London congress rested on very different premises from the anarchists' battle in the First International. Malatesta's new premise was the distinction between unions and political organizations. The residue of authoritarianism that he recognized in the anarchists' struggle for hegemony in the First International stemmed, in his view, from their failure to draw that distinction. Such failure to differentiate between unions and parties still characterized the marxist standpoint at the London congress. At the same time that Malatesta's new tactics were based on a criticism of anarchism in the old International, the theoretical foundations of his tactics made explicit elements that already set apart anarchists from marxists in the First International, such as voluntarism and a view of class solidarity as proceeding from ideals and values rather than from material interests alone.

Hence, Malatesta's new tactics implied both continuity and change with respect to the First International. There was continuity with elements that had always set apart anarchists from marxists. These only received new emphasis in Malatesta's theoretical foundations. The change consisted in moving further away from marxism. In fact, Malatesta often argued that a key trait of the anarchists' evolution was the riddance of marxist ideas, of which 'anarchists were once more consequential, if not more orthodox, supporters than those who declared themselves marxist and perhaps even than Marx himself' ('Decadenza').

The struggle at the London congress was rooted in this deepening theoretical contrast. The methodological focus on social wholes, the conflation between positive and normative, the idea that history had a knowable line of march, the rejection of ideals, and the role attributed to knowledge in setting aims and providing leadership—all epitomized by such notions as communism being 'the real movement'—were the marxist ground for positing a single, hegemonic working-class party, whose revolutionary political struggle subsumed the day-to-day economic struggle. In contrast, Malatesta's methodological individualism, his dualism between positive and normative, his emphasis on social indeterminacy, his propensity for moral vocabulary, and his voluntarism led him to posit a distinction between a plurality of working-class parties and single, inclusive unions.

Nor was this difference opportunistically dictated by the contingent circumstance that at that time socialists had the upper hand in the labor movement. The conflation of marxist party and working class was already advocated when the Communist League, for which the *Manifesto* was written, was a tiny formation. Conversely, Malatesta's separation between anarchist and labor organizations still held for the case of Spain, where anarchists were majoritarian in the workers' movement.

Explanations of the contrast between marxists and anarchists that fail to acknowledge such fundamental theoretical differences are bound to rest, one way or another, upon the attribution of irrationality.

SUSTAINABLE STRUGGLES AND STEADY GROWTH

For Italian anarchism, especially in its transnational segment, the London congress was part of the debate and propaganda drive for the spread of labor-oriented tactics that had begun before the congress, in parallel with a similar process in France, and that continued right after the congress.

In August 1896 Malatesta's 'anarchist-socialist group' edited in London the single issue 'L'Anarchia', a programmatic manifesto of the new tactics. The editors made clear that they spoke on behalf of a cohesive group, with no pretension to speak for the whole movement: 'If this is bound to determine a split—which, by the way, has already existed for years in a more or less latent state—let it come soon and be very clear, because nothing is more harmful than confusion and misunderstanding.' Luigi Fabbri, then a young anarchist militant in Central Italy, relates that 'L'Anarchia' exerted much influence on the Italian anarchist movement and 'laid the foundations of a whole well-defined and methodical orientation' (*Vida*, 134–6). Malatesta's article 'Errori e rimedi' (Errors and remedies) criticized the ideas of many self-styled anarchists about morals and violence. He argued that 'denying morals' altogether was meaningless, for no society or individual could be conceived without a moral whatsoever; and on the subject of violence he rejected as equally harmful the opposite errors of terrorism and passive resistance. Other contributors dealt with further themes of the new tactics: the anarchists' powerlessness due to divisions; the theoretical byzantinism and practical disorganization at the time of the Sicily and Lunigiana agitations; the need for a separation between advocates and opponents of organization; and the necessity to intermingle with the people, enter its organizations, and live its same life.

In a few months, the initiative would be directly transferred to the Italian soil.

In contrast to the alleged 'disappearances' and 'reappearances' of anarchism, the movements of such militants as Pietro Gori and Antonio Agresti provide a glimpse into the interplay between transnational anarchism and the movement at home. After a stay in London, Gori and Agresti participated in the debate before the congress from the United States. Both returned to London for the congress, where Gori represented Italian groups and workers' associations of North America and Agresti represented French workers. The latter was also among the editors of 'L'Anarchia'. Both were back in Italy by 1897, the year of Malatesta's return.

As for Malatesta, the Ancona anarchist Rodolfo Felicioli recalls that in 1896 Malatesta corresponded from London with Cesare Agostinelli in Ancona. Together they took the decision to start a periodical. In November 1896 Agostinelli and Emidio Recchioni returned to Ancona from *domicilio coatto* (Giulianelli; Dipaola, 'Recchioni'). This may have helped plans fall in place. Furthermore, Saverio Merlino's pronouncement of January 1897 in favor of parliamentary action reinforced and hastened plans for Malatesta's return and for the periodical's publication, so as to counter the potential negative effects of a change of tactics by such an influential figure (Luigi Fabbri, *Vida*, 137). In February 1897 *Freedom* announced the imminent publication of *L'Agitazione* ('International Notes'). Malatesta reached Italy in March, prudentially incognito, though his conviction of 1884 was to lapse within weeks. On 14 March the first issue of *L'Agitazione* appeared, under the editorship of Malatesta.

Without repudiating revolution and anti-parliamentarianism, *L'Agitazione* preached novel tactics for Italy, advocating the intervention of anarchist-socialists in labor struggles for immediate economic gains. Moreover, it maintained that political liberties could be obtained neither by abstention, nor parliamentarian means, but rather by direct and conscious action of the people (*Processo*, 13–14). The events of socialism in the previous half decade were the backdrop to the new tactics. The founding of a parliamentarian socialist party in Italy in 1892 had the two segments of socialism take different routes, with parliamentarians increasingly gaining momentum in Italy in workers' economic and legal resistance. Moreover, Malatesta's resolution that a clear-cut separation between anarchists was in order gave him a free hand in decidedly pursuing organizationist tactics and participation in the labor movement, challenging socialists on the ground where they had made progress.

The new tactics were based on a self-criticism on behalf of Italian anarchism, guilty of drawing away from the people. The juvenile mazzinian illusion that revolution could come soon by the action of a minority had made anarchists averse to any long and patient work to prepare and organize the people. Strikes were frowned upon and the labor movement only appreciated as a source of recruits for insurrection ('Evoluzione dell'anarchismo', *Agitazione*). The traditional forms of revolution, Malatesta argued, were still excellent, but in most situations they remained wishful thinking. The insurrectionary spirit still had great value, but by neglecting modest means of struggle one ended up being powerless. This was why legalitarians had gained momentum ('Anarchismo nel movimento'). Conversely, the anarchists' focus on insurrection exposed them to unnecessary persecutions and drew away the most advanced workers, who saw their own success in wresting improvements from their masters as a refutation of anarchist claims. These errors had reduced anarchism to such isolation and dissolution as to be unable to oppose any resistance to Crispi's reaction, and to raise any solidarity ('Evoluzione dell'anarchismo', *Agitazione*).

Revolution was a longer process than anarchists had believed. A long-term, daily commitment was required, made of practical work in trade unions, cooperatives, and educational societies ('1° Maggio'). The labor movement was to be the foundation of the anarchists' strength and the guarantee that the next revolution would be truly socialist and anarchist. In response to Pietro Gori's piqued reaction to Malatesta's claim that Italian anarchists had been indifferent to the labor movement, the latter stressed the difference between theoretical statements in favor of the labor movement, or sporadic attempts to organize workers, and a constant, methodic, generalized work.

The latter had never been undertaken in Italy or elsewhere, except in Spain. Malatesta recalled the reaction to the Sicilian Fasci as a case of anarchist prejudice against labor organizations that were not fully anarchist. At present, anarchists had a foothold in too few unions, notwithstanding their support to them (note to Gori, 'Postilla'). The struggle was still twofold, against government and capitalists. However, economic oppression took priority. The economic struggle implied the political one, though the reverse did not necessarily hold. The economic struggle was more difficult to suppress, because workers were indispensable for production. Hence, no matter how strong reaction was, it still remained possible to fight the bosses, and thus the government, which anarchists were powerless to attack head-on ('Alba').

Describing revolution as the end-point of a process, rather than a circumscribed event, involved clarifying the difference between the new tactics and reformism, to face both the anarchist charge of wasting time in 'agitations made of paper and chatter' ('Nostra'), and the socialist argument that anarchists were evolving toward them. For Malatesta, 'the workers' real condition at a given time depended—all the rest being equal—on the degree of resistance that they could oppose to the masters' demands' ('Leghe'). In contrast with the errors of classic revolutionaries, Malatesta argued that bourgeois institutions could still yield much before capitulating. In the past, both republicans and anarchists committed all expectations of social change to the overthrow of governments. This created a rift between present and future, which in practice meant that their day-to-day work was limited to propaganda and futile military preparations, awaiting the day of insurrection. Instead, Malatesta insisted, revolutionaries should be interested in wresting any possible concessions, both to diminish present sufferings and to hasten the final conflict. People were so much apter to revolution as their conditions were better and they developed confidence through resistance and struggle ('Decadenza'). Not only was there room for improvement within the bourgeois society, but, more importantly, every concession wrested from the bosses brought nearer the point of crisis at which violent conflict would be unavoidable.

The First of May agitations were a case in point. The key thing was for workers to get used to collectively asserting themselves, not the specific reforms that they demanded. As long as workers knew how to assert themselves, it would become easier to make them understand what they should really pursue. The eight-hour workday, for example, was indeed a poor reform, but it was a mistake for anarchists to deplore it, for the struggle would promote class consciousness. In order to bring one's arguments home to the workers, one had to live and fight with them. Neither could the people accept anarchist ideas at once, nor could society suddenly jump from hell to heaven. Still, every step was a real advantage, so long as it went in the right direction—the abolition of authority and individual property—and developed the workers' spirit and habit of free and voluntary cooperation ('Echi').

Malatesta further illustrated the value of labor struggles by commenting upon the Toulouse double congress of the *Bourses du Travail* and the *Confédération Générale du Travail*, held in September 1897. It was not an anarchist congress, and rightly so, as it was for all workers. Yet anarchist tactics prevailed, thus showing that 'the conscious part of the French proletariat, even when they do not comprehend or accept our general principles, can devise the way that must lead to the end of human exploitation'. The congress had accepted direct action methods: strikes, boycotts, ca'canny, and sabotage, many of which were new for Italy. These, Malatesta remarked, might seem petty means of struggle, only good for 'legalitarians'. However, the prejudice against such methods was due to the fact that in Italy the collective consciousness of class struggle had been lacking until recently, and hence antagonism had mostly found individual outlets. Socialists, including anarchists, had to foster the consciousness of class antagonism and of the need for collective struggle. To the extent that a new consciousness would spread, the tactics being adopted in France and long used in England would also become practicable and useful in Italy ('Anarchismo nel movimento').

Malatesta's ideas were criticized by Italian comrades, who accused him of wanting to introduce *inglesismo* (Anglicism) in Italy, by which they meant the fashion of struggling imported from British unions. Their argument was that legal resistance and slow organization were not suitable for Italy, where legal resistance, if successful at all, would soon escalate into riots. Malatesta pointed out that the alleged Italian revolutionary spirit had not manifested itself for decades, and he rejected the criticism: 'Forget about *inglesismo*. If this term means anything at all, it means economic resistance for its own sake, as it was practiced by the "old" trade unions, which—though they wanted to improve the workers' conditions—accepted and respected the capitalist system and all the bourgeois institutions.' In contrast, Malatesta believed that workers' organizations, economic resistance, and other more or less legal forms of resistance were means toward the total transformation of society, which ultimately, he restated, could not occur peacefully ('Nostra'). The substance of the matter was the long and patient work that Malatesta urged anarchists to undertake. However, the mistrust that 'foreign' tactics met with implicitly speaks to the broad-mindedness that transnationalism gave to anarchist exiles.

At the same time that he restated that class struggle could only have an insurrectionary solution, Malatesta placed new emphasis on sustainability. Though their ultimate aim was the complete transformation of society, anarchists were not to bite off more than they could chew. Thus, in the face of criticisms to *L'Agitazione*'s support to a campaign against a law that introduced *domicilio coatto* as an ordinary measure, Malatesta admitted the narrow character of the agitation and the anarchists' even narrower role: 'Yet what should be done, if the others do not want to do more, and we do not have the strength to do more ourselves?' In order to undertake more radical initiatives, such as riots and aggressive strikes, one had to be in a position to do so, or else have the patience to work and wait until that time would come: 'what those friends are suggesting to us has already been done, or attempted, by both us and them for years on end, without any success. And if we managed to morally survive and preserve our capability to do better, it was simply because we have always dearly paid in person for our deeds.' Malatesta and his comrades did not intend to eternally run through the same cycle: 'six months of quiet activity; then some microscopically tiny uprising, or more often simple threats of uprisings; and then arrests, escapes abroad, interruption of the propaganda, disbandment of the organization', only to start over again the same story two or three years later. 'Now', Malatesta concluded, 'we have persuaded ourselves—and yet it took us a long time!—that in order to act one must have the necessary strength for acting; and if time is required to gain such a strength, we will have the patience to wait for as long as it takes' ('Nostra').

The emphasis on sustainability involved a new attention to adjusting anarchist struggles to the horizon provided by the current legislation—a strikingly novel theme in its moderate and pragmatistic tone, which resonated awkwardly to many anarchist ears. The focus on sustainability involved carrying out as much propaganda as possible within legal boundaries, undertaking campaigns against the introduction of more repressive laws, such as *domicilio coatto*, or against existing laws, such as the infamous article 248 of the penal code, which equated anarchist organizations to associations of malefactors. Accordingly, a new emphasis was placed on defensive struggles. Malatesta discussed the anarchists' attitude toward the law in the article 'Il dovere della resistenza: Gli anarchici e la legge' (The duty of resistance: anarchists and the law). While the word 'insurrection' rarely appeared in *L'Agitazione*, 'resistance' was Malatesta's recurring term: 'economic resistance against the masters' exploitation; political resistance against the violations of freedom, and moral resistance against anything that contributes to let workers be considered or treated as an inferior caste.' Rebellion for its own sake had to be set aside; the focus was to be on the means conducive to victory. The conflict with the law was to be precipitated when the chances were in the anarchists' favor. For the time being, they were to do what could be done usefully: 'Since we have not been able to gain enough strength to resist the law, yet, at least let us resist—and incite the people to resist—within the limits of the law. That is already enough to take us a long way.'

Opposing legalitarian tactics to achieve emancipation did not mean shunning legal means. Indeed, Malatesta remarked, the law was the weapon of the privileged. Yet some laws were popular victories, because they replaced more oppressive ones, under collective pressure. It was indeed bad for people to be happy with a law, instead of imposing their full right; but it was even worse when people, after wresting a concession out of their masters' scare, quietly let it be taken back, only to fight the same struggles over and over again. Such was the situation in Italy, where all political liberties—freedom of press, association, and assembly, house inviolability, mail secrecy, personal freedom, and so on—were lost or about to be lost, unless a strong reawakening of the public opinion put a check on police arrogance. To such reawakening and resistance anarchists were most interested, because they were hardest hit, and above all because the loss of liberties would produce the huge harm of taking the struggle back from the economic to the political ground ('Dovere della resistenza'). Hence, it was legitimate for anarchists harmed by an abuse of power to demand that the law be respected, as Nino Samaja argued in the article 'In difesa della legge' (In defense of law).

Malatesta thus described the tactics of moral resistance that circumstances imposed on the anarchist movement:

> Since presently we cannot gain broader freedom, at least let us use whatever freedom the law leaves us: however, let us use it to its extreme limit. If the defenders of the law violate it against our persons and actions—as they unfortunately do—we will profit from the anti-legalitarian propaganda that spontaneously results from any abuse of power.
>
> ('In alto')

Entrenchment in popular and workers' movements and organization in broad daylight were the anarchists' weapons to counteract government repression. Before the attempts to take away freedom of association and to treat anarchists as an association of malefactors, these were to associate ever more, publicly and visibly, using public venues whenever possible, and publishing their program and the addresses of their groups, associations, and federations on the newspapers: 'Eventually, people will wonder who these new and strange *malefactors* are, which demand daylight instead of seeking obscurity, and willingly suffer for an openly avowed cause—and deep down every person of heart will feel a little bit like a malefactor.' Likewise, before attempts to take away the anarchists' right of free speech, these were to profit from every opportunity to let their voice be heard, or, where there was no opportunity, to create it. Anarchists were numerous enough to make persecutions powerless to halt their march, if they all fulfilled their duty: 'Great as the reactionary rage of our oppressors can be, they can jail, deport, or force to exile but a tiny part of us' ('In alto').

The continuity of Malatesta's tactics of 1897–98 should be emphasized along with their novelty. All the tactical tenets illustrated earlier on were still present, though their relative weight changed. Less emphasis was placed on insurrectionism, not because insurrection was no longer viable, but because the road to it was longer than previously hoped. In contrast, a renewed emphasis was placed on 'going to the people' and inclusiveness. Yet, as the importance of partial struggles for economic concessions and legal resistance was acknowledged, coherence between ends and means was reaffirmed, thus distinguishing Malatesta's tactics from pure and simple reformism. Economic and legal resistance were not so much important for the actual concessions being wrested, as for the way in which they were wrested and for the struggling habit induced in workers. Finally, as participation in the labor movement was advocated, anarchist autonomy was reaffirmed: 'This is our program', Malatesta wrote, 'against the masters, with all the workers; against the government, with all the enemies of the government; for anarchist socialism, with all the anarchist socialists' ('Lotta politica').

ANARCHISM, PARLIAMENTARIANISM, AND DECISION MAKING

The continuity of Malatesta's ideas was not only tactical, but also theoretical. At the same time that he emphasized the theme of sustainability, the importance of legal battles, the value of economic struggles for immediate objectives and reform, and the room for progress within the bourgeois society, he rejected parliamentarianism as strongly as ever, clarifying the common theoretical foundations of such rejection and his new tactics.

The opportunity for this clarification came from a long debate between Malatesta and Saverio Merlino about parliamentarianism and democracy, which had started in the press shortly before *L'Agitazione* appeared and continued in Malatesta's paper from its first issue throughout 1897. The controversy set out as a disagreement about tactics, but its scope soon extended, revealing a profound divide of methodological nature. It was one of the most insightful debates about anarchism and parliamentarianism of which we have written record, owing to the intellectual capacity of the opponents, the constructive atmosphere of mutual respect and friendship, and the extent of the debate that allowed the opponents to amply articulate arguments and objections. The opponents were probably as close as a supporter of anarchism and one of parliamentarianism could be; yet their differences proved irreconcilable. Hence, the debate provides an opportunity to assess what the nature of such differences was, as well as to analyze Malatesta's viewpoints on a number of tactical and theoretical issues that illuminate the foundations of his anarchism.

The controversy started when Merlino, in a letter to the daily *Il Messaggero* of 29 January 1897, proposed that Italian anarchists use their right to vote in the upcoming March elections. Merlino presented his proposal as a tactical one, maintaining that the real battle was to be waged outside of parliament. Still, he argued, there was no reason for not fighting that battle during elections, too. Bad as it was, parliamentarianism was better than absolutism. Anarchist socialists did not need to run for election, as they did not aim for power. Still, a socialist member of parliament was preferable to a reactionary one, and anarchist votes could make a difference ('Al partito').

While conceding that parliamentarianism was preferable to absolutism, Malatesta countered that political liberties were only obtained when the

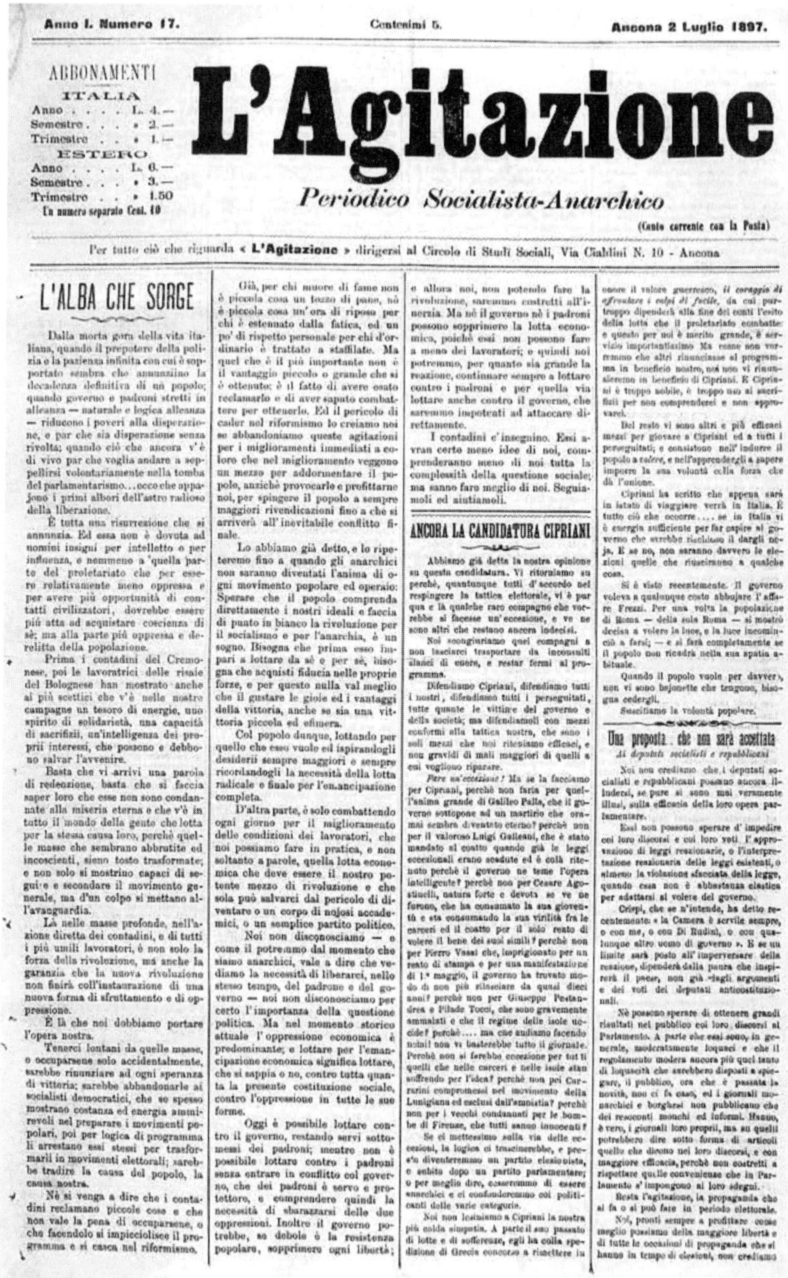

Anno I. Numero 17. Centesimi 5. Ancona 2 Luglio 1897.

ABBONAMENTI
ITALIA
Anno . . . . L. 4.—
Semestre . . . » 2.—
Trimestre . . . » 1.—
ESTERO
Anno . . . . L. 6.—
Semestre . . . » 3.—
Trimestre . . . » 1.50
Un numero separato Cent. 10

L'Agitazione

Periodico Socialista-Anarchico

(Conto corrente con la Posta)

Per tutto ciò che riguarda « **L'Agitazione** » dirigersi al Circolo di Studi Sociali, Via Cialdini N. 10 - Ancona

L'ALBA CHE SORGE

Dalla morta gora della vita italiana, quando il prepotere della polizia e la pazienza infinita con cui è sopportato sembra che annunziino la decadenza definitiva di un popolo; quando governo e padroni stretti in alleanza — naturale e logica alleanza — riducono i poveri alla disperazione, e par che sia disperazione senza rivolta; quando ciò che ancora v'è di vivo par che voglia andare a seppellirsi volontariamente nella tomba del parlamentarismo. . .ecco che appajono i primi albori dell'astro radioso della liberazione.

È tutta una risurrezione che si annunzia. Ed essa non è dovuta ad uomini insigni per intelletto o per influenza, e nemmeno a quella parte del proletariato che per essere relativamente meno oppressa e per avere più opportunità di contatti civilizzatori, dovrebbe essere più atta ad acquistare coscienza di sè; ma alla parte più oppressa e derelitta della popolazione.

Prima i contadini del Cremonese, poi le lavoratrici delle risaie del Bolognese han mostrato anche ai più scettici che v'è nelle nostre campagne un tesoro di energie, uno spirito di solidarietà, una capacità di sacrifizii, un'intelligenza dei proprii interessi, che possono e debbono salvar l'avvenire.

Basta che vi arrivi una parola di redenzione, basta che si faccia saper loro che esse non sono condannate alla miseria eterna e che v'è in tutto il mondo della gente che lotta per la stessa causa loro, perchè quelle masse che sembrano abbrutite ed incoscienti, sieno tosto trasformate; e non solo si mostrino capaci di seguire e secondare il movimento generale, ma d'un colpo si mettano all'avanguardia.

Là nelle masse profonde, nell'azione diretta dei contadini, e di tutti i più umili lavoratori, è non solo la forza della rivoluzione, ma anche la garanzia che la nuova rivoluzione non finirà coll'instaurazione di una nuova forma di sfruttamento e di oppressione.

È là che noi dobbiamo portare l'opera nostra.

Tenerci lontani da quelle masse, o occuparsene solo accidentalmente, sarebbe rinunziare ad ogni speranza di vittoria; sarebbe abbandonarle ai socialisti democratici, che se spesso mostrano costanza ed energia ammirevoli nel preparare i movimenti popolari, poi per logica di programma li arrestano essi stessi per trasformarli in movimenti elettorali; sarebbe tradire la causa del popolo, la causa nostra.

Nè si venga a dire che i contadini reclamano piccole cose e che non vale la pena di occuparsene, o che facendolo si impiccolisce il programma e si casca nel riformismo.

Già, per chi muore di fame non è piccola cosa un tozzo di pane, nè è piccola cosa un'ora di riposo per chi è estenuato dalla fatica, ed un po' di rispetto personale per chi d'ordinario è trattato a staffilate. Ma quel che è il più importante non è il vantaggio piccolo o grande che si è ottenuto: è il fatto di avere osato reclamarlo e di aver saputo combattere per ottenerlo. Ed il pericolo di cader nel riformismo lo creiamo noi se abbandoniamo queste agitazioni per i miglioramenti immediati a coloro che nel miglioramento veggono un mezzo per addormentare il popolo, anzichè provocarlo e profittarne noi, per spingere il popolo a sempre maggiori rivendicazioni fino a che si arriverà all'inevitabile conflitto finale.

Lo abbiamo già detto, e lo ripeteremo fino a quando gli anarchici non saranno diventati l'anima di ogni movimento popolare ed operaio: Sperare che il popolo comprenda direttamente i nostri ideali e faccia di punto in bianco la rivoluzione per il socialismo e per l'anarchia, è un sogno. Bisogna che prima esso impari a lottare da sè e per sè, bisogna che acquisti fiducia nelle proprie forze, e per questo nulla val meglio che il gustare le gioie ed i vantaggi della vittoria, anche se sia una vittoria piccola ed efimera.

Col popolo dunque, lottando per quello che esso vuole ed ispirandogli desiderii sempre maggiori e sempre ricordandogli la necessità della lotta radicale e finale per l'emancipazione completa.

D'altra parte, è solo combattendo ogni giorno per il miglioramento delle condizioni dei lavoratori, che noi possiamo fare in pratica, e non soltanto a parole, quella lotta economica che deve essere il nostro potente mezzo di rivoluzione e che sola può salvarci dal pericolo di diventare o un corpo di nojosi accademici, o un semplice partito politico.

Noi non disconosciamo — e come il potremmo dal momento che siamo anarchici, vale a dire che vediamo la necessità di liberarci, nello stesso tempo, del padrone e del governo — noi non disconosciamo per certo l'importanza della questione politica. Ma nel momento storico attuale l'oppressione economica è predominante; e lottare per l'emancipazione economica significa lottare, che si sappia o no, contro tutta quanta la presente costituzione sociale, contro l'oppressione in tutte le sue forme.

Oggi è possibile lottare contro il governo, restando servi sottomessi dei padroni; mentre non è possibile lottare contro i padroni senza entrare in conflitto col governo, che dei padroni è servo e protettore, e comprendere quindi la necessità di sbarazzarsi delle due oppressioni. Inoltre il governo potrebbe, se debole è la resistenza popolare, sopprimere ogni libertà; e allora noi, non potendo fare la rivoluzione, saremmo costretti all'inerzia. Ma nè il governo nè i padroni possono sopprimere la lotta economica, poichè essi non possono fare a meno dei lavoratori; e quindi noi potremmo, per quanto sia grande la reazione, continuare sempre a lottare contro i padroni e per quella via lottare anche contro il governo, che saremmo impotenti ad attaccare direttamente.

I contadini c'insegnino. Essi avran certo meno idee di noi, comprenderanno meno di noi tutta la complessità della questione sociale; ma sanno fare meglio di noi. Seguiamoli ed aiutiamoli.

ANCORA LA CANDIDATURA CIPRIANI

Abbiamo già detta la nostra opinione su questa candidatura. Vi ritorniamo su perchè, quantunque tutti d'accordo nel respingere la tattica elettorale, vi è pur qua e là qualche raro compagno che vorrebbe si facesse un'eccezione, e ve ne sono altri che restano ancora indecisi.

Noi scongiuriamo quei compagni a non lasciarci trasportare da inconsulti slanci di cuore, e restar fermi al programma.

Difendiamo Cipriani, difendiamo tutti i nostri, difendiamo tutti i perseguitati, tutte quante le vittime del governo e della società; ma difendiamoli con mezzi conformi alla tattica nostra, che sono i soli mezzi che noi riteniamo efficaci, e non gravidi di mali maggiori di quelli a cui vogliono riparare.

Fare un'eccezione! Ma se la facciamo per Cipriani, perchè non farla per quell'anima grande di Galileo Palla, che il governo sottopone ad un martirio che oramai sembra diventato eterno? perchè non per il valoroso Luigi Galleani, che è stato mandato al coatto quando già le leggi eccezionali erano scadute ed è colà ritenuto perchè il governo ne teme l'opera intelligente? perchè non per Cesare Agostinelli, natura forte e devota se ve ne furono, che ha consumato la sua gioventù e sta consumando la sua virilità fra le carceri ed il coatto per il solo reato di volere il bene dei suoi simili? perchè non per Pietro Vasai che, imprigionato per un reato di stampa e per una manifestazione di 1.° maggio, il governo ha trovato modo di non più rilasciare da quasi dieci anni? perchè non per Giuseppe Pestandrea e Pilade Tocci, che sono gravemente ammalati e che il regime delle isole uccide? perchè. . . . ma che andiamo facendo nomi! non vi basterebbe tutto il giornale. Perchè non si farebbe eccezione per tutti quelli che nelle carceri e nelle isole stan soffrendo per l'idea? perchè non pei Carrarini compromessi nel movimento della Lunigiana ed esclusi dall'amnistia? perchè non per i vecchi condannati per le bombe di Firenze, che tutti sanno innocenti?

Se ci mettessimo sulla via delle eccezioni, la logica ci trascinerebbe, e presto diventeremmo un partito elezionista, e subito dopo un partito parlamentare; o per meglio dire, cesseremmo di essere anarchici e ci confonderemmo coi politicanti delle varie categorie.

Noi non lesiniamo a Cipriani la nostra più calda simpatia. A parte il suo passato di lotte e di sofferenze, egli ha colla spedizione di Grecia concorso a rimettere in onore il valore guerresco, *il coraggio di affrontare i colpi di fucile,* da cui purtroppo dipenderà alla fine dei conti l'esito della lotta che il proletariato combatte: e questo per noi è merito grande, è servizio importantissimo. Ma come non vorremmo che altri rinunciasse al programma in beneficio nostro, noi non vi rinunzieremo in beneficio di Cipriani. E Cipriani è troppo nobile, è troppo uso ai sacrifizii per non comprenderci e non approvarci.

Del resto vi sono altri e più efficaci mezzi per giovare a Cipriani ed a tutti i perseguitati; e consistono nell'indurre il popolo a *volere*, e nell'apprendergli a sapere imporre la sua volontà colla forza che dà l'unione.

Cipriani ha scritto che appena sarà in istato di viaggiare verrà in Italia. È tutto ciò che occorre. . . . se in Italia vi è energia sufficiente per far capire al governo che sarebbe rischioso il dargli noja. E se no, non saranno davvero le elezioni quelle che riusciranno a qualche cosa.

Si è visto recentemente. Il governo voleva a qualunque costo abbujare l'affare Frezzi. Per una volta la popolazione di Roma — della sola Roma — si mostrò decisa a volere la luce, e la luce incominciò a farsi; — e si farà completamente se il popolo non ricadrà nella sua apatia abituale.

Quando il popolo vuole per davvero, non vi sono bajonette che tengono, bisogna cedergli.

Suscitiamo la volontà popolare.

Una proposta. che non sarà accettata

Ai deputati socialisti e repubblicani

Noi non crediamo che i deputati socialisti e repubblicani possano ancora illudersi, se pure si sono mai veramente illusi, sulla efficacia della loro opera parlamentare.

Essi non possono sperare d'impedire coi loro discorsi e coi loro voti l'approvazione di leggi reazionarie, o l'interpretazione reazionaria delle leggi esistenti, o almeno la violazione sfacciata della legge, quando essa non è abbastanza elastica per adattarsi al volere del governo.

Crispi, che se n'intende, ha detto recentemente: « la Camera è servile sempre, o con me, o con Di Rudinì, o con qualunque altro uomo di governo ». E se un limite sarà posto all'imperversare della reazione, dipenderà dalla paura che ispirerà il paese, non già dagli argomenti e dai voti dei deputati anticostituzionali.

Nè possono sperare di ottenere grandi risultati nel pubblico coi loro discorsi al Parlamento. A parte che essi sono, in generale, moderatamente loquaci e che il regolamento modera ancora più quel tanto di loquacità che sarebbero disposti a spiegare, il pubblico, ora che è passata la novità, non ci fa caso, ed i giornali monarchici e borghesi non pubblicano che dei resoconti monchi ed informi. Hanno, è vero, i giornali loro proprii, ma su quelli potrebbero dire sotto forma di articoli quello che dicono nei loro discorsi, e con maggiore efficacia, perchè non costretti a rispettare quelle convenienze che in Parlamento s'impongono ai loro sdegni.

Resta l'agitazione, la propaganda che si fa o si può fare in periodo elettorale.

Noi, pronti sempre a profittare come meglio possiamo della maggiore libertà e di tutte le occasioni di propaganda che si hanno in tempo di elezioni, non crediamo

FIGURE 7.1 **Front page from an issue of *L'Agitazione***
Source: Biblioteca Nazionale Centrale, Florence

people appeared determined to obtain them, and only lasted as long as governments felt that the people would not tolerate their abolition. Getting people accustomed to delegating the conquest and defense of their rights was the surest way to give rulers a free hand in acting arbitrarily. Likewise, parliamentarianism was better than absolutism only to the extent that it was a concession made out of fear: 'Between accepting and flaunting parliamentarianism, and enduring despotism with one's mind focused on reconquest, despotism is a thousand times better.' The two methods of struggle, inside and outside parliament, were at cross purposes, and by accepting both one fatally ended up sacrificing any other consideration to electoral interests. Merlino himself, Malatesta argued, showed awareness of the danger, when he claimed that anarchists did not need to have their own candidates. However, for Malatesta, this stance was untenable. If anything good could result from parliamentary action, why would anarchists let others take it? If anarchists did not long for power, why should they help those who did? If they had no use for power, what would others do with it, except use it against the people? 'Let Merlino rest assured', Malatesta concluded, 'if we told people to vote today, tomorrow we would tell them to vote for us' ('Socialisti e le elezioni').

The debate illustrated from the outset Malatesta's methodological individualism. He refused to assess parliamentarianism and absolutism as wholes, but broke them up into their components, the dispositions of social actors. His preference for a system depended on the dispositions of individuals that determined that system. He also displayed awareness of the 'heterogony of ends'. Merlino's argument was that, all the rest being equal, there was no reason for not using parliament as a means. Malatesta objected on the ground of coherence between ends and means. The struggles inside and outside parliament served different goals, as revealed by Merlino's own aversion to the anarchists' presence in parliament. Voting would serve anarchist goals only indirectly, by instrumentally furthering the goals of other parties. However, if parliamentarian tactics were seriously pursued, electoral considerations would eventually become predominant. Malatesta did not reject the usefulness of voting, but did reject Merlino's *ceteris paribus* clause, that is, the assumption that one could vote while everything else remained equal. The modification introduced in anarchist behavior by voting was a displacement of goals. The electoral struggle educated one to parliamentarianism, transforming those who practiced it into parliamentarians, including Merlino. Though Malatesta had no doubt about Merlino's honesty in denying ambitions to parliament, the inner logic of supporting parliamentarian tactics would be stronger, and he would end up accepting, if asked to ('Anarchia e parlamentarismo'). 'Abstentionism', Malatesta argued, 'is a question of tactics for us. Yet it is so important that, by giving it up, one ends up giving up the principles, too. This is so because of the natural connection between the means and the end' (note to Merlino, 'Da una questione').

Malatesta's methodological individualism was even more clearly spelled out in the continuation of the debate. When Merlino remarked that it was contradictory for anarchists to abstain from voting while expressing satisfaction for socialist electoral successes ('Poche'), Malatesta responded that he rejoiced not only in a socialist victory over bourgeois parties, but also in a republican victory over monarchists, or even of liberal monarchists over clerical monarchists. Still, that was no good reason for becoming oneself monarchist, liberal, or republican, when one deemed one's own belief to be more advanced (note to Merlino, 'Poche'). Likewise, with respect to Merlino's call in defense of parliamentarianism against the impending dangers of reaction, fostered by the discredit into which parliament was brought by the simultaneous attacks from clericists, Bourbonists, and anarchists ('Pericolo'), Malatesta retorted: 'Such a logic can go a long way, as no institution is so reactionary, harmful, and absurd that someone cannot be found who fights against it to the end of replacing it with something worse.' Instead, he argued, the best way to prevent a return to the past was to render the future ever more threatening for conservatives and reactionaries: 'There would be no constitutional monarchies, if kings had not been afraid of the republic . . . ' ('Difesa'). For Malatesta, the line of march of society depended on the various directions in which its components tended, which in turn depended upon the respective aims. Rather than being determined in advance, that line of march could be acted upon. Making one's aim depend on an assessment of the present society did not make one's action more effective. Rather, by watering down one's program to make it more pragmatic, a group simply weakened its own contribution to the overall direction of society, in favor of the contribution of other, more conservative forces. Hence, seemingly pragmatic moves, such as contributing to the electoral success of socialists or whatever electoral forces were most advanced, or defending parliamentarianism from the specter of reaction, actually bore a regressive character.

The debate soon extended to the role of parliamentarianism, majorities, and minorities in the anarchist society. The two opponents agreed that some decisions would be taken by majority, as unanimity could not always be expected. For Merlino, this amounted to admitting that some form of parliamentarianism would survive. Malatesta countered that any concession by a minority had to be the result of an act of free will, not a principle or a law automatically applied in all cases. For him, this was the difference between anarchy and government ('Da Londra'). Merlino retorted that either one believed in a kropotkinian providential harmony, which Malatesta admittedly rejected, or accepted some form of parliamentarianism ('Da una questione'). Malatesta responded that when minorities refused to yield and majorities abused their strength, anarchy was simply not possible. Likewise, if bullying and violence were rampant in society, the weak would end up invoking a police. Again, in a society of cowards and bullies, anarchy was not possible.

'However things stand, we, the anarchists, are not the whole of humanity, and cannot make all human history by ourselves. However, we can and must work to the realization of our ideas, striving to eliminate as much as possible mutual struggle and coercion from social life' (note to Merlino, 'Da una questione').

In an article for *Revue Socialiste* of June 1897, Merlino further articulated his effort to abandon doctrinaire formulas in favor of practicable socialist schemes, striking a middle path between anarchy and democracy. He argued that the two systems were in contrast only in their utopian versions. As soon as practical application was taken into account, qualifications had to be added, such that the only practicable system ended up being an intermediate form in which the two principles were reconciled. The acknowledgment of both individual intangible rights and indivisible collective interests resulted in a form of administration that left as little room as possible to the administrators' abuse of power ('Collectivisme'). For Malatesta, any attempt to reconcile democracy and anarchy ignored the difference of method: 'authority or freedom; coercion or consensus; compulsion or voluntarism' ('Collettivismo'). Merlino countered again that voluntarism, freedom, and consensus were incomplete principles, which could not account for the entire social organization, either presently, or for a long time to come. On the other hand, democratic socialists were not advocating authority, coercion, and compulsoriness across the board, without acknowledging the value of the principle of freedom. If both sides abandoned abstract principles to discuss concrete modes of organization, Merlino argued, they would come to an understanding. Even with respect to the revolutionary period, a complex social organization could be achieved neither by a newly constituted despotic power nor by the masses randomly gathered in the streets ('Per la conciliazione'). Malatesta could only restate the object of disagreement between socialists and anarchists: socialists advocated the law; anarchist advocated free agreement (note to Merlino, 'Per la conciliazione').

In sum, Merlino and Malatesta's arguments lay on different planes that could never intersect. There was no substantial divergence about values or empirical claims: Merlino shared Malatesta's value judgment on freedom versus coercion; Malatesta acknowledged that the full realization of anarchy was presently out of reach; and both aimed for whatever society came closest to the anarchist-socialist ideal. The divergence was methodological. Merlino started from a holistic assumption, in contrast to Malatesta's methodological individualism. As a consequence, they held symmetric and opposite views on the relationship between the descriptive and normative domains.

Merlino's point of departure was society as a whole, which did not depend on anyone's individual will. Accordingly, his arguments based normative statements on descriptions of society. In particular, his model of socialism started from an assessment of what practicable systems were collectively reachable from the present society. This ruled out utopian models where coercion was altogether absent, for they were too distant from present reality. Therefore, controversies over abstract models that were not presently attainable were futile for him. Accordingly, his preoccupation was to provide the blueprint of a practicable future society where coercion was reduced to a minimum, which he expected all reasonable socialists, parliamentarians, and anarchists alike, to agree upon and aim for.

In contrast, Malatesta looked at society as the effect of composition of all its members' oriented action. What each individual aimed for contributed to determine the overall direction of society. Accordingly, he started from an ideal model of society that fully realized anarchist-socialist principles, and maintained that all the efforts of anarchist-socialists should be aimed at approaching that model. To what extent that model could be approached was not known in advance. It depended on the anarchists' strength and ability to propagate their ideas. In any case, whatever the achieved result, that would be the best possible society that could be reached from the present one, given the current strength of the anarchist movement.

In brief, for Merlino, the kind of society that could be realistically attained was to determine what socialists aimed for. For Malatesta, what socialists aimed for was a factor in determining what society could be realistically attained.

Spelling out the theoretical foundation of Malatesta's arguments helps clear up such misunderstandings as can be found in the detailed analysis of the Malatesta–Merlino debate by Giampietro Berti, a foremost scholar of both opponents' thought. Berti claims that Malatesta's preference for endured despotism over flaunted parliamentarianism shows that he 'places moral requirements before political ones' (*Errico*, 259); his acknowledgment that minorities may have to yield to majorities was 'a crucial admission: the sharp and unequivocal recognition that it is impossible to exceed the democratic criterion of the majority's political and moral superiority...and to make anarchist pluralism work in circumstances of compulsory choice' (263); and his expectation that minorities surrender voluntarily would signal that 'he refuses to acknowledge that certain situations in which surrender is simply a must are objectively insurmountable' (264). For Berti, Malatesta insisted on the moral diversity between anarchism and democracy as a way out of his failure to argue for the former's political superiority. Berti's further remarks are variations on the theme of the contrast between politics and ethics: Malatesta allegedly made an epistemological mistake in contrasting the political principle of authority with the ethical one of freedom, 'since the two entities are ontologically different, and thus not comparable' (268); Merlino represented Weber's 'ethic of responsibility', in contrast to Malatesta's 'ethic of ultimate ends'; Malatesta was bound to an anthropological optimism, while realism and 'the historical responsibility of the present' prevailed in Merlino (270). In sum, for Berti, Malatesta's anarchism 'is indeed fideistic; it summarizes the utopian mentality, which always prioritizes "ought" over "is" and shirks any immediate reality check, by criticizing the present not in relation to its possible outcomes, but rather in relation to a hypothetical future' (272).

Politics is defined in two ways, as 'public life and affairs as involving authority and government' (*Concise*), and as activity aiming at the preservation of a society's 'safety, peace, and prosperity' (*Webster*). The two definitions are usually collapsed, as the promotion and preservation of the collective good is customarily identified with government. Obviously, under such identification the mutual exclusion between politics and anarchism becomes a truism. However, Malatesta himself rejected that identification in a response to the socialist Osvaldo Gnocchi Viani, who had commented upon the Malatesta–Merlino debate, arguing that anarchists were finally approaching the political struggle: 'Today', Malatesta wrote, 'there is a school that means by political struggle the conquest of political power through elections. However, Gnocchi Viani cannot ignore that logic imposes other methods of struggle to those who want to abolish political power instead of occupying it' ('Da Londra').

If the concern of politics is the collective good, Malatesta's anarchism and the role that ethics played in it were entirely political. Ethics has to do with individuals, but Malatesta's focus on ethics was dictated by his preoccupation with the best way of achieving collective goals. It did not proceed from a neglect of politics, but from his methodologically individualistic construal of society as an effect of composition and from his awareness of the heterogony of ends. Thus, regarding ethics and politics as ontologically different is a misunderstanding. Machiavelli did argue for the separation of ethics and politics. However, Machiavelli's book's title was *The Prince*: he addressed governors. Malatesta would have agreed with Machiavelli that governors have to learn how not to be good, and that ethics and power cannot go together. But his political concern with the collective good led him to hold on to ethics and reject power.

Nor was Malatesta's insistence on the moral diversity between anarchism and democracy an escape from politics. When he claimed that the majority rule was reasonable in some cases, but that it was to be voluntarily accepted by the minority, he was not simply keeping up anarchist appearances while tacitly admitting the political superiority of democracy. Instead, he was making a substantive point. While the majority rule was reasonable in some cases, in others it might be reasonable to adopt multiple solutions, or even for the majority to yield, if it was deemed that the issue at stake demanded unanimity. It would be up to those involved to adopt a criterion by free agreement, that is, an agreement about how to settle a disagreement. Establishing an a priori decision-making process and coercively enforcing it would be bound to induce some form of goal displacement. Were majority rule enforced, the common good would no longer be the immediate goal; rather, achieving a majority would become the immediate goal for a group, while holding a majority would become an incentive to ignore dissent. Conversely, should unanimity rule be in force, minorities would be encouraged to prioritize selfish interests over the common good.

Indeed, each political system has its own point of crisis. In anarchy, the inability to reach agreements is such a point, which makes anarchy impossible, as Malatesta acknowledged. Yet in democracy, too, there are circumstances that determine a systemic breakdown. As Carl Schmitt pointed out in his criticism of parliamentary democracy, 'the danger exists that democracy might be used in order to defeat democracy' (28). However, acknowledging the fragility of democracy does not amount to maintaining its lack of realism or impossibility. As is routinely claimed, democracy rests on the people's capability to live democratically. So does anarchy rest on people's capability to live anarchically. Anarchy stands in a similar relation to democracy as the latter to autocracy. In principle, in an autocratic system a full blueprint of society can be provided in advance, given that the entire decision-making process is managed autocratically. In contrast, an a priori 'democratic' blueprint of society would be a self-contradictory concept, since it is up to elective parliaments to pass laws. What is established in advance is the decision-making process, as enshrined in a constitution and thereafter coercively enforced. Anarchism goes one step further on the path of under-specification, and claims that the decision-making process itself cannot be pre-determined, but always depends on free agreements. A custom may arise, but it can never be coercively enforced. In brief, autocracy, democracy, and anarchy lie on a scale of progressive under-specification about the future society. Berti's charge that Malatesta escaped from providing political solutions could similarly be leveled by an advocate of autocracy to a democrat. Such a progressive scale of under-specification—and institutional fragility—coincides with the progressive scale of freedom. Berti's notion of politics, which implies the restricted sense of public life as involving authority, is realized to the extent that it moves away from freedom. In contrast, Malatesta's appeal to ethics was an appeal to the method of freedom as the best realization of politics in the broader sense of common good provision.

AN ANARCHIST MOBILIZATION DRIVE

In its escalation from a tactical disagreement about the expediency for anarchists to use the right to vote to a contrast between irreconcilable methodological and theoretical perspectives, Malatesta's debate with Merlino well illustrates the link between tactical and theoretical issues. Since Merlino first expressed his opinion on elections in January 1897, Malatesta immediately perceived the implications of his friend's tactical stand. Most importantly, as Fabbri notes, 'Merlino's intelligence and extraordinary culture, his evident good faith and the influence of his name' made his evolution toward parliamentarian socialism a serious threat for the destiny of the anarchist movement in Italy, on the eve of Malatesta's return to Italy and of the mobilization campaign he intended to undertake. Such concerns motivated the promptness and vigor of Malatesta's reaction, which eventually succeeded in averting the danger. 'Merlino remained isolated', Fabbri recalls, 'too revolutionary, eclectic, and independent to be looked on favorably in socialist circles, but too legalitarian for the anarchists, with which he kept the friendliest relationships until his death' (*Vida*, 137–8).

With upcoming elections, the reassertion of anti-parliamentarianism, which was central to the controversy with Merlino, was one of Malatesta's priorities at the time of his return to Italy. Such reassertion came with a manifesto of March 1897, endorsed by groups from 63 localities, half of which were in Marches, Tuscany, and Romagna, as *L'Agitazione* regularly documented throughout its first seven issues. Similarly to the manifesto of November 1890, which was the opening act of the 1891 mobilization campaign, including the Capolago congress and the First of May riots in Rome, the manifesto of March 1897 marked the beginning of the 1897–98 mobilization. The manifesto clearly sketched the new socialist-anarchist tactics: 'Do you want the freedom of association? Associate, and if the government dissolves you, keep associating all the same. Do you want the eight-hour workday? Organize, and refuse to work for longer than eight hours.' The manifesto was itself the first instance of the new tactics. Unlike the manifesto of November 1890, which was signed by anarchists abroad, this one was almost entirely signed by groups and individuals in Italy, to assert the movement's right to openly exist in the homeland ('Adesioni', 21 March 1897).

The extensive anarchist-socialist mobilization drive of 1897–98 was centered on *L'Agitazione* not only as a vehicle of propaganda and theoretical debate, but also to borrow from Lenin an expression that also applies to anarchist papers, as a 'collective organizer' (qtd in Woods, 120). Years later, in a letter of 12 June 1913 to Luigi Bertoni, Malatesta thus wrote about another editorial project: 'I attribute the greatest importance to the success of the newspaper, not only for the propaganda it will be able to carry out, but also because it will be useful as a means, and a cover-up, for work of a more practical nature' (*Epistolario*, 92). The same, with only less emphasis on the 'cover-up' function, held for *L'Agitazione* during the mobilization of 1897–98, which had very different characteristics from the insurrectionary projects of Malatesta's earlier stays in Italy. This time the focus was on the steady growth of the anarchist and labor movements through public activities. The mobilization can be split into two parts, before and after the Ancona bread riots of January 1898, which led to Malatesta's arrest and changed the nature of the mobilization. In 1897, this was centered on three themes: labor struggles; the growth of the anarchist-socialist movement; and legal struggles for civil liberties. The 1898 riots and the ensuing repression turned the anarchist struggle into one for survival, in the form of a legal struggle for the right of association. Malatesta remained a protagonist, though from jail. His trial became the focal point of the anarchists' country-wide struggle to assert their right to exist as a movement.

The foremost task of Malatesta's new tactics was 'going to the people', in the form of widespread, local participation in labor struggles. *L'Agitazione*'s weekly reports illustrate this activity. An article of 1 May 1897 explained Malatesta's views on unions:

> The workers of the same trade, or of various trades employed in the same factory, unite and struggle to improve their salary and other working conditions, or to prevent the boss from worsening the present ones, as well as to defend any of them who is the target of personal injustices or harassments. The various groups, conscious of the ever increasing solidarity among the interests of workers of all trades and countries, keep progressively uniting in local, national, and international federations of each trade, and in general federations of workers of the various trades, in order to make the struggle more effective and direct the means of all towards helping the specific fractions that are in turn engaged in a struggle.
>
> ('Leghe')

The outline superficially resembles Marx's description of how workers came together as a class through combination. However, Marx regarded the process as historically necessary. In contrast, for Malatesta the only necessity concerned the link between means and end. In order to prevent both illusion and skepticism, Malatesta illustrated the economic and moral import of strikes. Most often strikes ended up in compromises or defeats, or in victories for which an enormous price was paid, but the fear of them was the only check on the bosses' abuses. Yet the balance of strength obtained through strikes was constantly threatened by broader circumstances, such as economic crises, which were stronger than any workers' resistance and constantly endangered temporary gains. To secure a steady improvement of all workers' conditions, while unions engaged in the daily struggle, they also had to aim for the higher and more general goal of transforming the current system of property and production. At the same time, they had to get workers used to organizing and managing their own interests by themselves. Every act of resistance to the bosses had value, insofar as it went in the direction of forming a revolutionary class consciousness ('Leghe').

Such ideas were put in practice in the day-to-day unionization effort that anarchist-socialists undertook in Ancona. The choice of Ancona as Malatesta's base of operations was not casual. Ancona was a stronghold of organizationist anarchism. Malatesta's link with the city dated back to 1894 and would last until 1913–14. Moreover, as Pier Carlo Masini notes, the city was strategically located in the heart of the area where historically anarchism had strongest roots: Marches, Romagna, Emilia, Tuscany, Umbria, and Rome

TYPE OF GROUP	CITY		DISTRICT		TOTAL	
	Groups	Members	Groups	Members	Groups	Members
Anarchist-socialist	2	316	10	701	12	1,017
Socialist	2	36	6	309	8	345
Socialist-republican	—	—	5	364	5	364
Republican	33	3,384	30	2,244	63	5,628
Constitutionalist	5 ˙	750	6	598	11	1,348

TABLE 7.1   Number and size of political groups in the city and district of Ancona, June 1894

(*Storia . . . nell'epoca*, 87). Finally, the distribution of political forces in the city was favorable to Malatesta's project. Three years before the Prefecture of Ancona had compiled an overview of political groups in the district, summarized in Table 7.1. As biased as absolute figures may be, the relative weight of political currents can be taken to be more reliably represented. Four traits stand out: there was an overwhelming preponderance of revolutionary forces, mainly republican; anarchists had a minoritarian but sizable presence in the city and district; socialist presence was weak; and the strong presence of socialist-republicans indicates a social orientation among republicans. In brief, Ancona was an ideal terrain for anarchist propaganda, with a notable anarchist presence, potential for expansion provided by a socially oriented revolutionary milieu, and weak socialist competition.

The core of the city's urban proletariat comprised sugar mill workers, railway workers, and dockers, all categories among which anarchist-socialists were active (Santarelli, 'Azione', 252–3). On the same day on which Malatesta's above-mentioned article on unions appeared, a meeting took place in which over 200 workers of the Ancona sugar mill constituted a union ('Notizie'). However, it is the case of the Ancona dockers that best illustrates the role of anarchist-socialist propaganda in uniting workers, emphasizing the need for class solidarity, irrespective of skill or occupation, and seeking as much to overcome workers' rivalries as to foster antagonism to the bosses. In the port of Ancona labor was traditionally organized hierarchically. A form of monopoly allowed stevedores to hand down jobs from father to son and to temporarily subcontract work to casual laborers. A contract system gave control over stevedores' gangs to foremen, who negotiated contracts with shipping companies. The situation started to change in 1897, when the formation of new gangs organized as co-ops challenged the traditional monopoly (Santarelli, 'Azione', 253–5). *L'Agitazione* stood by the new gangs, arguing that instead of trying to preserve waning privileges at the expense of all other workers, the right course of action in the face of job shortage was for all stevedores to unite and demand decent salaries, while the result of competition would be to lower salaries, to the whole category's detriment ('In Ancona', 2 July 1897).

Enzo Santarelli acknowledges the effectiveness of the anarchist-social-ists' labor propaganda, arguing that their activism among stevedores turned thereafter this category into a stronghold of anarchist socialism in Ancona, shunning the influence of the republican party and the patronage system of foremen and brokers. Unfortunately, Santarelli's interpretation is also plagued by the marxist axiom that anarchism was a sign of backwardness. Thus, he argues that the stevedores' support for anarchist socialism was typ-ical of a social setting in which the limited development of industry, the predominance of handcraft occupations, the guild-based organization of la-bor, and the consequent individualism of dock workers provided the organic basis for the anarchist-socialist ideology: 'the plant of bakuninism still bears fruits in an environment in which the great modern industry has not arisen, yet. Anarchist preaching catches on with relative ease among the dockers, a privileged and widely diverse group of workers, inclined to an extremely individualistic vision of life, lacking discipline, and insufficiently "educated" by the use of machinery in their toil' ('Azione', 255–6).

Contrary to Santarelli's assertions, however, anarchist-socialists attacked precisely that individualism and the defense of craft privileges, promoting instead class unionism. Moreover, in contrast to Santarelli's charge of back-wardness and localism, Malatesta's strategy was backed by firsthand knowl-edge of a wide international context, which came with his transnationalism. His strategy had roots that went as far back as the late 1880s' labor struggles in Argentina, and had been deeply influenced by the Great Dock Strike. Notwithstanding the different sizes of the cities, the situation in Ancona pre-sented commonalities with that of the London docks in 1889. In both cases, casual labor was the central problem; the struggle against contract work also sparked the London strike; and the idea of general workers' unions enrolling all classes of skilled and unskilled workers, which Malatesta brought to the Ancona dock workers, was the same established by the new unionism that arose from the Great Dock Strike in the world's most advanced capitalist city (Lovell, 93–4, 101–5).

Malatesta was also keenly aware of the current European context. In par-ticular, it was not accidental that *L'Agitazione* held up as an example the dockers of Hamburg, where there were 'neither new nor old, but only con-scious workers in agreement, who were able to resist their bosses' ('In An-cona', 14 October 1897). A notable role in the Hamburg dockers' strike, which occurred from November 1896 to February 1897 ('End'), was played by Tom Mann, a leader of the Great Dock Strike and Malatesta's friend. In June 1896 Mann had become the president of the International Feder-ation of Ship, Dock, and River Workers, which promoted organization on international lines (Mann, 135). The Federation made its presence felt at the 1896 London congress with a manifesto foreshadowing an imminent international strike ('International Federation of Ship'). Then, Mann and others undertook a tour in various European ports, including Hamburg. In February 1897, shortly before Malatesta's departure for Italy, an international conference convened by Mann was held in London to the end of enforcing uniformity of treatment. The International Federation held another conference in London in June 1897, when the Ancona stevedores' controversy was under way (Tsuzuki, 113–16).

The European backdrop was familiar to Malatesta as he worked out his labor strategy for the port of Ancona. Another strike that *L'Agitazione* held up before the Ancona stevedores as an example of national and international solidarity was that of the Amalgamated Society of Engineers ('In Ancona', 21 October 1897). The strike lasted throughout the second half of 1897 and represented the first major national labor conflict in British history (Pelling, 109). Malatesta even considered starting a national fund-raising campaign for the British strikers, but he abandoned the idea, doubting that in Italy the initiative would be backed by socialist and workers' organizations (note to Gori, 'Postilla').

In brief, Malatesta's ideas may have grown on the bakuninist plant, but were also in unison with the most forward-looking labor strategies arising from the dockers' experience of a decade in the most industrially advanced European countries, which Malatesta had directly witnessed. In the end, Santarelli's claims undermine his own analysis. He argues that 'at the end of the century, the Ancona workers' movement was about to finally come out of a still immature phase of development, in which the old guild spirit confronted, with ever smaller success, the new and modern impulse toward association that resulted from maturing economic transformations and from the numerical increment of a still scarcely qualified proletariat' ('Azione', 256). Yet despite his depiction of anarchism as a lingering remnant of the past, he remarks: 'for long years, up to the Red Week and the uprisings of June 1920, anarchist traditions took root in the vivacious, restless, mobile mass of the dockers, and in their characteristic social and economic organization' (252). It is legitimate to question accounts involving death struggles so vital as to last longer than a movement's healthy life.

Throughout 1897, *L'Agitazione* supported the unionization efforts of various other categories, such as bakers, barbers, and shoemakers, helping to overcome divisions. For example, resistance to unionization existed in the Ancona printing industry, where past episodes of union malpractice had alienated workers, including anarchists. *L'Agitazione* issued repeated appeals in support of the renewed effort toward the printers' unionization ('In Ancona', 19 August 1897; 'Per l'organizzazione'; Smorti). The effort paid off, and in October a local section of the publishing industry national union was created ('In Ancona', 28 October 1897). By its local and ordinary character, the anarchist-socialists' involvement in the labor movement's life was an eloquent assertion of their new tactics. Their day-to-day activities were a living testimony of the concepts of inclusiveness, sustainability, organization, and collective action that were most contentious among anarchists.

The periodical even engaged in a controversy with the customs administration over grievances by its officers ('In Ancona', 9 December 1897). The episode, triggered by a letter from a custom officer to the periodical ('In Ancona', 2 December 1897), illustrates the local credit of *L'Agitazione* as an advocate of workers' rights, as well as the newspaper's willingness to support the grievances of all workers without distinction. Some anarchists protested that *L'Agitazione* had gone too far: Would they also defend policemen from the ill-treatment of higher-ranking officers? For Malatesta, the protest assumed 'a clear-cut separation between useful workers and exploiters or defenders of exploiters, with everyone being free to choose one's place'. However, he countered, no such separation existed: people were often forced by necessity to take up jobs they disliked; competition was everywhere; and everyone could be in turn oppressed and oppressor, exploited and exploiter. The point was not to draw untenable lines, but to fight oppression and exploitation wherever they occurred. Evil did not depend on the individuals' wickedness, but on the entire social constitution. Hence, the remedy did not consist in hating individuals, but in spreading the feeling that institutions must be changed. Malatesta concluded by restating his inclusive view of class and his humanism: anarchists were to especially instigate the organization of workers as a struggling class, but at the same time they were to bring a message of love and brotherhood to everyone ('Giustizia').

For Malatesta, taking root among workers was the anarchists' first priority, but in order to do so as anarchists they also had to organize among themselves. Along with their long-term, daily commitment to agitating among workers, Italian anarchist-socialists similarly attended to reorganizing their own movement, a task in which *L'Agitazione* acted as an informal correspondence committee. The effort took a different shape than at the time of Capolago. Its progress was reported by *L'Agitazione* in the column 'Movimento Socialista Anarchico'. The reference to a 'movement' rather than a 'party' had a double significance: the project of uniting all anarchists into a single organization had been abandoned, and anarchist-socialist organization was now looked upon as a gradual process. While in 1891 the creation of a party began the mobilization drive, in 1897 the creation of a party was expected to be the result of a mobilization drive. Thus, when in May the Lugano anarchists, the promoters of the Capolago congress in 1890, posed the issue of a national congress, *L'Agitazione* deemed the idea premature, giving priority to a bottom-up growth starting at the local and regional levels. Meanwhile, anarchists were to focus on taking firm root in the labor movement. 'Later on, after our organization will have extended throughout Italy and acquired a solid basis through the practice of local and regional work, we will finally have the means to start our national congresses, and be able to do so profitably' ('Congresso di anarchici').

The anarchist-socialists of Ancona set the example. By August, five new groups in the city had been added to the seven that endorsed the March manifesto, as can be gleaned from scattered references in the *Agitazione*. Further impulse to propaganda came from Malatesta's arrest and immediate release in November 1897. During the previous nine months of underground presence he had not remained in hiding, even lecturing out of town under the name of Giuseppe Rinaldi. However, after earlier convictions had lapsed, Malatesta was free to openly engage in spoken propaganda, as witnessed by the 'Anarchist-Socialist Movement' regular column in *L'Agitazione*, which weekly reported his activity throughout the Marches and Umbria. The same column, which throughout April had recorded the initial country-wide difficulty of organizing—reporting most often police persecutions, amid scant announcements of projected manifestos and publications—by January 1898 had a different tone, with spoken propaganda and the creation of new groups across Italy as predominant themes. The slow but steady progress that socialist-anarchists had envisaged was taking place.

An important event in that growth process was the congress of the Anarchist-Socialist Federation of Romagna in December 1897, the first of the regional congresses projected back in April. Twenty-seven groups from 15 localities participated, with endorsements from 9 more localities. The congress resolutions closely reflected the tactics advocated by *L'Agitazione*. Groups were to regularly report on unions and the anarchists' activity therein; in case of trials for criminal association, the existence of anarchist associations was to be admitted and claimed as a right; furthermore, solidarity with the defendants was to be publicly declared ('1.° Congresso'). Such provisions anticipated a scenario that would become reality in less than a month.

In addition to agitation among the working masses and the internal growth of the anarchist-socialist movement, the third kind of long and patient work that anarchist-socialists undertook was legal struggle, a terrain that offered opportunities for cooperation with other political forces. Throughout 1897, the new tactics of legal struggle took the form of a campaign against a bill that made *domicilio coatto* part of the permanent legislation, de facto introducing deportation for political reasons as an ordinary procedure. The agitations picked up after the bill, approved by the Senate, was scheduled for debate at the Chamber. From mid-July on, *L'Agitazione* urged anarchist-socialists to get involved. As Malatesta argued, 'this is an agitation in which we can agree with all participants, in terms of both ends and means... Let us take the initiative ourselves wherever we can; and where we cannot, or we have been preceded by others, let us loyally follow their initiative' ('Contro il domicilio'). Meanwhile, Malatesta wrote for *L'Agitazione* the series of articles 'Come si conquista quel che si vuole' (How one obtains what one wants), on such episodes as the 1893 Belgian struggle for universal suffrage, to illustrate the idea of legal struggles by popular action. The agitations went on for the rest of 1897. In August many local committees were formed with the contribution of socialists, anarchists, republicans, and occasionally other democratic and radical parties. Throughout September mass rallies were held or planned in Northern and Central Italy. A further wave of initiatives occurred between late November and early January 1898. All these development were regularly reported by *L'Agitazione*. Anarchist socialists were particularly active in Emilia, Romagna, and Marches (Marabini and Ortalli), in a spirit of cooperation with other progressive forces that brought them to share speaking platforms with socialists and republicans.

By early January 1898 the bill's menace was averted, and the agitations subsided. *L'Agitazione* of 30 December drew a balance sheet of the agitations. These were regarded as a popular victory over the reactionary plan of prime minister Di Rudinì's. They had been characterized by the concerted action of popular parties, and the hope was expressed that they would be the prelude to broader popular struggles. Still, they had been kept within the rules of the game imposed by the government. As for anarchist-socialists, their legitimate realism about their limited strength had tended to turn into excessive timidity and self-deprecation; the article ended by even voicing the conjecture that the ditching of the bill mainly owed to Di Rudinì's political indecisiveness, with popular agitations merely providing its 'decorative appearance'. The comment did not intend to belittle the agitation, but to urge anarchist-socialists to a more energetic action (Samaja, 'Agitazione').

During 1897 the food crisis that would spark the bread riots of the next year began to be felt. *L'Agitazione* started agitating the issue as early as August. Malatesta's article had a subdued tone, pointing to the present situation as avoidable, since the wheat shortage that caused the crisis was induced by a profit-driven economy ('Prezzo'). In the next weeks, as the agitations against *domicilio coatto* were gaining momentum, the first initiatives about the cost of bread in places of anarchist and socialist presence were also being taken. In Ancona, a well-attended rally was held in late September. In calling people to action, the anarchist Adelmo Smorti emphasized that such action should go to the root causes, rather than being misdirected to bakers ('In Ancona', 30 September 1897). It was for the government, he argued, to set a fixed price on wheat and to remove import duties, and for local authorities to remove consumption duties: 'Will governments and municipalities do any of these things? None, if we look feeble.' Socialist-anarchists were not fanning insurrectionary flames, but at the same time their call was for direct action aiming at capitalists and the government. This was the way to obtain reforms such as the abolition of duties, while at the same time building the workers' revolutionary collective strength.

The wave of bread riots that swept Italy for four months started in early January 1898 with revolts in southern villages (Del Carria, 1: 300–1). However, Ancona was the first urban center where major agitations occurred, and the Marches the first region where they widely propagated. The agitations lasted several days. Military occupation of the city put an end to them on 18 January. The socialist Bocconi, Malatesta, and other anarchists were arrested. On 19–20 January the revolt spread to numerous urban centers of the Marches (Santarelli, 'Azione', 261–5). As a result, bread prices were reduced and soup kitchens were arranged in the city. The next issue of *L'Agitazione*, promptly seized by the authorities, made the tongue-in-cheek remark that the authorities had acknowledged that the people's demands were legitimate ('In Ancona', 28 January 1898). Yet in the next three months the Ancona criminal court alone held 38 trials involving 243 people (Santarelli, 'Azione', 265–6). Meanwhile, the government temporarily reduced by one-third the import duty on wheat from 25 January to 30 April. *L'Agitazione* remarked that the temporary character of the decree was going to benefit speculators, who would buy cheap after January, to resell at a higher price after April ('Provvedimenti'). The repression that followed the agitations changed the nature of anarchist action. The 'anarchist-socialist movement' column, that had weekly recorded the movement's growth throughout 1897, was discontinued. At that juncture the priority was no longer to extend the movement, but, as expected, to defend its right to exist publicly and legally.

In the aftermath of the Ancona agitations, *L'Agitazione* argued that, in contrast to the attitude of all parliamentarian forces, the duty of the extreme parties, as parties of action, was 'to fight at the side of the people' ('Sfogliando'). The tone was quite different from that of 1893–94. No insurrectional scenario was evoked, but no check was placed on popular action either. The focus remained on collective direct action as a means to defend and extend concessions. The attitude toward socialists was notable. Unlike republicans, socialists were spared from criticism and the article made an inclusive appeal for common tactics to 'extreme parties' indistinctively. The article sheds light on the anarchists' role in the Ancona agitations, emphasizing the dynamic interplay between spontaneous popular action and conscious action of organized parties. While the agitations cannot be ascribed to the action of anarchists alone, their presence was crucial in making Ancona the leading city of the resistance. Santarelli's pre-packaged interpretation is that anarchists joined the agitations as 'a step to ascend to the longed-for social revolution, which they had always imagined to be imminent' ('Azione', 262–3). However, their whole tactics of this period were based on the premise that no immediate revolutionary prospect was in sight.

FIGURE 7.2   **Malatesta's 1898 police photographs**
Source: Archivio Centrale dello Stato, Rome, Casellario Politico Centrale, box 2952

After the Ancona agitations, the anarchists' struggle for the right of association focused on the trial of Malatesta and eight others that had been arrested, including the staff of *L'Agitazione*. The trial took place in Ancona from 21 to 28 April 1898. As planned, the defendants admitted the existence of their associations, claiming their right of expression and association. In mid-March the Romagnole Federation started a country-wide campaign for the right of association, centered on a collective, public declaration of solidarity with the comrades under arrest ('Per la libertà'). A protest manifesto *Al Popolo Italiano* (To the Italian People) was distributed to all groups throughout the country with the recommendation that it be signed by anarchists only. In this way anarchists wanted to make clear that the manifesto was not simply a generic sign of solidarity with their comrades on trial, but that they were unequivocally throwing down the gauntlet at the government. In a country where a repressive law on the right of association equated anarchist groups to criminal associations, the manifesto challenged that law by a collective declaration that amounted to self-incrimination. The manifesto was published in Ancona as a supplement of *L'Agitazione* on 24 April, in the middle of the trial, followed by individual names and places of 3,137 signatories from 116 localities across Italy. As with the abstentionist manifesto of a year before, emphasis was placed on the requirement that the signatories be individuals rather than groups, so as to underline the legal responsibility that each militant was taking. Though the initiative was part of the new tactics, it had precedents. When Malatesta, Merlino, and others were convicted for criminal association in 1884, 78 Florence internationalists signed a manifesto of solidarity (Masini, *Storia...Da Bakunin*, 331–3). They were indeed tried and convicted for 'contempt of the fundamental laws of the state' (Conti, 239). Fourteen years later the sheer number of signatories made any such measure impossible.

The trial had considerable echo outside of Italy. The Parisian *L'Aurore*, which a few months earlier had published Émile Zola's 'J'Accuse', dealt with it. In England an extensive campaign weeks ahead of the trial involved the *Daily Chronicle*, the *Daily News*, and the *Star* and was endorsed by delegates of many trades unions, Independent Labour Party, and Socialist Democratic Federation branches. An international protest manifesto was signed by Tom Mann, Keir Hardie, the writer Edward Carpenter, the painter Walter Crane, the journalist Henry W. Nevinson, and other intellectual and political figures ('Trial').

In Italy itself, however, the campaign for the right of association did not have the hoped-for following. A week after its start, *L'Agitazione* lamented that not even socialist and republican newspapers had publicized the campaign (Samaja, 'Agitazione'). However, the trial did have a national echo. For its duration, *L'Agitazione* published a daily supplement with a circulation of 8,000 copies. The trial did not end with the hoped-for acquittal: Malatesta was sentenced to seven months, the others to six months, with one person acquitted (*Processo*, 163). However, the criminal association charge against everyone was dropped, and this was regarded as a victory. Nevertheless, right after the trial *L'Agitazione* drew a first balance sheet of the agitation that expressed disappointment: 'Let us admit it at the outset: even in relative terms, the effect has been nearly nil.' The campaign mainly consisted of conferences held by anarchist-socialists, the paper complained. In the anarchist camp, the article continued, the criticism was raised that the initiative was semi-legalitarian and misleadingly focused solely on article 248, which equated anarchist organizations to associations of malefactors, rather than on the entire penal code. The reaction of other parties feebly consisted of protest resolutions. In the end, anarchist-socialists were left alone. Still, the support from their own ranks to the manifesto of the Romagnole Federation was a success. The convenient theory that one had to hide in order to act had been hard hit: 'we, who want to civilly live in the light of day like any other party, have set off on the right path' ('Bilancio').

The Ancona trial coincided with the onset of the 1898 bread riots. Agitations had occurred throughout Italy in the wake of the Ancona events of January (Del Carria, 1: 303–5). However, the situation was precipitated by a worsening of the food crisis due to the Spanish–American War, which reduced imports and increased the price of wheat. In the space of two weeks, between the last decade of April and the first decade of May, agitations spread as wildfire across Italy (Colajanni, 31–2). In Milan, what came to be known as *Fatti di Maggio* (May Events) started on 6 May and went on for four days. A state of siege was declared and General Bava Beccaris was put in command of the city. Heavy artillery was used and blanket orders to shoot were given to the troops. Counts and estimates of the casualties in Milan widely vary. An official count of 80 deaths is usually mentioned (Colajanni, 81). Louise Tilly raises the baseline to 264 victims, whose names she collected from local newspapers (267). Del Carria mentions further journalistic estimates ranging from 400 to 800 deaths (1: 330). In the following months, 129 trials were held by the Milan military tribunal, involving 828 defendants, of which 688 were convicted (Del Carria, 1: 337). Writing at the end of 1898, Napoleone Colajanni reported that the military tribunals of Florence, Milan, and Naples alone convicted approximately 2,500 people (254). Sources quoted by Del Carria report that civil and military courts together inflicted nearly 5,000 years of jail (1: 337).

Unfortunately, the time when anarchists could civilly live in broad daylight was yet to come. *L'Agitazione*'s balance sheet of the agitations for the right of association appeared only days before the *Fatti di Maggio*. Then, repression fell not only upon anarchists, but also upon socialists, republicans, radicals, and catholics, with greater brutality than in 1894. The suppression of the freedom of speech is well illustrated by the 12 May issue of *L'Agitazione*, whose four pages appeared entirely blanked, except for the last column of the last page, which contained the list of donations. The very denomination 'anarchist-socialist periodical' in the masthead was replaced by the word 'CENSORED'. Ironically, *domicilio coatto* was utilized more than ever, and colonies destined to that purpose were repopulated.

Pier Carlo Masini observes that 'in this situation, the anarchist movement, broken up, with its people put away and its means of communication confiscated, and banished from political life, should have disappeared. Instead, exactly the opposite happened . . . At the *domicilio coatto* islands the cream of Italian anarchism came to meet for the first time in a permanent congress . . . ' (*Storia...nell'epoca*, 127). The next year a one-off publication appeared, jointly edited by anarchist groups at *domicilio coatto* and significantly titled *I morti* (The dead). However, these were already the prodromes of the next 'reappearance' of Italian anarchism, while the anarchist-socialist experience of 1897–98 could be looked at retrospectively.

EPILOGUE: THE 'FATAL DICHOTOMIES' OF ANARCHISM

Such experience represented a remarkable tactical turn from 1893–94. The focus shifted from social indeterminacy to a sustainable growth of the anarchist movement as part of the labor movement's growth. The anarchist-socialist experience of 1897–98 was as remote as any from historiographical stereotypes that presuppose a dichotomy between two paths to social change: a pragmatistic, incremental, peaceful, reformist, and legal path, and a utopian, all-or-nothing, violent, revolutionary, and illegal one. The latter, it is alleged, was the path of anarchism, barred from the former path by its own nature, defined in a suitably narrow way for the historian's convenience. Effective and 'anarchist' means being mutually exclusive, the equally doomed options supposedly left to anarchists ranged from 'dynamiter' to 'dreamer', with no middle ground. However, real-life anarchists did not comply with a priori generalizations. The core idea of the anarchist-socialist experience of 1897–98 was to shed both dynamite and dreams without shedding either revolution or anarchy. That experience can only be understood on the basis of its own theoretical foundations, which were roomier than arbitrary stereotypes allow.

For Malatesta, the line of march of society was the composite result of multiple social forces. Anarchists were to exert whatever influence their strength allowed them. Their action was simultaneously revolutionary and reforming: they aimed to build the workers' revolutionary strength, for emancipation could only come by revolution; at the same time they contributed to wrest from the bourgeoisie whatever concessions could be obtained in the present society. Inclusiveness and coherence between ends and means characterized anarchist action. No effort or gain was too partial to be significant. Every labor struggle was worth fighting if class solidarity was its guiding principle. Conversely, no deflection from anarchist means was too small to be questioned, for it implied a displacement of goals: 'if we told people to vote today', Malatesta remarked to Merlino, 'tomorrow we would tell them to vote for us'. Every struggle fought by direct action was relevant. This did not necessarily mean illegality or violence. Struggles could be peaceful and within the bounds of law, so long as they were directly fought by those who had a stake in them. Legal struggles such as the ones against *domicilio coatto* and for the right of association were the clearest examples. Their objective was as pragmatic as the repeal of a law; their means were as peaceful as rallies and mass self-denunciation; yet what made them coherent with anarchist ends was their being fought in the streets and not in parliament. The workers' fighting habit and class consciousness were made through reforming but anti-parliamentarian struggles.

Violent and illegal means were not rejected, as anarchist participation in the bread riots shows. The standard dichotomy between peaceful and violent, legal and illegal means was meaningless to anarchists. For them, means were either coherent or in contrast with anarchist ends. The former case included all direct action, in a continuum that ranged from strikes to sabotage and from rallies to riots. Meaningful distinctions concerned sustainability and the way of 'going to the people'. Rather than agitating for insurrection as in 1893–94, anarchist-socialists focused on sustainable struggles. Yet they placed no check on the escalation of class struggle. Their attitude toward the 1898 bread riots illustrates their view of the dynamic relation between conscious minorities and masses. As Malatesta argued in 1889, anarchists were to 'take the viewpoint of the mass, reach down to its starting point, and thence push it forward' ('Altro'). This idea was put in practice in the anarchist-socialists' inclusive participation in day-to-day labor struggles, where talk of anarchy was out of the question. At the same time, as *L'Agitazione* argued in February 1898, in 'moments of general stir' the duty of the parties of action was to 'fight at the people's side, guide it, and defend its legitimate demands' ('Provvedimenti'). In the coexistence of such stances lay the originality of the 'going to the people' idea. Unlike anti-organizationists, anarchist-socialists believed their place to be in collective struggles. Hence, they took responsibility, as an advanced minority, to actively promote and direct those struggles in an anarchist direction. However, unlike marxists, they did not expect to hold the reins of those struggles. The difference was as evident in 1893–94 as in 1897–98, when the socialist Filippo Turati tried to persuade the Milan workers in revolt to disband (Tilly, 261–2). In contrast, anarchist-socialists expected as much to be steered by collective struggles as to steer them.

In contrast to the stereotypical dichotomy between reformism and revolution, in 1897–98 Italian anarchist-socialists experimented with progress within the bourgeois society. They advocated and practiced direct action that was meant to be both reforming and conducive to revolution. The lesson of experience was that the room for such progress was narrower than Malatesta had assumed. The unbearable hardships imposed by capitalism upon the popular masses and the government's willingness to crush any collective movement whose demands were not kept within the rules of the parliamentary game, even when those demands had no revolutionary character, thwarted the anarchist-socialists' project. In the end, the choice between gradual reform and insurrection, which stereotypes arbitrarily ascribe to the theoretical foundations of anarchism, was thrust upon anarchists by the government's repressiveness, epitomized by Bava Beccaris's cannons in Milan. Insurrectionism received empirical corroboration from the events of 1897–98. Malatesta had time to ponder the lesson of experience, for in September 1898, after serving his prison term, he was sent to *domicilio coatto*. He regained freedom in April 1899, and then only by escaping from Lampedusa Island. The results of his further tactical elaboration found expression shortly thereafter in the pamphlet *Contro la Monarchia*, which opened a new phase in Malatesta's anarchist struggle.

8

FROM THE OTHER SIDE OF THE
ATLANTIC OCEAN, 1899–1900

THE YEAR BETWEEN MALATESTA'S REGAINED FREEDOM IN APRIL 1899 AND HIS permanent return to London in April 1900 has the semblance of an intermission between two similar cycles, each constituted by a long exile in London, a return to Italy, the editing of a periodical in Ancona, and a year of agitation climaxing in ill-fated revolt. Such was the semblance of the 1894–98 years, and thus would appear the 1900–14 period.

However, such a Sisyphean look can be dispelled precisely by paying due attention to intermissions. Just as the apparently uneventful year following Malatesta's return from Italy in 1894 was the time he laid the ground for his tactics of the next half decade, so Malatesta's pamphlet *Contro la Monarchia* (Against the Monarchy), published in 1899, marked the beginning of a new tactical phase. Malatesta remained in London for the next 13 years, during which he did not join any popular mobilization in Italy. The circumstance speaks to the short-term lack of success of his new tactics. At the same time, not only did the pamphlet have lasting consequences for the evolution of Malatesta's anarchism, but the Red Week of 1914 followed the tactical model proposed in the 1899 pamphlet, revealing once more continuity where continuity is not immediately apparent.

Moreover, the period 1899–1900 was not only intellectually productive, but, unlike the 1894–95 'intermission', it was eventful. For the most part it was occupied by an eight-month journey to the United States, which superficially looks like a diversion in Malatesta's Europe-centered life of the previous decade, but was far from being one. Similarly to another transition period in Malatesta's life, the year 1889 that linked his stay in South America to his settling in London, the journey of 1899–1900 to North America was characterized by a set of themes that were steadily central to the mode of operation of Italian anarchism.

The journey included three main events. First was a controversy over the editorship of *La Questione Sociale* of Paterson, which had received an anti-organizationist direction from its editor Giuseppe Ciancabilla. After his arrival

Malatesta took on the editorship of the newspaper, and from its columns engaged in a debate on organization with the former editor. Then Malatesta undertook a speaking tour throughout the Eastern part of the United States. Finally, he accepted an invitation for another, shorter speaking tour in Cuba, recently passed from Spanish colonial domination to the United States control.

These events respectively provide the opportunity for systematic discussion of three themes that have run through the previous chapters: the controversy between Italian organizationists and anti-organizationists, which provided one of the trip's motives; anarchist transnationalism, which was most notably represented by the Italian anarchists in North America; and the anarchists' cross-national mutual involvement, most notably represented by Malatesta's affinity with Spanish anarchism.

The first theme sheds light on the practical issues that really mattered to anarchists, in contrast to charges of utopianism; the second theme is key to understanding the continuity of anarchist action; and the third theme is crucial to put the debate of national anarchist movements, such as the ones on organization in Italy and on collectivism versus communism in Spain, in a broader perspective.

All such themes characterized not only Malatesta's journey to North America, but his entire militant life.

An impromptu escape?

Malatesta's route to North America was a circuitous one, that took him first from Lampedusa Island to Tunisia, Malta, and London. Malatesta escaped from Lampedusa Island on the night between 26 and 27 April 1899 (Leonardi), after seven months in prison and eight at *domicilio coatto*, where he was supposed to spend four years. According to Luigi Fabbri, what made the escape easier was that 'Malatesta inspired such confidence in the director of the penal colony, that the latter granted all kinds of facilities to Malatesta and all the political detainees, closing an eye on everything... The preparations for the escape could be easily made.' Fabbri mentions that Malatesta 'got some help from the socialist Oddino Morgari, who once visited the colony in his capacity of Member of Parliament'. On the set night, 'amidst the most complete obscurity and with a rough sea, Malatesta, comrade Vivoli from Florence, and a civil detainee swam to a fishing boat anchored some way out—with the Sicilian socialist Lovetere aboard—boarded it and set sail for Malta' (*Vida*, 142–4).

Malatesta's escape from Lampedusa Island illustrates the problems that trouble the historiography of anarchism even at the level of factual accuracy, as Vernon Richards points out in reviewing James Joll's potted biography of Malatesta. This sort of event tends most easily to trigger romanticized accounts. An amusingly extreme but representative example comes from the memoirs of the Scotland Yard inspector Herbert T. Fitch, where Malatesta is transfigured into a Count of Monte Cristo:

> He had managed to smuggle into his cell a small stone-breaking tool, with which he picked and wrenched a hole large enough to admit his body. One stormy night he clambered through it, made his way to the harbour, swam out to a tiny fishing smack which was riding at anchor, and succeeded in navigating it himself as far as Malta in a sea in which practised seamen refused to put out in pursuit because of its danger. (46–7)

On the other hand, accounts such as Fabbri's tend to be reticent or incomplete. The emphasis on odd figures such as the director of the Lampedusa penal colony looks like a diversion from a full account of people and events, for reasons of discretion. In contrast to simplistic or romanticized accounts, a closer look at the events illustrates the working of the anarchist network.

To begin with, the loose surveillance, and even cooperation, by the penal colony's director was not simply a matter of personal relationship with Malatesta. Oddino Morgari related years later how things went (55–60). Malatesta, made aware that the director could be corrupted, asked for financial help from Giovanni Bergamasco, a participant of the 1891 Capolago congress who had money at his disposal. Bergamasco had been himself at *domicilio coatto*, possibly at Lampedusa with Malatesta for a short time. In turn, Bergamasco, who had generously supported the socialist newspaper *Avanti!* in the past, contacted its administrator, Morgari, asking for aid in delivering the money to Malatesta. Morgari was eager to help, and visited Malatesta during a tour of the *domicilio coatto* islands in February–March 1899. At a meeting in Lampedusa with Malatesta and the director the money was delivered and the agreement made.

Malatesta's plan was to escape to Tunisia, then to Malta, with London as final destination. The plan required organization, and it must have been prepared for some time. As his roommate Amedeo Boschi relates, more than once Malatesta's attempts to approach Greek captains of sponge-fishing vessels had been reported to the colony director and reports about Malatesta's plans had reached the Ministry of Interior (56–8). Eventually, on 27 April 1899 a police inspector arrived on Lampedusa to transfer Malatesta, but he could only ascertain that Malatesta and two other detainees had just escaped (Bolis). It is not clear who made the arrangement with the vessel that took Malatesta to Tunisia. According to information from the Italian Consul in Marseille, a sum of money was paid to the owner of the sponge-fishing vessel by Nicolò Converti and Nicolò Ponzio, two Italian anarchists resident in Tunis ('Circa'). Converti later admitted to holding a correspondence with Malatesta during the latter's sojourn in Lampedusa, but he predictably denied discussing any escape plan ('Procès').

Malatesta and the other two fugitives disembarked on the shore of Sousse, in Tunisia. Being outside of the Italian soil meant by no means being safe. Tunisia was then a French protectorate. Three years earlier, six anarchists, including Galileo Palla, Francesco Pezzi, and Giovanni Bergamasco, had escaped from *domicilio coatto* to Tunisia. Breaking a tradition of granting the right of asylum, the French-Tunisian authorities had turned the fugitives back to the Italian government (Bettini, 2: 265). Given this precedent, it was crucial for Malatesta and his comrades to keep their presence in Tunisia as secret as possible. A plan had been laid out in advance for this purpose. Anarchists in Paris were assigned the task of spreading the rumor, after the escape, that Malatesta was safe on the British soil of Gibraltar ('Errico', *Questione Sociale*). The rumor caught on well: by 5 May the news of Malatesta in Gibraltar appeared in *Le Temps* of Paris, and got as far as New York, where it was published in the *Evening Sun* of the same day. Malatesta confirmed himself to be the source of the false news in a letter of 1 July 1899 to Max Nettlau: 'The news that I was in Gibraltar was false. I had it spread myself, because I was still in danger of being arrested and I wanted to sidetrack the government' (Nettlau Papers). On 7 May Malatesta and Vivoli embarked for Malta ('Note').

The organization of Malatesta's stay in Malta and his passage to London were taken care of by a circle of militants linked to Giuseppe De Felice Giuffrida. Though in Malta Malatesta was finally safe from arrest, foreigners could stay undisturbed for no longer than eight days, after which police would summon and examine them, as well as require that a deposit be paid and security be given by a Malta citizen. In order to preserve Malatesta's safety, Filippo Lovetere, a Palermo lawyer who had been involved in the Fasci, placed him under the care of a friend, an actor who was then in Malta with his theater company (Vitti). Eventually, the actor's help proved unnecessary. Two friends of De Felice Giuffrida, residents of Malta, arranged a passage to London for Malatesta before the eight days went by (Grandi, 'Enrico'). On May 14 Malatesta boarded a ship due to reach London in ten days (Grandi, telegram). On 26 May the Italian ambassador in London reported to the Ministry of Interior: 'I am informed by the English Police that the registered anarchist Malatesta arrived here on the 24th of the current month, and took domicile at his old address...' (De Renzis).

In the light of the above, one can better appreciate the inaccuracy and deceptiveness of accounts such as Woodcock's, especially for their implicit outlook on anarchism: 'One stormy day [Malatesta] and three of his comrades seized a boat and put out to sea in defiance of the high waves. They were lucky enough to be picked up by a ship on its way to Malta, whence Malatesta sailed to the United States' (329–30). In contrast to such pervasive and obstinate emphasis on spontaneism and lack of organization percolating down even to personal events, Malatesta's escape reveals the existence of a complex solidarity network, extending beyond anarchist circles, and capable of effective concerted action. Malatesta's escape was not an isolated episode. Within a year, another prominent figure of Italian anarchism, Luigi Galleani, escaped from Pantelleria Island, following a familiar plan. As Ugo Fedeli relates, 'the boat that carried him had Tunisia as its destination. He disembarked in Sousse, whence, with a false passport in the name of Antonio Valenza, he embarked again…and reached first Malta, then Alexandria in Egypt. This was the old itinerary of the refugees of Italian *Risorgimento*' (*Luigi*, 105). The money to fund Galleani's escape was collected among London exiles by Emidio Recchioni, a co-editor of *L'Agitazione* who was at *domicilio coatto* with Galleani and migrated to London in 1899 (Dipaola, 'Recchioni').

The level of organization and effective action that could be reached in such undertakings was a function of both the resources that anarchists under restraint could call upon through their connections, and, conversely, the resources that autonomous initiatives of solidarity from outside summoned in their favor. Both variables were highest for prominent figures such as Malatesta and Galleani. Arguably, those two complementary factors combined into a selective mechanism whereby leaders were helped first in emergency situations such as the 1898 repression. Of course, 'leadership' is to be intended as an informal, spontaneous acknowledgment on the part of anarchist militants, not a formal, hierarchical relationship. However, such an acknowledgment existed and had consequences. Figures such as Malatesta and Galleani were considered, and arguably were, especially, important for the anarchist movement. Accordingly, their freedom was especially valued by their comrades.

In brief, spontaneous, decentralized activities could effectively self-organize into a complex and oriented whole, such as is usually associated with centralized planning and hierarchical party discipline.

Anarchist tactics and the lesson of experience

During his brief stay in London between the end of May 1899 and the beginning of August, when he left for America, Malatesta published the pamphlet *Contro la Monarchia* (Against the Monarchy), in which the overthrow of the monarchy was set as a priority for a revolutionary strategy in Italy. Since the pamphlet was dated August 1899 and Malatesta set sail for the United States on August 5—as he announced in a letter to Max Nettlau the day before (Nettlau Papers)—its completion must have immediately preceded Malatesta's departure.

The pamphlet began with a brief overview of the state of oppression in which Italy languished. The analysis was framed in general terms that could be agreed upon by all the 'progressive people' addressed in the pamphlet's subtitle. Little mention was made of class antagonisms and only passing references to government as an instrument of capitalism. Rather, the focus was on the contrast between national interests and the Savoy monarchy. The

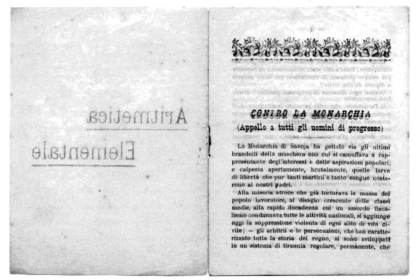

FIGURE 8.1   First page of *Contro la Monarchia*. The pamphlet's cover bore the false title *Aritmetica Elementale* to avoid police seizure
Source: Massimo Ortalli private archive

latter, Malatesta argued, had lost legitimacy and turned into an autocratic regime, which promoted disastrous policies and suppressed the civil liberties 'that cost so much martyrdom and blood to our fathers'. Malatesta pointed out the endemic poverty of the working people, 'the increasing hardships of the middle classes', and the inability of parliament 'to safeguard even the interests of the class it represents'. Malatesta's overview insisted on national rather than class interests, with references to 'oppressive taxes', a customs system that favored certain classes at the expense of 'the mass of citizens and national production', 'useless public works', 'huge armaments', 'pompous politics', and 'alliances imposed by dynastic interests in contrast to the national sympathies and interests'. In brief, Malatesta argued, Italy found itself in a situation that could not last without dragging the country 'in such a state of abjection as to make it forever incapable of raising itself up again to the dignity of a civilized life' (3–5).

Then Malatesta set out to demonstrate that the tyranny could only be overthrown by insurrection, arguing that 'it is a general characteristic of the ruling classes to persist so much more in wrongdoing as they are threatened with ruin', and that 'the monarchy can count on nothing but the sword, and to the sword it will commit its own defence and that of the class that has solidarized with it'. 'Hence', Malatesta argued, 'it is a matter of opposing force to force...' In contrast to so many past uprisings that were easily repressed and offered pretexts for a ferocious reaction because of their lack of preparation, coordination, and clarity of objective, it was necessary to match the opponent's strength with equal strength in order to make a successful insurrection (6–8).

At this point Malatesta issued his appeal for a common insurrectionary front among all the enemies of the monarchy. In Italy there were various parties, which all sincerely aimed for the common good, but radically differed in their judgments about the causes and remedies of social evils. However, given that they had a common enemy in the monarchy, while none was strong enough to overthrow it alone, the common interest was to unite 'in order to get rid of this obstacle that prevents any progress and any improvement'. No party was to give up ideas, hopes, and autonomous organization to merge into a single formation. Mutual differences were too serious for that (8–9). However, differences need not prevent distinct parties from uniting for a specific aim of common interest. Furthermore, since popular rage, to which all subversive parties had a duty to contribute, was bound to break out anyway, 'would it not be a huge mistake to act each by oneself outside of any agreement, running the risk of paralyzing each other to the advantage of the common enemy, instead of seeking, by concerted action, to secure the material victory that is the necessary condition of any transformation of the present state of affairs?' (10–12).

Afterwards, 'if all will have the respect for freedom that they claim to have, and will grant to everyone the right and the means to propagate and experiment with their own ideas, freedom will yield what it can yield, with the triumph of those methods and those institutions that best meet the current material and moral conditions'. At the very least 'the fall of the monarchy will still represent the suppression of the worst enemy, and the struggle will restart, only in more humane and civilized conditions' (12–13). The last part of the pamphlet outlined the multiple tasks that a successful insurrection posed to its participants, and strongly advocated tactical coordination and military preparation (13–15).

The propounded tactics were not new, and were subsumed by the wider theme, frequent in Malatesta's writings, of the anarchists' attitude toward the 'kindred parties', socialists and republicans. The Capolago resolutions of 1891 already envisaged a possible cooperation with the republicans 'in deeds of a revolutionary character' involving no 'compromise on the Party's principles' ('Risoluzioni', 191). In his letter of 10 March 1896 to Converti, Malatesta speculated again about a similar tactical alliance:

> If republicans were willing to take action, it seems to me that we could do no better than massing with them. Once the sleep into which Italy seems to have fallen is broken, we could raise our banner again and continue the struggle in our own way and for our own ideals.
>
> (*Epistolario*, 75)

In January 1897 Malatesta explained his ideas about 'tolerance towards kindred parties' in *La Questione Sociale* of Paterson. He expressed disapproval for intolerance and exclusivism and remarked that tolerance should not be confused with abdication. Parties must separately organize, each with its own program. However, 'there are innumerable circumstances in which giving priority to narrow party interests would be a crime, and in which the hearty cooperation of all those who aspire to human emancipation is a duty' ('Tolleranza').

Malatesta's proposal reaffirmed all his tactical tenets: insurrectionism, inclusiveness, coherence between means and ends, and anarchist autonomy. In this respect, one can see continuity with the tactics of 1897–98. Yet the proposal represented a dramatic tactical turn, thus illustrating how his tactical tenets delimited a coherent but broad space within which different tactics were possible. The import of such a turn is thrown into relief by a comparison between Malatesta's respective justifications for his tactics of 1897 and 1899.

In 1897 he distanced himself from the mazzinian illusion of a short-term revolution accomplished by a minority, which had made anarchists averse to any long and patient work of popular preparation and organization; he pointed out the pitfalls of the past focus on enrolling forces for the armed insurrection; he emphasized that the barricades erected without a certain consciousness in the people can only lead to the replacement of one government with another, and that such a consciousness could only develop gradually; and he argued that bourgeois institutions could yield much before reaching the point of crisis.

In 1899 an insurrection to topple the monarchical institution was presented as an absolute and immediate priority, in a country where 'every illusion of peaceful progress has become impossible'. Accordingly, all enemies of the monarchy were called to a work of tactical and military preparation concerning the provision of weapons and agreements on how to distribute military tasks, ensure simultaneous action, and so on.

Such a radical change of perspective had been determined by the events of 1898 in Italy. One can gauge the distance between expectations and reality from Malatesta's article on the First of May 1897. After lamenting the present state of the Italian workers' movement and pointing out the anarchists' past mistakes, he described the long-term, constant, daily work to which he called all anarchists. 'This is what we promise to our comrades', he stated, 'and this is what we demand of them.' Then he concluded: 'If we all earnestly undertake that work, the next First of May will find us in quite different conditions' ('1° Maggio'). Malatesta kept his promise during the following year, obtaining a favorable response not only from the majority of the Italian anarchist movement, but also outside of it. The First of May 1898 indeed found Malatesta and the Italian anarchists in a different condition than a year before, but, ironically, not quite in the hoped-for direction. At that date

Malatesta was in jail, and a few days later, the heavy artillery of General Bava Beccaris killed hundreds of people in the streets of Milan. Arrests and convictions followed by the thousand, and Italian anarchists, who had hoped to 'civilly live in broad daylight', had to live in large numbers at *domicilio coatto* for long months.

In brief, Malatesta's hope for a steady growth of the anarchist movement, based upon a long and patient work within the workers' movement, was irreparably shattered.

If the earlier experiment of 1897–98 has been characterized as innovative, progressive, and forward-looking, its ultimate failure does not generally receive equal emphasis. Likewise, the conviction of Malatesta and his comrades is often referred to as a political victory, because the charge of criminal association was dropped. Still, Malatesta, who had made continuity of action and sustainability the key tenets of his new tactics, was put in a condition of inactivity for 15 months, as many of his comrades were, and would return to Italy only 15 years later. In such conditions, one could have held on to the same tactics and restarted from the beginning, but this would have been a self-defeating move, as the very purpose of such tactics was to achieve a steady and continuous growth.

Instead of cyclically and unchangingly repeating the same mistakes, as the historiographical stereotype would have it, Malatesta learned the lesson of experience. His changed outlook was illustrated by the article 'Il compito degli anarchici' (The anarchists' task), of December 1899, which asked the classic question: 'What is to be done?' The best tactics would be to systematically undertake the propaganda of anarchist ideas, 'to kindle the spirit of association and resistance in the proletarians with all possible means and to arouse in them ever growing demands', in an incremental and continuous process, eventually giving anarchists enough strength to rise up autonomously and win. However, several obstacles intervened. Propaganda could not progress indefinitely in a given environment, for a point of saturation was always reached, at which only a transformation of the environment itself could bring new social strata into the reach of effective propaganda. The same reasons limited the effectiveness of workers' organization. A strong anarchist organization found an obstacle in the lack of means and in government repression. And even admitting such an indefinite progress as theoretically possible, 'every day, and well before we get to have that strength, political situations arise, in which we are obliged to intervene, not only on pain of renouncing the advantages that can be obtained from them, but also of losing any influence on the people, of destroying part of the work already done, and of making the future work more difficult'.

Thus, the problem was to find a way of determining the modifications of the environment needed by the progress of propaganda, 'and to profit from the struggles among the various political parties and from any occasions that present themselves, without giving up any part of our programme'. At that point Malatesta discussed the short-term scenario of an insurrection against the monarchy, the result of which would certainly not be anarchist socialism, and he asked: 'Should we take part in preparing and undertaking this insurrection? And how?' Malatesta warned against the opposite errors of abstaining from any tasks short of the full anarchist goal, and of temporarily setting aside anarchist goals to merge with the republicans in pursuit of immediate aims. In advocating participation, Malatesta reiterated that, for anarchists, republic and monarchy were equivalent, for all governments equally tended to extend their power. Yet the weaker a government was, or equivalently, the stronger resistance it encountered, the greater freedom and opportunities for progress were. By contributing to the fall of the monarchy, anarchists could oppose the constitution or consolidation of a republic, remain armed, and refuse obedience to the new government, as well as make attempts at expropriation and libertarian organization of society. 'We could', he concluded, 'prevent the revolution from halting after its first step, and the popular energy just awakened by the insurrection from subsiding again' ('Compito').

The article contained obvious references to the context of 1897–98, such as the observation about the tactics of 'kindling the spirit of association and resistance in the proletarians with all possible means and to arouse in them ever growing demands'. Significantly, Malatesta was now casting doubts on the possibility of indefinitely extending propaganda and workers' organization within the present social context. The purported reasons made equally evident reference to 1898. The extension of anarchist organization, even when aimed at propaganda, was limited by government repression, as the events had demonstrated. And, at any rate, social unrest independently arose, in which anarchists were obliged to intervene, as had been the case with the bread riots.

In what light should Malatesta's new tactical turn be seen? Giampietro Berti regards it as a return to the past: 'Now, after the events of 1898, in his view the classical insurrectionary perspective seemed to present itself again with renewed vigor. The barricades in Milan, nearly a revival of the similar ones of 50 years earlier, seemed to make the idea of an immediate and violent revolution current again.' Berti further remarks: 'Although it was reaffirmed "that republic and monarchy are equivalent" emphasis was placed on the necessity for the anarchists to participate in a popular action, so as not to leave the anti-monarchy movement in the hands of socialists, republicans, and bourgeois democrats.' What makes the pamphlet interesting, for Berti, is that 'it put back on the agenda an insurrectional hypothesis that seems almost written for the days of 1848' (*Errico*, 313–14).

Berti's analysis, which repeats the stereotyped image of Malatesta as a nostalgic proponent of an obsolete insurrectional model, is utterly misleading. First of all, there is as much justification, or arbitrariness, in linking Malatesta's insurrectionary tactics to the past uprisings of 1848 as to the future capture of the Winter Palace in October 1917, which was indeed an insurrection undertaken by a coalition of forces. Regarding Malatesta as backward- or forward-looking is a matter of choice.

More importantly, Malatesta's proposal was not a revival of the 'classical' insurrectionary perspective. It could not be a revival, simply because Malatesta had never abandoned the insurrectionary perspective, as he kept reasserting even in 1897, though he did not posit it as an immediate objective. At the same time, the current perspective on insurrection implied a break with the past. In contrast to both Berti's claim that the barricades in Milan revamped the idea of an immediate revolution, and to the anarchists' past belief in such a prospect, for Malatesta those barricades had a totally different meaning: they proved that the linear path to revolution he had earlier envisioned was problematic. In contrast to his hope of 1897 that anarchist could gradually build revolutionary strength within the present society, the key point he was now making was that such a process was bound to be interrupted long before it could come to a hoped-for completion, precisely because popular agitations such as those of Milan would inevitably intervene before the conditions for a truly revolutionary outcome were reached.

Malatesta's tactical turn was neither a return to the past, nor a rejection of the ideas recently advocated in *L'Agitazione*. In fact, the key intuitions that had led to the new tactics of 1897 were preserved and further articulated in the new tactical turn of 1899. The proposal for an insurrectionary alliance was an instance of Malatesta's inclusive attitude toward 'kindred parties' that had been prominent in the anarchist-socialist tactics of 1897–98. Furthermore, Malatesta had maintained that the barricades erected 'without a certain consciousness in the people can only lead to the replacement of one government with another'. Now, Malatesta was advocating insurrection in the short term. Yet his earlier point was not forgotten. In fact, he made clear that the next insurrection would not result in anarchist socialism. In 1897 he had argued that people's consciousness 'can only develop gradually, through the daily struggle, which cannot be the one fought on the barricades'. Now, the purpose of the insurrection was precisely to remove the obstacles in the way of such a gradual process, and to bring about a transformation of the environment that could bring new social strata into the reach of propaganda. In 1897, Malatesta had claimed that bourgeois institutions could still yield much before reaching the point of crisis. Now, it was still not a matter of abolishing bourgeois institutions altogether, but of replacing the monarchy with less repressive bourgeois institutions.

Though Berti seems to regard Malatesta's claim that republic and monarchy were equivalent as paradoxical or contradictory, Malatesta explained clearly how they could be both equivalent and different in the very paragraph in which he made that claim. They were equivalent from the point of view of rulers, which all had an equal tendency to extend their power as much as possible. They were different because rulers, against their will, could be stronger or weaker depending on the degree of resistance they encountered. In turn, different degrees of freedom and opportunity for progress could be found in different societies, depending on the rulers' degree of weakness. What really made the difference between Malatesta's ideas of 1897 and 1899 was the lesson of experience, especially the realization that not even the conditions for sustainable struggles for simple economic improvements existed in Italy. As he remarked in *Contro la Monarchia*: 'To put an end to an agitation that, after all, amounted to unarmed demonstrations and small-scale riots, which the abolition of customs and few other insignificant concessions would have easily calmed down, the government did not hesitate to massacre citizens by the hundred' (13).

In sum, Malatesta returned to the idea of insurrection by moving further away from the old idea of insurrection that was equated with revolution. Instead, the gap between insurrection and revolution became wider. Short-term insurrectionary prospects were contrasted with the long-term prospects of an anarchist revolution. Insurrection came to be incorporated into the gradual process that led from the present society to anarchy. This led Malatesta to the thoroughly novel and unconventional idea that the next step in the process toward the anarchist revolution was a non-anarchist insurrection. This contrasted with the oft-repeated claim that 'the revolution will be anarchist or will not be at all', against which Malatesta would still be arguing in 1922 ('Ancora'). It was not just a matter of supporting a non-anarchist insurrection that was likely to happen anyway, as Malatesta somewhat deceivingly made it appear in his article of December 1899, probably because he was wary of publicly revealing such plans as his own. Rather it was a matter for anarchists to promote such an insurrection as a priority, as Malatesta actually did in *Contro la Monarchia*, which had been published anonymously.

Furthermore, commentators have often emphasized the novelty of Malatesta's tactics, by pointing out his realism in proposing tactics suitable for anarchism as a minoritarian movement. However, it should be remarked that his proposal was not simply a sort of tactical makeshift solution for low-ebb times. Malatesta's claim was much stronger and crucial: anarchists were essentially and necessarily bound to be a minority within bourgeois society. If anarchists were to stick to their own principles and tactics—as Malatesta was adamant they should—crises were bound to happen long before they could become majoritarian. These would not be abortive attempts, but rather crises that would bring about a freer society without immediately bringing about the anarchist society, yet. In this conception, one can discern the seed of the idea of 'anarchist gradualism' that Malatesta would fully express a quarter of a century later.

Such gradualist awareness was clearly expressed a few months after *Contro la Monarchia* and a week after Malatesta's article on the anarchists' task, in the article 'Verso l'anarchia' (Toward anarchy), which has rightly become one of Malatesta's most reprinted and translated articles. In contrast to the prejudice, traceable even in their own ranks, that anarchists expected anarchy to come with one stroke, and to the associated belief that anarchy thus conceived was impossible, Malatesta argued that the essence of anarchy was that it could not be forcibly imposed, but it could only triumph when all human beings had developed an anarchist conscience—a process which could only happen gradually. Hence, 'anarchy cannot come but little by little, slowly, but surely, growing in intensity and extension'; 'it is not a matter of achieving anarchy today, tomorrow, or within ten centuries, but of walking toward anarchy today, tomorrow, and always.' The problem lay in knowing how to choose the path that approached the ideal's realization, without confusing real progress with hypocritical reforms. Though anarchists might not be able to overthrow the present government, or to prevent another one from arising in its place, every weakening of authority that they could achieve would be a progress toward anarchy. Anarchists could not soon abolish private property, and perhaps they would still not be able to in the next insurrectionary movement. Still, every victory against the bosses, every decrease of exploitation, would be a step on the road of anarchy.

Even after the right of force had disappeared and the means of production had been placed under the producers' management, anarchy would only be for those who wanted it, and only in those things that they could accomplish without the cooperation of the non-anarchists. Anarchists did not intend to destroy anything but what could be replaced, as such replacement became gradually possible. As bad as collective services such as food distribution, mail, and schools were present, they could only be destroyed to the extent that something better could be put in their place. In sum, 'to arrive at anarchy, having the material force to make a revolution is not enough; it is also essential that the workers, grouped according to the various branches of production, become able to ensure by themselves the functioning of social life, without the need of capitalists or governments.' Ultimately, anarchist ideas were 'the experimental system brought from the field of research to that of social realization' ('Verso').

New Jersey: taking care of Italian business

Malatesta expounded these ideas while he was in the United States, during that 'intermission' between two cycles of his struggle. In fact, far from being a temporary disengagement from the anarchist movement in Italy, Malatesta's journey was motivated precisely by issues of crucial importance to that movement. Such importance can be appreciated by giving due attention to two fundamental aspects of Italian anarchism: the centrality of the controversy on organization; and the role of the movement's transnational segment. Both aspects were key to Malatesta's trip, which also provides evidence of how cross-national ties among worldwide-mobile militants of different countries were upheld over time.

As Luigi Fabbri relates, Malatesta was invited to the United States by his old Spanish friend Pedro Esteve, who lived in Paterson, New Jersey (*Vida*, 145). Esteve tried to contact Malatesta with urgency, as soon as news of Malatesta's escape spread. In the editorial mail column ('Piccola Posta') of *La Questione Sociale* of 27 May, we find the following message: 'London—E. M. [Errico Malatesta]—Esteve wrote to your address and to that of K. [probably Kropotkin] He hopes for a prompt response.' Less than a month later, the project had already taken shape. On 24 June Malatesta wrote to Domela Nieuwenhuis that in five or six weeks he would leave for the United States, where he was engaged with the Italian and Spanish comrades in a speaking tour, and where he would remain for six months (Nieuwenhuis Papers, file 177). The editorship of *La Questione Sociale*, of which Esteve was the typesetter, was a key issue that prompted Malatesta to undertake his trip. At that time *La Questione Sociale* was directed by Giuseppe Ciancabilla, who had come from Europe nine months earlier and had given an anti-organizationist direction to the periodical. The import of the question for Malatesta, as well as for Esteve, can be fully appreciated in the context of the situation in which Italian anarchism found itself in the homeland at that time.

The aftermath of the 1898 riots in Italy was one of those periods in which the role of the transnational anarchist press became especially crucial. The anarchist press had been completely silenced in Italy, and worldwide there existed only two Italian language periodicals at the time of Malatesta's trip to America: *La Questione Sociale* of Paterson and *L'Avvenire* of Buenos Aires (Bettini). In this context, one can understand how serious it was for Malatesta that during his captivity one of the two surviving voices of Italian anarchism worldwide had been given an anti-organizationist direction.

The editorship of *La Questione Sociale* had been contentious for some time after Ciancabilla took it on. A meeting of February 1899 declared that *La Questione Sociale* was 'the organ of all comrades in the United States and outside of Italy', and, upon Ciancabilla's proposal, adopted the formula that the periodical be an open forum for discussion, in which both organizationist and anti-organizationist tendencies would have a voice ('Riunione'). However, discussion in the Paterson group continued. After Malatesta's arrival in Paterson, the editorship issue was put again on the agenda and settled relatively quickly. The editing group 'Diritto all'Esistenza' (Right to exist) called a meeting in which the inclusive open forum approach was rejected as unsatisfactory. As Malatesta reported, it was acknowledged that effective propaganda required a clear direction and the vast majority of the group declared itself for organizationist tactics, such as creating anarchist federations ('Separazione'). Ciancabilla resigned the editorship, and with a small group

of dissidents he founded a new periodical, *L'Aurora* (Ciancabilla, Della Barile, and Guabello). On 9 September the new series of *La Questione Sociale*
started under Malatesta's editorship. Significantly, the first issue of the new
series started the publication of an anarchist program ('Nostro'), which was
one of the most contentious subjects between the supporters and the opponents of organization.

In the wake of the split at *La Questione Sociale* came one of those episodes
that constitute juicy opportunities for historians interested more in colorful
than in insightful accounts of anarchism. During a meeting Malatesta was
shot in a leg by an anti-organizationist opponent, fortunately without serious
consequences. In George Woodcock's account the episode sums up Malatesta's whole journey to North America:

> Malatesta sailed to the United States. There his life once again took a
> sensational turn, which this time almost brought it to an end. He be-
> came involved in a dispute with the individualist anarchists of Paterson,
> who insisted that anarchism implied no organization at all, and that
> every man must act solely on his impulses. At last, in one noisy de-
> bate, the individual impulse of a certain comrade directed him to shoot
> Malatesta, who was badly wounded but obstinately refused to name his
> assailant. The would-be assassin fled to California, and Malatesta even-
> tually recovered: in 1900 he set sail for London . . . (330)

The detail that 'the would-be assassin fled to California' indicates that
Woodcock gives credit to Max Nomad's faulty account (30) that identifies
the assailant with Ciancabilla, who did eventually move to California but
had no part in the shooting.

Trivializing accounts such as Woodcock's reduce the interest of the controversy between Malatesta and Ciancabilla to the sensation of associated
events, that is, Malatesta's shooting and the bitter personal character that
the controversy eventually took on. However, its real historical value is
that, before turning sour, the debate was an articulate exposition of the
arguments of organizationists and anti-organizationists as made by two
brilliant advocates.

ORGANIZATION AND OLIGARCHY: AN ANARCHIST DEBATE

As Malatesta's debate of two years before with Merlino on anarchism and
parliamentarianism, the debate with Ciancabilla provides an opportunity to
review opposing arguments and systematically discuss Malatesta's views on
the central issue of organization. This was the object of the most heated,
divisive, and long-lasting controversy of Italian anarchism. The issue was
discussed in Malatesta's writings for over four decades, from 1889 down to
1927–30, when Malatesta, the life-long champion of anarchist organization

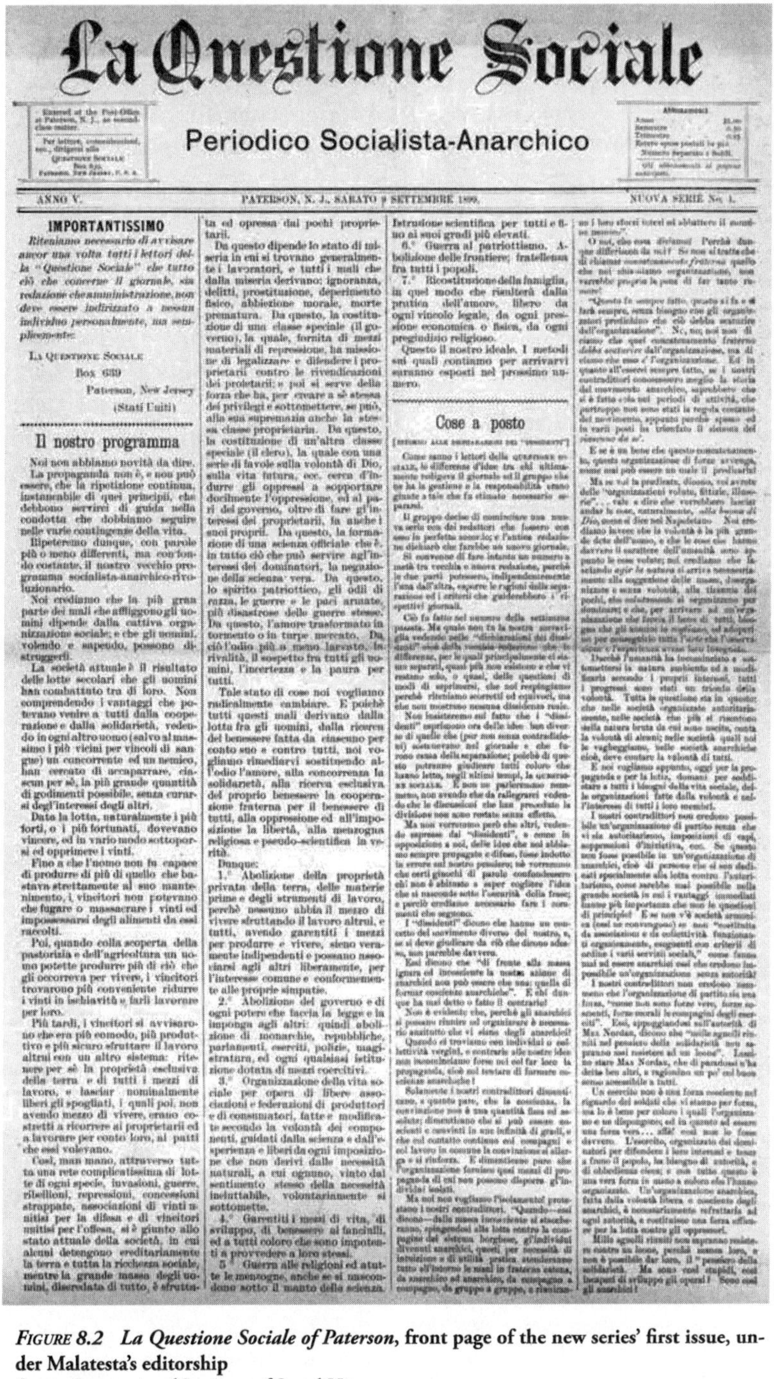

La Questione Sociale

Periodico Socialista-Anarchico

ANNO V. | PATERSON, N. J., SABATO 9 SETTEMBRE 1899. | NUOVA SERIE N. 1.

IMPORTANTISSIMO

Riteniamo necessario di avvisare ancor una volta tutti i lettori della "Questione Sociale" che tutto ciò che concerne il giornale, sia redazione che amministrazione, non deve essere indirizzato a nessun individuo personalmente, ma semplicemente:

LA QUESTIONE SOCIALE
Box 639
Paterson, New Jersey
(Stati Uniti)

Il nostro programma

Noi non abbiamo novità da dire.

La propaganda non è, e non può essere, che la ripetizione continua, instancabile di quei principii, che debbono servirci di guida nella condotta che dobbiamo seguire nelle varie contingenze della vita.

Ripeteremo dunque, con parole più o meno differenti, ma con fondo costante, il nostro vecchio programma socialista-anarchico-rivoluzionario.

Noi crediamo che la più gran parte dei mali che affliggono gli uomini dipende dalla cattiva organizzazione sociale; e che gli uomini, volendo e sapendo, possono distruggerli.

La società attuale è il risultato delle lotte secolari che gli uomini han combattuto tra di loro. Non comprendendo i vantaggi che potevano venire a tutti dalla cooperazione e dalla solidarietà, vedendo in ogni altro uomo (salvo al massimo i più vicini per vincoli di sangue) un concorrente ed un nemico, han cercato di accaparrare, ciascun per sè, la più grande quantità di godimenti possibile, senza curarsi degl'interessi degli altri.

Data la lotta, naturalmente i più forti, o i più fortunati, dovevano vincere, ed in vario modo sottoporsi ed opprimere i vinti.

Fino a che l'uomo non fu capace di produrre di più di quello che bastava strettamente al suo mantenimento, i vincitori non potevano che fugare o massacrare i vinti ed impossessarsi degli alimenti da essi raccolti.

Poi, quando colla scoperta della pastorizia e dell'agricoltura un uomo potette produrre più di ciò che gli occorreva per vivere, i vincitori trovarono più conveniente ridurre i vinti in ischiavitù e farli lavorare per loro.

Più tardi, i vincitori si avvisarono che era più comodo, più produttivo e più sicuro sfruttare il lavoro altrui con un altro sistema: ritenere per sè la proprietà esclusiva della terra e di tutti i mezzi di lavoro, e lasciar nominalmente liberi gli spogliati, i quali poi, non avendo mezzo di vivere, erano costretti a ricorrere ai proprietarii ed a lavorare per conto loro, ai patti che essi volevano.

Così, man mano, attraverso tutta una rete complicatissima di lotte di ogni specie, invasioni, guerre, ribellioni, repressioni, concessioni strappate, associazioni di vinti unitisi per la difesa e di vincitori unitisi per l'offesa, si è giunto allo stato attuale della società, in cui alcuni detengono ereditariamente la terra e tutta la ricchezza sociale, mentre la grande massa degli uomini, diseredata di tutto, è sfruttata ed oppressa dai pochi proprietarii.

Da questo dipende lo stato di miseria in cui si trovano generalmente i lavoratori, e tutti i mali che dalla miseria derivano: ignoranza, delitti, prostituzione, deperimento fisico, abbiezione morale, morte prematura. Da questo, la costituzione di una classe speciale (il governo), la quale, fornita di mezzi materiali di repressione, ha missione di legalizzare e difendere i proprietarii contro le rivendicazioni dei proletarii; e poi si serve della forza che ha, per creare a sè stessa dei privilegi e sottomettere, se può, alla sua supremazia anche la stessa classe proprietaria. Da questo, la costituzione di un'altra classe speciale (il clero), la quale con una serie di favole sulla volontà di Dio, sulla vita futura, ecc. cerca d'indurre gli oppressi a sopportare docilmente l'oppressione, ed al pari del governo, oltre di fare gl'interessi dei proprietarii, fa anche i suoi proprii. Da questo, la formazione di una scienza officiale che è, in tutto ciò che può servire agl'interessi dei dominatori, la negazione della scienza vera. Da questo, lo spirito patriottico, gli odii di razza, le guerre e le paci armate, più disastrose delle guerre stesse. Da questo, l'amore trasformato in tormento o in turpe mercato. Da ciò l'odio più o meno larvato, la rivalità, il sospetto fra tutti gli uomini, l'incertezza e la paura per tutti.

Tale stato di cose noi vogliamo radicalmente cambiare. E poichè tutti questi mali derivano dalla lotta fra gli uomini, dalla ricerca del benessere fatta da ciascuno per conto suo e contro tutti, noi vogliamo rimediarvi sostituendo all'odio l'amore, alla concorrenza la solidarietà, alla ricerca esclusiva del proprio benessere la cooperazione fraterna per il benessere di tutti, alla oppressione ed all'imposizione la libertà, alla menzogna religiosa e pseudo-scientifica la verità.

Dunque:

1.° Abolizione della proprietà privata della terra, delle materie prime e degli strumenti di lavoro, perchè nessuno abbia il mezzo di vivere sfruttando il lavoro altrui, e tutti, avendo garentiti i mezzi per produrre e vivere, sieno veramente indipendenti e possano associarsi agli altri liberamente, per l'interesse comune e conformemente alle proprie simpatie.

2.° Abolizione del governo e di ogni potere che faccia la legge e la imponga agli altri: quindi abolizione di monarchie, repubbliche, parlamenti, eserciti, polizie, magistratura, ed ogni qualsiasi istituzione dotata di mezzi coercitivi.

3.° Organizzazione della vita sociale per opera di libere associazioni e federazioni di produttori e di consumatori, fatte e modificate secondo la volontà dei componenti, guidati dalla scienza e dall'esperienza e liberi da ogni imposizione che non derivi dalle necessità naturali, a cui ognuno, vinto dal sentimento stesso della necessità ineluttabile, volontariamente si sottomette.

4.° Garentiti i mezzi di vita, di sviluppo, di benessere ai fanciulli, ed a tutti coloro che sono impotenti a provvedere a loro stessi.

5.° Guerra alle religioni ed a tutte le menzogne, anche se si nascondono sotto il manto della scienza. Istruzione scientifica per tutti e fino ai suoi gradi più elevati.

6.° Guerra al patriottismo. Abolizione delle frontiere; fratellanza fra tutti i popoli.

7.° Ricostituzione della famiglia, in quel modo che risulterà dalla pratica dell'amore, libero da ogni vincolo legale, da ogni pressione economica o fisica, da ogni pregiudizio religioso.

Questo il nostro ideale. I metodi sui quali contiamo per arrivarvi saranno esposti nel prossimo numero.

Cose a posto

Come sanno i lettori della QUESTIONE SOCIALE, le differenze d'idee tra chi ultimamente redigeva il giornale ed il gruppo che ne ha la gestione e la responsabilità erano giunte a tale che fu stimato necessario separarsi.

FIGURE 8.2 ***La Questione Sociale of Paterson*, front page of the new series' first issue, under Malatesta's editorship**

Source: International Institute of Social History

in the face of charges of authoritarianism, critiqued the authoritarian content of the *Platform*, the model of anarchist organization advocated by Nestor Makhno and other Russian anarchists.

The crux of the controversy between organizationists and anti-organizationists was whether anarchists should organize in any institutional form.

As Ciancabilla explained in parting from *La Questione Sociale*, anti-organizationists claimed that an aim 'spontaneously directs towards itself the efforts of those who struggle to the same end, without this implying the binding acceptance of a common program of struggle, which would be impossible to follow without mutual concessions and curtailments by individuals with diverse temperaments and ways of thinking, viewing, and feeling, for the sake of complying with a majority'. For them, 'party' meant a sect. Admission, excommunication, and exclusivism were its fatal consequences (Ciancabilla, Della Barile, and Guabello). Similarly, Luigi Galleani, the most influential representative of anti-organizationism, argued in 1925 that 'a political party, any political party, has its program, that is its constitutional charter; in assemblies of group representatives, it has its parliament; in its management, its boards and executive committees, it has its government.' In short, it was 'a true hierarchy, no matter how disguised, in which all stages are connected by a single bond, discipline, which punishes infractions with sanctions that go from censure to excommunication, to expulsion' (*End*, 45).

In contrast, organizationists argued for the creation of anarchist federations. In the three-part article 'L'organizzazione' of June 1897—his most comprehensive work on the subject—Malatesta argued that it was only natural that individuals sharing a common goal 'make agreements, join forces, distribute tasks, and take all those appropriate measures to reach the goal that constitutes the object of an organization'. In contrast, he argued, isolation meant 'dooming oneself to powerlessness, wasting one's energy in small, ineffective acts, and soon losing faith in the goal and falling into complete inaction'. Organizationists emphasized that their model of organization had no authoritarian element, for nobody had the right to impose one's will, or committed oneself to resolutions that one had not previously accepted. Members only had the moral duty to see through their commitments and to do nothing that would contradict the accepted program. Within those boundaries, individual members could express any opinion and use any tactics.

The controversy was rooted in opposite perspectives about the relationship between individual and society.

The fundamental value of anti-organizationists was individual autonomy, the ability to only act in conformity with one's own will. 'We aspire to realize the *autonomy of the individual within the freedom of association*', Galleani wrote, 'the independence of his thought, of his life, of his development, of his destiny, freedom from violence, from caprice and from the domination of the majority, as well as of various minorities.' Anti-organizationists, Galleani continued, referred to libertarian communism as a way 'to find an economic *ubi consistam* [where should I stand] in which this political autonomy of the individual may find an enlightened and happy reality' (*End*, 35–6). Obviously, they were aware that individual autonomy was limited in the bourgeois society. However, for them this was one more reason for treasuring such autonomy in the sphere of political action. In contrast to stereotypical representations, anti-organizationists neither advocated acting solely on one's impulses nor egoism, that is, the exclusive concern for their own individual interest. On the contrary, they were thoroughly egalitarian and advocates of solidarity. Likewise, the distinction between anti-organizationists and organizationists should not be confused, as it frequently is, with more popular distinctions, such as between individualists and communists. The two most influential anti-organizationists argued otherwise: Ciancabilla claimed that individualism and anarchism were contradictory terms (Ciancabilla, Della Barile, and Guabello), while Galleani preferred to argue that between communism and individualism there was no contradiction; at any rate, neither rejected communism.

While anti-organizationists placed emphasis on individual autonomy, organizationists considered association the fundamental human trait. For Malatesta, organization was a necessity of life: 'organization' and 'society' were near synonyms. The isolated man was so impotent that he could not even live the life of a brute. Having to unite with other men, or rather finding himself already united as a consequence of the species' prior evolution, he had three options: submit to others and be a slave; impose one's will on others and be an authority; or live in brotherly agreement for the greatest welfare of all, thus being an associate. For Malatesta, 'no one can get out of this necessity' ('Organizzazione', pt. 1). The fact that present institutions were authoritarian was not to obscure that they addressed social needs: 'all institutions that oppress and exploit man had their origin in a real need of human society' ('I nostri propositi: II'). The anarchist society was at the same time the society where organization was at its highest, and authority at its lowest. Significantly, Malatesta added: 'if we believed that there can be no organization without authority, we would rather be authoritarian, because we would still prefer authority, which hinders and aggrieves life, to disorganization, which makes it impossible' ('Organizzazione', pt. 1). Thus, for Malatesta man was unavoidably a social being, always immersed in a web of social relations.

However, Malatesta shunned holistic outlooks on society. For him, two models of organization existed, corresponding to two concepts of human society. All acknowledge, he argued, that man needs man, and that society is the result of this need. However, some maintain 'that the aim of association and cooperation among men is to contribute to the well-being and improvement of "society," and that the individual good must be sacrificed to the "collective good" '. This view was based on an analogy with complex organisms, in which 'the work of cells and of the various organs is done to the service of the entire organism, which alone has a conscience and is properly capable of pleasure and pain'. Since, in human society, 'each individual has a conscience, while no collective conscience exists, the "collective good" of which the abovementioned theorists talk means, in practice, the good of those who rule'. In contrast, 'others think that the aim of society must be the well-being and self-development of all its members, and hence that all must have equal rights and equal means, whereas nobody can oblige someone else to do anything against their own will' ('Principio'). Missing the distinction between the sociological and methodological planes is a source of confusion about Malatesta's view. For example, Sharif Gemie contrasts Bakunin's claim that the 'isolated individual' is a fiction and society an 'eternal reality', with Malatesta's claim that 'the real thing is man, the individual' ('Counter-Community', 352). For Gemie the two claims are mutually contradictory. Yet Malatesta maintained both: no living individual existed outside of society, but 'society' denoted no undivided whole.

From the axiomatic value respectively attributed to autonomy and association, anti-organizationists and organizationists derived opposite views about permanent collective structures. For the former, membership in any such structure—no matter how free from coercion—amounted by definition to accepting external constraints on autonomy, and was therefore rejected. For the latter, organization was a necessity, or more simply a fact of life, beyond individual choice. What was indeed a matter of choice was whether people organized in an authoritarian or egalitarian way. Accordingly, they gave little consideration to individual autonomy as an abstract value, for in practice it amounted to unsustainable isolation. Rather, they aimed to prevent anyone from being forced to obey someone else's individual will. For anti-organizationists, external norms limited individual autonomy and therefore were authoritarian. For organizationists, such norms were both necessary and harmless, as long as they were self-imposed and modifiable. Such difference in theoretical premises determined a sort of asymmetry between the respective attitudes to the debate. Organizationists, for whom organization was a necessity for everyone, whether one admitted it or not, regarded the debate as lacking real ground, while anti-organizationists emphasized the gap between them and their opponents and turned organization into a question of principle.

The issue of organization had far-reaching ramifications, concerning especially the relationship between anarchist and labor movements: in a nutshell, for anti-organizationists there was mutual exclusion and discontinuity, for organizationists inclusion and continuity. 'In the face of the unconscious and unaware mass', Ciancabilla argued, 'our action of anarchists can be only one: to form anarchist consciences.' He described the process of becoming anarchist as one of 'separating from the unconscious mass' (Ciancabilla,

Della Barile, and Guabello). Ciancabilla's language illustrates an outlook on the formation of anarchist consciousness as an individual, not a collective process; not as gradual, but as happening at once; and finally, as a process of separation from the unaware mass. Galleani conveyed a similar idea when he remarked that 'the anarchist movement and the labour movement follow two parallel lines, and it has been geometrically proven that parallels never meet' (*End*, 47). Nevertheless, Galleani maintained that anarchists should join unions 'whenever we find it useful to our struggle and wherever it is possible to do so under *well defined pledges and reservations*' (49). His viewpoint was epitomized by his foremost role in the Paterson silk strike of June 1902, which cost him a bullet in the face and forced him to escape to Canada (Avrich, *Anarchist Portraits*, 168). Galleani's pledges and reservations were largely shared by organizationists. Malatesta claimed to be 'almost completely in agreement with Galleani' on the subject ('Fine dell'anarchismo'). However, Galleani's stance was mainly instrumental. Unions were environments for anarchist propaganda, and possibly for anti-capitalist direct action, but no intrinsic value was attributed to their ends and means, both deemed inconsistent with anarchism.

In contrast, Malatesta observed in 1897 that workers could never emancipate themselves until they found in union the moral, economic, and physical strength to overcome their enemy. He remarked that some anarchists were hostile to any organization that did not explicitly aim for anarchy and follow anarchist methods. Hence, some kept aloof from all unions, or meddled with them with the avowed goal of disorganizing them; while others admitted that one could join existing unions, but considered nearly as defection any attempt to organize new ones. In contrast to the belief that any forces organized for less than revolutionary goals took away from revolution, Malatesta maintained that aloofness from unions doomed anarchism to perpetual sterility. Propaganda, he argued, was to be done among the people, and unions provided the most receptive ground for that. In addition, propaganda could only have a limited effect, as anarchist consciousness could seldom be reached at once. Organization was a worker's means to gradually and collectively approach anarchism through class consciousness:

> To become an anarchist for good, and not only nominally, he must start to feel the solidarity that links him to his comrades; learn to cooperate with the others for the defence of the common interests; and, struggling against the masters and the government that supports the masters, understand that masters and governments are useless parasites and that workers could manage by themselves the social enterprise. When he has understood all this, he is an anarchist, even if he does not carry the denomination.
>
> ('Organizzazione', pt. 3)

Most importantly, the support for popular organizations was not only good tactics, but also a consequence of anarchist ideas, and as such it should be inscribed in the anarchist program. Authoritarian parties were interested in organizing the people only to the extent that it was necessary to get them in power, either electorally or militarily, depending on a party's parliamentarian or revolutionary tactics. In contrast, anarchists did not believe in emancipating the people, but rather in people emancipating themselves. Hence, it mattered for them that all interests and opinions have a voice in collective life through conscious organization and that as many people as possible be accustomed to organizing and managing their interests. 'Social life', Malatesta argued, 'admits no interruption. During the revolution—or insurrection, whatever we want to call it—and immediately after, one must eat, dress, travel, print, cure sick people, etc., and all these things do not get done by themselves.' Once government and capitalists were driven out, those tasks fell upon workers. 'And how could these workers provide for the urgent needs if they were not already accustomed to meet and deal together with the common interests, and were not already prepared to take upon themselves the heritage of the old society?' ('Organizzazione', pt. 3.)

Malatesta acknowledged the authoritarian risks of unions. In 1897 he discussed the issue of salaries in socialist enterprises, such as newspapers and unions, comparing the options of paid staff versus volunteer personnel. He illustrated the risk of creating a privileged class of employees by the examples of the German SPD and the English trade unions. He pragmatically suggested the middle course that paid staff should be limited as much as possible, gain no more than in one's regular profession, and in any case not more than manual workers ('Salario'). A similar proposal was renewed in 1913, when Malatesta added that unions' executive staff should change as frequently as possible. Still, he attributed increasing importance to anarchist full involvement in unions ('Anarchici e le leghe'). In 1921 he argued that anarchists should not simply participate passively as workers, but also accept responsibilities compatible with their beliefs. He acknowledged that this course of action was not immune from risks of 'taming, deviation, and corruption', but he also argued that such risks could be minimized by prescribing a specific line of conduct, and by exercising a 'continuous, mutual control among comrades' ('Anarchici nel movimento'). In 1923 he returned to the subject of anarchists' executive positions in unions, suggesting again a middle course between extreme options: 'I believe that in general and in quiet times this would be better avoided. However, I believe that the harm and the danger does not lie so much in occupying an executive position—which in certain circumstances may be useful and even necessary—as in perpetuating oneself in that position' ('Condotta').

Finally, in an article of 1927 Malatesta drew a clear line between anarchist and authoritarian organization in response to the pamphlet *Organizational Platform of the General Union of Anarchists*, published the year before in France by a group of exiled Russian anarchists, including Nestor Makhno and Peter Arshinov. Malatesta's response, which complements the debate with anti-organizationists and provides a fuller picture of his outlook on organization, expressed long-held ideas that, as often happened, he fully formulated only when the need to do so arose from current debates in the anarchist movement. Malatesta's main target was the 'principle of collective responsibility' introduced by the executive organ of the newly formed Anarchist Union, according to which 'the entire Union will be responsible for the political and revolutionary activity of each member; in the same way, each member will be responsible for the political and revolutionary activity of the Union as a whole' (Dielo Trouda). If the Union was responsible for what each member did, Malatesta objected, how could it leave individual members the freedom to apply the common program as they thought best? Being responsible for someone's action meant being in a position to prevent it. Hence, Malatesta continued, the Executive Committee would need to monitor the action of individual members and order them what to do or not do. Conversely, how could an individual accept responsibility for the actions of a collectivity before knowing what they would be and if he could not prevent what he disapproved of? Moreover, what did 'the will of the Union' stand for? Once again, Malatesta rejected any holistic concept of an undivided collective, on the ground that decisions would always ultimately come from a set of individuals; if this was not the set of all members, in which case unanimity would be required, it was bound to be a group, either a majority or a minority, which imposed its will on the others ('Project'). Malatesta did not object to the need for unity, but rather, as he had done in his debate of 1897 with Merlino, to the blind acceptance of a binding decision process, even by majority rule.

Ultimately, and in contrast to irrationalist interpretations of anarchism as unconcerned with practical means, the whole debate on organization concerned precisely the relation between anarchist ends and means. As Malatesta repeated in his criticism of the Platform, 'it is not enough to want something; one also has to adopt suitable means; to get to a certain place one must take the right path or end up somewhere else' ('Project'). That organizationists and anti-organizationists shared common goals was always understood throughout the debate, which concerned the best means to achieve them: in particular, by focusing on the possibly authoritarian outcome of anarchist organization, even beyond the intentions of its advocates, the debate was about the displacement of goals. Yet, despite its breadth, the debate has gone largely unnoticed outside of anarchist circles. Part of the reason may be that the debate, as was characteristic of the anarchist movement, was almost entirely carried out in anarchist periodicals, thus severely limiting its circulation outside of the anarchist movement and its transmission to the posterity. In any case, the crude cliché of anarchists simply rejecting organization out of hand is still predominant. At the same time, many ideas debated between organizationists and anti-organizationists have become common currency in the sociological literature.

This is due, in particular, to the German sociologist Robert Michels, whose *Political Parties*, of 1911, has been defined 'one of the twentieth century's most influential books' and 'a classic of social science' (Lipset, 20). Michels's 'fundamental sociological law of political parties', better known as the 'iron law of oligarchy', is clearly linked with the foregoing discussion: 'it is organization which gives birth to the domination of the elected over the electors, of the mandataries over the mandators, of the delegates over the delegators. Who says organization says oligarchy' (365). A socialist in his early years, Michels grew disillusioned with German Social Democracy and turned against parliamentarianism. From 1904 on he developed intellectual ties with French syndicalists and anarchists, and in 1907 he obtained a professorship in Italy. In brief, Michels had a first-hand acquaintance with the ideas of the anarchist movement, especially the Italian movement (Linz, 5–11). He acknowledged that 'anarchists were the first to insist upon the hierarchical and oligarchic consequences of party organization. Their view of the defects of organization is much clearer than that of socialists and even than that of syndicalists' (325). The historian Carl Levy argues that Michels specifically used Malatesta's ideas on bureaucracy in workers' organizations ('Malatesta in Exile', 274). The similarity exists, but Malatesta's points about labor bureaucracy were pressed even more forcefully by anti-organizationists. In other words, Michels's arguments reflected ideas that were the common denominator of organizationists and anti-organizationists alike. Those ideas were only the background to their controversy.

In fact, organizationists differed most from Michels, because, unlike anti-organizationists, they believed that the law of oligarchy was not as iron-made as Michels claimed. Specifically, Malatesta and Michels diverged in their outlook on the masses.

Michels thus expressed his 'scientific conviction':

> the objective immaturity of the mass is not a mere transitory phenomenon which will disappear with the progress of democratization *au lendemain du socialisme*. On the contrary, it derives from the very nature of the mass as mass, for this, even when organized, suffers from an incurable incompetence for the solution of the diverse problems which present themselves for solution—because the mass *per se* is amorphous, and therefore needs division of labor, specialization, and guidance. (367)

From this belief Michels derived his rejection of anarchism. He approvingly quoted Walter Borgius, who, commenting on Johann Most's claim that 'only the dictatorial and the servile could be sincere opponents of anarchism', remarked that 'in view of the natural endowments of human beings, it seems probable that the majority will always continue to belong to one or other of the two types here characterized by Most' (370).

In contrast, Malatesta believed that the incompetence of the masses was curable; or, at least, he agnostically refrained from either postulating any natural endowment of human beings, or venturing into historical prophecies.

A NATIONAL MOVEMENT SPANNING CONTINENTS

The theoretical articulation of the Malatesta–Ciancabilla debate of 1899 on organization made it a highlight in a controversy that spanned several decades. That a foremost episode in such a long-lasting and momentous controversy for the Italian anarchist movement in the homeland took place abroad speaks to the transnational dimension of that movement.

'Nostra patria è il mondo intero' (Our homeland is the whole world), declares a popular song by the Italian anarchist Pietro Gori. That line expresses hope for a future in which the whole world would be a homeland without borders; it also expresses the anarchists' internationalist disposition to solidarity toward workers and oppressed of all countries; but above all it expresses a factual truth. The mode of operation of the Italian anarchist movement was as transnational as Malatesta's life. Furthermore, that the Malatesta–Ciancabilla debate took place in the United States epitomizes that country's prominence in the geography of Italian transnational anarchism worldwide. Far from being a diversion, Malatesta's journey to North America took him to one of the sources of the strength and continuity of the anarchist movement in Italy. An unsigned article in the first issue of the *Questione Sociale* under Malatesta's editorship emphasized such a link, addressing an appeal to the Italian anarchists in North America and pleading for transnational solidarity, which it called an 'anarchist duty' ('Dovere anarchico').

Despite its importance for the working of the movement, the transnational dimension of Italian anarchism has fallen through the cracks of histories of national scope: just as it has been neglected by historians restricted to an Italian national perspective, so it has been largely lost on American historians who have leveled their own charges of detachment from empirical reality against Italian anarchists. Thus, George Carey remarked that *La Questione Sociale* 'was continually caught between the interests of its local group constituents in improving the conditions of their lives through local union related activities, and leadership imported from abroad—however distinguished—which sought blindly to apply to American conditions formulae forged in the European context'. Such an exclusive focus on North America is misleading, and Carey himself concedes that 'study of the American context in the absence of the Italian is insufficient' (296–7).

In fact, the relationship between Italian anarchists in North America and the homeland was a two-way cooperative relationship. Militants from Europe—such as Malatesta and before him Francesco Saverio Merlino and Pietro Gori—contributed to propaganda and periodicals in North America. Conversely, in times of repression in Italy, it fell upon the anarchist press abroad to carry on propaganda in Italian. *La Questione Sociale* appeared in July 1895, when the reaction of the Crispi government was raging in Italy. At that time, no anarchist periodical existed in Italy (Bettini). Therefore the appearance of *La Questione Sociale* in Paterson, in relatively unhampered conditions, fulfilled a fundamental role in the Italian anarchist movement worldwide. North American militants, besides being readers, regularly subsidized a large distribution of the paper in Italy and other countries.

The reciprocity of the relationship between Italian anarchists across the ocean is illustrated by the support from North America for the anarchist press in Italy and elsewhere, through subscriptions and donations. The following data, which I have directly gleaned from their sources, illustrate the relative weight of donations from the United States to four major periodicals, *L'Associazione*, *L'Agitazione*, *La Rivoluzione Sociale*, and *Volontà*, edited by Malatesta between 1889 and 1915, as regularly reported in the periodicals themselves. All periodicals were weekly or fortnightly. Only direct donations to the periodicals are considered, as opposed to collections on such accounts as propaganda tours or political prisoners. In each case the country of publication and the United States were the two highest-contributing countries, although their relative order varied. The United States ranked highest with *La Rivoluzione Sociale*, published in London in 1902–03, with contributions at 41.5 percent, as against 17 percent from the United Kingdom. Since Italy was the country of highest circulation, contributions from the country of publication were predictably higher for periodicals published in Italy, such as *L'Agitazione* and *Volontà*, respectively, published in 1889–90 and 1913–15. The former's contributions from Italy and the United States were, respectively, 68.7 percent and 17.1 percent, and the latter's were 42.4 percent and 40.0 percent, respectively.

The case of *Volontà* is particularly significant. Contributions from the United States, though significant throughout the periodical's life span, really soared after a financial crisis forced *Volontà* to suspend publication in mid-October 1914. The editors attributed the crisis to a drop in readership with the outbreak of World War I, and a few weeks before ceasing publication they issued an appeal for help to their comrades in North America, where the war's effects were not felt yet ('Ai nostri'). A massive response came from the United States and elsewhere, allowing the periodical to resume publication on 14 November, continuing until July 1915, when publication ceased shortly after Italy's declaration of war. While donations to *Volontà* from Italy and the United States before the suspension were, respectively,

59.5 percent and 14.9 percent, thus being comparable to those of *L'Agitazione* in 1897–98, after World War I broke out contributions from the United States became absolutely predominant, soaring to 67.4 percent, as against 23.6 percent from Italy, and showing again that country's fundamental role in bridging periods of difficulty for the movement.

Transatlantic integration also found organizational expression. Debates and projects affecting the movement in Italy could be decisively influenced by initiatives in North America. The opacity of anarchist organization makes it difficult to provide systematic evidence. However, institutional manifestations of Italian anarchism show a steady participation from North America. For example, the signatories of the abstentionist manifesto of November 1890 ('Socialisti-anarchici al Popolo') included the New York anarchists Napoleone Carabba and Vito Solieri—the latter being Malatesta's old comrade, expelled with him from Switzerland in 1879 and fellow exile in London in 1881. In January 1891 the anarchists of the United States were represented at the Capolago congress ('Congresso Socialista'). Solieri was also in the editorial staff of *La Questione Sociale*, the prospective organ of the newly created party ('Stampa socialista'). Another pro-abstention manifesto published by *L'Agitazione* in March 1897 was subscribed by 43 New York militants ('Adesioni', 25 April 1897).

Such episodes document that Italian anarchists in North America were both interested and influential in the Italian movement in Europe, as well as organizationally closer than the physical distance might lead us to believe. Their sustained contribution of militants, resources, and ideas must be reckoned with in assessing the strength of Italian anarchism, to avoid the pitfall of exchanging mobilization campaigns in Italy for cyclical and short-lived episodes of spontaneous combustion. As we have seen, the same sort of integration and resource exchange also existed for other countries around the Atlantic Ocean and the Mediterranean Sea. In fact, for European countries—especially those neighboring Italy—cooperation across the border was an ordinary mode of operation.

Transnational support for the anarchist press is quantitatively illustrated by the worldwide contributions to the same four periodicals referred to for the United States. The peak of transnational contributions was reached by *La Rivoluzione Sociale*, with 83 percent of contributions from outside the country of publication. *L'Associazione* and *Volontà* follow on a par, with contributions from outside the country of publication of 57.5 percent and 57.6 percent, respectively. Ironically, the least impressive total, 31.3 percent of foreign contributions for *L'Agitazione*, is probably also the most significant, for three reasons. First, the figure concerns a relatively long period, covering 52 weekly issues, thus providing more valuable data than shorter-lived periodicals, in terms of both statistical reliability and significance as a financially viable periodical. Second, the periodical was published in Italy. Hence one can expect contributions from the country of publication to be highest. Finally, unlike *Volontà*, whose figures were partly due to an exceptional wartime situation, *L'Agitazione* reflected a relatively ordinary situation. It is true that solidarity to the periodical was partly spurred by governmental repression in 1898, including Malatesta's arrest. However, this can hardly be considered exceptional. In fact, Malatesta rarely resided in Italy longer than a year without being arrested or escaping arrest by going underground or fleeing the country. In brief, *L'Agitazione* exhibits a steady contribution from abroad of nearly one-third of overall donations in standard conditions, thus providing a baseline from which one can generalize and claim that contributions from abroad were crucial for the viability of any Italian anarchist periodical. For similar reasons, *L'Agitazione* better illustrates the worldwide spread and balance of contributions in ordinary times. For example, it illustrates the importance of contributions from South America, on a par with Europe and Africa. Contributions from these three areas together amounted to 14.3 percent, coming close to the volume of contributions from the United States. In contrast, those three areas are not given justice in the case of *Volontà*, being comparatively dwarfed by the United States.

Predictably, the highest-contributing countries overlap with those of highest Italian immigration. This intersection defines the map of Italian anarchist transnationalism: France, Switzerland, and the United Kingdom in Europe; Egypt and Tunisia in Africa; Argentina, Brazil, and Uruguay in South America; and the United States in North America. However, no hard-and-fast correlation can be established. This is readily apparent by comparing North and South America, with the former having a much higher volume of contributions, in contrast to the latter's higher Italian immigrant population. A comparison between the rate of overall contributions from abroad and the rate of Italian population abroad is also instructive. As of 1 January 1901, the population on the Italian territory amounted to 32,447,474, while Italians abroad were 3,344,548 around that year (Ministero di Agricoltura et al., 53, 164–5). Therefore the latter comprised 9.3 percent of the Italian worldwide population, which strikingly contrasts with the 31.3 percent rate of contributions to *L'Agitazione* from abroad. While better economic conditions of workers abroad may partly explain this gap, further causes were at work with anarchist transnationalism, of which government repression was foremost. As a consequence, the proportion of exiles among Italian anarchists was higher than that of migrants among Italian workers. Suffice it to mention that, according to an extensive biographical dictionary of Italian anarchists, approximately 60 percent of them emigrated at least once for longer than six months (Antonioli et al., vi). Clearly, anarchist exiles were attracted to areas of Italian migration, both because they were workers themselves, and because those areas provided a more fertile ground for their political activity. However, the relevance of transnationalism for their movement exceeded the transnationalism of Italians at large.

The Italian anarchist press was also transnational in another way: periodicals were also locally published in those same areas of Italian migration. Besides their local readership, they also had a wider circulation, thus fulfilling a fundamental propaganda role. A statistical survey of Italian anarchist periodicals and single issues published worldwide between 1889 and 1913 reveals that nearly 40 percent of the periodicals were published outside of Italy, in those same countries of Italian immigration and anarchist concentration. South America—represented by Argentina, Brazil, and Uruguay—is particularly prominent, with a share of 14 percent of all periodicals, remarkably higher than the 9.5 percent share of North America. The discrepancy between the rates of periodicals and single issues published abroad is worth noting: less than 25 percent of single issues were published abroad, in contrast to nearly 40 percent of periodicals; or, to put things in a different but equivalent perspective, 59 percent of anarchist publications in Italy were single issues, as against only 41 percent abroad (Bettini).

This discrepancy is remarkable. How to explain it? Why were Italian anarchists more prone to publish single issues in Italy than abroad?

The rate of single issues is an indicator of the difficulties that the press encountered in an area. Sometimes publications were intentionally given the form of single issues, when the need to comment on specific questions arose. However, more often than not publishing a single issue was a necessity, or simply the unforeseen outcome of an aborted editorial project. In many cases it was a fallback solution when resources were not sufficient for a serial publication. In other cases, what we call single issues were simply planned periodicals that ceased publication after the first issue, for lack of funds or police harassment. For example, in 1897 *La Protesta Umana* was immediately seized by the authorities and its editor Luigi Fabbri was prosecuted (Bettini, 1: 132). Relatedly, single issues could be stratagems to circumvent police prohibition: the title of a serial publication was changed at every issue so as to be formally unrelated to the previous issues and circumvent legal problems. This is what *L'Agitazione* did for three consecutive issues in April–May 1897. In sum, rather than representing a discrepancy, the figures on periodicals and single issues complement each other in showing that publishing anarchist press was easier abroad than in Italy: periodicals had a less troubled life abroad, and therefore they had a longer life span. Conversely, fewer single issues, or fewer aborted periodicals, were published abroad.

The circulation of anarchist ideas was not limited to the press. Anarchist literature, especially pamphlets, was another crucial component, though constructing a systematic analysis is more problematic in this case. However, we can catch a glimpse using Malatesta's pamphlets as a case study. Since they were steadily popular throughout the period under consideration, in all areas of anarchist presence, and among anarchists of all tendencies, they can be regarded as a fairly representative sample. The most popular was undoubtedly

Fra Contadini (Between Peasants), which was reprinted so often and for so long that its figures are large enough to have statistical significance, even limiting ourselves to editions in Italian. The data I have gleaned from various bibliographies, catalogs, and original pamphlet editions show that 25 editions were published between 1884 and 1913, including both new editions and simple reprints, but excluding serializations in periodicals. The editions printed in Italy were less than half, amounting to 12. The United States follow with eight editions, then the rest of Europe with three, and South America with two. Places of publication tended to be repetitive: three Italian editions appeared in Turin, and three more in Messina; two editions came out of London; and six of the eight North American editions were published in Paterson. Such places of publication correspond to those of major anarchist periodicals, such as *L'Avvenire Sociale* in Messina, and *La Questione Sociale*, then renamed *L'Era Nuova*, in Paterson. More generally, pamphlets almost invariably came out of the printing presses of periodicals, further confirming both the broader propaganda tasks associated with newspapers, and the importance of places as Paterson, Buenos Aires, São Paulo, Tunis, London, and Paris for a wider range of anarchist activities than publishing periodicals. Printing presses lasted longer than periodicals, and thus the production of pamphlets, which required less resources but were more durable and exchangeable propaganda vehicles than some local and ephemeral periodicals, is an even stronger indicator of the continuity of transnational propaganda provided by those centers.

Why was anarchist propaganda easier abroad than at home?

The Catalan historian Joan Casanovas argues that Spanish anarchists enjoyed greater freedom of organization and expression in the United States than in Spain, partly because of the difficulty of the United States administration to censor the press and infiltrate groups that used foreign languages (20). The argument could clearly be extended to other countries. On this note, in 1905 an Italian police agent in London reported a telling episode. At the time a strong, anarchist-oriented, Jewish labor movement existed in London. The Yiddish anarchist paper *Der Arbayter Fraynd* (Workers' Friend) had recently reached sales of 6,000 copies. The circumstance worried the London chief of police, who sent 300 policemen to attend Yiddish classes, so as to monitor speeches and street conversations among Russian and Polish Yiddish-speaking refugees ('Relazione'). Clearly, such a language barrier probably hampered police surveillance of Italian anarchists as well.

Furthermore, it is often assumed that countries with liberal traditions, such as Great Britain and Switzerland, were 'safe havens' for anarchist exiles. Data about the number of expulsions from Switzerland between 1879 and 1902 cast doubts on this assumption, though. Overall, 241 individuals were expelled in that period, 141 of whom were Italian. The peak was in 1898, the year of *Fatti di Maggio*, when repression in Italy determined a wave of exiles, which in turn spurred the Swiss government's reaction: 87 expulsions occurred, of which 76 concerned Italians. Most people expelled in those 23 years were anarchists: Malatesta was expelled in 1879; the only expulsion of 1881 was that of Kropotkin; other notable cases were Galleani in 1890, Schicchi in 1891, Gori in 1895, and Ciancabilla in 1898 (Langhard, 472–9). In brief, Switzerland was by no means a 'safe haven'. Nor was the Swiss republican government unconcerned with anarchist activities targeting the Italian monarchy: Malatesta's expulsion of 1879 was determined by a manifesto against the king of Italy after Passannante's attempt; and in 1900 arrests were made in Switzerland, in connection with the publication of Malatesta's pamphlet Contro la Monarchia. Still, anarchists in Switzerland were comparatively safer from the clutches of the Italian government, for the Swiss government was not inclined to accede to the requests of the Italian monarchy, at the same time that it had little tolerance for anarchist activity. So, while Malatesta was expelled from Switzerland and imprisoned for violating the order of expulsion in 1891, on that occasion the Swiss government rejected Italy's request of extradition. Similarly, the London Metropolitan Police kept a tight watch on Italian anarchists, but was reluctant to act upon information provided by the Italian embassy when it was solely about crimes or plans concerning Italy.

Malatesta and the Italian anarchists were aware of the importance of transnationalism. They consciously relied on it and turned it into an ordinary component of organization and struggle on the Italian soil, as many initiatives in which Malatesta was involved in the 1890s illustrate: the Capolago congress of 1891; the Rome riots of the same year, sparked by a foremost figure of transnational anarchism, Galileo Palla; and the 1893 circular 'To the Italian Workers Abroad', issued by Malatesta's London group La Solidarietà, which urged Italian anarchists to form groups abroad that would correspond among themselves and with Italy ('Á los anarquistas'). Transnationalism helped carry out openly illegal propaganda in Italy. When the manifesto Al Popolo d'Italia reached Italy from London in March 1894, while Crispi's repression was raging, the Italian authorities prosecuted many recipients of the placards, including well-known anarchists, but the defendants invariably ended up being acquitted, as long as they could claim, as they all unfailingly did, that they had not solicited the mailing ('Stampa straniera'). The episode illustrates a sort of division of labor between militants in Italy and abroad, which shielded the former from government persecution.

Malatesta reiterated the importance of transnationalism from the columns of La Questione Sociale. After the first issue of the Questione Sociale had called for the 'anarchist duty' of transnational solidarity, he addressed a further appeal to the Italian anarchists of North America two weeks later, on the eve of a propaganda tour. Malatesta clearly expressed the essence of anarchist transnationalism as follows:

As bad as conditions may be here in the United States, they are still exceptionally favorable to us, compared to continental Europe: there are more resources than elsewhere, and there is opportunity for an activity that can be expanded slowly, perhaps, but without too much danger of being suddenly interrupted by the government. We must take advantage of the present circumstances to build up a strength that, now and later on, in one way or another, can come to the aid of our cause where the opportunity arises, especially in Italy, which is the country we come from, whose language we speak, and where consequently we can exert our influence more effectively.

('Federazione')

The reference to a slow but continuous expansion was crucial, coming in the aftermath of the 1898 repression in Italy, which abruptly ended Malatesta's effort to undertake precisely that kind of expansion in the homeland.

In sum, borders did not necessarily work against anarchism. Italian borders circumscribed not only the territory inside of which the Italian government ruled, but also that outside of which it could not rule. Italian anarchists, whose homeland was 'the whole world', lived on either side of the border, while the Italian government had a limited reach beyond it. For example, the International Anti-Anarchist Conference of 1898 in Rome was a largely unsuccessful attempt by the Italian government to cope with anarchist transnationalism. The domestic policy of countries like Switzerland and Great Britain was not more liberal toward Italian anarchists than that of Italy. However, the foreign policy of those countries made Italian anarchists safer there than in Italy, in the narrow sense of being out of the Italian government's reach.

THE CROSS-NATIONAL DIMENSION OF ANARCHISM

Transnationalism was not a peculiarity of Italian anarchism. Emigration was a lot that Italians shared with other workers, as was exile for Italian anarchists and those of other countries. A consequence of the simultaneous transnationalism of the anarchists movements of different countries was their cross-national mutual involvement, as the example of Italians and French in London in the mid-1890s illustrates. An even closer affinity and long-standing mutual involvement characterized Malatesta's relationship with Spanish anarchism, especially in its majoritarian collectivist current. Malatesta's journey of 1899 to North America was a significant episode in such relationship, though standard accounts do not give adequate prominence to this aspect of the journey.

As we have seen, Pedro Esteve was instrumental in bringing Malatesta to the United States. Moreover, a significant part of the journey was devoted to Spanish-speaking workers. Biographies usually mention Malatesta's brief

ENRICO MALATESTA,
CÉLEBRE AGITADOR ANARQUISTA.

Figure 8.3 **Malatesta's photograph taken around the year 1900**
Source: *Nuevo Mundo* (Madrid), 11 September 1901

propaganda tour in Cuba, but this was preceded by initiatives arranged by
Esteve in the United States, to which biographies make little or no reference.
Malatesta spoke at the *Círculo de Trabajadores* (Workers' Club) of Brooklyn
toward the end of September, as the *Despertar* of 20 October 1899 recorded.
Subsequently, the New York Spanish-language union of cigarmakers entrusted him with the task of going to Tampa, Florida, to promote the idea of a
country-wide federation of tobacco workers, among whom ethnic lines often
separated Cubans from Spaniards ('Federación', 30 January 1900).

In February 1900 Malatesta spent several days in Tampa, trying in vain
to smooth out local conflicts among workers and promoting the tobacco
workers' federation ('Por la posta'). He met with Italian workers too, many
of whom were exiles of the 1893 Fasci, and he lectured in Key West. In late
February he reached Cuba, where he was received by Adrián del Valle, whom
he had met during his 1891–92 tour in Spain and again in London, whence
del Valle emigrated to America. Malatesta was forced to cut his speaking tour
short, due to harassment from the authorities. As he boarded the steamship
that took him back to New York, he greeted del Valle: 'First in Barcelona,
then in London, now in Havana. Where shall we meet next?' (del Valle, 400.)

At the end of March Malatesta reported back to the *Círculo de Traba-jadores* in New York about his mission. Tampa workers, he said, displayed a remarkable combativeness, but their effectiveness was hindered by political and patriotic divisions. The same problem could be observed in Cuba. A successful effort to promote the Federation of tobacco workers would have to overcome this hard barrier ('En el Círculo').

The Spanish-language leg of Malatesta's stay in America speaks to the continuity of his relation with Spanish anarchism and again illustrates the working of the anarchist network. The manifestations of Malatesta's cross-national cooperation with the Spaniards were chronologically and geographically scattered, as his farewell to del Valle well expressed. Hence, its continuity cannot be detected through recurring occasions or circumscribed places, but rather through the intersecting, transnational trajectories of individuals. Most importantly, Malatesta's affinity with Spanish anarchists throws a bridge between the controversies that divided the respective movements, that is, the Italian controversy on organization and the Spanish one on collectivism and communism. The figures of Malatesta, Esteve, and Ciancabilla epitomize how the two debates intersected. In the years around 1889 Malatesta took great interest in the Spanish debate, which spurred his pluralist stance on the collectivism–communism controversy. Likewise, Esteve took interest in the Italian controversy, as his involvement with *La Questione Sociale* and his role in Malatesta's coming to Paterson illustrate. However, the respective standpoints intersected in non-obvious ways that defy standard categorizations. Both Malatesta and Ciancabilla were anarchist-communists, while Esteve was an anarchist-collectivist. Yet, the greatest affinity bound together Malatesta and Esteve, who stood in the same camp in both the Spanish and the Italian controversies and jointly opposed Ciancabilla. By analyzing the ground of the affinity between Malatesta and Esteve one can identify commonalities between the two national debates and put both in a broader perspective.

Standard accounts of the Spanish controversy are based on some kind of Spanish exceptionalism. For example, George Richard Esenwein remarks that the transition from collectivism to communism in Europe did not generate anything like the controversy that preoccupied the Spanish anarchists for two decades. He attributes this to the peculiar way in which anarchism developed in the Spanish context. In the rest of Europe, Esenwein argues, anarchists had never secured a foothold within the trade union movements. Hence collectivism was easily displaced by a doctrine like communism, which did not rely on the support of organized labor groups. In Spain, however, anarchist collectivism had from the beginning been identified with the trade union movement and this identification persisted in time, thus allowing collectivism to survive longer in Spain than elsewhere (109–10). In pointing out the association between collectivism and organized labor, Esenwein emphasizes that the controversy was not simply about the future society, but also concerned anarchist tactics in the present, though he does not explain what the necessary link was.

In fact, the first dissidence arose in Andalusia on the tactical ground, out of irritation with gradualist tactics based on labor organizations. As Esenwein argues, those who criticized the 'legalist' orientation, which focused on an open and legal trade union movement, did not reject the collectivist creed at first; only later, with the penetration of anarchist-communist ideas from abroad, did these dissident elements become the disciples of the new ideology (113). The theoretical controversy between anarchist collectivism and anarchist communism concerned distribution in the socialist society, which for collectivists was to be done according to work performed and for communists according to needs. On the tactical ground, Esenwein attributes the following tenets to communists: they were 'intractably opposed to trade unions, which were viewed as essentially reformist bodies' and 'as being invariably accompanied by the three most iniquitous features of capitalism: bureaucracy, hierarchy, and corruption'; they preferred to 'set up small, loosely federated groups composed of dedicated militants'; and they held a profound faith in the power of spontaneous revolutionary acts. 'Quite understandably', Esenwein concludes, 'they tended to shun strikes and other forms of economic warfare in favor of violent methods, extolling above all the virtues of propaganda by the deed' (108–9).

There is evident similarity between the tactics advocated by Spanish anarchist-communists and Italian anti-organizationists. The tactical rift was as sharp in Spain as in Italy, but the divide on collectivism and communism, though nominally more relevant, was blurred. Max Nettlau remarks that, on reading the journals published in Madrid from 1885 on, one can hardly distinguish whether they were collectivist or communist (*Short*, 195). Most notably, from the second half of the 1880s, Catalan anarchists strove to overcome the controversy and in 1889 *El Productor* argued that the various economic systems were a secondary aspect of anarchist theory (Piqué i Padró, 134–7). The outcome of such a trend was the idea of a tolerant 'anarchism without adjectives', akin to Malatesta's pluralism (Nettlau, *Short*, 198). The group of *El Productor* discussed such questions in an open letter to the Parisian *La Révolte*, published in September 1890 under the title 'Questions de Tactique'. Significantly, while the article advocated a pluralist solution, it criticized the French comrades for their exclusive emphasis on individual initiative, strongly contrasting this to the tactics adopted in Spain, which were based on federative organization, action among the proletarian masses, and association for resistance to capital. Just as the tactics of the anarchist-communist dissidents were akin to those of Italian anti-organizationists, the above outline clearly foreshadows the perspectives of Italian organizationists.

In brief, tactics were not just an important but accessory component of
the controversy in Spain, but its very core. In this light, commonalities between Spain and Italy become more than simple similarities: the core of the
debate was the same. Hence, it becomes problematic to look at Spain as an
exceptional case, one where the bakuninist heritage of collectivism lingered
for longer than elsewhere. Rather, the same crucial tactical issues were debated in Spain as in other major countries for decades to come. Relatedly, if we
acknowledge that organization and labor involvement were the key ideas at
stake, then the claim that such ideas lingered in Spain because Spanish anarchists identified with trade unions is a tautology rather than an explanation.
Moreover, if those were the ideas really at stake, they did not just 'linger' in
Spain, but remained key ideas for half a century, eventually turning Spanish
anarchism into a powerful mass movement.

Identifying the cross-national link between the controversies in Spain and
Italy helps clarify both.

The Italian communist Malatesta and the Spanish collectivist Esteve
agreed in advocating organization. In 1898 Esteve remarked that it was a
serious mistake to consider Spanish anarchism a deviating branch. Instead,
he argued, its distinctive trait was that it remained within the lines drawn by
the International ('Schiarimenti'). It was this essentially associationist tradition, based on organization and the labor movement, that Spanish anarchists
shared with Italian organizationists. Indeed, collectivism was part of that
heritage, which is why Spanish anarchism was born collectivist. However,
collectivism was ultimately the accessory part of that heritage as the eventual
agreement on pluralism between Malatesta and Esteve illustrates.

In the opposite camp we equally find agreement between Italian and
Spanish anti-organizationists. However, unlike their opponents, they retained the link between communism and anti-organizationism.

The situation can be summarized as follows: communism was a necessary requirement for anti-organizationists and organization was a necessary
requirement for collectivists. However, in the middle there were organizationists who could be either communist or pluralist. For example, Malatesta was both. However, there was no such thing as an anti-organizationist
advocacy of pluralism. Why did anti-organizationists posit that link so
forcefully?

The explanation proceeds from the respective values of anti-organizationists and organizationists: individual autonomy and association. The contrasting principles of communism and collectivism about consumption had
different implications for those values. The communist principle that each
should receive according to one's needs assumed abundance, which made
it possible to take from the hypothetical and thus controversial 'inexhaust-
ible stockpile'. In such conditions, the criterion of consumption, need, was
entirely individual and free from constraints. As such it was consistent with
individual autonomy. In conditions of abundance the choice between the

communist and collectivist principles became irrelevant, given that each could receive enough to satisfy all needs, regardless of one's contribution to production. The collectivist principle only became relevant in conditions of scarcity, where the problem of consumption became one of distribution of the social product. The worth of each individual's labor was determined with respect to the whole social product available: it was the portion to which each was entitled. In this respect, and in contrast to the communist principle, the collectivist principle of distribution was inherently relative and socially determined. In implying the notion of social organization it offended the anti-organizationist principle of individual autonomy. On the other hand, while collectivism implied social organization, the reverse was not true: social organization was equally compatible with collectivism and communism. In brief, individual autonomy required communism, collectivism required social organization, and social organization itself was compatible with a pluralist stance.

The commonality of themes debated by Italian and Spanish anarchists has important implications for a charitable interpretation of anarchism. Rather than by exceptionalism and the weight of tradition, the persistence of collectivism in Spain proceeded from reasons shared by anarchists in other countries and concerning not the future society but disagreement about practical means. Moreover, that both debates were rooted in a shared contrast of basic values, individual autonomy and association, throws into relief both the diversity of the anarchist movement and the internal coherence of competing versions of anarchism. Contrasts were not based on dogmas, but on complex, interconnected, and rational arguments. The anarchist movement was neither monolithic nor inconsistent. By acknowledging that coherent but contrasting versions of anarchism coexisted, one can replace irrationalist explanations in terms of alleged contradictions, implausible changes of course, or unreasonable attachment to tradition by national anarchist movements by a rational comprehension of the steady and consistent evolution of alternative, cross-national anarchist traditions.

Epilogue: the proper scope of anarchist history
On 4 April Malatesta finally left for London (Branchi).

The different parts of his activity in America show a variety of themes: organization, the key issue of Italian anarchists; patriotism and national independence, which divided Spanish and Cuban workers; and anarchist participation in unions. Malatesta and the anarchist tobacco workers advocated a brand of unionism based on solidarity across ethnic and occupational lines, which coupled immediate gains with the long-term goal of overthrowing capitalism. Five years later such ideas would be made current in North America by the founding of the Industrial Workers of the World.

Despite such variety and relevance of themes, standard accounts present Malatesta's stay in America as the trip in which the knight errant of Anarchy got shot in the leg. By focusing on the anecdotal, the exotic, and the sensational such accounts portray anarchist action as made up of disconnected, unplanned, and unpredictable events, from which an image of anarchism as ultimately irrational results. In contrast to such trivializations, in which sensationalism and the 'enormous condescension' stigmatized by E. P. Thompson replace rational understanding, a charitable reading reveals complexity, interconnection, and orientation as ordinary features of anarchist theory and action.

Once we take the trouble of looking into the premises of Malatesta's journey to the United States, his reasons for undertaking it, and his ties with anarchists in that continent, we realize that it was not a bizarre diversion from his engagement in Europe, nor was his tour in Cuba a diversion from his journey to the United States. Both were part of a transnational and cross-national engagement that knew no temporal or spatial interruption.

Once we look at European anarchism from the other side of the Atlantic Ocean, a whole new scenario opens up, and we realize how much we miss by remaining confined to a national framework of analysis. We catch a glimpse of the extent to which anarchism in Italy drew its life blood from that segment of the movement that was forced out of the national borders but remained committed to the struggle in the homeland, in a sort of reverse nationalism. Love for their country led them to fight, not to aggrandize, their country's state. More broadly, when we look at Malatesta's and Pedro Esteve's involvement in each other's 'national' movements, when we investigate the mutual influence and ties between the respective debates, we realize how much richer our understanding of each movement becomes in this broader context. The proper scope of anarchist history is transnational and crossnational. The anarchists' life was never easy. They had to travel to far-away countries and learn new languages. The historians' life cannot be too easy either, as they need to follow anarchists in their transatlantic itineraries.

On 13 April 1900 Malatesta arrived in London, where he remained for the next 13 years. At 46, he had been an anarchist militant for nearly 30 years. The eight-month American 'intermission' at the turn of the century, in the middle of his adult life and militancy, was probably his most definitive turning point. While his theoretical and tactical evolution did not stop there, all the theoretical elements from which his subsequent evolution stemmed had been put in place.

On the basis of Malatesta's trajectory from 1889 to 1900, it is possible to finally attempt a comprehensive interpretation of the system of beliefs that gave sense and coherence to his anarchism.

9

MALATESTA'S ANARCHISM:
A CHARITABLE INTERPRETATION

THE CONCEPT OF 'ANARCHIST GRADUALISM', WHICH MALATESTA WORKED OUT in the 1920s, was the final outcome of his theoretical and tactical elaboration.

The two decades after his return of 1900 to London were by no means idle or intellectually unproductive, as a brief excursus of his activity shows: in 1902–03 he edited *La Rivoluzione Sociale*, in which historians such as Pier Carlo Masini have seen 'an involutional phase', in contrast with the 'politics of realism and pragmatism' of earlier years (*Storia...nell'epoca*, 212–15), but which still in the 1920s Malatesta himself considered both important and underrated (Luigi Fabbri, 'Per una raccolta'); in 1907 Malatesta was a protagonist of the international anarchist congress of Amsterdam; in 1913–14 he was back in Italy, where he edited *Volontà* and had a key role in the 'Red Week' insurrectional movement; and in 1914–16, during World War I, Malatesta reaffirmed anti-militarism as a cornerstone of the anarchist coherence between ends and means, in dramatic opposition to Kropotkin.

Still, the core ideas of anarchist gradualism are clearly traceable in Malatesta's writings of 1899, as such articles as 'Verso l'anarchia' illustrate. Hence, gradualism provides a vantage point from which Malatesta's evolution in 1889–1900 can best be assessed, because it fully spells out the implications of ideas germinated in that period.

ANARCHIST GRADUALISM

By stereotypical standards, 'anarchist gradualism' may seem a contradictory concept, or at least a thoroughly revisionistic one that sheds the 'impossibilist' assumptions typical of anarchism. Yet it was the outcome of Malatesta's coherent trajectory of half a century, begun with the First International. It thus provides the opportunity to reassess the substance of Malatesta's anarchism and to discuss how it 'made sense'.

The task consists of showing how anarchist ends and means were interconnected, and what beliefs provided the backbone that supported and justified those interconnections. Such reappraisal of the rationality of anarchism can be best accomplished by a critical comparison of its 'good' reasons with ideas and theories of collective action that have become current in the social sciences of the twentieth century. This way anarchism can be rescued from the cultural *domicilio coatto* in which it is often segregated. By bringing to the fore similarities and connections with 'sensible' theories outside of the anarchist tradition, the intellectual sophistication of anarchist theory can be vindicated and the attribution of irrationality, usually made easy by conveniently confining anarchism to the rank of an intellectual aberration, becomes more problematic and questionable.

Malatesta summed up the trajectory of Italian anarchism in an article of 1931, a year before his death. He recalled that 60 years earlier, at the outset of their movement, anarchists believed that anarchy and communism could come about as a direct, immediate consequence of a victorious insurrection and that their establishment would be the very initial act of the social revolution. 'This was indeed the idea that, after being accepted a little later by Kropotkin, was popularized and almost established by him as the definitive program of anarchism' ('A proposito di "revisionismo"'). That confidence rested on the beliefs that the people had the innate capacity to self-organize and provide for their own interests and that anarchists interpreted the deep instincts of the masses. As time went by, study and experience proved that many such beliefs were wishful thinking.

The historian Richard Hostetter regards that early belief in the 'instinctive revolutionism of the masses' as the kernel of an inescapable 'anarchists' dilemma' that by 1882 had already determined the 'ideological liquidation' of the Italian International (409–10). However, in spite of the 'obsequies of the Italian anarchist movement' that end Hostetter's book (425), anarchist theory and tactics had more resources and potential than many historians would like to believe.

As Malatesta remarked in his 1931 article, the key realizations that neither the mass had all the virtues attributed to it nor that propaganda had all the potential that anarchists had believed were the starting point of a new outlook on the social struggle. Anarchists realized that only a limited number of people could be converted in a given environment; then, finding new members became increasingly difficult, until economic and political occurrences created new opportunities.

'After reaching a certain point', Malatesta observed, 'numbers could not grow except by watering down and adulterating one's program, as happened to the democratic socialists, who were able to gather imposing masses, but only at the price of ceasing to be real socialists.' Anarchists came to understand their mission differently, based on the conviction that the aspiration to integral freedom, or the 'anarchist spirit', was the cause of humanity's progress, while political and economic privileges pushed humanity back into a barbaric condition, unless such privileges found an obstacle in a more or less conscious anarchism. Anarchists understood that 'anarchy could only come gradually, to the extent that the mass could understand and desire it, but it would never come except under the impulse of a more or less consciously anarchist minority, acting so as to prepare the necessary environment'. Remaining anarchists and acting as anarchists in all circumstances, before, during, and after a revolution, was the duty they set to themselves ('A proposito di "revisionismo" ').

Malatesta had summarized what anarchists were to do before, during, and after a revolution in his 1925 article 'Gradualismo'.

For Malatesta, anarchy could still be seen as absolute perfection, and it was right that this concept should remain in the anarchists' minds, like a beacon to guide their steps, but obviously such an ideal could not be attained in one sudden leap. Nor, conversely, were anarchists to wait till everyone had become anarchist to achieve anarchy. On the contrary, they were revolutionary precisely because they believed that under present conditions only a small minority could conceive what anarchy was, while it would be chimerical to hope for a general conversion before the environment changed. Since anarchists could neither convert everybody at once, nor remain in isolation from the rest of society, it was necessary to find ways to apply anarchy, or that degree of anarchy that became gradually feasible, among people who were not anarchist, or were such to different degrees, as soon as a sufficient amount of freedom was won, and anarchist nuclei existed with enough numerical strength and capabilities to be self-sufficient and spread their influence locally.

Before a revolution, Malatesta argued, anarchists were to propagate their ideas and educate as widely as possible, rejecting any compromise with the enemy and keeping ready, at least mentally, to grab any opportunity that could present itself.

What were they to do during a revolution? They could not make a revolution alone, nor that would be advisable, for without mobilizing all spiritual forces, interests, and aspirations of an entire people a revolution would be abortive. And even in the unlikely case that anarchists were able to succeed alone, they would find themselves in the paradoxical position of either pushing forward the revolution in an authoritarian manner or pulling back and letting someone else take control of the situation for their own aims. Thus, anarchists should act in agreement with all progressive forces and attract the largest possible mass, letting the revolution, of which anarchists would only be one component, yield whatever it could. However, anarchists were not to renounce their specific aim. On the contrary, they were to remain united as anarchists and distinct from other parties and fight for their own program: the abolition of political power and the expropriation of capitalists. If, notwithstanding their efforts, new powers succeeded in establishing themselves, hindered popular initiative, and imposed their will, anarchists should disavow those powers, induce the people to withhold human and material resources from them, and weaken them as much as possible, until it became possible to overthrow them altogether. In any case, anarchists were to demand, even by force, full autonomy, and the right and means to organize and live their own way, and experiment with the social arrangements they deemed best.

The aftermath of a revolution, after the overthrow of the existing power and the final triumph of the insurgents, was the terrain in which gradualism was to become really crucial. All practical problems of life were to be studied—concerning production, exchange, means of communication, and so on—and each problem was to be solved in the way that was not only economically most convenient, but also most satisfactory from the point of view of justice and freedom, and left the way open to future improvements. In the case of conflict between different requirements, justice, freedom, and solidarity were to be prioritized over economic convenience. While fighting against authority and privilege, anarchists were to profit from all the benefits of civilization. No institution that fulfilled a need, even imperfectly, was to be destroyed until it could be replaced with a better solution to provide for that need. While anarchists were intransigent against any imposition and capitalistic exploitation, they were to be tolerant toward any social plans prevailing in the various groupings, as long as such plans did not infringe the equal freedom of others. Anarchists were to be content with progressing gradually, in step with the people's moral development and as material and intellectual means increased, doing at the same time all they could, by study, work, and propaganda, to hasten the development toward ever more advanced ideals. Solutions would be diverse, according to circumstances, but would always conform, as far as anarchists were concerned, to the fundamental principle that coercion and exploitation were to be rejected ('Gradualismo').

Ultimately, as Malatesta wrote in an open letter of 1929 to Nestor Makhno,

> The important thing is not the victory of our plans, our projects, our utopias, which in any case need the confirmation of experience and can be modified by experience, developed and adapted to the real moral and material conditions of the age and place. What matters most is that the people, men and women lose the sheeplike instincts and habits which thousands of years of slavery have instilled in them, and learn to think and act freely. And it is to this great work of moral liberation that the anarchists must specially dedicate themselves.
>
> ('A proposito della "Plateforme" ')

Anarchist gradualism was the outcome of a long itinerary started in 1889. It was built upon the new foundations for anarchism that Malatesta first laid down in *L'Associazione*. All the stages of Malatesta's subsequent evolution were preserved and merged together in his gradualist conception.

Its primary motivation was provided by Malatesta's disenchanted outlook on the masses that he began to express in his 1889 articles in which he urged anarchists to 'go to the people' and take the masses as they were. Malatesta's realism found expression not only in the idea that a limited number of people could be converted to revolutionary ideals in a given environment, but also in his belief that the mere defense of economic interests did not necessarily turn into a revolutionary force. 'After all'—Malatesta argued in 1922 in contrast with syndicalist theories—'interests are always conservative; only the ideal is revolutionary.' He meant that economic interests were by nature divisive, as the example of controversies among dockers, which he had dealt with in 1897, still illustrated a quarter of a century later: the closed-shop and freedom of work, each expressed workers' legitimate but conflicting interests. A revolutionary consciousness could only be achieved by transcending both ('Lotta economica').

Though Malatesta acknowledged the relevance of material needs, he recognized that immediate, personal, material interests often clash with future, general, moral ones. Every person who fought social evils had to address this tension. Though examples of self-sacrifice and even martyrdom abounded, the spirit of sacrifice could not be expected of large masses. Still, economic resistance helped create a fertile terrain for the germination of revolutionary ideals ('Interesse').

Gradualism was Malatesta's ultimate response to the conundrum of anarchist collective action, whereby the conscious participation of the masses was necessary to any truly emancipatory revolution, while at the same time revolutionary consciousness could not be the prerogative of large masses under the existing material constraints of exploitation and oppression.

In Malatesta's gradualist view, the uplifting of consciousness and the increase of freedom, equality, and well-being fed each other in a dynamic, iterative, and open-ended process.

A SOCIALIST OPEN SOCIETY

A leading theme of Malatesta's anarchism that received full expression in his gradualist view was experimentalism. Anarchists ideas were 'the experimental system brought from the field of research to that of social realization' ('Verso').

This made the method of freedom paramount.

Only by letting social experiments flourish could the best solutions arise and be recognized. Anarchy was not 'perfection' or an 'absolute ideal', but 'the way open to all progress and all improvements for the benefit of everybody'. In a pluralist perspective, as Malatesta advocated in 1889, 'utopias' and specific solutions pertained to individuals and groups, rather than to a shared anarchist doctrine. In a letter of 20 July 1896 to Hamon, Malatesta thus summarized his view on the issue of collectivism and communism, from which his pluralism originated: 'I am communist only at the condition that I do not have to be. That is to say that I consider collectivism as a necessary alternative to ensure the libertarian character of communism' (Hamon Papers, file 109). Social experimentation was to act as a filter, discarding unviable solutions and selecting viable ones, which might not necessarily coincide with anyone's specific utopia, but result rather from their interplay.

The keystone of anarchist gradualism was the notion of anarchism as a method, another idea that Malatesta first expressed in 1889 ('I nostri propositi: I'), and whose import is best appreciated retrospectively, in the light of his subsequent trajectory. The anarchist method not only characterized anarchist action in the present, but became the substance of anarchy itself, no longer identified with one or the other blueprint, but with the society where the search for the best solution to social problems was carried out by the method of freedom. As Peter Marshall remarks, 'not only do the means influence the ends, but means are ends-in-the-making' (637).

In brief, the method of freedom was both a method of struggle and the very substance of anarchy. In this perspective, anarchy characterizes a decision-making process, rather than a specific social arrangement, similarly to the notion of democracy. In either case, it would be a category mistake to require a detailed description of society, for the essence of such notions is that the specific shape of a society be left to its members.

There was a necessary link between anarchist gradualism and anarchism as a method. It consisted in defining society in terms of the aggregation of individual dispositions. In this perspective, anarchy was recast as a society of anarchists, that is of individuals holding anarchist dispositions. Aiming for the welfare of all human beings, practicing the method of freedom, and being motivated by solidarity were all intentional stances that could be predicated of individuals rather than of whole societies. Anarchy was a society where solidarity and the method of freedom were generalized. Still, before reaching that point, all kinds of intermediate stages existed, where solidarity and the method of freedom were limited to sectors of society, or even minorities.

In other words, the methodological shift—in the dual sense of defining anarchism as a method and of understanding society in methodological individualistic terms—enabled a view of anarchy as a gradual process. Anarchism became one of the forces whose interaction the direction of society resulted from. The stronger the anarchist force, the more society would steer toward anarchy.

The theoretical breadth of anarchism as a method can be appreciated by pointing out similarities with contemporary theories outside the anarchist tradition, such as Karl Popper's 'open society' and Robert Nozick's 'framework for utopia'.

Popper's approach to politics abandons the positive task of determining 'who should rule' for the negative one of devising political institutions that prevent tyranny (*Open*, 120–1). For him, theories of sovereignty recall the 'paradox of freedom', for sovereignty can always be exercised in a self-defeating manner, for example, by people choosing to be ruled by a tyrant (123). In contrast, Popper seeks to develop a theory of democratic control that does not proceed from a doctrine of the righteousness of majority rule, but from the baseness of tyranny (124). Though no foolproof institutions can ever be developed, Popper regards elections and representation as reasonable safeguards against tyranny, 'always open to improvement, and even providing methods for their own improvement' (125). A self-sustainable search for the viable rather than for the absolutely best also motivates Popper's piecemeal approach to social engineering, for social life, he maintains, is too complex for anyone to judge a blueprint for social engineering on a grand scale (159). By its approach made up of experiments, readjustments, and readiness to learn from mistakes, Popper argues, piecemeal social engineering would mean the introduction of scientific method into politics (163).

Nozick is likewise interested in principles of institutional design such that 'bad men at their head can do little harm' (298). He discusses the minimal state from the perspective of utopian theory. For Nozick, 'there will not be *one* kind of community existing and one kind of life led in utopia'. Rather, 'utopia will consist of utopias, of many different and divergent communities in which people lead different kinds of lives under different institutions'. Hence, utopia becomes 'a framework for utopias, a place where people are at liberty to join together voluntarily to pursue and attempt to realize their own vision of the good life in the ideal community but where no one can *impose* his own utopian vision upon others' (311–12). For Nozick, utopia as meta-utopia, as the environment in which experiments may be tried out, and which must be realized first if more particular utopian visions are to be realized stably, is equivalent with the minimal state (333). In this framework, the best society is sought by a combination of 'design devices' and 'filter devices'. Specific models of community are generated and promoted by individuals and groups, while the support, or lack thereof, to such proposals works as a filtering process (313–14).

There are clear commonalities between these two models and Malatesta's gradualism: there is a basic distrust for power as a means to achieve positive goals; no description of the best institutions is provided; a method is described that makes an open-ended process of improvement possible, leaving its accomplishment to the responsibility and aggregate initiatives of individuals; and the process is experimental, upon the assumption that the complexity and diversity of society makes it impossible to collectively, intentionally pursue an a priori blueprint. In particular, Popper's concern to make the method of freedom self-sustainable and avoid the paradoxes of freedom and sovereignty is also the concern of anarchists, for whom those paradoxes were the very substance of any society where people alienate their freedom to a government. Just as they exposed the oppressive nature of government, they emphasized that its main pillar was people's submission, the 'voluntary servitude' of Étienne de La Boétie. Such affinity between Popper and anarchism is confirmed by a 1982 interview in which Popper expresses sympathy with anarchism, which he dismissed in *The Open Society*. It is, he says, an unrealizable ideal, but the closer we can get to it, the better off freedom is (Hacohen, 505, n. 210).

In turn, Nozick emphasizes the fundamental role of utopia as individual and collective motive, in a framework that is not utopian itself but pluralistically open to all utopias, insofar as they do not endanger the framework itself.

Clearly, fundamental differences separate Malatesta from Popper and Nozick. However, these are not so much about the dynamics of the framework, which bears striking resemblances, as about the conditions that make its working possible, which are more stringent for Malatesta. He spelled out such differences in *Anarchy*, where he defined liberalism as 'a kind of anarchy without socialism'. For him, the liberal method 'relies on free individual enterprise and proclaims, if not the abolition, at least the reduction of governmental functions to an absolute minimum; but because it respects private property and is entirely based on the principle of each for himself and therefore of competition between men, the liberty it espouses is for the strong' (46). Far from producing harmony, this method leads to exploitation and domination. In brief, for Malatesta, the method of freedom shared by Popper and Nozick is not self-sustainable without solidarity.

Malatesta's references to socialism and solidarity make it clear that recasting anarchy as a decision-making process does not mean turning it into a hollow and formalistic notion. It is worth recalling Malatesta's definition of anarchy as having equality of conditions as its point of departure, solidarity as its beacon, and freedom as its method (*Anarchy*, 46–7). Though the definition gave no description of an anarchist society, it was far from vacuous. In fact, it drew a line even within anarchism. The point of departure in the pursuit of the well-being of all was the equality of conditions, as provided by the abolition of private ownership of the means of production. Malatesta thus reasserted a socialistic and substantial notion of equality based on the satisfaction of material needs, in contrast to the formal notion of liberal democracy. Yet socialism was only a starting point. Different paths were open and diverse solutions might be tried, so long as their motive was solidarity. This apparently obvious statement was crucial. In contrast with the marxist tradition, Malatesta was claiming human dispositions as the substance of the socialist society. At the same time, in contrast with the liberal tradition, he claimed that the common good could only be achieved by intentionally aiming for it. Finally, in contrast with egoistic versions of anarchism, he maintained that there could be no anarchy without solidarity.

THE REJECTION OF 'GOOD BY FORCE'

Just as anarchism as a method was not a formalistic notion, neither did it become an unchanging standpoint detached from concrete situations, or an aimless and merely individual moral stance without political goals.

Malatesta's methodological individualism was coupled with the assumption that humans were eminently social beings, and this constituted the main divide from anti-organizationism. Though Malatesta did not disavow the legitimacy and possible usefulness of individual deeds, for him anarchist action was preeminently collective and had to be constantly adjusted to fit the current conditions of the people, with the aim of fostering their material and moral uplifting. Malatesta's crucial step was his inclusive interpretation of the principle of coherence between ends and means, whereby anarchists could do anything that did not contrast with their principles. A range of initiatives, such as labor struggles and insurrectionary alliances, which others regarded as compromises that watered down anarchist principles, were legitimate for Malatesta, as well as crucial in drawing the masses to anarchist practices. Thus, anarchism as a method was thoroughly situated in the social context, in virtue of its collective dimension.

Most importantly, insurrection remained a goal of anarchist collective action. It might be more or less distant in time, but it was the single most definite task on the anarchist agenda. On the one hand, though some progress was possible within bourgeois society, open insurrection was the unavoidable outcome of class struggle, if further progress was to be made. On the other hand, though Malatesta increasingly regarded insurrection as only the beginning of a revolutionary process, the direction of society after a successful insurrection was indeterminate and open-ended; setting goals for the post-insurrectional stage could only be conjectural. Hence, insurrection was the one aim firmly in sight. Malatesta's evolution toward gradualism did not affect this belief. Gradualism evolved from a changing outlook on the revolutionary potential of the masses, not on the coercive potential of governments. It originated from the increasing abandonment of the identification between insurrection and revolution. Hence, it concerned more social evolution after a successful insurrection than before it. In fact, gradualism arose precisely from the combination of an evolutionary outlook on social change, as spelled out in 1897, with the awareness of the limited scope of such evolution within a bourgeois society, as emphasized in *Contro la Monarchia*.

By shifting focus from the end-point of anarchy to the process by which to approach it, whether or not the end-point was fully attainable, anarchist gradualism throws into relief Malatesta's predominant concern for practical means in the pursuit of ultimate goals. His outlook on means is summarized by a concise formula: the rejection of 'good by force', as Malatesta put it ('Bien'). This was the root of the asymmetry between the tactics of anarchists and those of all parties aiming at political power. The latter's goal was ultimately to achieve enough strength to be able to enforce what they regarded as the common good. In contrast, the anarchists' aims were limited to spreading the anarchist ideal through propaganda and example, and to removing the obstacles that hindered the method of freedom. As Malatesta tirelessly pointed out, the constructive task of building new social institutions was equally important as destroying the evil ones, but that task could not be committed to anarchists alone, or to any party or minority, on behalf of a passive majority. Such institutions could only be built by those directly affected by them, insofar as they were morally equipped for the task. Hence, anarchy could only be realized to the extent that such moral readiness was widespread among the population. In brief, anarchists aimed for the collective good without aiming to gain the strength to impose it. Herein lay the difference from other parties, and what I have termed the conundrum of anarchist collective action, which can be restated as follows: anarchists strove for an aim that could never be entirely up to them to realize.

From this asymmetry, it followed that insufficient forces and defeat were a matter of course to be reckoned with. Indeed, anarchists did not look upon defeat as an unqualified liability. There was a greater failure than defeat, and that was the forsaking of anarchist principles. Coherence between ends and means had priority over winning. In 1914, in the heat of the debate among anarchists about World War I, Malatesta argued that in those circumstances where socialists were powerless to act efficaciously to weaken the State and the capitalist class their duty was to 'refuse any voluntary help to the cause of the enemy, and stand aside to save at least their principles—which means to save the future'. In 1924, discussing terror as a revolutionary weapon, he argued: 'the revolution has to be defended and developed with an inexorable logic; but it must not and cannot be defended with means that contradict its own ends . . . If, to win, we have to set up the gallows in the public square, I would prefer to lose.' And in 1931 he reiterated: 'we must always act as anarchists, even at the risk of being defeated, thus giving up a victory that might be the victory of our persons, but would be the defeat of our ideas' ('A proposito di "revisionismo" ').

This attitude toward defeat did not proceed from a dogmatic attachment to abstract values, but from the preoccupation to stay on the right path. Anarchists were concerned not only about which means were adequate, but most importantly about which ones were not and led elsewhere than desired, that is about the unintended consequences of their action. This concern reveals a side of anarchism that is seldom pointed out, and could be described as its conservative dimension. The advocacy of coherence between ends and means, the rejection of self-defeating means such as parliamentarianism, the mistrust of reformism, the acceptance of defeat, the rejection of formal organization by some, all point to a predominant preoccupation with not going in the wrong direction. At the root of such preoccupation was a keen awareness of the issue of the heterogony of ends, which had characterized the anarchists since the time of the International.

As with the anarchists' general attitude toward defeat, the rejection of specific means was based on pragmatic reasons. For example, in contrast to the blanket rejection of organization customarily attributed to anarchists, the question of organization was not just about organizing or not, but rather about formal organization. Anti-organizationists opposed the conformity to rules induced by bureaucracy, a question whose importance has been later pointed out by sociologists like Robert K. Merton. In 'Bureaucratic Structure and Personality', Merton argues that the adherence to rules required for bureaucracy to operate successfully, and originally conceived as a means, becomes transformed into an end-in-itself, in a process of displacement of goals, such that devotion to rules interferes with the achievement of the organization's purposes (562–3). Anti-organizationists claimed that formal structure added nothing valuable to the advantages of organization, and shunned organization at the point where it generated bureaucracy. Aside from that, all anarchists did organize. Malatesta's most frequent objection to anti-organizationists was that, despite their claims, when they wanted to get something accomplished they did organize, sometimes better than self-proclaimed organizationists. The most common form of organization was the common denominator between organizationists and anti-organizationists, the anarchist network.

A MORALITY-DRIVEN SPONTANEOUS PROCESS

The link between Malatesta's outlook on social evolution as a gradual, experimental process characterized by the method of freedom and the anarchists' adherence to the principle of coherence between ends and means can be brought forth by redescribing social evolution, as viewed by Malatesta, as an incremental invisible-hand process driven by morality, which could unfold to the degree that coercive visible hands hindering the process were removed from its way.

Again, a comparison with twentieth-century theories that discuss invisible-hand processes is useful to illustrate such an interpretation of Malatesta's view of social dynamics. A good starting point for discussing the relation between invisible-hand processes and the method of freedom is the work of F. A. Hayek, which contains an articulate defense of that method.

'The case for individual freedom', Hayek contends, 'rests chiefly on the recognition of the inevitable ignorance of all of us concerning a great many of the factors on which the achievement of our ends and welfare depends.' If there were omniscient men, Hayek argues, there would be little case for liberty (*Constitution*, 29). Instead, through mutually adjusted efforts, more knowledge is utilized than any individual possesses. Dispersed knowledge makes greater achievements possible than any single mind can foresee. 'It is because freedom means the renunciation of direct control of individual efforts that a free society can make use of so much more knowledge than the mind of the wisest ruler could comprehend' (30–1). In contrast, when the exclusive right to try alternatives is conferred to one agency, presumed to hold superior knowledge, the process ceases to be experimental and beliefs held at a given time may hinder the advancement of knowledge (37). Hayek's key example of how dispersed knowledge works is the distribution of products in a competitive market, which informs individuals in what direction their several efforts must aim in contributing to the total product. For Hayek, human civilization depends on the spontaneous extended order of human cooperation known as capitalism (*Fatal*, 6–7).

Hayek's view belongs to the class of the so-called invisible-hand explanations. In turn, these are a special case of what Raymond Boudon calls explanations that feature 'perverse effects', which include not only unintended collective benefits, but also unintended collective problems (*Unintended*, 5–6). In fact, much of the study of collective action and the provision of public goods has concerned 'the working of the back of the invisible hand', that is, the failure to secure greater collective interests in seeking private interests (Hardin, *Collective*, 6). Similar concerns motivated the anarchists' preoccupation with coherence between ends and means and solidarity.

The affinity between Hayek's case for individual freedom and Malatesta's advocacy of the method of freedom as 'the experimental system brought from the field of research to that of social realization' should be apparent. Incidentally, given such affinity between Hayek and an advocate of socialism who belonged to the First International, it is ironic that the Left, especially British, has recently engaged with Hayek's ideas in an effort to renew the socialist project (Griffiths).

However, there are two fundamental differences between Hayek's and Malatesta's appeal to the method of freedom.

The first is the scope of its application. When it comes to preventing coercion, Hayek is satisfied that 'the exclusive right to try alternatives is conferred to one agency'. He no longer commits the advance of reason to freedom and unpredictability, but to control and predictability. In fact, his pre-condition to prevent coercion is the recognition of a private sphere, including most crucially private property, to be protected against interference by everyone's acceptance of rules enforced by a government (*Constitution*, 139–40).

In contrast, anarchists advocated the method of freedom across the board. For them, knowledge dispersion was valid not only in the economy, but also in politics. Carl Schmitt characterizes liberalism as a 'consistent, comprehensive metaphysical system' that is not limited to the economic sphere in applying a general principle: that 'the truth can be found through an unrestrained clash of opinion and that competition will produce harmony' (35). In this light, the anarchists' across-the-board advocacy of freedom would be a consequent interpretation of the liberal principle, though one Popper, Nozick, and Hayek would deny.

The second difference between Malatesta and Hayek is that they hold diametrically opposed views on the role of solidarity. For Hayek solidarity and altruism are 'a remnant of the instinctual, and cautious, micro-ethic of the small band'. In a large group, 'the old impulse to follow inborn altruistic instincts actually hinders the formation of more extensive orders'. Hence, implicit in Hayek's account is a normative urge to abstain from solidarity, so as to let the 'spontaneous' extended order work for the collective good (*Fatal*, 80–1). Herein lies the self-referential paradox of an agent who is invited to pursue the collective good by intentionally abstaining from pursuing it.

Instead, for Malatesta freedom led to exploitation and domination when individuals were motivated by self-interest rather than solidarity. For him, the collective good could only arise from its intentional pursuit. However, insofar as an invisible-hand process is one in which the end result is unpredictable, unplanned, and unintended by anyone, Malatesta's pursuit of the collective good was one such process. No individual or group could hold the knowledge necessary to plan or predict what the end result would be. The outcome could only be the result of free experimentation. Even competition was not absent from Malatesta's scenario, insofar as different ideas of the collective good competed to gain predominance, just as different scientific theories compete in pursuit of the common aim of truth. 'If the day came', Malatesta wrote, 'that all fully agreed on the advantages of a given thing, it would mean that any possible progress with respect to that thing would be exhausted' ('Da Londra'). In brief, the common good would arise as a spontaneous social result of its intentional individual pursuit. Hayek's self-referential paradox did not arise for Malatesta, while the non-controlled character of the process was preserved.

In Malatesta's view, the concern for the well-being of all humanity was the substance of the anarchist morals. Thus, his invisible-hand process of social evolution can be described as being driven by morality. Malatesta regarded this disposition as ultimate and fundamental. He thus refrained from any attempt to derive it from other principles: 'We could cease to be communist or anarchist', Malatesta argued in 1913, 'if it seemed to us to have found a better solution, but the force that sustains and drives us would still remain the love of humanity. Such love is either felt or not felt: it comes neither from science nor from philosophy. However, it is often a latent feeling, that can be brought forth and set in motion: this is the main goal of propaganda' ('Base', *Volontà*).

Likewise, Malatesta refrained from deriving explicit, universal rules of conduct from this disposition, as his argument against the principle of non-violence, which kept tolstoyans from defending the oppressed, expressed well: 'For myself, I would violate every principle in the world in order to save a man: which would in fact be a question of respecting principle, since, in my opinion, all moral and sociological principles are reduced to this one: the good of humanity, of all humanity' ('Errori').

Though Malatesta refrained from philosophical abstractions, his formulation echoes Kant's principle of humanity as an end in itself. The idea of love as the ultimate foundation of anarchy, even above justice, was thus argued for in a letter of 18 May 1931 to Luigi Fabbri: 'Strictly speaking, justice means giving to the others the equivalent of what they give to you; it means Proudhon's *échange égal*... Instead love gives all it can and wishes it could give ever more, without counting, without calculating... It seems to me that there are two contrasting feelings in the human mind: the feeling of sympathy, or love, for one's fellow human beings, which is always beneficial; and the feeling of justice, which gives rise to unending strife, because everyone finds it fair what suits him best' (*Epistolario*, 316–17).

For Malatesta, morality was pervasive in society and inherent in intentional action. As he argued in 'Errori e rimedi', one could choose which morals to follow, but could not help holding a moral view of some kind. Thus he charged anarchists who affected to reject morality altogether with forgetting that 'in order to reasonably fight some morals, one must oppose superior morals to them, in theory and in practice'. For him, 'morals are the rule of conduct that each individual considers good'. One could reject specific moral views, but a society without any morals whatsoever could not be conceived, nor could an individual who acted consciously without a criterion for discriminating good from bad, for himself and for others. Thus, in fighting the present society, anarchists 'oppose the morals of love and solidarity to bourgeois individualistic morals of struggle and competition'. In upholding the centrality of morals, Malatesta rejected the claim that the social environment prevented one from acting morally, at the same time that he acknowledged the overwhelming constraints that limited such action:

> Certainly every anarchist, every socialist understands the economic fatality that today forces man to fight against man, and every good observer sees the impotence of individual rebellion against the preponderant force of the social environment. However, it is equally certain that without the rebellion of the individual, who associates with other rebellious individuals to resist the environment and strive to transform it, such an environment would never change.

'All of us, without exception', Malatesta acknowledged, 'are obliged to live, more or less, in contradiction with our ideals; but we are anarchists and socialists because, and in so far as, we suffer by this contradiction, and seek to make it as small as possible.' The day one adapted himself to the environment, one would end up losing the desire to change it, thus turning into an ordinary bourgeois; perhaps penniless, Malatesta concluded, but nevertheless a bourgeois in one's acts and intentions ('Errori').

Though not always easy to practice, solidarity was a widespread sentiment for Malatesta. If hate, competition, and war had been the exclusive or dominant factors in human relationships, he argued, humanity could not have developed and progressed; there would not even be any humanity to speak of, but only brutes. By setting a limit that conflicts could not cross without arousing repugnance, human sympathy was morality in the making. Along with the awareness of the practical advantages that stem from its fulfillment, that sympathy yielded the ideas of 'justice', 'right', and 'morals' that, notwithstanding endless hypocrisy and lies, represented an ideal toward which humanity advanced. 'This "morality" is fickle and relative', Malatesta maintained; 'it varies with different times, peoples, classes, and individuals; people use it to serve their own personal interests and that of their families, class or country. But discarding what in official "morality" serves to defend the privilege and violence of the ruling class, there is always something left which is in the general interest and is the common achievement of all humanity, irrespective of class and race.' For Malatesta, the fact itself that the privileged felt the need to justify their status by a 'morality', however contradictory, was already a step toward a superior morality, and evidence that privilege did not feel secure on the mere basis of brute force ('Morale').

At any rate, Malatesta's anarchism did not rest upon such empirical observations. It made no appeal to any supposed human nature or law of social evolution, but equally—and this was the aim of his observations—it rejected human nature or social evolution as the basis for normative statements.

At the same time, grounding anarchism on an ethical choice that did not proceed from scientific or philosophical theories did not imply reducing it to an absolute principle independent of any appraisal of empirical reality, as often argued by commentators. For example, commenting upon the Malatesta–Merlino debate of 1897, Giampietro Berti utilizes Max Weber's fundamental distinction between 'ethic of ultimate ends' and 'ethic of responsibility', which, in Berti's view, were respectively epitomized by Malatesta and Merlino. For Malatesta, Berti argues, 'nothing was worth struggling for except the full realization of the anarchist idea'; in contrast, Merlino was allegedly driven by 'the present historical responsibility' (*Errico*, 270).

By trivializing Weber's distinction into a dichotomy between idealism and realism, Berti does justice to neither Weber nor Malatesta. Both Weber's concepts, as his choice of words makes clear, partake of an ethically oriented conduct, in which 'some kind of faith must always exist' (43). Neither one is identical with irresponsibility nor the other with unprincipled opportunism (46–7). Rather, Weber claims, the two 'are not absolute contrasts but rather supplements, which only in unison constitute a genuine man—a man who *can* have the "calling for politics" ' (54). Such combination is found in Malatesta. Not only his concern for the consequences of one's action was evident in his argument for violence and against tolstoyism, but also his urge to 'take the people as they are' epitomized Weber's claim that 'a man who believes in an ethic of responsibility takes account of precisely the average deficiencies of people'.

The anarchists' 'conservative' concern for the consequences of one's action was expressed in general form by their principle of coherence between ends and means rather than by any attempt to calculate the consequences of singular initiatives. This view was akin to Popper's, who assigns social sciences the task 'to trace the unintended social repercussions of intentional human actions', rather than to propound historical prophecies as a pre-requisite to conducting politics in a rational way ('Prediction', 336, 342). Similarly, for Malatesta the task of social sciences was to uncover the necessary laws resulting from the interaction of men living together ('Volontà'). At the same time, his emphasis on social indeterminacy implied that social evolution was not predictable and that the consequences of singular initiatives were only foreseeable to a limited degree.

By recasting anarchist gradualism as an invisible-hand process driven by the individual pursuit of the collective good, it is possible to grasp the connection between two aspects of anarchist theory, spontaneism and morality, which are usually addressed separately by commentators. When their connection is severed, both aspects are misunderstood and criticized as obviously irrational. Spontaneism is misconstrued as the unrealistic and unreasonable assumption of a benign human nature and the expectation that the collective good be provided without being intentionally aimed for. Morality is misconstrued as an individual stance that stubbornly ignores the social nature of the provision of collective goods.

However, the anarchists' struggling for the full realization of their ideal was not based on self-deception about what was directly reachable from the present society, but on their understanding of the dynamics of collective action. For Malatesta, social change was a function of the strength and direction of each component involved. If anarchists aimed for a more moderate goal, the result would also be a lesser change. Moreover, nobody knew exactly what was reachable from the present society. The standard relation between the desirable and the possible was reversed. For 'realists', the set of reachable possible worlds was an independent variable, to which individuals adjusted their goals. For anarchists, individual goals were the independent variable. If all were anarchist, anarchy would become possible, or rather real.

In brief, for Malatesta, aiming for the full anarchist ideal and adhering to anarchist morals came neither from an unrealistic apprehension of reality nor from a retreat from politics. Instead, spontaneism and morality together comprised the anarchist's outlook on the political problem. On the one hand, he regarded the provision of the common good as the spontaneous and socially unplanned result of individual intentional efforts. On the other hand, morality was the individual stance intentionally embraced in pursuit of the common good. Spontaneism did not rely on the assumption of a benign human nature or on the substitution of fideistic wishful thinking for empirical analysis. It relied on a rational understanding of social evolution as an invisible-hand process of the same kind that social theorists invoke in the description of market economy and many other social phenomena described as effects of composition. Conversely, morality was the sort of individual behavior socially conducive to the common good as an unplanned effect of composition.

Such conscious connection between spontaneism and morality constituted the essence of Malatesta's voluntarist theory of collective action.

THEORIES OF COLLECTIVE ACTION: A COMPARISON

The poignancy of Malatesta's theory of collective action can be best assessed by comparing it with competing theories in the mainstream traditions of rational-choice theory and marxism, especially with respect to each theory's outlook on the relation between positive and normative statements. The comparison shows that such ideas as coherence between ends and means, voluntarism, morality, and social indeterminacy were not accessory eccentricities of anarchist theory, but necessary elements that marked off the anarchist path from alternative ones.

Rational-choice theory starts from the methodologically individualistic premise that any social phenomenon is the effect of individual decisions, actions, attitudes, and so on. Second, actors are assumed to be rational, that is, their action is caused by reasons that derive from the actors' consideration of the consequences of their action. Third, actors are egoist, that is, they are concerned mainly with the consequences to themselves of their own action. Finally, they aim to maximize their benefits, that is, they are assumed to be able to distinguish the costs and benefits of alternative lines of action and to choose the one with the most favorable balance (Boudon, 'Beyond', 3–4).

A key theme of rational-choice theory is the conflict between individual and collective rationality, in contrast to what has been called the 'fallacy of composition', that is, the presumption that a group with a common interest takes action to further that interest (Hardin, *Collective*, 2). The conflict has been clearly formulated in Mancur Olson's influential book *The Logic of Collective Action*. Olson argues that, unless a group is small, or unless there is coercion or some separate incentive, 'rational, self-interested individuals will not act to achieve their common group interest' (2). The reason is that an individual's action has no perceptible effect in a large group. In such situations, the model of individual rationality is the 'free rider', that is, the individual who enjoys an indivisible collective good without contributing to its provision (35).

Olson's argument fits game theory's Prisoners' Dilemma model, in which the contrast between individual and collective rationality has received formal expression. In this model, two players can choose between a 'defection' and a 'cooperation' strategy. Either player gets the highest payoff by defecting when the other player cooperates and vice versa. Mutual defection and mutual cooperation yield intermediate payoffs, with mutual defection paying off lower than mutual cooperation (Taylor, 13–15). The environmental problem is a typical example of our times: if we all were environmentally minded we would all enjoy the best possible world, whereas if we all polluted our survival itself would be threatened. The problem, however, is that the optimal strategy for each of us individually is to keep reaping the benefits of polluting, while everyone else pays the costs of being environmentally minded.

The Prisoners' Dilemma model is regarded as the paradigm of collective action problems, that is, problems of joint action in pursuit of a collective good. For example, Russell Hardin claims that 'the problem of collective action in social contexts...is the Prisoners' Dilemma writ large' (*Collective*, xiii); and for Jon Elster politics is 'the study of ways of transcending the Prisoners' Dilemma' (qtd in Taylor, 19–20).

What are the normative implications of rational behavior models?

Some theories explicitly claim their prescriptive motivation. For example, John Charles Harsanyi states that his theory 'deals with the question of how each player *should* act in order to promote his own interest most effectively' (qtd in Sen, 68). Other models claim to explain and predict actual behavior. They do so by first characterizing rational behavior, and then arguing that 'while actual behavior can, in principle, take any form, it is reasonable to assume that much of the time it will, in fact, be of the kind that can be described as "rational" ' (Sen, 68).

However, even descriptive models, by their predictive power, must have normative implications. The most obvious and relevant for the present discussion is that, since an anarchist society is empirically shown to be impossible or utterly undesirable, we should not be anarchist. As Olson clearly states, the idea that a large group 'can be natural, harmonious, and voluntary, and thus stand in contrast to the coercive state, is mistaken' (130). In fact, the Prisoners' Dilemma model has been used to restate Hobbes's argument that government is necessary, because otherwise people would not voluntarily cooperate to provide themselves with basic public goods, such as peace and security (Taylor, 1–2).

Thus, in its methodological individualism, the Prisoners' Dilemma model of rational behavior provides both a term of comparison and a challenge to Malatesta's approach to collective action. However, the argument for the desirability of government appears in a different light if we require that its positive and normative domains be self-contained and identical, that is, that the set of actors that enter the described scenario are the same that enter the prescribed scenario.

Under this requirement the argument for the desirability of government clearly becomes circular, for the same set of actors is both described and prescribed to. Since we all act to maximize our own benefits, government is necessary; that is to say, since we are not anarchist, we should not be anarchist.

Moreover, the claim that government yields universal cooperation is based on a departure from methodological individualism, for government is regarded as an unanalyzed entity external to the game. Yet, as anarchists have relentlessly pointed out, governments are made up of individuals. Hence, they should be amenable to rational-choice analysis as every other actor in the game. At that point government can no longer be regarded as an agent that imposes cooperation on all players, for government members are not bound themselves by cooperation, and therefore they constitute a residuum of defectors. In brief, the result of introducing government is not the collectively optimal outcome.

In fact, free-riding and government are two sides of the same coin, rather than being mutually exclusive as the theory argues. Free riders live off cooperators. Their ideal situation is for everyone else to cooperate. Hence, a free-rider's best condition is to be able to enforce cooperation. Conversely, actors in a position to enforce cooperation must be assumed to seek to maximize their own benefit, on pain of making the theory self-contradictory. In brief, both free-riding and government imply defection and rest on everyone else's cooperation. So, government does not remove free-riding, but monopolizes it.

Finally, as Michael Taylor argues, government 'exacerbates the conditions that are supposed to make it necessary' (168–9). Malatesta made the even stronger point that 'a police force where there are no crimes to solve or criminals to apprehend, will invent both, or cease to exist' (*Anarchy*, 33).

In sum, the argument for the desirability of government is tenable only insofar as it avoids self-referentiality. Otherwise, its black and white distinction between a described scenario of universal defection and a prescribed scenario of universal cooperation incurs empirical, logical, and methodological problems. Empirically, the argument is made that the need for government is self-fulfilling, as dispositions to voluntary cooperation are discouraged and thwarted by the very existence of government. Logically, it follows from rational-choice theory's own assumptions that government monopolizes free-riding rather than preventing it. Methodologically, the simultaneous consideration of descriptive and prescriptive statements makes the argument self-fulfilling in an even stronger way, as the same dispositions are described and prescribed at the same time.

The anarchists' approach to situations modeled by the Prisoner's Dilemma was a straightforward and unconditional adherence to collective rationality: as Malatesta claimed, their actions aimed at the well-being of all humanity; their ideal was a society characterized by universal voluntary cooperation, which, unlike the monopoly of free-riding by a government, represents the

232 MAKING SENSE OF ANARCHISM

optimal outcome in the Prisoner's Dilemma; and through the principle of coherence between ends and means their every action in the here and now was driven by collective rationality.

By framing the problem of collective action in methodological individualistic terms, as the effect of composition of individual action, the Prisoner's Dilemma illuminates the political import of morality. For example, it has been argued that a solution to Prisoners' Dilemma situations would be to become Kantians: since none could rationally will that all choose a self-benefiting alternative, each would choose an altruistic alternative (Parfit, 38). In other words, the anarchist advocacy of morals was a way of transcending the Prisoner's Dilemma.

The iterative version of the Prisoner's Dilemma, that is, a sequence of games where each player knows the strategies chosen by all players in all previous games, sheds further light on the strategic dimension of morality. Anarchists did not only practice collective rationality, but equally focused on propaganda and example. As Michael Taylor argues, altruism may be encouraged by the observation of altruism (168–75). At the same time that they were the 'early adopters' of collective rationality, anarchists also recognized that most actors' disposition to cooperate was constrained by the struggle for survival. Hence, in addition to educating by propaganda and example, they focused on removing government and the private ownership of the means of production, the obstacles that prevented actors from embracing collective rationality.

The anarchists' solution to the Prisoners' Dilemma, as well as their larger claims about solidarity, are often charged with neglecting how real actors behave. For example, Olson contrasts his theory with the alleged 'anarchistic fallacy' of believing that 'once the existing, repressive, exploitive state was overthrown, a new, voluntary, natural unity would somehow emerge to take its place', which he regards as 'evidence of hopeless eccentricity' (130–1). However, Olson's own work demonstrates that anarchism is not so far outside the mainstream as it is portrayed. His argument that 'action taking' groups tend to be small (53–4) reflects a key argument of anti-organizationists. At the same time Olson argues that 'federal' groups constitute an exception to his theory (62–5). Again, federation was the standard form of large anarchist organizations. Thus Olson, unwittingly, since he does not understand anarchism, brings grist to the anarchist mill.

Furthermore, anarchists maintained that solidarity was pervasive in society. Kropotkin's studies of mutual aid are well-known and Malatesta himself regarded association as the fabric of society. However, anarchists most strongly refuted the claim that self-interest was universal by their own existence. They were a living example of solidaristic behavior in the present society. Olson's theory is again relevant here. Referring to utopian mass movements, which he discusses later in the book (161–2), he claims:

'There is paradoxically the logical possibility that groups composed of either altruistic individuals or irrational individuals may sometimes act in their common group interests' (2). Olson dismisses this 'logical possibility' as being 'usually of no practical importance'. Yet, with its own existence as a mass movement, anarchism refuted Olson's empirical claim, lending practical importance to the logical possibility. The implied argument was self-fulfilling, like the hobbesian one, but, unlike the latter, it was explicitly and unproblematically so. In a nutshell, the two sides respectively argued: 'we must be egoist since everyone is' and 'anyone can be altruist since we are'. The 'realist' argument grounds normative statements on allegedly empirical assumptions and is made unsound by its being self-referential. The voluntarist argument is self-contained and made sound precisely by its being self-referential.

If the assumption of universal self-interest is dropped, univocal normative statements can no longer be inferred from the Prisoners' Dilemma. Each actor makes a choice between individual and collective rationality in a game whose structure and outcome are indeterminate, depending on the aggregate choice of all actors. This is the very situation that Malatesta outlined when he claimed that the choice between egoism and solidarity confronted every individual and could only be consciously made. Through this claim he rejected the opposite and equally unwarranted beliefs in the necessity of government and in a natural harmony among individuals.

In sum, rather than exposing the 'anarchistic fallacy' purported by Olson, the Prisoner's Dilemma corroborates Malatesta's approach to collective action. Unlike government's advocates, anarchists aimed for the optimal solution from the point of view of collective rationality. And unlike hobbesians, Malatesta made no assumption about human nature. By their own existence, anarchists proved that living morally was a feasible course of action; by their example and propaganda, they spread the preference for collective rationality; and by the growth of their movement they increased the likelihood of an anarchist outcome. As Hobbes had claimed, if a multitude of people could live morally 'we might as well suppose all Man-kind to do the same' (86, orig. edn). By being anarchist, that is by embodying and propagating collective rationality, anarchists were the living proof that anarchy, or the realization of collective rationality, was possible. Even E. J. Hobsbawm, certainly no anarchist, makes a similar point when he argues that utopianism is probably a necessary social device to generate a revolution, because 'revolutionary movements and revolutions appear to prove that almost no change is beyond their reach'. Revolutionaries, Hobsbawm continues, carry a higher standard of morality into practice, the implied message being: 'If this is possible within their movement, why not everywhere?' (60–2).

The tension between positive and normative statements is also at the core of the contrast between marxist and anarchist theories of collective action.

Marxists were normatively driven by the analysis of historical processes, while anarchists were driven by the coherence between ends and means. The contrast is often portrayed as being between 'scientific' and 'utopian' social-ism, the one allegedly based on empirical knowledge and the other shunning it. However, this is misleading. Both theories concerned the relation between theory and practice, but differed radically in the appraisal of that relation. Marxists tended to conflate descriptive and prescriptive statements, while anarchists drew a sharp line between them. Again, the issue of self-reference is central to understanding the respective versions of self-aware rationality. The key question is whether empirical knowledge can concern one's own beliefs and actions.

At the heart of the question is the notion of reflexive beliefs, thus charac-terized by the sociologists William I. and Dorothy Swaine Thomas: 'If men define situations as real, they are real in their consequences' (572).

Reflexivity proceeded directly from the tenets of historical materialism, when the theory was invoked as a guide to social action. By conflating the positive and normative spheres, 'self-understanding', on which histor-ical materialism founded normative statements, amounted to self-fulfill-ing belief, for beliefs were both constitutive of reality and derived from it. For historical materialism, history had a knowable line of march; the agency of the proletariat was a key determinant of that line of march; at the same time the proletariat was to embrace the mission assigned by the course of history and deemed to be independent from anyone's will. The marxist philosopher György Lukács describes the process as the proletariat self-referentially becoming 'both the subject and the object of knowledge' (20). Others have acknowledged the dualism between the descriptive and prescriptive domain in marxist theory, but have sought to explain it. For example, A. W. Gouldner speaks of two marxisms, one 'scientific' and one 'critical', respectively deterministic and voluntaristic; and Steven Lukes speaks of a paradox in marxism's view of morality, proceeding from the fact that morality is claimed to be a form of ideology while marxist writings abound in moral judgments (2–3), but he 'resolves' the paradox by drawing a distinction between 'the morality of *Recht* and the morality of *emanci-pation*' (27). In contrast, the former marxist philosopher of science Imre Lakatos openly and unceremoniously points out the self-fulfilling character of marxist theory:

> Marx's greatest weakness…was that he advocated both historical de-terminism and then human freedom. For his whole theory it was vital to encourage the working class by showing that they are supported by historical necessity; on the other hand he was afraid that if they take this argument really seriously they will find out that they do not have to make a revolution and suffer for it, since the revolution will come anyway. Therefore Marx is for historical necessity on even pages and

for freedom of the will on odd pages, so that revolutionaries should know that without their efforts historical determinism will stop working. (369)

Determinism and voluntarism, which were conflated in marxist theory, were kept sharply apart in Malatesta's anarchism. On the issue of determinism and free will, Malatesta's standpoint was a characteristic suspension of judgment and unresolved dualism. What was remarkable in this stance was precisely the implicit avoidance of self-referentiality: the observer Malatesta embraced determinism, but he stopped its application where the will of the actor Malatesta began. A rift between the observer and the actor was retained, rather than building a theoretical system encompassing one's own beliefs as possible objects of belief. Incompleteness on the descriptive side and unwarranted assumptions on the prescriptive side were accepted. Inconsistency between descriptive and prescriptive systems was not ruled out. However, the consistency between Malatesta's theory and action might well rest upon not making any claim about their consistency.

In its cautiousness, which seems to verge on the inconsequent, Malatesta's standpoint is remarkably in step with recent formal results in belief logic. Recasting Kurt Gödel's metamathematical theorems in terms of systems that can reason about their consistency and inconsistency, Raymond Smullyan has proven that such systems cannot consistently believe in their own consistency: 'if the reasoner is consistent, he can never know that he is consistent; or, stated otherwise, if the reasoner ever believes that he cannot be inconsistent, he will become inconsistent!' (101). The soundness and sophistication of Malatesta's viewpoint can also be appreciated by comparison with a current philosophical thesis about the mind–body relationship, Donald Davidson's 'anomalous monism', which 'resembles materialism in its claim that all events are physical, but rejects the thesis, usually considered essential to materialism, that mental phenomena can be given purely physical explanations' (*Essays*, 214).

While the marxist theory of collective action was implicitly based on self-fulfilling beliefs, Malatesta's was explicitly so. This was the essence of his voluntarism. Malatesta positively advocated a version of the 'Thomas theorem': 'If men define anarchy as real', the theorem could be paraphrased, 'anarchy is real in its consequences.'

A question thus arises: if, after all, both Marx's and Malatesta's theories of collective action hinged upon self-fulfilling beliefs, what set them apart? The difference consisted in the opposite views about what beliefs were legitimate. Marx and Malatesta agreed that the working class had numbers, but in order to turn those numbers into a revolutionary movement a revolutionary consciousness was also required. The two radically differed as to how that consciousness was to be formed.

For Marx, revolutionary consciousness could only be the consciousness of the working class's historical mission, as uniquely identified through knowledge of the concrete totality's real movement, and summarized by the notion of 'self-understanding'. Self-understanding was a complex process in the light of Marx's own theory of ideology, which made knowledge of the concrete totality by actors who were part of it a contradictory notion. Only an external observer could soundly undertake the task of 'letting the world perceive its own consciousness by awaking it from dreaming about itself'. In fact, it was the responsibility of the philosopher, or of the marxist party, to make the proletariat aware of its historical mission. Since there was one definite line of march of history, which dictated one definite mission, only one path was admitted. No other successful course of action was deemed to be open to the proletarian actors.

However, the matter was not just to interpret the world, but to change it. The task of marxist philosophy was not only to make the proletariat aware of its mission, but to lead it in its fulfillment. In brief, the task was both to define that unique path as real and to make it real in its consequences, as per the Thomas theorem.

Yet defining situations as real is not a purely 'objective' operation, when one can have beliefs about one's own beliefs under certain conditions. As has been pointed out in the current sociological debate about reflexive beliefs, these have more profound implications than making originally false conceptions come true. For example, Emile Grunberg remarks that phenomena often characterized as self-fulfilling beliefs, such as minority stereotypes, do not concern reflexive public predictions—that is, predictions made public to agents whose behavior they refer to and who therefore can either falsify or fulfill those predictions by their actions—but rather private predictions or expectations about others. These motivate their holders to behave in a certain way, which, in turn, self-fulfillingly engenders the expected reaction by those others (480). In a similar vein, it has been argued that 'consciousness, beliefs, ideals, imaginings, prejudices, values...enter essentially and constitutively into the being of the reality studied in the social sciences' (Krishna, 1107). So, in defining situations as real there is room for indeterminacy and arbitrariness. In fact, Raymond Smullyan has demonstrated, using a metamathematical theorem due to Martin Löb, that self-fulfilling beliefs are logically demonstrable in formalized belief systems (146). One can get a glimpse of Löb's original theorem from the very succinct version that the author himself sketched: let A be any arbitrary sentence and let B be the sentence "if this sentence is true, then so is A'. If B is true, then so is A; that is, B is true; hence, A is true.

The above findings imply that the issue of reflexivity has not only epistemological relevance, but it also crucially concerns the relation between the beliefs and actions of an observer–actor, which was the context of the controversy between marxism and anarchism. In a nutshell, Löb's theorem proves that what 'goes on before our eyes' depends on a choice, which in turn can be 'demonstrated' within our belief system. Furthermore, as has been noted, 'the likelihood of a prediction becoming self-fulfilling increases with the proximity of the man of knowledge to the reins of power', for in that case intellectuals 'possess the resources to alter future social conditions so that their predictions may be fulfilled' (Avison, 76).

The relevance of the above discussion is obvious in the case of marxist parties. They attributed themselves the role of providing the proletariat with knowledge, from which an objectively ascertainable and uniquely viable path, a 'historical mission', could allegedly be inferred. At the same time they claimed to represent 'the working class organized as a party', and, in that capacity, they aimed at exercising a dictatorship of the proletariat, whereby that historical mission was fulfilled.

In contrast, for Malatesta history had no knowable line of march, nor was there any mission set by history. As he wrote in 1920, 'society moves forward or backward depending on which forces and wills prevail, mocking any of those "historical laws" that may explain past events more or less adequately (more often inadequately than not), but are useless in predicting future events' ('Leggi'). Missions, aims, and normative concepts pertained to individuals. They were collective and socially relevant to the extent that they were widespread and spurred collective organization in their pursuit. For Malatesta, collective action admitted as many self-fulfilling paths as collective projects. Each 'utopia' was a possible path, in principle; the extent to which each succeeded depended on the ascendancy it gained in the social arena. Malatesta's approach was steeped in incomplete knowledge, social indeterminacy, and arbitrary choice of aims, which, however, could be held by all actors within a social system. In other words, the very cognitive completeness and determinacy of the marxist approach prevented it from being universalizable; and the very cognitive incompleteness and indeterminacy of the anarchist approach made it amenable to universalization.

In sum, an inherent link between theory and practice existed for both Marx and Malatesta. For Marx, the link was between historical materialist theory and authoritarian practice. The latter was not an accessory trait, but the result of extending historical materialism from the descriptive to the prescriptive domain. In the latter domain, the issue of reflexivity arose, and authoritarianism was the way historical materialism dealt with it. Conversely, the libertarian practice of Malatesta's anarchism had a counterpart in his suspension of judgment and unresolved dualism on the controversy between determinism and voluntarism, which *de facto* prevented the issue of reflexivity from arising. Authoritarianism resulted from the pretension to be simultaneously observer and actor with respect to the same concrete totality. In contrast, anarchist voluntarism resulted from universalizing the mutual exclusion between observing and acting posited for individuals.

EPILOGUE: LESS IS MORE

The comparison between the anarchist theory of collective action and those of rational-choice theory and marxism throws into relief the soundness of the former in the area where it is least given credit, the relation between theory and practice. There was more to anarchist theory than the 'hopeless eccentricity' attributed to it by Olson (130–1) or the 'schoolboy's asininity' by which Marx branded Bakunin's voluntarism ('On Bakunin', 607).

The two comparisons point in the same direction, revealing the central role of self-reference as a crucial test bed for the adequacy of theories of collective action.

Both rational-choice theory and marxism base their conclusions upon empirical claims and dismiss anarchist theory for its empirical inadequacy and voluntarist arbitrariness. However, for both rational-choice theory and marxism the pretension to derive normative from positive statements breaks down in the face of self-reference. Both theories have to resort to exogenous agents in their accounts of the relation between theory and practice. The argument for the desirability of government does so by departing from the methodological individualistic assumption on which it is based, and marxism does so by the very nature of its methodological holism, when it posits a party that represents the working class 'for itself'. On the practical side, in both cases the resort to an exogenous agent amounts to the provision of the common good by authoritarian means. Both hobbesians and marxists advocate 'good by force' as a political solution.

In contrast, anarchist voluntarism deals unproblematically with self-reference. The anarchist theory of collective action is consistent and self-contained, involving no resort to exogenous agents, and correspondingly advocating the method of freedom as a political solution to the provision of the common good.

In brief, when abstract theorizing is to be replaced by a sound approach to the relation between theory and practice, the anarchist lesson is that less is more.

10
CONCLUSION:
A COMPLEX, RATIONAL BUSINESS

HISTORIANS HAVE PORTRAYED ANARCHIST ACTION AS UNPLANNED, UNORGANized, spontaneistic, aimless, futile, cyclical, and unchanging; their aims as purist, 'all-or-nothing', utopian, 'pie-in-the-sky', and impossibilist; and their beliefs as backward, stubborn, romantic, fideistic, infantile, primitive, and millenarian. Each qualification is based on evidence but at the same time interprets evidence in a way that denies anarchists the benefit of common sense. As a result, anarchism has appeared doomed, eccentric, absurd, contradictory, or stupid. In the face of such appearance, two paths lay open. The uncharitable historian is content with concluding that anarchists appeared irrational because they were so, and sets out to causally explain the anarchists' irrationality in terms of socio-psychological motives. No doubt E. J. Hobsbawm's most unobjectionable claim about millenarian movements is the following: 'Those who cannot understand what it is that moves them—and even some who do—may be tempted to interpret their behaviour as wholly irrational or pathological, or at best as an instinctive reaction to intolerable conditions' (60).

In step with Hobsbawm's authoritative guidelines, the charitable historian assumes that anarchism appears irrational because it has been interpreted in a faulty way, and sets out to reinterpret evidence in a way that grants common sense to anarchism. In the process, the attribution of rationality is used as a criterion to filter interpretations and challenge appearances. The aim is a self-contained explanation of anarchism in terms of reasons. This has been the task of this work in investigating the ideas and action of Errico Malatesta. A charitable account of Malatesta's anarchism is at the same time an account of the historians' pitfalls about anarchism.

The pillars of Malatesta's anarchism were his methodologically individualist view of social action and his concept of anarchism as a method. These ideas, which Malatesta began expounding in 1889, were the key to his evolution in the next four decades. For Malatesta, social action was 'the resultant of initiatives, thoughts, and actions of all individuals who make up society'. The resultant depended on the aim to which the different social components were directed and on the strength of each. The rise of an anarchist society was a gradual process. Society would become increasingly anarchist as the component acting in the direction of anarchy became increasingly strong. Both anarchism as a movement and anarchy as a result were characterized by freedom as the method of social action. In the light of these ideas many traits of anarchism commonly interpreted in irrationalist terms can be reframed and made sense of.

The canonical objection on which anarchism supposedly founders concerns the possibility of anarchy. Accordingly, the standard irrationalist interpretation is that anarchists had unrealistic expectations, based on unwarranted optimistic beliefs. Alternatively, the obvious unattainableness of the full anarchist objective has led commentators to the conclusion that anarchist action was aimless. Such interpretations assume a 'holistic' view of anarchy, according to which either anarchy is realized or it is not, without any middle ground. For Malatesta anarchy was indeed possible, though its feasibility was not committed to an alleged benign human nature, but to the degree of the moral development of the people. At any rate, it did not really matter whether anarchy could be fully realized or not. On the ground of a methodological individualist assumption, the objection was by-passed as simply misplaced. For Malatesta, anarchists were to strive for the full realization of their ideal, even if anarchy was not an immediate possibility, and whether or not it could ever be realized. In a way, he literally urged anarchists to be impossibilist, in the spirit of Max Weber's remark that 'all historical experience confirms the truth—that man would not have attained the possible unless time and again he had reached out for the impossible' (55). The key point was that the anarchist method ensured the best possible world to be experimentally attained, without knowing in advance what that world might be. For Malatesta, there was no gain in watering down the anarchist program, which would simply weaken the anarchists' impact on the overall direction of society. Instead, the anarchists' struggle for their entire program was the surest way to steer as much as possible the progress of humanity toward their ideal. In brief, anarchism did not theoretically stand or fall with the feasibility of its ideal society; and anarchist action was neither impossibilist nor aimless, but reforming.

The standard irrationalist interpretation of anarchist 'impossibilism' is an exclusive one, such that anarchism was for 'all-or-nothing'. Thus, for Woodcock the anarchist future 'was a kind of revolutionary pie-in-the-sky, and one was expected to fast until mealtime'. For him, anarchists 'displayed an infinite and consistent contempt for piecemeal reform...' (447). However, though Malatesta rejected any transgression of principles, his anarchism was inclusive. He did not overlook partial gains, but for him uncompromising direct action was the best way to obtain legal reform or to wrest concessions from the bosses, at the same time that it fostered revolutionary consciousness. Laws and concessions were the result of a balance of strength; force and fear were the only means of persuasion effective on rulers. Demanding a full meal was the most effective way to obtain snacks, but these were not to replace a full meal as the workers' objective.

Underlying Malatesta's 'impossibilism' were considerations of social indeterminacy, another theme that differentiates individualistic from holistic approaches to understanding social action. Indeterminacy arises in contexts of strategic interaction, which is to say 'in virtually all social contexts', as Russell Hardin argues. In such contexts, he explains, an actor can only choose a strategy, not an outcome. The latter depends on the choices of other actors, which are not known in advance (*Indeterminacy*, 1). That collective action can have apparently paradoxical outcomes is a point further elaborated by game-theoretic 'threshold' models. As Mark Granovetter argues, 'groups with similar average preferences may generate very different results' (1420). Knowing the norms, preferences, motives, and beliefs of participants in collective behavior is not sufficient to explain collective action outcomes, which also crucially depend on the variation of norms and preferences within the interacting group (1421). Two groups almost identical in composition may yield very different outcome results, due to differences in the respective processes of aggregation, among which the presence of 'instigators' may be crucial (1424–5). Anarchist 'impossibilism' did not reflect expectations about actual outcomes, but strategic considerations in situations of limited knowledge. More generally, Malatesta rejected any pretense to comprehend social processes as wholes. The same attitude characterizes modern methodological individualistic arguments, such as the criticisms of holistic social engineering by Hayek (*Counter-Revolution*, 91–2) and Popper (*Poverty*, 67–9), foreshadowed by anarchist arguments since the First International.

Considerations of strategic interaction were also at the heart of Malatesta's voluntarism.

Writing about the revolutionary theory of Andalusian anarchism, Hobsbawm asks: 'How would the great change come about? Nobody knew. At bottom the peasants felt that it must somehow come about if only all men declared themselves for it at the same time' (88). In a similar vein, Irving Horowitz argues: 'Isn't it true, as Plekhanov and others have insisted, that anarchism is simply a form of utopianism, a longing for a world of human perfection independent of the agencies for getting to such a perfect condition? And therefore, would it not be more rational to conceive of anarchism as a religious expression, a messianic critique, of the social world as it is?' (585). Hobsbawm and Horowitz's arguments illustrate the stereotypical interpretation of voluntarism, which was a trait of anarchism since the First International, where it contrasted with the marxist focus on historical necessity. Such contrast is usually interpreted as being between a messianic expectation that overlooked actual agencies and a due consideration given to empirical reality.

Hobsbawm's argument is not groundless. In fact, the unconscious feeling that he attributes to Andalusian anarchists corresponded to Malatesta's explicit claim that the day everyone was anarchist, anarchy would be real. Obviously he did not expect that all would become anarchist at once, or even that everyone would eventually become anarchist. However, he did construe anarchy in terms of the actors' anarchist dispositions. Again, methodological individualism allows one to make sense of anarchist voluntarism, in contrast to irrationalist interpretations. The emphasis on oriented action as the matter of social reality, which is inherent to methodological individualism, implies that beliefs, ideals, and values are essential and constitutive of that reality. In the social sciences of the twentieth century such a focus is most evident in the study of reflexive belief, summarized by the Thomas theorem: what is conceived to be real also tends to become real. Yet by reading the Thomas theorem normatively one obtains a statement of voluntarism. For Malatesta, anarchy became real to the extent that people became anarchist. In brief, the social science idea of self-fulfilling prediction and voluntarism express the same statement, of which they respectively constitute the descriptive and prescriptive interpretations.

In contrast to the misconception that anarchism ignored real agencies, Malatesta's voluntarism was coupled with a strong realism about the choices that situated individuals could make. Anarchist gradualism precisely arose from a realist outlook on the masses and the consciousness that a mass conversion to anarchism was out of the question. In fact, Malatesta's voluntarism and realism proceeded in parallel and reinforced each other. To the extent that Malatesta committed revolution and anarchy to conscious choices, he correspondingly refrained from comforting analyses that committed social progress to allegedly empirical trends, be they kropotkinian evolutionary laws or marxist historical necessities. Malatesta held a realistic outlook on class consciousness formation. He realized that propaganda had limited power on masses constrained by harsh material conditions. At the same time, he did not expect capitalist development to create the proletariat as a revolutionary force, nor mere economic interests to unite the working class into a compact army. For Malatesta, interests tended to be conservative, while only the ideal was revolutionary. Unlike Marx, he did not believe that interests and capability for collective action proceeded in parallel, and did not subscribe to the 'group theory' idea that 'groups will act when necessary to further their common or group goals' (Olson, 1). Much of his anarchism consequently proceeded from such realist appraisal of social dynamics.

The 'fundamental vagueness about the actual way in which the new society will be brought about', which Hobsbawm considers typical of millenarian movements (58–60), concerns not only the revolutionary process, but also the revolutionary program. Likewise, Woodcock argues that the anarchists' 'disinclination to attempt specific proposals led to their producing a vague and vapid vision of an idyllic society' congenial to 'primitive and evangel-ically minded people like the Andalusian peasants', with their 'millenarian longings for the earthly Kingdom of God' (446–7). In Malatesta's case, the 'vagueness' of the anarchist program was not the symptom of a primitive and evangelical frame of mind, but the original result of nearly two decades of theoretical elaboration. What came to characterize his anarchism from the 1890s on was the method of freedom, not a blueprint of society. Anarchists were indeed to discuss solutions for the future, and in the 1920s Malatesta lamented that such discussions had been largely wanting in the anarchist movement. However, no blueprint of society was to be inscribed in the an-archist program, which was to be deliberately limited to outlining a method. For Malatesta, those who expected detailed answers in advance about the future society, beyond the scope of personal opinions, did not really under-stand what anarchy was about (*Anarchy*, 44–5).

The core of his anarchism as a method was the idea that the most col-lectively rational society would be brought about not by implementing a pre-conceived blueprint, but by free experimentation aimed at the collective good. The much-maligned anarchist spontaneism can be reframed in the light of such notion. The idea of a spontaneous self-ordering process, which is, as we have seen, ubiquitous in social sciences and taken for granted in liberal theory, is looked upon as problematic when it is advocated by anar-chists. The anarchist appeal to spontaneity is regarded as either a utopian and futile expectation that all actors agree upon a universally accepted plan, or a fideistic belief in a pre-established harmony, such that social mechanisms run smoothly while actors are only intent on following private impulses. The only 'realistic' alternative to such unrealistic expectation is deemed to be so-cial chaos. In contrast, the process described by Malatesta was spontaneous, but bore no such traits. No faith in a benign human nature that had only to be freed from unnatural fetters was involved. The process was unplanned, but it consisted of oriented action.

The idea of an invisible-hand process driven by solidarity is one of those concepts that run counter to standard categorizations, for it fits neither of the mutually exclusive blocs separated by the conceptual Berlin Wall mentioned in the preface. Liberal theory advocates individualism across the board, both methodologically and ethically. Marxist socialism is for holism all along the line. Anarchism fits neither side. The originality of Malatesta's anarchism stemmed precisely from his advocacy of methodological individualism and ethical holism at the same time. Social action was the effect of composition of individual actions; but the fundamental principle of anarchist action was that it be aimed at the collective good. Malatesta advocated the method of freedom as against centralized planning, but at the same time he made so-cialism a precondition of that method. Unfortunately, anarchism is not only overlooked, but also misconstrued as contradictory in terms of dichotomies that were alien to its own conceptual framework.

However, ethical holism, social indeterminacy, and voluntarism made up a coherent theory of collective action that approached the contrast between individual and collective rationality, as modeled by the Prisoner's Dilemma, in empirically adequate and theoretically sound terms. In this context ethical holism was not an ungrounded moral stance, but could be motivated in a utilitarian fashion. The anarchist theory of collective action squarely contrasts with the standard charge that anarchists ignored reality or made arbitrary assumptions about human nature, and provides an alternative to the allegedly more sophisticated approaches of mainstream rational-choice theory and marxism. The relation between theory and practice, deemed to be the greatest weakness of anarchism, reveals its greater sophistication and consistency in addressing crucial questions of observer–actor self-reference and self-fulfilling beliefs.

Anarchism as a method bridged the gap between the future anarchist society and anarchist action in the present, redefining anarchism as a continuous process, rather than the attainment of a static end-result. If anarchism was a method and means were ends-in-the-making, the essence of anarchism was constituted more by its means than by its utopias. In fact, notwithstanding the misrepresentation of anarchism as unconcerned with practical means, debates over different ways of organizing and struggling took priority among anarchists over controversies about different models of the future society. The most profound division of Italian anarchism concerned the issue of organization. Ultimately, the debate was about different interpretations of the fundamental anarchist principle of coherence between ends and means.

This principle has been misinterpreted as a form of purism. However, coherence with ends was not just a straitjacket imposed upon anarchist means. Instead it expressed the anarchists' pragmatic preoccupation with the consequences of their action. Anarchists were not only concerned about which means were adequate, but most importantly about which ones led elsewhere than desired. Their concern for the displacement of goals and the unintended consequences of their action represented their conservative side. The constraints placed by the principle of coherence between ends and means on anarchist action varied with its interpretation. With his inclusive tactics and advocacy of organization, Malatesta stood in the most possibilist wing of the anarchist spectrum, often lamenting the paralyzing concerns of anti-organizationists. His own interpretation was that all means were good except those that either implied the imposition of 'good by force' or a displacement of goals, which in turn amounted to indirectly furthering anarchist goals by furthering other goals that implied 'good by force'. Still, the 'conservative' preoccupation was present in Malatesta, too. An example was his piecemeal approach to post-revolutionary reconstruction: no institution, no matter how imperfect, was to be destroyed until a better solution was found to fulfill the need in question ('Verso'; 'Gradualismo').

'Impossibilism' and 'purism' represented opposite but complementary aspects of anarchist action. Both stemmed from the anarchist awareness of social indeterminacy. Actors chose strategies, but could not foresee the outcome of strategic interaction. In the absence of any such knowledge, anarchists were to exert their social influence in the 'impossible' direction of anarchy, and refrain from any means that led in any other direction. Both aspects of anarchist action have been irrationalistically interpreted as forms of millenarian detachment from empirical reality.

Ultimately, millenarian interpretations fail to realize that anarchists were aware of the gap between their ultimate end and their present means. Though such interpretations still have currency among historians, they received the clearest and fullest refutation as early as 1899, when Malatesta pointed out the misconception that anarchists expected anarchy to come with one stroke and the associated belief that anarchy, thus conceived, was impossible. In contrast, he claimed, 'anarchy cannot come but little by little, slowly, but surely, growing in intensity and extension'. It was not a matter of 'achieving anarchy today, tomorrow, or within ten centuries, but of walking toward anarchy today, tomorrow, and always'. Hence, 'every victory against the bosses, every decrease of exploitation, would be a step on the road of anarchy' ('Verso').

Along that road, ultimate ends gave perspective to the anarchists' action. They looked not only at immediate gains, but also at long-term consequences. In this, a key concern was to stay on the right path, avoiding entry of dead ends that barred future progress. This led them to 'conservative' tactics that, in the short term, looked ineffective and hardly conducive to revolution. Yet in undertaking actions that were a far cry from their ultimate ends, anarchists were realistically gauging the distance. The stereotype of anarchists as doomed and fighting for lost causes is the irrationalistic counterpart of their awareness that they struggled for an aim they could not accomplish alone, and that the self-defeat of entering a wrong path was more irrecoverable that any setback along the right path.

If the substance of anarchism was no longer a blueprint, but the forms in which anarchist action unfolded, the history of anarchism becomes the practical illustration of how the method of freedom was applied and anarchism creatively made. Such experimental making of anarchism was not carried out in insulated colonies, but amid society and through collective action. Anarchists were always to adopt the method of freedom and to pursue the full realization of the anarchist ideal, without any transgression of their principles. However, constancy of method and aim did not imply that anarchism was an endless repetition of an unchanging pattern of action, irrespective of circumstances.

Thus Malatesta's activity illustrates a wide array of tactics. He gave priority to collective action, though individual deeds and affinity groups were not ruled out. Anarchist action could be carried out in many ways: underground or openly; on economic or political ground; autonomously by anarchists or as part of larger agitations with non-anarchist objectives; violently or peacefully; legally or illegally; and in pursuit of immediate partial gains or broader insurrectionary aims. Over time, Malatesta promoted, joined, or praised various kinds of tactics: guerrilla warfare, such as the Benevento uprising of 1877; affinity groups' propaganda by the deed, as advocated in *L'Associazione* in 1889; economic general strikes, such as the London dockers' strike of 1889; urban guerrilla, as advocated on the First of May in Paris in 1890, and practiced the next year in Rome; political general strikes, such as the one for universal suffrage in Belgium in 1893; popular riots, such as the Sicilian Fasci of 1893 and the bread riots of 1898; legal struggles to repel laws, such as the campaign against *domicilio coatto* in 1897; peaceful campaigns of self-denunciation, such as the manifesto for the right of association in 1898; labor struggles for immediate demands, such as in Argentina in the late 1880s and in Ancona in 1897; full-scale insurrectional initiatives, such as the one initiated in Lunigiana in 1894 and the Red Week of 1914; and individual deeds, including Bresci's assassination of Humbert I and forms of theft. Malatesta even undertook a hunger strike in jail in 1921, and by refusing to leave Italy during Fascism and living in an undeclared condition of house arrest, he foreshadowed the figure of the 'dissident'. Yet there was unity in all such tactics, which were all inscribed in the space defined by his tactical principles: insurrectionism, coherence with ends, inclusiveness, 'going to the people', and anarchist autonomy. Diversity and coherence practically illustrate the range and potential of the anarchist method.

The uncharitable historians' conclusion that unconcern for practical means, lack of organization, cyclicity, and spontaneism were the unchanging features of a doomed and irrational anarchist movement is consistent with the empirical evidence. Between 1889 and 1900 the only attempt at a country-wide Italian anarchist organization was the short-lived party created at Capolago in 1891. During that period anarchist activism peaked in 1891, in 1893–94, and in 1897–98. The highlights of each onset were respectively the Rome riots of 1 May 1891, the Carrara uprising of January 1894, and the bread riots of 1898. However, such analyses fail to explain how the anarchist movement lasted, for its sheer duration is testimony of its sustainability. The same evidence upon which anarchism is declared doomed and irrational motivates the charitable historian to look for anarchist rationality beyond the framework of formal and public organization within national bounds. Outside of that framework lies the realization that the very characteristics that made anarchist collective action seem discontinuous were precisely the ones that made it sustainable. These were organizational opacity and transnationalism.

Whenever we pierce through the appearance of casual and unplanned events, a web of connections is revealed that speaks to a more complex reality. Even individual episodes of Malatesta's life speak to this. In 1889, his return to Europe, his founding a periodical in Nice, and his hasty escape to London bore a casual and impromptu appearance. Questioning this appearance reveals that London, a hub of anarchist exiles, was Malatesta's center of gravity from the outset; that ongoing plans existed to establish a periodical in Nice by Malatesta's old Florentine comrades of the early 1880s; and that Malatesta had steady contacts throughout Europe. An even more striking contrast is offered by his escape from Lampedusa Island in 1899. The romantic tale of a brave and lucky individual who defies the waves of a stormy sea in a tiny boat must be replaced by the reality of a well-thought-out and carefully executed plan involving comrades in various countries. In contrast to the appearance of an isolated individual at the mercy of events, the reality was that of a dense network through which Malatesta made plans and kept abreast of events even from the other side of the Atlantic or from captivity.

At the level of collective action, the appearance of spontaneism and lack of organization must be replaced by the reality of opaque organization, as the events of 1890–92 illustrate. In Italy a stream of underground agitations for the First of May 1891 surfaced under the appearance of a spontaneous commotion of an inflammable crowd aroused by an unknown speaker. In Spain an articulate and far-reaching organization effort is hardly mentioned in accounts of Spanish anarchism, the historical stage being stolen, as it were, by yet another apparently spontaneous commotion of an inflammable crowd, the Jerez uprising of January 1892. That effort remains confined to a few lines in Malatesta's biographies, while historians are left to debate about his role in the uprising that thwarted the very project that brought him to Spain. However, reality was made of preparation and organization carried out from one First of May to the next, without interruption and across national borders. Yet the necessarily underground character of such work makes it disappear from historical accounts.

As E. P. Thompson has argued for Luddism, there was an intentional side to the opacity of anarchist organization, for this was the very precondition of effective action. The counterpart of the opacity of organization was the spontaneous semblance of popular agitations. One cannot assume that behind any seemingly spontaneous 'mob' there lay anarchist organization. But where such work did take place, the image of a spontaneous mob was an indicator of its effectiveness. That an agitation appeared to be carried out by a mob speaks to the popular participation to it; and that the agitation seemed spontaneous speaks to the ability of anarchists to work underground. Neglecting anarchist opacity and limiting one's scope of analysis to what rises to the surface, attempting to simply connect public events, is likely to provide distorted interpretations. Correcting such views is not simply about providing sympathetic interpretations. Paradoxically, these interpretations tend to endorse official versions, given that authorities were inclined to regard anarchist agitations as the outcome of pre-ordained, highly organized, and far-reaching conspiracies. Giampietro Berti's and Temma Kaplan's respective interpretations of the events in Italy and Spain are cases in point. The issue with opacity is not to reinterpret available evidence, but to question it and probe beneath the surface, so as to capture complexity and rationality concealed by simple and odd appearances.

In contrast to simplistic views of anarchist tactics, the events of Italy and Spain in 1891–92 point out internal divisions and tactical divergences within the anarchist movement, which in turn point to a range of alternative tactical options. Obviously, such divisions were a weakening factor. However, acknowledging the shortcomings of the anarchist initiatives under discussion does not invalidate the rationality argument. A failed insurrection is a failed insurrection. In hindsight, it is clear that the means employed by the anarchists in those circumstances were inadequate. However, there is a significant difference between ascribing such inadequacy to the inherent incoherence between anarchist means and ends and ascribing it to contingent overpowering circumstances. The latter attribution complies with the principle of charity, but the former does not.

The anarchists' lack of formal organization does not mean that anarchists did not organize, but rather that they did not organize formally. Thus, the historian cannot simply look for congresses, party programs, and party structures, but rather has to look also at the dense network of links between individuals and groups to study how anarchism functioned as a collective movement. In the sustained and multi-directional personal links between individuals and groups one can find the coordination and continuity that is usually looked for in the impersonal structure and fixed roles of formal organizations.

In addition to overlooking the informal and opaque character of anarchist organization, historians have neglected the movement's transnationalism. The use of analytic frameworks of national scope is responsible for the seeming cyclical pattern of advance and retreat, according to which the Italian anarchist movement seemed to disappear in the wave of arrests, exiles, shutdown of periodicals, and disbandment of groups after each struggle's onset, only to resurface years later in a new cycle of agitations. The movement did not vanish, it just moved from one sphere to another. Italian anarchism was characterized by intense transnational mobility of militants, resources, and ideas across the Atlantic Ocean and the Mediterranean Sea.

A transnational perspective provides the appropriate context in which the individual lives of militants should be placed. Malatesta's life is paradigmatic in this respect. From a national perspective his exiles through Europe, North Africa, and the Americas may appear as the wanderings of a knight errant in and out of his country, an alternation of engagements with and disengagements from anarchism in Italy. From a transnational perspective the same movements represent a coherent itinerary within Italian anarchism, either in Italy or outside of Italy, with no interruption and no disengagement.

Moreover, transnationalism is key to understanding how anarchism functioned as a movement. Anarchist mobility had its own dynamics and was not a simple function of the mobility of the Italian population at large. However, anarchist transnationalism was indeed rooted in the areas of Italian immigration. The steady presence of Italian anarchists in such areas was relied upon by comrades in the homeland and elsewhere in the world. The transnational segment of Italian anarchism provided financial resources for propaganda in Italy, most notably by supporting the anarchist press. It also had a key role in publishing its own periodicals and pamphlets. Such periodicals were transnational in various ways: not only were they published abroad, but they were also meant for distribution outside of their country of publication; and their content was itself considerably transnational, thanks to regular correspondences from comrades in other countries.

Transatlantic organizational integration characterized Italian anarchism, as best exemplified by the relations with militants in the United States, which was visited by most Italian anarchist leaders, with the purpose of strengthening the anarchist movement and press in that country. The sustained editorship of *La Questione Sociale* of Paterson by a steady stream of foremost anarchists over a long period of time constitutes a singular pattern of cooperation. Conversely, militants from overseas locations regularly participated in the collective life of the Italian movement, as institutional events like the Capolago congress of 1891 illustrate. Groups in New York, Buenos Aires, São Paulo, Tunis, and Alexandria, with their periodicals and their steady participation to the life of the homeland movement, were by all means integral parts of it. Transnational anarchism in Europe had an even closer role. A sort of division of labor existed, whereby a significant amount of the organizational and propaganda workload, such as arranging congresses and printing materials, could be taken up by groups outside of Italy, especially when such activities were likely to incur government repression. Conversely, exiles like Malatesta were always ready to clandestinely reenter Italy, when circumstances required it.

Transnationalism was a crucial factor for the anarchist movement's sustainability. In times of repression, it provided continuity to the movement that had been beheaded in the homeland, and its press abroad took up the task of carrying on propaganda in the Italian language. However, transnationalism was not just an emergency mode of operation in exceptional times. Rather, it was a built-in characteristic of the movement, closely related to the nature of its tactics. Italian anarchists were aware of the role of transnationalism and relied on it. Insurrectionary tactics required preparation and organization. The more this work could be carried out quietly and covertly, the more effective it could be. Hence, in the division of labor between anarchists in Italy and abroad, the latter were more suited to carry out such preparations. Conversely, direct action tactics were as effective as they could be sudden and widespread. Thus, direct action tactics, opacity of organization, and transnationalism together provide an alternative pattern of explanation to the advance-and-retreat or appearance-and-disappearance patterns.

Abandoning a national framework of analysis also means being able to grasp the cross-national links between movements of different countries and to look at national debates in a new light. Thus, the parallel process occurring in Italy and France in the mid-1890s sets syndicalism in a broader context of labor-oriented anarchism. The similarity of themes between the Spanish controversy about collectivism and communism and the Italian debate on organization reveals the real content of the debate in Spain, thus refuting the theory of Spanish exceptionalism and confirming that means were the real matter of debates even when these appeared to be about models of the anarchist society.

On the basis of this understanding of anarchism, standard categorizations should be reframed. Distinctions based on organization and the labor movement are more revealing than those based on pairs like collectivism–communism or communism–individualism. Malatesta's case illustrates well the negative effect of inappropriate categorizations. He is often portrayed as a communist and a defender of anarchist purism in contrast to syndicalism, at the Amsterdam congress of 1907, and to platformist organizationism. This picture becomes awkward, though, if Malatesta is categorized as an organizationist and hence as primarily a supporter of both labor involvement and organization.

Transnationalism and cross-nationalism enriched Malatesta's theoretical and tactical evolution, as did his direct experience of workers' struggles in four continents. That evolution, from an early faith in the revolutionary virtue of the people to anarchist gradualism, was a long process forged in the crucible of social struggles. Each tactical formula was put to the test of collective action; and each failed insurrectional attempt, repressed popular movement, or missed revolutionary opportunity occasioned a reformulation of Malatesta's tactics. Such was the case of the London Dock Strike of 1889, the First of May agitations of 1890–92, the Sicilian Fasci movement of 1893–94, and the labor struggles and bread riots of 1897–98. Rather than to an endless cycle of advance and retreat, the process can be more appropriately likened to the method of trial and error. Tentative solutions were put to the test of experience and revised accordingly. In this sense, those attempts can be truly regarded as Malatesta's experiments with revolution.

None of those experiments was victorious. However, even in defeat, Malatesta's work was not useless. As historians of anarchism have begun to show, anarchists, the early adopters of collective rationality, had an impact on society (Shaffer, *Anarchism*; M. Thomas). However, this impact was not in contrast with their 'impossibilist' ends but in step with them. Moreover, from a voluntarist perspective, the protracted existence and sustainability of the anarchist movement provides historical evidence that self-fulfillingly reinforces the viability of anarchism as a political proposal. If anarchism can exist, then anarchy can be real. Arguably, the same logic, used in the opposite direction, tacitly underpins the eagerness of many historians to present anarchism as a necessarily doomed movement. The normative implication would be that anarchism is politically unviable.

Notwithstanding the impact and sustainability of anarchism, the lack of success was painfully present to Malatesta's mind. In his last years, seriously ill, he wrote to Luigi Bertoni about the 'intimate tragedy' of his heart: 'I am moved by the great affection that the comrades have for me and at the same time I am tormented by the thought to have done so little to deserve it.' Still, self-defeat overrode defeat in the anarchists' consideration. For Malatesta, the anarchists' last stand was to save their principles when they were materially powerless to further their cause, for that meant saving the future. The very last sentence of *Anarchy* was: 'If today we fall without compromising, we can be sure of victory tomorrow.' The sentence was not galvanizing rhetoric or a rationalization of defeat. It expressed the essence of anarchist action.

In hindsight, eight decades after Malatesta's death, the historian can dismiss his belief as naïve and his hope as ill-conceived and irrational. Still, the voluntarist Malatesta could rejoin that the historian's own assessment is another example of self-fulfilling belief, for tomorrow is yet to come.

References

List of Abbreviations

ACS	Archivio Centrale dello Stato, Rome
APP	Archives de la Préfecture de Police, Paris
ASDMAE	Archivio Storico Diplomatico del Ministero degli Affari Esteri, Rome
CPC	Ministero dell'Interno, Direzione Generale Pubblica Sicurezza, Casellario Politico Centrale
DAP	Ministero di Grazia e Giustizia, Direzione Generale degli Affari Penali, delle Grazie e del Casellario, Divisione Affari Penali
DGPS	Ministero dell'Interno, Direzione Generale Pubblica Sicurezza, Divisione affari generali e riservati, Archivio generale, Categorie annuali

Works by Errico Malatesta

'Il 1° Maggio', *Agitiamoci per il Socialismo Anarchico*, 1 May 1897; rpt. in *Lavoro lungo*, 45–6.

'L'alba che sorge', *L'Agitazione*, 2 July 1897; rpt. in *Lavoro lungo*, 143–4.

'Un altro sciopero', *L'Associazione*, 16 October 1889.

'L'Anarchia', parts 1–3, *La Questione Sociale* (Florence), 4–18 May 1884.

'Anarchia e parlamentarismo', *L'Agitazione*, 14 March 1897; rpt. in *Lavoro lungo*, 7–10.

'Gli anarchici e le leghe operaie', *Volontà*, 20 September 1913.

'Gli anarchici nel movimento operaio', parts 1–3, *Umanità Nova*, 26–28 October 1921.

Anarchismo e democrazia (with F. S. Merlino; Ragusa: La Fiaccola, 1949; rpt., 1974).

'L'anarchismo nel movimento operajo', *L'Agitazione*, 7 October 1897; rpt. in *Lavoro lungo*, 247–9.

The Anarchist Revolution, ed. V. Richards (London: Freedom Press, 1995).

Anarchy, trans. V. Richards (London: Freedom Press, 1974); originally published as *L'Anarchia* (London: Biblioteca dell'Associazione, 1891).

'Ancora sulla rivoluzione in pratica', *Umanità Nova*, 14 October 1922.

'Andiamo fra il popolo', *L'Art. 248*, 4 February 1894.

Appello (Nice: Tipografia del giornale 'L'Associazione', 1889).

'A propos d'Aigues-Mortes' (with F. S. Merlino), *La Revue Anarchiste*, 30 September 1893.

'A proposito della "Plateforme"', *Il Risveglio*, 14 December 1929; trans. in *Anarchist Revolution*, 106–11.

'A proposito di "revisionismo" ', *L'Adunata dei Refrattari*, 1 August 1931.

'A proposito di uno sciopero', *L'Associazione*, 6 September [*recte* October] 1889.

'L'arbitrato', *La Rivoluzione Sociale*, 1 December 1902.

'La base morale dell'anarchismo', *Umanità Nova*, 16 September 1922; partly trans. in *Errico Malatesta: Life and Ideas*. 'La base morale dell'anarchismo', *Volontà*, 18 October 1913.

'Le bien par la force', *L'Idée*, 15 October 1894; rpt. in *Le Réveil*, 1 May 1937.

'Collettivismo, comunismo, democrazia socialista e anarchismo', *L'Agitazione*, 6 August 1897; rpt. in *Lavoro lungo*, 176–8.

'Come si conquista quel . . . che si vuole', parts 1 and 2, *L'Agitazione*, 12 April 1897 and *L'Agitatore Socialista Anarchico*, 25 April 1897; rpt. in *Lavoro lungo*, 46–52.

'Come si conquista quel che si vuole: Caso pratico', *L'Agitazione*, 6 August 1897; rpt. in *Lavoro lungo*, 179–80.

'Communications et correspondance', *La Révolte*, 3 September 1892.

'Il compito degli anarchici', *La Questione Sociale* (Paterson), 2 December 1899.

'La condotta degli anarchici nel movimento sindacale', *Fede*, 30 September 1923.

'Un congresso di anarchici italiani', *Agitatevi per il Socialismo Anarchico*, 8 May 1897; rpt. in *Lavoro lungo*, 83–4.

'Contro il domicilio coatto', *L'Agitazione*, 6 August 1897; rpt. in *Lavoro lungo*, 175–6.

Contro la Monarchia (London, 1899). 'Da Londra: Cose a posto', parts 1 and 2, *L'Agitazione*, 14 and 21 March 1897; rpt. in *Lavoro lungo*, 13–17.

'La decadenza dello spirito rivoluzionario e la necessità della resistenza' (signed 'Giuseppe Rinaldi'), *L'Agitazione*, 23 September 1897; rpt. in *Lavoro lungo*, 228–30.

'Una difesa del Parlamentarismo', *L'Agitazione*, 11 November 1897; rpt. in *Lavoro lungo*, 288–91. 'Dove mena il movimento operajo', *Volontà*, 28 February 1914.

'Il dovere della resistenza', *L'Agitazione*, 30 May 1897; rpt. in *Lavoro lungo*, 106–8.

'The Duties of the Present Hour', *Liberty*, August 1894.

'Echi del 1 Maggio', *Agitatevi per il Socialismo Anarchico*, 8 May 1897; rpt. in *Lavoro lungo*, 81–3.

Epistolario. Lettere edite e inedite 1873–1932, ed. R. Bertolucci (Avenza: Centro Studi Sociali, 1984).

'È possibile la rivoluzione?' *Volontà*, 18 April 1914.

Errico Malatesta: His Life and Ideas, ed. V. Richards (London: Freedom Press, 1965; rpt., 1993).

'Errori e rimedi', *L'Anarchia*, August 1896.

'Evoluzione dell'anarchismo', *L'Agitazione*, 14 October 1897; rpt. in *Lavoro lungo*, 253–7. 'L'evoluzione dell'anarchismo', interview by G. Ciancabilla, *Avanti!*, 3 October 1897; rpt. in *Lavoro lungo*, 240–7.

'Federación Internacional Socialista Anárquica Revolucionaria', *El Corsario* (Corunna), 11 April 1895.

'Federación Internacional, Socialista-Anárquica Revolucionaria', *El Despertar*, 10 March 1895.

'Federazione Socialista-Anarchica', *La Questione Sociale* (Paterson), 23 September 1899.

'"La fine dell'anarchismo" di Luigi Galleani', *Pensiero e Volontà*, 1 June 1926.

'Fine e mezzi', *Tribuna dell'Operaio*, 4 August [*recte* September] 1892.

'The First of May', *Commonweal*, 1 May 1893.

'Galileo Palla ed i fatti di Roma', *La Rivendicazione*, 23 May 1891.

'The General Strike and the Revolution', *Torch*, August 1894.

'Giuseppe Mazzini', *Umanità Nova*, 11 March 1922.

'Giustizia per tutti', *L'Agitazione*, 16 December 1897; rpt. in *Lavoro lungo*, 303–5.

'Gradualismo', *Pensiero e Volontà*, 1 October 1925; trans. in *Anarchist Revolution*, 82–7.

'La guerra contro i lavoranti stranieri', *La Rivoluzione Sociale*, 27 January 1903.

'Ideale e realtà', *Pensiero e Volontà*, 1 February 1924.

'"Idealismo" e "materialismo" ', *Pensiero e Volontà*, 15 January 1924.

'In alto i cuori', *Agitiamoci per il Socialismo Anarchico*, 1 May 1897; rpt. in *Lavoro lungo*, 72–4. 'Interesse ed ideale', *Umanità Nova*, 2 December 1922.

'International Federation of Revolutionary Anarchist Socialists', *Liberty*, February 1895, and *Torch*, 18 February 1895.

'Un lavoro lungo e paziente': Il socialismo anarchico dell'Agitazione, 1897–1898, ed. D. Turcato, with an introduction by R. Giulianelli (Milan: Zero in Condotta and Ragusa: La Fiaccola, 2011).

'Les Leçons du 1er Mai', *La Révolte*, 10 May 1890. 'Leghe di resistenza', *Agitiamoci per il Socialismo Anarchico*, 1 May 1897; rpt. in *Lavoro lungo*, 77–80.

'Le leggi storiche e la rivoluzione, *Umanità Nova*, 17 July 1920.

'Liberty and Fatalism, Determinism and Will', *Man!*, February 1935; originally published as 'Libertà e fatalità: Determinismo e volontà', *Volontà*, 22 November 1913.

'Lotta di classe o odio tra le classi?', *Umanità Nova*, 20 September 1921.

'La lotta economica in regime capitalistico', *Umanità Nova*, 21 October 1922.

'La lotta per la vita: Egoismo e solidarietà', *L'Associazione*, 23 January 1890.

'Lotta politica e lotta economica', *L'Agitazione*, 11 June 1897; rpt. in *Lavoro lungo*, 127–9.

'Morale e violenza', *Umanità Nova*, 21 October 1922. 'Un "nemico della rivoluzione" ai padroni della stessa', *Umanità Nova*, 20 October 1921.

'La nostra tattica', *L'Agitazione*, 11 November 1897; rpt. in *Lavoro lungo*, 286–7.

'I nostri propositi: I. L'Unione tra comunisti e collettivisti', *L'Associazione*, 30 November 1889.

'I nostri propositi: II. L'Organizzazione', *L'Associazione*, 7 December 1889.

'Il nostro programma', *La Questione Sociale* (Paterson), 9 September 1899.

'La nuova Internazionale dei Lavoratori' (signed 'Un vecchio Internazionalista'), *La Rivoluzione Sociale*, 15 November 1902.

'L'organizzazione', parts 1–3, *L'Agitazione*, 4–18 June 1897; rpt. in *Lavoro lungo*, 112–20.

'Un peu de théorie', *L'En Dehors*, 21 August 1892.

'Peter Kropotkin', *Freedom Bulletin*, July 1931.

Postcard to E. Molinari, London, 20 February 1894. MS, Ettore Molinari Papers, Biblioteca A. Mai, Bergamo.

Preface to Nettlau, *Bakunin*, xv–xxxi.

'Il prezzo del pane', *L'Agitazione*, 12 August 1897; rpt. in *Lavoro lungo*, 182–3.

'La Prima Internazionale', *Umanità Nova*, 9 September 1922.

'Il principio di organizzazione', *La Questione Sociale* (Paterson) 7 October 1899.

'Programma', *L'Associazione*, 6 September [*recte* October] 1889.

Programma e Organizzazione dell'Associazione Internazionale dei Lavoratori (Florence: Tipografia Toni, 1884).

'A Project of Anarchist Organization', in *Anarchist Revolution*, 93–103; originally published as 'Un progetto di organizzazione anarchica', parts 1 and 2, *Il Risveglio*, 1–15 October 1927.

'La propaganda a fatti', *L'Associazione*, 16 October 1889.

'Questione economica', *La Questione Sociale* (Florence), 29 June 1884.

'Questions de tactique', *La Révolte*, 1 October 1892.

'Questions révolutionnaires', *La Révolte*, 4 October 1890.

'Il salario nelle aziende socialiste e nelle organizzazioni operaie' *L'Agitazione*, 4 June 1897; rpt. in *Lavoro lungo*, 120–2.

'Science and Social Reform', *Man!*, March 1935; originally published as 'Scienza e riforma sociale', *Volontà*, 27 December 1913.

'Separazione', *La Questione Sociale* (Paterson), 2 September 1899.

'Should Anarchists Be Admitted to the Coming International Congress?' *Labour Leader*, 11 July 1896.

'Il signor Malatesta si spiega', *Il Progresso Italo Americano*, 23 August 1899.

Socialismo y anarquía (Madrid: Ayuso, 1975).

'I socialisti e le elezioni: Una lettera di E. Malatesta', *Il Messaggero* (Roma), 7 February 1897; rpt. in *Lavoro lungo*, 3–4.

'La sommossa non è rivoluzione', *L'Associazione*, 27 October 1889.

'La Tolleranza Verso i Partiti Affini', *La Questione Sociale* (Paterson), 30 January 1897.

'Verso l'anarchia', *La Questione Sociale* (Paterson), 9 December 1899.

'La Volontà', *Volontà*, 3 January 1914.

OTHER REFERENCES

'Il 1. Congresso della Federazione Socialista-Anarchica Romagnola', *L'Agitazione*, 30 December 1897; rpt., 6 January 1898.

A40, Excerpt from memo to French police, Geneva, 18 November 1893. MS, box BA 913, APP.

'Adesioni al manifesto astensionista', *L'Agitatore Socialista-Anarchico*, 25 April 1897.

'Adesioni al manifesto astensionista', *L'Agitazione*, 21 March 1897.

Agli Operai Italiani, placard (London, 1893). 'Ai nostri compagni residenti in America', *Volontà*, 5 September 1914.

'Á los anarquistas italianos del extranjero', *El Productor*, 1 June 1893.

Al popolo d'Italia, in Dadà, 219–22.

Al Popolo Italiano, special supplement of *L'Agitazione*, 24 April 1898.

Anarchici e anarchia nel mondo contemporaneo (Turin: Fondazione Luigi Einaudi, 1971).

'Anarchistes résidant à Londres', n.p., December 1894. TS, box BA 1509, APP.

'Anarchistes résidant à Londres au 1ᵉʳ Avril 1896', n.p., [1896]. MS, box BA 1509, APP.

'Anarchists and the Labour Movement', *Commonweal*, 7 November 1891.

André, G., 'Rapport', Paris, 22 May 1895. MS, box BA 1510, APP.

Antonioli, M., 'Norsa, Augusto Cesare', in Antonioli et al.

Antonioli, M., et al., eds., *Dizionario biografico degli anarchici italiani*, 2 vols (Pisa: Biblioteca Franco Serantini, 2003–04).

Aragno, G., 'Bergamasco, Giovanni', in Antonioli et al. Avison, W. R., 'On Being Right versus Being Bright', *Pacific Sociological Review*, 21 (1), 67–84 (1978).

Avrich, P., *Anarchist Portraits* (Princeton University Press, 1988).

———, *Anarchist Voices* (Princeton University Press, 1995).

'Azione popolare', *L'Agitazione*, 28 January 1898.

Bakunin, M., 'God and the State', in *Bakunin on Anarchism*, ed., trans. and with an introduction by S. Dolgoff (Montreal: Black Rose, 1980), 225–42.

Bantman, C., 'Internationalism without an International?', *Revue Belge de Philologie et d'Histoire*, 84 (4), 961–81 (2006).

Baron, L., 'The International Workers' Congress', *Liberty*, January 1896.

'Bava socialista', *L'Ordine* (Turin), 6 January 1894.

Beauregard, F., Memo to Italian foreign minister, Nice, 18 October 1889. MS, Polizia Internazionale, box 3, ASDMAE.

Beauregard, F., Telegram to Italian foreign minister, Nice, 11 September 1889. MS, Polizia Internazionale, box 3, ASDMAE.

'The Belgian Agitation and Franchise Reform', *Times* (London), 19 April 1893.

Berti, G., *Errico Malatesta e il movimento anarchico italiano e internazionale, 1872–1932* (Milan: Franco Angeli, 2003).

———, *Francesco Saverio Merlino* (Milan: Franco Angeli, 1993).

Bertolucci, R., *Milleottocentonovantaquattro* (Carrara: Gruppi Anarchici Riuniti, 1981).

Bettini, L., *Bibliografia dell'anarchismo*, 2 vols (Florence: Crescita Politica, 1972–76).

'Between Ourselves', *Liberty*, October 1895. 'Il bilancio della nostra agitazione', supplement to *L'Agitazione*, 30 April 1898.

Blatchford, R., 'At the Conference', *Clarion*, 1 August 1896.

'Blatchford, Robert Peel Glanville', in *The Encyclopedia of the British Press, 1422–1922*, ed. D. Griffiths (New York: St. Martin's Press, 1992).

Bolis, F., Telegram to minister of interior, Girgenti, 1 May 1899. MS, CPC, box 2949, ACS.

Borghi, A., *Errico Malatesta* (1947; rpt., Catania: Edizioni Anarchismo, 1978).

Bornibus, Memo to French police, Paris, 18 May 1895. MS, box BA 1510, APP.

Boschi, A., *Ricordi del domicilio coatto* (Turin: Seme Anarchico, 1954).

Boudon, R., *The Art of Self-Persuasion* (Cambridge: Polity Press, 1994).

———, 'Beyond Rational Choice Theory', *Annual Review of Sociology*, 29 (1), 1–21 (2003).

———, *The Origin of Values* (New Brunswick, NJ: Transaction, 2001).

———, *Theories of Social Change* (Cambridge: Polity Press, 1986).

———, *The Unintended Consequences of Social Action* (London: The Macmillan Press, 1982).

Bouhey, V., *Les Anarchistes contre la République* (Presses universitaires de Rennes, 2008).

Branchi, G., Telegram to Italian ministry of Interior, New York, 3 April 1900. MS., CPC, box 2949, ACS.

Brocher Papers, International Institute of Social History, Amsterdam.

Cafagna, L., 'Anarchismo e socialismo a Roma negli anni della "febbre edilizia" e della crisi, 1882–1891', *Movimento operaio*, 4 (5), 729–88 (1952).

Canadian Security Intelligence Service, *Anti-Globalization – A Spreading Phenomenon*, Perspectives, Report No. 2000/08, http://www.csis.gc.ca (home page), date accessed 25 November 2011.

Canovan, M., *Populism* (London: Junction, 1981).

Caraman, Memo to French police, Paris, 18 May 1895. MS, box BA 1510, APP.

Carey, G., 'La Questione Sociale', in *Italian Americans*, ed. L. Tomasi (Staten Island, NY, 1985), 289–97.

Carr, R., 'All or Nothing', *New York Review of Books*, 24 (16), 22, 27 (1977).

Casanovas i Codina, J., 'Pere Esteve, 1865–1925', *L'Avenc* (Barcelona), (162), 18–22 (1992).

Ceccarelli, A., 'Primo Maggio 1891 in Roma', *Il Risveglio Anarchico*, 1 May 1936.

Centurione, E., Memo to Italian foreign minister, Nice, 20 May 1889. MS, Polizia Internazionale, box 3, ASDMAE.

Centurione, E., Memo to Italian foreign minister, Nice, 15 June 1889. MS, Polizia Internazionale, box 3, ASDMAE.

Cerrito, G., *I Fasci dei Lavoratori nella provincia di Messina* (Ragusa: Sicilia Punto L, 1989).

Ciancabilla, G., G. Della Barile, and A. Guabello, 'Idee e tattica', *La Questione Sociale* (Paterson), 2 September 1899.

'Circa l'evasione dall'isola di Lampedusa . . . ', Memo from Italian consulate in Marseille to ministry of interior, Marseille, 6 May 1899. MS, CPC, box 2949, ACS.

'Circulaire du Congrès de Sonvilier', in Freymond, 2: 265.

'Club Life in Nineteenth Century Fitzrovia', *Fitzrovia Neighborhood News*, December 1986.

Colajanni, N., *L'Italia nel 1898*, 3rd edn (Casalvelino Scalo: Galzerano, 1998).

Colombo, E., *Los desconocidos y los olvidados* (Montevideo: Nordan Comunidad, 1999).

Commissariato di Lugano, arrest report, 12 June 1891. MS, Justiz, Bundesanwaltschaft, Polizeidienst, E 21, Ds. 7113, Schweizerisches Bundesarchiv, Bern.

Commissariato di Lugano, interrogation report, 15 June 1891. MS, Justiz, Bundesanwaltschaft, Polizeidienst, E 21, Ds. 7113, Schweizerisches Bundesarchiv, Bern.

'A Comrade who was present', "The Capolago Congress", *Freedom*, March 1891.

'Communications et correspondance', *La Révolte*, 10 September 1892.

'Communications et correspondance', *La Révolte*, 8 April 1893. 'Comunicati', *L'Ordine* (Turin), 23 December 1893.

The Concise Oxford Dictionary of Current English, 8th edn, ed. R. E. Allen (Oxford: Clarendon Press, 1990).

Congrès International Ouvrier Socialiste Tenu à Bruxelles du 16 au 23 Août 1891 (Geneva: Minkoff Reprint, 1977).

Congrès International Socialiste et des Chambres Syndicales Ouvrières. Londres

26 Juillet – 2 Août 1896 (Geneva: Minkoff Reprint, 1980).

'El Congreso Amplio', *El Productor*, 2 April 1891.

'Congress Notes. Anarchists', *Justice, Special Daily Congress Issue*, 28 July 1896.

'Il Congresso Operaio Internazionale del 1896', *La Questione Sociale* (Paterson), 15 September 1895.

'Congresso Socialista Rivoluzionario Italiano', *La Rivendicazione* (Forlì), 10 January 1891.

Conti, E., *Le origini del socialismo a Firenze, 1860–1880* (Rome: Rinascita, 1950).

Cortesi, L., 'Il Partito Socialista e il movimento dei Fasci', *Movimento Operaio*, 6 (6), 1067–110 (1954).

'Il covo degli anarchici a Nizza', *Gazzetta Piemontese*, 6 July 1894.

Dadà, A., *L'anarchismo in Italia* (Milan: Teti, 1984).

Damiani, A., Telegram to Italian embassy in London, Rome, 9 August 1889. MS, Polizia Internazionale, box 39, ASDMAE.

Damiani, A., Memo to chargé d'affaires of Italian embassy in London, Rome, 15 August 1889. MS, Polizia Internazionale, box 39, ASDMAE.

Davidson, D., *Essays on Actions and Events*, 2nd edn (Oxford: Clarendon Press, 2001).

———, *Inquiries into Truth and Interpretation*, 2nd edn (Oxford: Clarendon Press, 2001).

———, *Problems of Rationality* (Oxford: Clarendon Press, 2004).

De Renzis, F., Memo to Italian minister of interior, 26 May 1899. MS, CPC, box 2949, ACS.

Del Carria, R., *Proletari senza rivoluzione*, 2nd edn, 2 vols (Milan: Oriente, 1970).

del Valle, A. [Palmiro de Lidia, pseud.], 'Visita de Malatesta a La Habana en 1900', *La Revista Blanca* (Barcelona), 10 (229), 400–2 (1932).

Della Peruta, F., 'L'Internazionale a Roma dal 1872 al 1877', *Movimento Operaio*, 4 (1), 5–52 (1952).

Di Lembo, L., 'Cioci, Giuseppe', in Antonioli et al.

Di Lembo, L., 'Talchi, Giovanni', in Antonioli et al.

Dielo Trouda, *The Organisational Platform of the Libertarian Communists* (n.p.: Workers Solidarity Movement, 2001).

Dipaola, P., 'Italian Anarchists in London, 1870–1914' (Ph.D. Dissertation, Goldsmith College, University of London, 2004).

Dipaola, P., 'Recchioni, Emidio', in Antonioli et al.

'The Disturbances in Italy', *Times* (London), 18 January 1894.

'The Disturbances in Sicily', *Times* (London), 5 January 1894.

Domanico, G. [Jehan Le Vagre, pseud.], *Un trentennio nel movimento socialista italiano* (Prato: Tipografia Brogi e Buccianti, 1910).

Dommanget, M., *Histoire du Premier Mai* (Paris: Tête de Feuilles, 1972).

'Il dovere anarchico', *La Questione Sociale* (Paterson), 9 September 1899.

'Elenco dei destinatari di un manifesto incendiario stampato a Londra il 1

Marzo 1894 dal Gruppo Anarchico Solidarietà', n.p., (1894). MS, DAP, box 105, ACS.

'En el Círculo de Trabajadores: Conferencia Malatesta', *El Despertar*, 1 May 1900.

'End of the Hamburg Dock Strike', *Times*, 8 February 1897.

Engels, F., 'The Congress of Sonvillier and the International', in *Anarchism and Anarcho-Syndicalism*, ed. K. Marx, F. Engels, and V. Lenin, 60–6.

'England. The International Socialist Workers Congress of 1896', *Torch*, 18 September 1895.

'Errico Malatesta', *La Questione Sociale* (Paterson), 27 May 1899.

Esenwein, G. R., *Anarchist Ideology and the Working-Class Movement in Spain, 1868–1898* (Berkeley: University of California Press, 1989).

Esteve, P., 'Constatazione', *La Questione Sociale* (Paterson), 7 September 1901.

———, 'Schiarimenti', part 1, *La Questione Sociale* (Paterson), 28 February 1898.

Eureka, Memo to French police, London, 20 May 1895. MS, box BA 1510, APP.

'European Disarmament', *Times* (London), 26 March 1894.

Excerpt from police report, Paris, 24 August 1888. MS, box BA 30, APP.

Fabbri, Luce, *Luigi Fabbri, storia d'un uomo libero* (Pisa: Biblioteca Franco Serantini, 1996).

Fabbri, Luigi, *Malatesta: L'uomo e il pensiero* (1951; rpt., Catania: Edizioni Anarchismo, 1979).

———, 'Per una raccolta degli scritti di E. Malatesta', *Studi Sociali* (Montevideo), 3 (21), 8 (1932).

———, *La vida de Malatesta* (Barcelona: Guilda de Amigos del Libro, 1936).

'I Fasti della Fasciocrazia Siciliana', *L'Ordine* (Turin), 6 January 1894.

Fedeli, U., *Luigi Galleani* (Cesena: L'Antistato, 1956).

'La Federación', *El Despertar*, 30 January 1900.

Felicioli, R., 'Episodi anconitani', *Umanità Nova, 1853–1953*, December 1953.

Felzani, E., 'Comizio in Piazza S.Croce in Gerusalemme', memo to minister of interior, Rome, 6 May 1891. MS, DGPS, 1879–1903, box 2, ACS.

Felzani, E., 'Setta anarchica. Disordini del 1 Maggio', memo to the public prosecutor, Rome, 14 May 1891. MS, DGPS, 1879–1903, box 2, ACS.

Felzani, E., 'Setta anarchica. Disordini del 1 Maggio', memo to the public prosecutor, Rome, 21 May 1891. MS, DGPS, 1879–1903, box 2, ACS.

Fitch, H. T., *Traitors Within* (London: Hurst and Blackett, 1933).

'Una franca parola agli pseudo-anarchici', *L'Ordine* (Turin), 23 December 1893.

Freymond, J., ed., *La Première Internationale*, 4 vols (Geneva: Librairie E. Droz, 1962–71).

G. A., 'Comunicaciones', *El Productor*, 20 July 1888.

Galleani, L., *The End of Anarchism?* (Orkney: Cienfuegos Press, 1982).

――――, [Minin, pseud.], 'È morto Cipriani', *Cronaca Sovversiva*, 20 April 1918.

Gemie, S., 'Counter-Community: An Aspect of Anarchist Political Culture', *Journal of Contemporary History*, 29 (2), 349–67 (1994).

――――, 'Historians, Anarchism and Political Culture', *Anarchist Studies*, 6 (2), 153–9 (1998).

Gestri, L., 'Dieci lettere inedite di Cipriani, Malatesta e Merlino', *Movimento Operaio e Socialista* (Genoa), 17 (4), 309–30 (1971).

Giulianelli, R., 'Agostinelli, Cesare', in Antonioli et al.

Gori, P., 'Il Congresso Internazionale Operaio Socialista di Londra', in *Scritti Scelti*, vol. 2 (Cesena: L'Antistato, 1968), 206–18.

――――, 'Postilla alla polemica sull'evoluzione dell'anarchismo', *L'Agitazione*, 4 November 1897.

Gouldner, A. W., *The Two Marxisms: Contradictions and Anomalies in the Development of Theory* (New York: Seabury Press, 1980).

Grandi, 'Enrico Malatesta', memo to Italian foreign minister, Malta, 31 August 1900. MS, Serie Z, box 51, ASDMAE.

Grandi, Telegram to minister of interior, Malta, 15 May 1899. MS, CPC, box 2949, ACS.

Granovetter, M., 'Threshold Models of Collective Behavior', *American Journal of Sociology*, 83 (6), 1420–43 (1978).

Griffiths, S., '"Comrade Hayek" or the Revival of Liberalism?', *Journal of Political Ideologies*, 12 (2), 189–210 (2007).

Grunberg, E., 'Predictability and Reflexivity', *American Journal of Economics and Sociology*, 45 (4), 475–88 (1986).

Gruppo La Solidarietà, *Agli Anarchici d'Italia* (London, 1893).

Guillaume, Memo to French police, Paris, 18 May 1895. MS, box BA 1510, APP.

Hacohen, M. H., *Karl Popper: The Formative Years, 1902–1945* (Cambridge University Press, 2000; rpt., 2002).

Hamon, A., *Le socialisme et le Congrès de Londres* (1897; rpt., Genève: Minkoff Reprint, 1977).

Hamon Papers, International Institute of Social History, Amsterdam.

Hanneman, R. A., and M. Riddle. *Introduction to Social Network Methods* (University of California, Riverside, 2005), http://faculty.ucr.edu/~hanneman/, date accessed 25 November 2011.

Hardin, R., *Collective Action* (Baltimore: Johns Hopkins University Press, 1982).

――――, *Indeterminacy and Society* (Princeton University Press, 2003).

Hayek, F. A., *The Constitution of Liberty* (University of Chicago Press, 1960).

――――, *The Counter-Revolution of Science* (London: Collier-Macmillan, 1955).

――――, *The Fatal Conceit* (University of Chicago Press, 1988).

Herschel de Minerbi, Memo to Italian foreign minister, London, 7 March

1893. MS, CPC, box 1519, folder 'Cova Cesare', ACS.

Hobbes, T., *Leviathan* (1651; rpt., London: Penguin Books, 1985).

Hobsbawm, E. J., *Primitive Rebels* (Manchester University Press, 1959).

Hollis, M., 'The Limits of Irrationality', in *Rationality*, ed. B. R. Wilson (Oxford: Basil Blackwell, 1977), 214–20.

Holmes, C., *John Bull's Island* (Basingstoke: Macmillan Education, 1988).

Horowitz, I. L., postscript to edited volume *The Anarchists* (New York: Dell, 1964; rpt., 1970), 581–603.

Hostetter, R., *The Italian Socialist Movement* (Princeton, NJ: D. Van Nostrand, 1958).

'Huelga, no manifestación', *El Productor*, 30 April 1890. 'In Ancona', *L'Agitazione*, regular weekly feature.

'The International Federation of Ship, Dock, and River Workers', *Conference Record*, 27 July 1896; rpt. in *Congrès International Socialiste*, 294–5.

'International Notes', *Freedom*, February 1897. *International Socialist Workers and Trade Union Congress. London, 1896. Report of Proceedings, List of British and Foreign Delegates, and Balance Sheet* (London: Twentieth Century Press, n.d.); rpt. in *Congrès International Socialiste*, 191–271.

'The International Workers' Congress', *Liberty*, May 1896.

'The International Workers' Congress. Anarchist Committee', *Liberty*, February 1896.

'Italy', *Times* (London), 10 January 1894.

Jackson, Memo to French police, London, 20 May 1895. MS, box BA 1509, APP.

Joll, J., 'Anarchism between Communism and Individualism', in *Anarchici e anarchia*, 269–84.

———, *The Anarchists*, 2nd edn (Cambridge, MA: Harvard University Press, 1980).

———, *The Second International, 1889–1914* (New York: Harper and Row, 1966).

Jones, G. S., *Languages of Class* (Cambridge University Press, 1983).

Julliard, J., *Fernand Pelloutier et les origines du syndicalisme d'action directe* (Paris: Éditions du Seuil, 1971).

Kant, I., *Groundwork of the Metaphysics of Morals*, in *Practical Philosophy*, ed. M. J. Gregor (Cambridge University Press, 1996), 37–108.

Kaplan, T., *Anarchists of Andalusia 1868–1903* (Princeton University Press, 1977).

Krishna, D., '"The Self-Fulfilling Prophecy" and the Nature of Society', *American Sociological Review*, 36 (6), 1104–7 (1971).

Kropotkin, P., 'Anarchism', in *Kropotkin's Revolutionary Pamphlets*, 283–300; originally published in *The Encyclopedia Britannica*, 11th edn.

———, 'Le Congrès Ouvrier de 1896', *Les Temps Nouveaux*, 3 August 1895.

———, *Kropotkin's Revolutionary Pamphlets*, ed. with an introduction by R. N. Baldwin (1927; rpt., New York: Dover, 1970).

————, 'Modern Science and Anarchism', in *Kropotkin's Revolutionary Pamphlets*, 145–94.

————, 'The Workers' Congress of 1896', *Liberty*, September 1895.

La Boétie, E., *The Politics of Obedience: The Discourse of Voluntary Servitude*, 2nd rev. edn (Montreal: Black Rose, 1997).

'The Labour Question', *Times* (London), 2 May 1891.

Labriola, A., 'To F. Engels', 1 July 1893, in *La corrispondenza di Marx e Engels con italiani 1848–1895*, ed. G. Del Bo (Milan: Feltrinelli, 1964), 487–90.

Lakatos, I., 'To P. Feyerabend', 29 January 1974, in I. Lakatos and P. Feyerabend, *For and Against Method* (University of Chicago Press, 1999), 366–72.

Langhard, J., *Die anarchistische Bewegung in der Schweiz* (1903; rpt., Glashütten im Taunus, 1975).

Lapeyre, Memo to French police, London, 22 May 1895. MS, box BA 1509, APP.

Lear, J., *Workers, Neighbors, and Citizens* (Lincoln: University of Nebraska Press, 2001).

'La legalidad es una farsa', *El Productor*, 7 May 1891.

Leonardi, Memo to Italian ambassador in Madrid, Rome, 31 December 1900. MS, CPC, box 2949, ACS.

Levy, C., 'Italian Anarchism, 1870–1926', in *For Anarchism*, ed. D. Goodway (London: Routledge, 1989), 25–78.

————, 'Malatesta in Exile', *Annali della Fondazione Luigi Einaudi*, 15, 245–80 (1981).

————, 'Malatesta in London: The Era of Dynamite', in *A Century of Italian Emigration to Britain. 1880s to 1980s. Five Essays*, ed. L. Sponza and A. Tosi, supplement to *The Italianist*, 13 (2), 25–42 (1998).

Linebaugh, P., and M. Rediker, *The Many-Headed Hydra* (Boston: Beacon Press, 2000).

Linz, J. J., *Robert Michels, Political Sociology, and the Future of Democracy* (New Brunswick, NJ: Transaction, 2006).

Lipset, S. M., Introduction to Michels, 15–39.

Littlechild, J. G., Memo, London, 27 April 1891. MS, FO 45/677, Public Record Office, London.

Löb, M. H., 'Solution of a Problem of Leon Henkin', *Journal of Symbolic Logic*, 20 (2), 115–18 (1955).

'Lo de Jerez', *El Corsario* (Corunna), 24 January 1892.

'Lo de Jerez', *El Productor*, 14 January 1892.

López Estudillo, A., 'Conflictividad social agraria y crisis finisecular. Republicanismo y anarquismo en Andalucía, 1868–1900', (Doctoral diss.; Bellaterra: Universitat Autónoma de Barcelona, 1994).

Lovell, J. C., *Stevedores and Dockers* (London: Macmillan, 1969).

Lozovsky, A., *Marx and the Trade Unions* (New York: International Publishers,

1935).

Lukács, G., 'What is Orthodox Marxism?', in *History and Class Consciousness* (Cambridge, MA: MIT Press, 1971).

Lukes, S., *Marxism and Morality* (Oxford: Clarendon Press, 1985).

Machiavelli, N., *The Prince*, in *Selected Political Writings*, ed. David Wootton (Indianapolis: Hackett, 1994), 5–80.

Maffei, C. A., Memo to Spanish Ministry of State, Madrid, 25 February 1892. MS, Orden Público, H2756, Archivo Historico, Ministerio de Asuntos Exteriores, Madrid.

Maitron, J., *Le mouvement anarchiste en France*, vol. 1 (Paris: Maspero, 1975).

Malato, C., *De la commune à l'anarchie* (Paris: Stock, 1894).

———, *Les Joyeusetés de l'Exil* (1897; rpt., Mauléon: Acratie, 1985).

Mann, T., *Tom Mann's Memoirs* (London: Labour Publishing Company, 1923).

Marabini, T., and M. Ortalli, 'Lacchini, Vivaldo', in Antonioli et al.

Marshall, P., *Demanding the Impossible*, rev. edn (London: HarperCollins, 1993).

Martin, M., and L. C. McIntyre, Introduction to part 4, 'Rationality', of edited volume *Readings in the Philosophy of Social Science* (Cambridge, MA: MIT Press, 1994).

Marucco, D., 'Processi anarchici a Torino tra il 1892 ed il 1894', in *Anarchici e anarchia*, 217–41.

Marx, K., 'A Correspondence of 1843', in *Selected Writings*, 43–5.

———, 'The Conspectus of Bakunin's Book *State and Anarchy*', in K. Marx, F. Engels, and V. Lenin, 147–52.

———, 'Inaugural Address to the First International', in *Selected Writings*, 575–82.

———, 'On Bakunin's Statism and Anarchy', in *Selected Writings*, 606–9.

———, *The Poverty of Philosophy*, in *Selected Writings*, 212–33.

———, 'Preface to *A Critique of Political Economy*', in *Selected Writings*, 424–8.

———, *Selected Writings*, ed. D. McLellan, 2nd edn (Oxford University Press, 2000).

———, 'To J. Weydemeyer', 29 November 1864, in K. Marx and F. Engels, *Collected Works*, 43–5.

———, 'To P. Lafargue', 19 April 1870, in K. Marx, F. Engels, and V. Lenin, 45–6.

Marx, K., and F. Engels, *Collected Works*, vol. 42 (New York: International Publishers, 1987).

———, *The Communist Manifesto*, in K. Marx, *Selected Writings*, 245–72.

———, *The German Ideology*, in K. Marx, *Selected Writings*, 175–208.

Marx, K., F. Engels, and V. Lenin, *Anarchism and Anarcho-Syndicalism* (New York: International Publishers, 1972).

Masini, P. C., *Storia degli anarchici italiani: Da Bakunin a Malatesta* (Milan: Rizzoli, 1969).

————, *Storia degli anarchici italiani nell'epoca degli attentati* (Milan: Rizzoli, 1981).

Mella, R., '8 Enero 1892–10 Febrero 1893. Los Sucesos de Jerez', in *Forjando un mundo libre*, ed. Vladimir Muñoz (Madrid: Ediciones de La Piqueta, 1978), 169–212.

Merlino, S., 'Al partito socialista', *Il Messaggero*, 29 January 1897; rpt. in Malatesta and Merlino, *Anarchismo e Democrazia*, 29–33.

————, 'Collectivisme, Communisme, Social-Démocratie et Anarchisme', *La Revue Socialiste*, June 1897.

————, 'Da una questione di tattica ad una questione di principii', *L'Agitazione*, 28 March 1897; rpt. in Malatesta, *Lavoro lungo*, 29–34.

————, 'Marzo–Maggio 1871', *La Rivendicazione*, 11 April 1891.

————, 'Il pericolo', *L'Italia del Popolo*, 3–4 November 1897; rpt. in Malatesta and Merlino, *Anarchismo e Democrazia*, 145–9.

————, 'Per la conciliazione' *L'Agitazione*, 19 August 1897; rpt. in Malatesta, *Lavoro lungo*, 193–9.

————, 'Poche parole per chiudere la polemica', *L'Agitazione*, 18 April 1897; rpt. in Malatesta, *Lavoro lungo*, 59–65.

Merton, R. K., 'Bureaucratic Structure and Personality', *Social Forces*, 18 (4), 560–8 (1940).

————, 'The Unanticipated Consequences of Purposive Social Action', *American Sociological Review*, 1 (6), 894–904 (1936).

Michels, R., *Political Parties*, with an introduction by S. M. Lipset (New York: Free Press and London: Collier–Macmillan, 1962).

Ministero degli Affari Esteri, Memo to chargé d'affaires of Italian embassy in London, 21 October 1889. MS, Polizia Internazionale, box 39, ASDMAE.

Ministero degli Affari Esteri, Memo to chargé d'affaires of Italian embassy in London, 24 October 1889. MS, Polizia Internazionale, box 39, ASDMAE.

Ministero degli Affari Esteri, Memo to chargé d'affaires of Italian embassy in London, 26 October 1889. MS, Polizia Internazionale, box 39, ASDMAE.

Ministero degli Affari Esteri, Memo to Italian consul in Nice, 26 October 1889. MS, Polizia Internazionale, box 3, ASDMAE.

Ministero di Agricoltura, Industria e Commercio. Direzione Generale della Statistica, *Annuario Statistico Italiano, 1905–1907. Fascicolo Primo* (Rome, 1907).

Mintz, J. R., *The Anarchists of Casas Viejas* (Chicago, IL: University of Chicago Press, 1982).

Miscelánea', *El Productor*, 19 July 1889.

'Miscelánea', *El Productor*, 15 November 1889.

'Misceláneas', *El Productor*, 7 January 1892.

'More Rioting in Sicily', *Times* (London), 6 January 1894.

Moreau, A., 'L'anarchisme en France', Paris, September 1897. MS, F/7, Police Générale, box 13053, Archives Nationales, Paris.

Morgari, O., 'Come conobbi gli anarchici', *Almanacco Socialista 1934*, 55–60.

Moulaert, J., *Le mouvement anarchiste en Belgique, 1870–1914* (Ottignies: Quorum, 1996).

'Mouvement Social. Italie', *La Révolte*, 26 October 1889.

'Mouvement Social. Italie', *La Révolte*, 13 August 1892.

'Mouvement Social. Suisse', *La Révolte*, 12 August 1893.

'El movimiento de Mayo', parts 1–3, *El Productor*, 14–28 May 1891.

'El movimiento obrero de Mayo', *El Productor*, 7 May 1891.

'Movimiento Obrero. Exterior. Inglaterra', *El Productor*, 12 May 1892.

'Movimiento Obrero. Interior. Valladolid', *El Productor*, 9 June 1892.

Musarra, N., 'Dati statistici sulla consistenza dei Fasci dei Lavoratori: Gennaio 1894', *Rivista storica dell'anarchismo*, 1 (1), 63–86 (1994).

———, Introduction to Cerrito, 5–27.

———, 'Schicchi, Paolo', in Antonioli et al.

Negri, C., 'Galileo Palla', memo to Italian foreign minister, Paris, 13 May 1891. MS, Polizia Internazionale, box 27, ASDMAE.

'Nelle Nostre File', *Il Nuovo Combattiamo* (Genoa), 21 September 1889.

'Nelle Nostre File', *Il Nuovo Combattiamo* (Genoa), 12 October 1889.

Nelson, B. C., *Beyond the Martyrs* (New Brunswick, NJ: Rutgers University Press, 1988).

Nettlau, M., *Bakunin e l'Internazionale in Italia dal 1864 al 1872* (Geneva: Edizione del Risveglio, 1928).

———, *Errico Malatesta: La vida de un anarquista* (Buenos Aires: La Protesta, 1923).

———, *Die erste Blütezeit der Anarchie, 1886–1894* (Vaduz: Topos, 1981).

———, 'Prólogo', preface to Malatesta, *Socialismo y anarquía*, 7–42.

———, *A Short History of Anarchism*, trans. by I. P. Isca, ed. H. M. Becker (London: Freedom Press, 1996).

Nettlau Papers, International Institute of Social History, Amsterdam.

Nicotri, G., *Rivoluzioni e rivolte in Sicilia*, 3rd edn (Turin: Unione Tipografico-Editrice Torinese, 1910).

'Ni vencedores ni vencidos', *El Productor*, 14 May 1891.

Nieuwenhuis Papers, Russian State Archive for Social and Political History, Moscow.

Nomad, M., 'Errico Malatesta, or The Romance of Anarchism', in *Rebels and Renegades* (1932; rpt., Freeport, N.Y.: Books for Libraries Press, 1968), 1–47.

'Note', Memo from Tunis police to Italian consul in Tunis, (1899). MS, CPC box 2949, ACS.

'Noticias. Republica Argentina', *La Solidaridad* (Seville), 3 March 1889.

'Notizie', *Agitatevi per il Socialismo Anarchico*, 8 May 1897.

Nozick, R., *Anarchy, State, and Utopia* (New York: Basic Books, 1974).

Nye, R. A., *The Anti-Democratic Sources of Elite Theory: Pareto, Mosca, Michels* (London: Sage, 1977).

Oliver, H., *The International Anarchist Movement in Late Victorian London* (London: Croom Helm, 1983).

Olson, M., *The Logic of Collective Action* (Cambridge, MA: Harvard University Press, 1965).

Pages from Errico Malatesta's address book, [c. 1900]. MS, CPC, box 2953, ACS.

Parfit, D., 'Prudence, Morality, and the Prisoner's Dilemma', in *Rational Choice*, ed. J. Elster (New York University Press, 1986), 34–59.

Pearson, W. G., 'In Defence of "Intolerance"', *Clarion*, 8 August 1896.

Pease, E. R., *The History of the Fabian Society*, 3rd edn (London: Frank Cass, 1963).

Pelling, H., *A History of British Trade Unionism*, 5th edn (London: Macmillan, 1992).

Pelloutier, F., 'Lettre aux anarchistes', in Julliard, 415–9.

———, 'La situation actuelle du socialisme', in Julliard, 342–7.

'Per la libertà d'associazione', *L'Agitazione*, 7 April 1898.

'Per l'organizzazione dei tipografi', *L'Agitazione*, 7 October 1897.

Pernicone, N., *Italian Anarchism, 1864–1892* (Princeton University Press, 1993).

Perrot, M., 'The First of May 1890 in France', in *The Power of the Past*, ed. P. Thane, G. Crossick, and R. Floud (Cambridge University Press, 1984), 143–71.

'Piccola Posta', *La Questione Sociale* (Paterson), 27 May 1899.

Pierson, M.-A., *Histoire du Socialisme en Belgique* (Bruxelles: Institut Emile Vandervelde, 1953).

Piqué i Padró, J., *Anarco-col·lectivisme i anarco-communisme* (Barcelona: Publicacions de l'Abadia de Montserrat, 1989).

'Pisacane e i Mazziniani', *La Questione Sociale* (Florence), 29 December 1883.

Poe, Edgar Allan, 'The Murders in the Rue Morgue', in *Thirty-Two Stories*, 130–58.

———, 'The Purloined Latter', in *Thirty-Two Stories*, 256–71.

———, *Thirty-Two Stories*, ed. S. Levine and S. F. Levine (Indianapolis: Hackett, 2000).

Popper, K. R., *The Open Society and Its Enemies*, vol. 1, 5th rev. edn (Princeton University Press, 1966; rpt., 1971).

———, *The Poverty of Historicism*, rev. edn (London: Routledge and Kegan Paul, 1961; rpt., 1974).

———, 'Prediction and Prophecy in the Social Sciences', in *Conjectures and Refutations*, 5th rev. edn (London: Routledge, 1989; rpt., 1995).

'Por la posta', *El Despertar*, 20 May 1900.

Prefecture of Ancona, 'Elenco delle società politiche della provincia di Ancona', 8 June 1894. MS, DAP, box 103, ACS.

'Procès Verbal', Tunis, 18 May 1899. MS, CPC, box 2949, ACS.

Il processo Malatesta e compagni (1908; rpt., Pescara: Samizdat, 1996).

'I provvedimenti del governo', *L'Agitazione*, 28 January 1898.

Puccioni, E., Memo to chargé d'affaires of Italian embassy in London, Rome, 22 April 1889. MS, Polizia Internazionale, box 39, ASDMAE.

Quail, J., *The Slow Burning Fuse* (London: Granada Publishing, 1978).

'¿Que ha sido lo de Jerez?', *La Anarquía*, 15 January 1892.

'Questions de Tactique', parts 1 and 2, *La Révolte*, 6 and 13 September 1890.

Quine, W. V. O., *Word and Object* (Cambridge, MA: The MIT Press, 1960; rpt., 1997).

Rebérioux, M., *Le socialisme belge de 1875 à 1914*, in *Histoire Générale du Socialisme. Tome II: De 1875 à 1918*, ed. J. Droz (Paris: Presses Universitaires de France, 1974), 321–31.

Register of readers' signatures for temporary admission to the British Museum Reading Room. MS, British Museum Central Archive, London.

'Relazione del movimento dei sovversivi in Londra nei mesi marzo ed aprile', 21 May 1905. TS, DGPS, 1905, box 22, ACS.

'Report of Anarchist Conference', *Freedom*, August–September 1896.

Ressman, C., Two telegrams to Italian foreign minister, Paris, 18 December 1893. MS, Polizia Internazionale, box 27, ASDMAE.

'Résumé de la Réunion International Anarchiste', parts 1 and 2, *La Révolte*, 7 and 14 September 1889.

'Réunion Anarchiste Internationale', *La Révolte*, 27 July 1889.

Richards, V., 'Anarchism and the Historians', *Anarchy* (London), 4 (46), 357–67 (1964).

Ridley, F. F., *Revolutionary Syndicalism in France* (Cambridge University Press, 1970).

'Risoluzioni del Congresso generale di Capolago', in Santarelli, *Socialismo*, 190–3.

'La Riunione di West Hoboken', *La Questione Sociale* (Paterson), 18 February 1899.

Rocker, R., *En la Borrasca* (Buenos Aires: Americalee, 1949).

———, 'Errico Malatesta', *Der Syndicalist* (Berlin), 14 (32), 2 (1932).

———, *The London Years* (London: Anscombe, 1956).

Romano, S. F., 'Alcuni documenti inediti sugli anarchici di Palermo, 1892', *Movimento Operaio*, 2 (April–May 1950), 188–92.

———, *Storia dei Fasci siciliani* (Bari: Laterza, 1959).

Samaja, N. (Kristen Larsen, pseud.), 'In difesa della legge', *L'Agitazione*, 11 June 1897.

———, (Kristen Larsen, pseud.), 'L'agitazione contro il domicilio coatto', *L'Agitazione*, 30 December 1897.

Sandri, N., 'Il congresso socialista', *La Rivendicazione*, 3 January 1891.

————, 'I fatti di Roma', *La Rivendicazione*, 9 May 1891.

————, 'La Festa del Lavoro', *La Rivendicazione*, 4 April 1891.

————, 'La sommossa non è rivoluzione', *La Rivendicazione*, 5 October 1889.

Santarelli, E., 'L'azione di Errico Malatesta e i moti del 1898 ad Ancona', *Movimento Operaio*, 6 (2), 248–74 (1954).

————, *Il socialismo anarchico in Italia* (Milan: Feltrinelli, 1959).

Scavino, M., 'Galleani, Luigi', in Antonioli et al.

Schmitt, C., *The Crisis of Parliamentary Democracy* (Cambridge, MA: MIT Press, 1985).

Sen, A., 'Rational Behavior', in *The New Palgrave: A Dictionary of Economics*, ed. J. Eatwell, M. Milgate, and P. Newman, vol. 4 (London: Macmillan, 1987), 68–76.

Serantoni, F., 'Ancora rettificando la storia', *L'Aurora* (Spring Valley), 7 September 1901.

Sernicoli, E., Memo to C. Ressman, Paris, 9 September 1889. MS, Polizia Internazionale, box 27, ASDMAE.

Sernicoli, E., Memo to L. F. Menabrea, Paris, 13 May 1891. MS, Polizia Internazionale, box 27, ASDMAE.

'Sfogliando i giornali', *L'Agitazione*, 3 February 1898.

Shaffer, K. R., *Anarchism and Countercultural Politics in Early Twentieth-Century Cuba* (Gainesville: University Press of Florida, 2005).

————, 'Havana Hub: Cuban Anarchism, Radical Media, and the Trans-Caribbean Anarchist Network, 1903–1915', *Caribbean Studies*, 37 (2), 45–81 (2009).

Shipley, S., *Club Life and Socialism in Mid-Victorian London* (n.p.: History Workshop Pamphlets, 1971).

'La Sicilia e gli Anarchici', *L'Art.* 248, 7 January 1894.

'The Situation in Belgium', *Times* (London), 20 April 1893.

Smorti, A., 'Per l'organizzazione dei tipografi', *L'Agitazione*, 14 October 1897.

Smullyan, R., *Forever Undecided* (New York: Alfred A. Knopf, 1987).

S. N. T., 'Revista Internacional', *La Bandera Roja* (Madrid), 1 January 1889.

I socialisti anarchici ai lavoratori italiani in occasione delle elezioni, in Dadà, 232–6.

I socialisti-anarchici al Popolo Italiano: Non votate!, in Santarelli, *Socialismo*, 179–82.

Solé, R., and D. Valbelle, *The Rosetta Stone* (London: Profile, 2001).

Solidarietà con la Sicilia, in Vatteroni, 103–4.

'Sommes-nous a la hauteur des événéments?', *La Révolte*, 4 May 1893.

Sonn, R. D., *Anarchism and Cultural Politics in Fin de Siècle France* (Lincoln: University of Nebraska Press, 1989).

'Stampa socialista ed opuscoli di propaganda', *1 Maggio* (Naples), 29 March 1891.

'Stampa straniera sediziosa', folder. DAP, box 105, ACS.

Stancanelli, E., 'Malatesta, l'anarchico amico di Bakunin che morì a Prati piantonato dagli squadristi', *La Repubblica*, Rome ed., 20 February 2011.

Stekloff, G. M., *History of the First International*, trans. by E. and C. Paul (1928; rpt., New York: Russell and Russell, 1968).

Stella, E., 'Sedicente Fernandez', memo to Italian foreign minister, Barcelona, 28 April 1891. MS, Polizia Internazionale, box 46, ASDMAE.

Stueber, K. R., 'Understanding Other Minds and the Problem of Rationality', in *Empathy and Agency*, ed. H. H. Kögler and K. R. Stueber (Boulder, CO: Westview Press, 2000), 144–62.

Taylor, M., *The Possibility of Cooperation* (Cambridge University Press, 1987).

Thomas, M., *Anarchist Ideas and Counter-Cultures in Britain, 1880–1914* (Aldershot: Ashgate, 2005).

Thomas, P., *Karl Marx and the Anarchists* (London: Routledge and Kegan Paul, 1980).

Thomas, W. I., and D. S. Thomas, *The Child in America* (New York: Alfred A. Knopf, 1928; rpt., 1932).

Thompson, E. P., *The Making of the English Working Class*, rev. edn (Harmondsworth: Penguin Books, 1968; rpt., 1974).

Tilly, L. A., *Politics and Class in Milan 1881–1901* (Oxford University Press, 1992).

Tornielli, G., 'Anarchici. Servizio dell'Agente Segreto', memo to Italian foreign minister, London, 12 March 1894. MS, Polizia Internazionale, box 39, ASDMAE.

Trachtenberg, A., *History of May Day*, rev. edn (New York: International Publishers, 1947).

Tranfaglia, N., *La prima guerra mondiale e il fascismo* (Turin: UTET, 1995).

'The Trial of Italian Anarchists as Malefactors', *Freedom*, May 1898.

Tsuzuki, C., *Tom Mann, 1856–1941* (Oxford: Clarendon Press, 1991).

'Universales. Republica Argentina', *El Productor*, 23 December 1887.

Unsigned memo 'N 1', Paris, 14 December 1893. MS, F/7, Police Générale, box 12723, Archives Nationales, Paris.

Vaihinger, H., *The Philosophy of 'As If'*, 2nd edn (1935; rpt., New York: Barnes and Noble, 1966).

Vallina, P., *Crónica de un revolucionario* (Paris: Solidaridad Obrera, 1958).

Varias, A., *Paris and the Anarchists* (New York: St. Martin's Press, 1996).

Vatteroni, G. *'Abbasso i dazi, viva la Sicilia': Storia dell'insurrezione carrarese del 1894* (Sarzana: Industria Grafica Zappa, 1993).

'La Víspera', *El Productor*, 30 April 1890.

Vitti, A., 'Enrico Malatesta ed io', *La Tribuna Illustrata*, 16–23 September 1917.

Vizetelly, E. A., *The Anarchists* (1911; rpt., New York: Kraus Reprint, 1972).

Watkins, J. W. N., 'Ideal Types and Historical Explanation', in *Readings in the Philosophy of Science*, ed. H. Feigl and M. Brodbeck (New York:

Appleton–Century–Crofts, 1953), 723–43.

W. B. P., 'International Notes. Spain', *Commonweal*, 6 February 1892.

Weber, M., *Politics as a Vocation* (Philadelphia: Fortress Press, 1965; rpt., 1972).

Webster's Revised Unabridged Dictionary, ed. N. Porter (G & C. Merriam Co., 1913), http://machaut.uchicago.edu/websters, date accessed 6 December 2011.

Winks, R. W., ed., *The Historian as Detective* (New York: Harper & Row, 1968).

Woodcock, G., *Anarchism* (1962; rpt., Harmondsworth: Penguin Books, 1971).

Woods, A., *Bolshevism: The Road to Revolution* (London: Wellred, 1999).

Wundt, W., *Outlines of Psychology* (Leipzig: Wilhelm Engelmann, 1897).

Zagorin, P., Review of *The Anarchists* by James Joll, *Journal of Modern History*, 38 (4), 441 (1966).

Zaragoza, G., *Anarquismo argentino, 1876–1902* (Madrid: Ediciones de la Torre, 1996).

Z N° 6, Memo to French police, London, 19 April 1893. MS, box BA 1508, APP.

Z N° 6, Memo to French police, London, 3 July 1893. MS, box BA 1508, APP.

Z N° 6, Memo to French police, London, 5 February 1894. MS, box BA 1509, APP.

Z N° 6, Memo to French police, London, 21 February 1894. MS, box BA 1509, APP.

INDEX

vs. marxism, 234–8; descriptive completeness vs. prescriptive universality, 237; historical materialism and self-fulfilling beliefs, 234–5; reflexivity and authoritarianism, 237; 'self-understanding' as self-fulfilling belief, 236

collective action theories, Malatesta vs. rational-choice theory, 229–33, 238; anarchists as collective rationality pursuers, 231; self-referentiality, impact on normative statements, 231; self-referentiality, not a problem for voluntarism, 233; self-referentiality and self-fulfilling arguments, 233

freedom as method and Hayek's 'invisible-hand' explanations, 223–5

gradualism and Nozick's 'framework for utopia,' 219–20

gradualism and Popper's 'open society,' 218–20, 228

voluntarism, determinism, and Davidson's 'anomalous monism,' 235

Malatesta's tactical themes

anarchist autonomy, 61, 65, 100

anti-parliamentarianism, 154, 156–7

coherence between ends and means, 21–2, 64, 244; and anarchist 'conservatism,' 222–3, 245; and heterogony of ends, 24–5, 156; contrast with marxism, 22, 25

economic struggle and political struggle, 62–3, 146–7

'going to the people,' 60, 62, 65, 100, 107–8, 163

inclusiveness, 64–5, 101

insurrection, 63–4, 93, 181–2, 187; and partial struggles, 74–5

involvement in labor movement, 123, 149

legal struggles, 152–3, 168–9

moral resistance, 123, 153

propaganda by the deed, 15, 74–6

strikes, 163

sustainability of anarchist struggle,151–2

tactical alliances, 112, 168, 182–3

Malatesta's theoretical themes

anarchism as method, 56, 66, 69, 218, 239–40

anarchist morals, 148; as driver of spontaneous processes, 228–9; concern for common good, 225–6

anarchy, definition, 55–6

class consciousness, 29–32, 59

conscious minorities and masses, 60–3, 68, 70, 74, 78, 142

direct action's reforming power, 105–6, 150, 170, 174–5

ethical holism, 244

ethics and politics, 159–61, 228–9

experimentalism, 188, 217

freedom as method, 66, 161, 217, 243, see also under Malatesta's ideas,

comparative analyses freedom vs. coercion, 158

gradualism, 187–8, 213–7; and anarchism as method, 218; implications for anarchist action, 215–6; and methodological individualism, 218; motivations, 214, 216–17, see also under Malatesta's ideas, comparative analyses

humanism, 34, 167

indeterminacy of social action, 61, 72–3, 106, 110, 127, 145–6, 241, 245; in French Revolution, 72, 121

interests and ideals, 59

majorities and minorities, 157

methodological individualism, 66–9,145, 156–8, 193–4, 197, 239–40; society as effect of composition, 159

'moral communism,' 54

people, 32–4; and proletariat, 33–4

Support **AK Press!**

AK Press is one of the world's largest and most productive anarchist publishing houses. We're entirely worker-run

& democratically managed. We operate without a corporate structure—no boss, no managers, no bullshit. We publish close to twenty books every year, and distribute thousands of other titles published by other like-minded independent presses from around the globe.

The Friends of AK program is a way that you can directly contribute to the continued existence of AK Press, and ensure that we're able to keep publishing great books just like this one! Friends pay $25 a month directly into our publishing account ($30 for Canada, $35 for international), and receive a copy of every book AK Press publishes for the duration of their membership! Friends also receive a discount on anything they order from our website or buy at a table: 50% on AK titles, and 20% on everything else. We've also added a new Friends of AK ebook program: $15 a month gets you an electronic copy of every book we publish for the duration of your membership. Combine it with a print subscription, too!

There's great stuff in the works—so sign up now to become a Friend of AK Press, and let the presses roll!

Won't you be our friend? Email friendsofak@akpress.org for more info, or visit the Friends of AK Press website: www.akpress.org/programs/friendsofak